Golden Treasury

Francis Turner Palgrave (1824–1897) was an English critic and poet.

FRANCIS TURNER PALGRAVE
1824–1897

The
Golden Treasury

OF THE BEST SONGS AND LYRICAL POEMS IN THE ENGLISH LANGUAGE

Selected and arranged by
FRANCIS TURNER PALGRAVE

With an Introduction and additional
Poems selected and arranged by
C. DAY LEWIS
Poet Laureate

RUPA

Published by
Rupa Publications India Pvt. Ltd 2001
7/16, Ansari Road, Daryaganj
New Delhi 110002

Sales centres:
Allahabad Bengaluru Chennai
Hyderabad Jaipur Kathmandu
Kolkata Mumbai

ISBN: 978-81-716-7553-1

Eleventh impression 2021

15 14 13 12 11

The moral right of the author has been asserted.

Printed at Saurabh Printers Pvt. Ltd, Noida

ACKNOWLEDGMENTS

Cordial acknowledgments are here tendered to the following authors, owners of copyright, publishers and literary agents who have given permission for poems to appear in these pages :

GEORGE ALLEN & UNWIN LTD. for *Dead* from the *Poetical Works of Lionel Johnson.*

GEORGE ALLEN & UNWIN LTD. for *Water Music* from *Ha! Ha! Among the Trumpets* by Alun Lewis.

ROY CAMPBELL and CURTIS BROWN LTD. for *Choosing a Mast* and *Zebras* by Roy Campbell.

EXECUTORS OF LILIAN BOWES LYON and JONATHAN CAPE LTD. for *A Shepherd's Coat* from *Collected Poems* by Lilian Bowes Lyon.

MRS. W. H. DAVIS and JONATHAN CAPE LTD. for *The Kingfisher* and *Born of Tears* from *The Collected Poems of W. H. Davies.*

C. DAY LEWIS and JONATHAN CAPE LTD. for *Is it far to go?* and *The Christmas Tree* from *Poems 1943-47* by C. Day Lewis.

ROBERT FROST and JONATHAN CAPE LTD. for *to Earthward, Reluctance, The Runaway* and *The Road not Taken* from *The Complete Poems of Robert Frost.* Also for the same poems, HENRY HOLT & CO. INC. Copyright 1930, 1945 by Henry Holt & Co. Inc. Copyright 1942 by Robert Frost.

HENRY REED and JONATHAN CAPE LTD. for extract from *The Place and the Person* from *A Map of Verona* by Henry Reed.

ANDREW YOUNG and JONATHAN CAPE LTD. for *Wiltshire Downs* and *The Fear* from *The Collected Poems of Andrew Young.*

EXECUTORS OF WILFRED OWEN, CHATTO & WINDUS and NEW DIRECTIONS INC. for *Futility, Miners* and *Anthem for Doomed Youth* by Wilfred Owen.

THE CLARENDON PRESS for *I have loved flowers that fade, Thou didst delight my eyes* and *Winter Night-fall*, from *The Poetical Works of Robert Bridges.*

CONSTABLE & CO. LTD. for *Should thy love die*, extract from *Love in the Valley* and extract from *Modern Love*, by George Meredith.

PADRIAC COLUM for *She Moved through the Fair* by Padriac Colum.

JOHN SOUTAR and ANDREW DAKERS for *The Tryst* by William Soutar.

WALTER DE LA MARE and FABER & FABER LTD. for *The Listeners, To a Candle, Autumn* and *Farewell* by Walter de la Mare.

MISS D. E. COLLINS, J. M. DENT & SONS LTD. for *The Donkey* by G. K. Chesterton from *The Wild Knight.*

THE LITERARY EXECUTORS OF DYLAN THOMAS, J. M. DENT & SONS LTD. and NEW DIRECTIONS INC. for *Fern Hill* by Dylan Thomas.

MRS. GEORGE BAMBRIDGE, MACMILLAN & CO. LTD., THE MACMILLAN CO. OF CANADA for *The Way through the Woods* from *Rewards and Fairies* by Rudyard Kipling; for the same poem DOUBLEDAY & CO. INC. Copyright 1910 by Rudyard Kipling. Also for *Cities and Thrones and Powers* from *Puck of Pook's Hill* by Rudyard Kipling; for the same poem, DOUBLEDAY & CO. INC. Copyright 1906 by Rudyard Kipling.

LAURIE LEE and HOGARTH PRESS LTD. for *The Wild Trees* by Laurie Lee. Also DOUBLEDAY & Co. INC. for the same poem from *The Sun My Monument* by Laurie Lee. Copyright 1944 by Laurie Lee.

GERALD DUCKWORTH & Co. LTD. for *The Early Morning* from *Sonnets and Verse* by Hilaire Belloc.

W. H. AUDEN and FABER & FABER LTD. for *Fish in the Unruffled Lakes* from *Look Stranger* by W. H. Auden; also for *Lay your Sleeping Head my Love* and *Song: Warm are the still and lucky miles* from *Another Time* by W. H. Auden.

T. S. ELIOT and FABER & FABER LTD. for *Journey of the Magi, Marina* and *Hollow Men II* from the *Collected Poems of T. S. Eliot*.

LOUIS MACNEICE and FABER & FABER LTD. for *June Thunder* from *The Earth Compels* by Louis MacNeice; also for *A Toast* from *Plant and Phantom* by Louis MacNeice and *Nostalgia* from *Spring Board* by Louis MacNeice.

GEORGE BARKER and FABER & FABER LTD. for *To My Mother* from *Eros in Dogma* by George Barker; also for *Summer Son* from *News of the World* by George Barker.

STEPHEN SPENDER and FABER & FABER LTD. for *Seascape* and *Poor Girl Inhabitant of a strange land* from *Poems of Dedication* by Stephen Spender; also for *Prisoners* from *Poems* by Stephen Spender.

EDWIN MUIR and FABER & FABER LTD. for *The Child Dying* and *The Combat* from *The Labyrinth* by Edwin Muir.

SACKVILLE-WEST and HOGARTH PRESS for *The Greater Cats* by V. Sackville-West.

WILLIAM HEINEMANN LTD. for the *Chorus: Before the Beginning of Years* from *Atlanta in Calydon* by Algernon C. Swinburne; also for *A Forsaken Garden* and *A Match* from *Swinburne's Collected Poetical Works*.

ALFRED A. KNOPF INC. for *Bells for John Whiteside's Daughter* from *Selected Poems* by John Crowe Ransom. Copyright 1924, 1945 by Alfred A. Knopf Inc.

JOHN LANE THE BODLEY HEAD LTD. for *In Romney Marsh* by John Davidson from *Ballads and Songs*.

JOHN LEHMANN LTD. for *April Rise* by Laurie Lee; also for *Winter Garden* by David Gascoyne.

EXECUTORS OF ANDREW LANG for *The Odyssey* from *Poems* by Andrew Lang.

TRUSTEES OF THE HARDY ESTATE and MACMILLAN & Co. LTD. for *After a Journey, After a Visit, At Castle Boterel, Regret not me, The Haunter, The Self-Unseeing* by Thomas Hardy.

MACMILLAN & Co. LTD. for *The Old Jockey* by F. R. Higgins from *The Gap of Brightness*.

RALPH HODGSON and MACMILLAN & Co. LTD. for *Eve* from *Poems* by Ralph Hodgson.

MRS. STURGE MOORE for *The Dying Swan* from the *Collected Poems of T. Sturge Moore* Vol. 2, p. 7.

MRS. JAMES STEPHENS and MACMILLAN & Co. LTD. for *The Rivals* from *Collected Poems* of James Stephens.

MRS. W. B. YEATS, THE MACMILLAN Co. N.Y. and MACMILLAN & Co. LTD. for *An Acre of Grass, Death, Down by the Salley Gardens, Solomon to Sheba, The Rose Tree* and *The Wild Swans at Coole* from *Collected Poems* of W. B. Yeats.

MACMILLAN & CO. LTD. for *For a Dead Lady* from *The Collected Poems of E. A. Robinson*.

DR. JOHN MASEFIELD, THE SOCIETY OF AUTHORS and THE MACMILLAN Co. N.Y. for *Cargoes* from *Story of the Round House* by John Masefield.

FRANCIS MEYNELL for *The Daisy* by Francis Thompson.

MRS. HAROLD MONRO for *Thistledown* by Harold Monro.

JOHN BETJEMAN and JOHN MURRAY LTD. for *East Anglian Bathe* and *Upper Lambourne* from *Selected Poems* by John Betjeman.

NOEL NEWTON-WOOD for *Dragon Flies* and *Talking with Soldiers* by W. J. Turner.

EDMUND BLUNDEN for *The Sunlit Vale*, *What is Winter?* and *Midnight Skaters*.

DR. EDITH SITWELL and THE VANGUARD PRESS for *Once my heart*, *Heart and Mind* and *The Swans* by Edith Sitwell.

MRS. FRIEDA LAWRENCE and WILLIAM HEINEMANN LTD. for *The Humming Bird* by D. H. Lawrence; also THE VIKING PRESS INC. for the same poem, from *Birds, Beasts and Flowers* by D. H. Lawrence. Copyright 1923 by Thomas Seltzer Inc., 1951 by Frieda Lawrence.

EZRA POUND for *What thou lovest well remains*.

ROUTLEDGE & KEGAN PAUL LTD. for *William Wordsworth* by Sidney Leyes from *The Collected Poems of Sidney Keyes*.

SIEGFRIED SASSOON for *Prelude: The Troops*.

EXECUTRIC OF J. E. FLECKER and MARTIN SECKER & WARBURG LTD. for *Stillness* and *The Old Ships* by J. E. Flecker.

SIDGWICK & JACKSON, DODD MEAD & CO. and MCCLELLAND & STEWART LTD. for *Heaven* by Rupert Brooke.

MRS. HELEN THOMAS and FABER & FABER LTD. for *The Gallows* and *Lights Out* by Edward Thomas.

SOCIETY OF AUTHORS as the Literary Representative of the Trustees of the Estate of the late A. E. Housman and JONATHAN CAPE LTD. publishers of A. E. Housman's *Collected Poems* for *Tell me not here*, *Far in a western brookland* and *The night is freezing fast* by A. E. Housman. Also for the same poems, HENRY HOLT & CO. INC. Copyright 1922, 1940 by Henry Holt & Co. Inc. Copyright 1936, 1950 by Barclays Bank Ltd.

MRS. BINYON and THE SOCIETY OF AUTHORS for *The Burning of the Leaves I* by Lawrence Binyon.

EXECUTORS OF MARY COLERIDGE for *On Such a Day*, *The Witch* and *Unwelcome* from *Poems* by Mary Coleridge.

ROBERT GRAVES for *The Cool Web*, *In the Wilderness* from *Collected Poems* (1914-47) and *The Foreboding* by Robert Graves.

HER GRACE THE DUCHESS OF WELLINGTON for *The Buried Child* by Dorothy Wellesley.

TO ALFRED TENNYSON
POET LAUREATE

THIS book in its progress has recalled often to my memory a man with whose friendship we were once honoured, to whom no region of English Literature was unfamiliar, and who, whilst rich in all the noble gifts of Nature, was most eminently distinguished by the noblest and the rarest,—just judgement and high-hearted patriotism. It would have been hence a peculiar pleasure and pride to dedicate what I have endeavoured to make a true national Anthology of three centuries to Henry Hallam. But he is beyond the reach of any human tokens of love and reverence; and I desire therefore to place before it a name united with his by associations which, whilst Poetry retains her hold on the minds of Englishmen, are not likely to be forgotten.

Your encouragement, given while traversing the wild scenery of Treryn Dinas, led me to begin the work; and it has been completed under your advice and assistance. For the favour now asked I have thus a second reason: and to this I may add, the homage which is your right as Poet, and the gratitude due to a Friend, whose regard I rate at no common value.

Permit me then to inscribe to yourself a book which, I hope, may be found by many a lifelong fountain of innocent and exalted pleasure; a source of animation to friends when they meet; and able to sweeten solitude itself with best society,—with the companionship of the wise and the good, with the beauty which the eye cannot see, and the music only heard in silence. If this Collection proves a storehouse of delight to Labour and to Poverty,—if it teaches those indifferent to the Poets to love them, and those who love them to love them more, the aim and the desire entertained in framing it will be fully accomplished.

F. T. P.

May, 1861.

Εἰς τὸν λειμῶνα καθίσας,
ἔδρεπεν ἕτερον ἐφ' ἑτέρῳ
αἱρόμενος ἄγρευμ' ἀνθέων
ἁδομένᾳ ψυχᾷ.
[Eurip. *frag.* 754.]

[' He sat in the meadow and plucked with glad heart
the spoil of the flowers, gathering them one by one.']

CONTENTS

INTRODUCTION

FRANCIS TURNER PALGRAVE was born at Great Yarmouth on September 28th, 1824. His father was a historian and antiquarian of considerable reputation, a friend of Southey, Samuel Rogers, Macaulay and Sir Walter Scott. Palgrave's mother, a woman of culture and intellectual distinction, did much to foster the liking for art and literature which her son showed from an early age: at the same time, the high standard she set for her children led to a certain forcing of his development. She frequently complained of the child that he was childish and too fond of play. When he was only three years old, she remarked impatiently, " Frank does not make a rapid progress in his book at present—he seems unable to understand that the letters are the symbols of the *sound*. . . . His memory is excellent, and he knows many little poems by heart." Such intellectual forcing induces precocity: it may be the making of a good critic, but it may also nip a creative talent in the bud. At any rate, Palgrave's own verse—he published several books—is negligible. His childhood, nevertheless, was a happy one. The family home was in Hampstead; but frequent visits were paid to Yarmouth, and at the age of fourteen he was taken, with his brother Gifford, for the first of his many trips to Italy. This country inspired him with a passion which throughout his life never faltered. His early studies in Italian art and Greek and Roman literature formed the basis of that ' classical ' taste to which his contemporaries paid tribute.

Palgrave was educated at Charterhouse and Balliol, where he won a scholarship and became a pupil of Jowett. Amongst his Oxford friends were numbered Matthew Arnold and A. H. Clough; and it was Oxford that gave scope to his unusual gift for interesting people in all that he himself admired—a gift of enthusiasm which, regulated by his purity and independence of judgment, was to make him an exceptional anthologist. The influence Palgrave first showed at Oxford enlarged itself afterwards into wider circles, so that Churton Collins was able to write of him: " It may be questioned whether, after Arnold, any other critic of our time contributed so much to educate public taste where in this country it most needs such education. . . . He had no taint of vulgarity, of charlatanism, of insincerity. He never talked or wrote the cant of the cliques or of the multitude. He understood and loved what was excellent; he had no toleration for what was common and second-rate." There are few 'popularisers' of literature for whom so much can be said.

Although he read Classics, obtaining a First in 1847 and being elected Fellow of Exeter College, Palgrave found time for the private study not only of art and literature, but of history and theology—like his parents, he held strong Tractarian sympathies. He had spent 1846 as assistant private secretary to Gladstone. On March 31st, 1849, he first met Tennyson; and two days later he records in his journal, " In the afternoon to A. Tennyson's . . . he read me songs to be inserted in the ' Princess,' and poems on A. Hallam, some exquisite." He now entered the Education Office in Whitehall, where, including a five-year period as Vice-Principal of Kneller Hall training college for schoolmasters, under Frederick Temple, he worked till 1884. In 1862 he married Cecil, daughter of James and Mary Milnes-Gaskell. He was a devoted husband and an indulgent father. The Palgraves lived in London; but in 1872 they bought a house near Lyme Regis as a second home. In 1885, with Browning and Arnold among his supporters, Palgrave was elected to the Chair of Poetry at Oxford, holding it for the next ten years: some of his lectures were printed under the title of *Landscape in Poetry*. His wife died in 1890. " I shall be very happy with you," he said to his daughters towards the end of his life, " only you must not be my slaves." He died in 1897, and was buried in the cemetery on Barnes Common.

*　　*　　*　　*　　*　　*

Apart from his family ties, the most important relationship in Palgrave's life was his friendship with Tennyson. His feeling for the poet was one of frank hero-worship. His affection was fully reciprocated, though there were times when Tennyson became exasperated by his young friend's overzealous solicitude. One such occasion was during a tour they made through Cornwall and the Scillies in 1860, when " Palgrave, who felt himself bound by instructions, which he imagined he had received from Emily, never to let the poet out of his view, for fear that through his short sight he might fall over a cliff or come to some similar harm, was perpetually pursuing him over the rocks and calling out, ' Tennyson! Tennyson! '—which drove poor Alfred to frenzy."[1] However, this tour produced more than Tennyson's irritation with " Palgrave's voice like a bee in a bottle, making the neighbourhood resound with my name." It brought forth the idea of *The Golden Treasury*. Tennyson encouraged his friend to compile this selection of " the best original Lyrical pieces and

[1] *Alfred Tennyson.* By Sir Charles Tennyson (Macmillan).

Songs in our language, by writers not living." Tennyson's own taste is clearly reflected in the volume: " all poems suggested for inclusion were submitted to him at a ten-days' conference held at Farringford in December of this year, when he read each one aloud twice before passing final judgment." It would be wrong, though, to think of Palgrave as a mere enthusiastic retriever, laying his finds at the Master's feet for him to approve or reject. On the contrary, he had a rare faculty for discerning the good both in unfamiliar new work and in the neglected old: he was one of the first to realise the full genius of Tennyson himself and to recognise that of William Barnes; he did much to revive interest in such poets as Herrick and Vaughan, while the large representation of Wordsworth in *The Golden Treasury* helped to restore that poet to the high place he has never since lost.

Published in 1861, *The Golden Treasury* was an immediate success. Ninety years later, it still holds its own among the flood of anthologies which have followed it. How are we to account for this? Notice that word ' best ' in its title. Few present-day anthologists, certainly not the compiler of the supplement in this new edition, would dare to make such a claim. But Palgrave had the Victorian confidence and the classical idea of objective, formal criticism, which enabled him to believe that the ' best ' could be sifted from the less good by a fine discrimination, and *permanently* assessed. We may not approve all his choices in *The Golden Treasury*. We may wonder on what principle Collins's *Ode to Evening*, say, which Palgrave included, can be rated as ' better ' than Blake's *Night*, which he did not: they are, both, poems of grace and power, but so different that one can neither hope nor desire to find a basis of comparison between them. Nevertheless, Palgrave's insistence upon finish and wholeness,[1] strengthened by Tennyson's even severer judgment, is justified by the result—a selection of poems which as a whole transcends literary foibles and fashions, giving the reader the delight that comes from seeing something superlatively well done.

The Golden Treasury commends itself, not only by the formal perfection, and therefore the durability, of the work it presents, but also by its arrangement. To dispose poems of many different writers in such a way that each poem gains from its context and throws light upon those around it, is the supreme gift of the anthologist. In no other way do taste, sensibility, learning, and a fine ear for subtle shades of meaning so clearly reveal themselves. A satisfying arrangement of poems requires a special talent which can be fairly called ' creative.' It is a rare talent: in our own day, Mr. de la Mare possesses it: Palgrave had it too. His

[1] c.f. para. 3 of the Original Preface.

grouping of his material into successive but overlapping themes, within the period that each of his four Books covers, was done with great delicacy, is never obtrusive, and enables the reader both to get more from individual poems and to receive general impressions about the style and poetic interests of each period.

At the same time, as Palgrave says, the book does not attempt to be representative of English poetry as a whole. This is, perhaps, its greatest strength—the limiting of the contents to a given field. It is not, and cannot be, a clearly-defined field, since the word ' lyrical ' has no exact or stabilised meaning. Palgrave, in his Preface, lays down certain principles by which he was guided, and we are not likely to quarrel with these: a lyrical poem " shall turn on some single thought, feeling, or situation ": narrative, descriptive and didactic poems are to be excluded, " unless accompanied by rapidity of movement, brevity, and the colouring of human passion ": he has also left out " what is strictly personal, occasional and religious "; " and, again," he wrote in a letter of March 10th, 1890, " I have excluded from it the poetry of *doubt.*" The distinction between ' strictly personal ' and work with ' the colouring of human passion ' is illuminated in a letter to Lord Lyttleton (February 5th, 1863), when Palgrave defends himself for having omitted the last stanza of Shelley's *Stanzas Written in Dejection Near Naples*: " the very beauty and personal quality of that stanza seemed to me to render the poem less *universal* in interest—to bring it more within the class of individual or occasional poems—to place it among those which require *biographical* notes, and thus to remove it from the class of poems which Tennyson and I wished to unite in the selection." Again, in a letter to Tennyson (October 30th, 1860), we find Palgrave exercised as to whether " *Elegies* such as Gray's, and *Sonnets* should properly be included. They are lyrical in structure, and sonnets have always ranked as lyrical: but their didactic tone appears to me not decisively lyrical in whatever strictness of sense so vague a word can bear."

That Palgrave should not have included Donne, though regrettable, is hardly surprising. The omission of Blake from the 1861 edition is the most unexpected one; and it is the more unaccountable because Palgrave was one of the few men of his age who put a very high value on Blake's poetry. Whether he felt it to come too much within the ' religious ' category, or whether an apparent roughness of form seemed to make it ineligible for *The Golden Treasury,* I do not know. At any rate, I have repaired the omission by starting the new Supplement with a selection of Blake's poems.

*   *   *   *   *   *

The original *Golden Treasury* contained no work by poets living at the time of its compilation. Palgrave revised and enlarged it in 1891: but most subsequent editors have thought it best to take over from where he left off in the 1861 edition. We have, therefore, rather more than a hundred years of verse to choose from in making a new Supplement. Blake, Beddoes, Emily Brontë, George Darley[1] and Poe are the only poets I have included who, being dead by 1860, were eligible for the first edition. One's judgment of contemporaries is so peculiarly fallible that I might have been well advised to follow Palgrave and print no living writer in my Supplement: as it is, I have included little by poets born since 1910: these will have their turn, in twenty-five years or so, when *The Golden Treasury* is supplemented once again, and their work can be viewed in better perspective.

In choosing from the poetry of the last hundred years, I have been guided by two principles only—that the poems should be lyrical, and that they should be good. I have tried to be limited by the first of these rather more rigorously than was Palgrave (one wonders, for instance, how Milton's sonnet *To The Lady Margaret Ley* could have crept past the barriers he erected against non-lyrical and occasional verse). Such a limitation means that I cannot claim my chosen poems to be the best written during the period, or even, necessarily, the best which their authors wrote. It has involved me, too, in special difficulty with the poetry written since about 1917, for this poetry has on the whole tended more and more away from the lyric, or from what most of us still feel as the lyrical note, towards irony, greater complexity, deeper self-consciousness. In the last thirty years, an inordinate number of poems have been printed under the title, *Song*, which by no conceivable exercise of the imagination or the larynx could be made to justify their title; while some of the period's central poems—Yeats's *The Second Coming*, for example, Owen's *Strange Meeting*, or Eliot's *Gerontion*—are outside the lyrical class.

Lyricism, though indefinable, is not difficult to recognise when we meet it. Whether a poem's theme be slight or profound, whether its verbal texture be elaborate or simple, if it is a true lyric it will always manifest itself as such by a certain tone and a certain kind of rhythm. The lyrical impulse makes words sing. The music may be light or grave, pure or heavily orchestrated, thoughtful or rhapsodic, melodious or to some ears discordant; but we are aware of a singing tone—a tone of voice at the opposite

---

[1] Palgrave was misled into printing one of his poems, ' It is not beauty I demand,' attributed to Anon, amongst his selections from the seventeenth century in Book II.

extreme from that of the voice reasoning, arguing, describing. This is not to say that a strong colloquial element may not be present. Browning, Hardy and Robert Frost have, each in his different way, written poems in which the lyrical intonation is reconciled with colloquial phrasing and made as it were to grow out of it. The grafting of the colloquial upon the lyrical is, indeed, one of the most remarkable developments of our period, though we cannot, with some of Donne's poetry in mind, call it an original one. The result is ' impure ' lyric, certainly; but its effect, in successful poems of this kind, is the same as that of purer poetry—we feel that the writer has disappeared into his form, and even if it is a personal one, we are not aware of his personality.

The second mark of the truly lyrical is to be found in the rhythm. As Palgrave realised, the regular iambic pentameter, either rhyming or in blank verse, is the rhythm least amenable to lyric: the one exception seems to be the sonnet form, which still retains vestiges of its musical source; but here the language must be highly and consistently lyrical to compensate for the heaviness of the metre. On the whole, the lyric requires either a shorter line—three or four stresses rather than five or six if the lines are of uniform length; or, in stanzas of differing line-lengths, a strongly-marked rhythmical movement; or, if the lines are longer, an anapaestic rather than an iambic metre. The lyric impulse makes words dance, not stroll or march. With the true lyric, even when there are no refrains, we always expect a refrain and often seem to be hearing one. We may be fairly sure that one reason why Tennyson read aloud each poem submitted to him by Palgrave was to discover whether or no it had this lyrical rhythm.

Many long poems in English contain lyrical passages of great beauty; but I have included only four long poems of our period —ones in which the lyrical tone seems to be sustained throughout: *The Forsaken Merman, The Orphan's Song, The High Tide on the Coast of Lincolnshire, My Lost Youth.* For reasons of space, I am unable to give the whole of *Love in the Valley,* another poem which falls into this category; and I have given extracts from a few more long poems which could not be printed in full: these extracts are, I believe, able to stand by themselves. Of the poets represented here, rather more than half were born before 1870, or came to their maturity in the nineteenth century. The minor poetry of the Victorian age, though it is on the whole less vigorous, less varied and enterprising in subject, less challenging than that of the twentieth century, offers a greater choice of the pure lyric. As to major poets, some to-day would accept the claims to this title of Tennyson, Browning, Arnold, Hopkins, Whitman, Hardy and Yeats, while others might also allow the claims of Dickinson, Meredith, Frost, Eliot and Auden. At any rate, I have tried to give all these a good showing, though it has sometimes put a considerable strain upon my interpretation of 'lyrical.' The reader may feel, again, that the lyrical is subordinate to a philosophic, a dramatic or a descriptive element in such poems as *Modern Love*, *The Combat*, *London Snow*, and *Prelude: the Troops*. It may be so: but, for me, the lyric tone comes through in these poems; and an anthology confined entirely to *pure* lyricism would give too narrow a view of the field we are concerned with.

The period covered by this Supplement takes us from the last flickers of Augustanism in Landor and Bryant, through the long sunset and twilight of the Romantic Movement, up to the so-called neo-Classicism and neo-Romanticism of the 1930's and 1940's. If no poet can be found in the Supplement, apart from Blake, of the highest imaginative scope, the period does at least reveal the vitality, exuberance and variety of English verse, while it is distinguished by the rapid maturing of a poetic tradition in America. It is particularly rich in eccentrics—Clare, Beddoes, Emily Brontë, Barnes, and Melville—who stood outside the main movements of their time, and in poets like Browning, Hopkins, Eliot and Pound whose originality or experimentation has noticeably influenced the tradition.

I would like to thank the publishers, and particularly Mr. G. F. Maine, for their encouragement and help in the preparing of this edition. While reading through the material chosen for it, familiar and unfamiliar, old favourites and (to me) new finds, I returned with readier assent to Palgrave's own words: " As he closes his long survey, the Editor trusts he may add without egotism, that he has found the vague general verdict of popular Fame more just than those have thought, who, with too severe a criticism, would confine judgments on Poetry to ' the selected few of many generations.' "

C. Day Lewis

PREFACE

THIS little Collection differs, it is believed, from others in the attempt made to include in it all the best original Lyrical pieces and Songs in our language, by writers not living,—and none beside the best. Many familiar verses will hence be met with; many also which should be familiar:—the Editor will regard as his fittest readers those who love Poetry so well, that he can offer them nothing not already known and valued.

The Editor is acquainted with no strict and exhaustive definition of Lyrical Poetry; but he has found the task of practical decision increase in clearness and in facility as he advanced with the work, whilst keeping in view a few simple principles. Lyrical has been here held essentially to imply that each Poem shall turn on some single thought, feeling, or situation. In accordance with this, narrative, descriptive, and didactic poems,—unless accompanied by rapidity of movement, brevity, and the colouring of human passion,—have been excluded. Humorous poetry, except in the very unfrequent instances where a truly poetical tone pervades the whole, with what is strictly personal, occasional, and religious, has been considered foreign to the idea of the book. Blank verse and the ten-syllable couplet, with all pieces markedly dramatic, have been rejected as alien from what is commonly understood by Song, and rarely conforming to Lyrical conditions in treatment. But it is not anticipated, nor is it possible, that all readers shall think the line accurately drawn. Some poems, as Gray's 'Elegy,' the 'Allegro' and 'Penseroso,' Wordsworth's 'Ruth' or Campbell's 'Lord Ullin,' might be claimed with perhaps equal justice for a narrative or descriptive selection: whilst with reference especially to Ballads and Sonnets, the Editor can only state that he has taken his utmost pains to decide without caprice or partiality.

This also is all he can plead in regard to a point even more liable to question;—what degree of merit should give rank among the Best. That a Poem shall be worthy of the writer's genius,—that it shall reach a perfection commensurate with its aim,—that we should require finish in proportion to brevity,—that passion, colour, and originality cannot atone for serious imperfections in clearness, unity, or truth,—that a few good lines do not make a good poem,—that popular estimate is serviceable as a guidepost more than as a compass,—above all, that Excellence should be looked for rather in the Whole than in the Parts,—such and other such canons have been always steadily regarded. He may however add that the pieces chosen, and a far larger number rejected, have been carefully and repeatedly considered; and that he has been aided throughout by two friends of independent and exercised judgement, besides the distinguished person addressed in the Dedication. It is hoped that by this procedure the volume has been freed from that onesidedness which must beset individual decisions:—but for the final choice the Editor is alone responsible.

It would obviously have been invidious to apply the standard aimed at in this Collection to the Living. Nor, even in the cases where this might be done without offence, does it appear wise to attempt to anticipate the verdict of the Future on our contemporaries. Should the book last, poems by Tennyson, Bryant, Clare, Lowell, and others, will no doubt claim and obtain their place among the best. But the Editor trusts that this will be effected by other hands, and in days far distant.

Chalmers' vast collection, with the whole works of all accessible poets not contained in it, and the best Anthologies of different periods, have been twice systematically read through: and it is hence improbable that any omissions which may be regretted are due to oversight. The poems are printed entire, except in a very few instances (specified in the notes) where a stanza has been omitted. The omissions have been risked only when the piece could be thus brought to a closer lyrical unity: and, as essentially opposed to this unity, extracts, obviously such, are excluded. In regard to the text, the purpose of the book has appeared to justify the choice of the most poetical version, wherever more than one exists: and much labour has been given to present each poem, in disposition, spelling, and punctuation, to the greatest advantage.

For the permission under which the copyright pieces are inserted, thanks are due to the respective Proprietors, without whose liberal concurrence the scheme of the collection would have been defeated.

In the arrangement, the most poetically-effective order has been attempted. The English mind has passed through phases of thought and cultivation so various and so opposed during these three centuries of Poetry, that a rapid passage between Old and New, like rapid alteration of the eye's focus in looking at the landscape, will always be wearisome and hurtful to the sense of Beauty. The poems have been therefore distributed into Books corresponding, I to the ninety years closing about 1616, II thence to 1700, III to 1800, IV to the half-century just ended. Or, looking at the Poets who more or less give each portion its distinctive character, they might be called the Books of Shakespeare, Milton, Gray, and Wordsworth. The volume, in this respect, so far as the limitations of its range allow, accurately reflects the natural growth and evolution of our Poetry. A rigidly chronological sequence, however, rather fits a collection aiming at instruction than at pleasure, and the Wisdom which comes through Pleasure:—within each book the pieces have therefore been arranged in gradations of feeling or subject. The development of the symphonies of Mozart and Beethoven has been here thought of as a model, and nothing placed without careful consideration. And it is hoped that the contents of this Anthology will thus be found to present a certain unity, ' as episodes,' in the noble language of Shelley, ' to that great Poem which all poets, like the co-operating thoughts of one great mind, have built up since the beginning of the world.'

As he closes his long survey, the Editor trusts he may add without egotism, that he had found the vague general verdict of popular Fame more just than those have thought, who, with too severe a criticism, would confine judgements on Poetry to ' the selected few of many generations.' Not many appear to have gained reputation without some gift or performance that, in due degree, deserved it: and if no verses by certain writers who show less strength than sweetness, or more thought than mastery in expression, are printed in this volume, it should not be imagined that they have been excluded without much hesitation and regret,—far less that they have been slighted. Throughout this vast and pathetic array of Singers now silent, few have been honoured with the name Poet, and have not possessed a skill in words, a sympathy with beauty, a tenderness of feeling, or seriousness in reflection, which render their works, although never perhaps attaining that loftier and finer excellence here required,— better worth reading than much of what fills the scanty hours that most men spare for self-improvement, or for pleasure in any of its more elevated and permanent forms.—And if this be true of even mediocre poetry, for how much more are we indebted to the best! Like the fabled fountain of the Azores, but with a more various power, the magic of this Art can confer on each period of life its appropriate blessings: on early years Experience, on maturity Calm, on age Youthfulness. Poetry gives treasures ' more golden than gold,' leading us in higher and healthier ways than those of the world, and interpreting to us the lessons of Nature. But she speaks best for herself. Her true accents, if the plan has been executed with success, may be heard throughout the following pages:—wherever the Poets of England are honoured, wherever the dominant language of the world is spoken, it is hoped that they will find fit audience.

F. T. P.

THE GOLDEN TREASURY
BOOK FIRST

1

SPRING

Spring, the sweet Spring, is the year's pleasant king;
Then blooms each thing, then maids dance in a ring,
Cold doth not sting, the pretty birds do sing,
    Cuckoo, jug-jug, pu-we, to-witta-woo!

The palm and may make country houses gay,   5
Lambs frisk and play, the shepherds pipe all day,
And we hear ay birds tune this merry lay,
    Cuckoo, jug-jug, pu-we, to-witta-woo!

The fields breathe sweet, the daisies kiss our feet,
Young lovers meet, old wives a-sunning sit,   10
In every street these tunes our ears do greet,
    Cuckoo, jug-jug, pu-we, to-witta-woo!
      Spring! the sweet Spring!

T. NASH

2

SUMMONS TO LOVE

      Phœbus, arise!
     And paint the sable skies
     With azure, white, and red:
Rouse Memnon's mother from her Tithon's bed
That she thy càreer may with roses spread: 5
The nightingales thy coming each-where sing:
     Make an eternal spring,
Give life to this dark world which lieth dead;
     Spread forth thy golden hair
In larger locks than thou wast wont before,   10
     And emperor-like decore
With diadem of pearl thy temples fair:
     Chase hence the ugly night
Which serves but to make dear thy glorious light.

—This is that happy morn,   15
That day, long-wishéd day
Of all my life so dark,
(If cruel stars have not my ruin sworn
    And fates my hopes betray),
    Which, purely white, deserves   20
An everlasting diamond should it mark.
This is the morn should bring unto this grove
My Love, to hear and recompense my love.
    Fair King, who all preserves,
    But show thy blushing beams,   25
    And thou two sweeter eyes
Shalt see than those which by Peneus' streams
    Did once thy heart surprise.
Now, Flora, deck thyself in fairest guise:
    If that ye, winds, would hear   30
A voice surpassing far Amphion's lyre,
    Your furious chiding stay;
    Let Zephyr only breathe,
    And with her tresses play.
    —The winds all silent are,   35
    And Phoebus in his chair
    Ensaffroning sea and air
    Makes vanish every star:
    Night like a drunkard reels
Beyond the hills, to shun his flaming wheels;   40
The fields with flowers are deck'd in every hue,
The clouds with orient gold spangle their blue;
    Here is the pleasant place—
And nothing wanting is, save She, alas!

W. DRUMMOND OF HAWTHORNDEN

3

TIME AND LOVE

I

When I have seen by Time's fell hand defaced
    The rich proud cost of out-worn buried age;
When sometime lofty towers I see down-razed,
    And brass eternal slave to mortal rage;

When I have seen the hungry ocean gain   5
   Advantage on the kingdom of the shore,
And the firm soil win of the watery main,
   Increasing store with loss, and loss with store;

When I have seen such interchange of state,
   Or state itself confounded to decay,   10
Ruin hath taught me thus to ruminate—
   That Time will come and take my Love away:

—This thought is as a death, which cannot choose
But weep to have that which it fears to lose.

                    W. SHAKESPEARE

4

II

Since brass, nor stone, nor earth, nor boundless sea,
   But sad mortality o'ersways their power,
How with this rage shall beauty hold a plea,
   Whose action is no stronger than a flower?

O how shall summer's honey breath hold out   5
   Against the wreckful siege of battering days,
When rocks impregnable are not so stout
   Nor gates of steel so strong, but time decays?

O fearful meditation! where, alack!
   Shall Time's best jewel from Time's chest lie hid?   10
Or what strong hand can hold his swift foot back,
   Or who his spoil of beauty can forbid?

O! none, unless this miracle have might,
That in black ink my love may still shine bright.

                    W. SHAKESPEARE

5

THE PASSIONATE SHEPHERD TO HIS LOVE

Come live with me and be my Love,
And we will all the pleasures prove
That hills and valleys, dale and field,
And all the craggy mountains yield.

There will we sit upon the rocks   5
And see the shepherds feed their flocks,
By shallow rivers, to whose falls
Melodious birds sing madrigals.

There will I make thee beds of roses
And a thousand fragrant posies,   10
A cap of flowers, with a kirtle
Embroider'd all with leaves of myrtle.

A gown made of the finest wool,
Which from our pretty lambs we pull,
Fair linéd slippers for the cold,   15
With buckles of the purest gold.

A belt of straw and ivy buds
With coral clasps and amber studs:
And if these pleasures may thee move,
Come live with me and be my Love.   20

Thy silver dishes for thy meat
As precious as the gods do eat,
Shall on an ivory table be
Prepared each day for thee and me.

The shepherd swains shall dance and sing   25
For thy delight each May-morning:
If these delights thy mind may move,
Then live with me and be my Love.

C. MARLOWE

6

A MADRIGAL

Crabbed Age and Youth
Cannot live together:
  Youth is full of pleasance,
Age is full of care;
  Youth like summer morn,   5
Age like winter weather,
  Youth like summer brave,
Age like winter bare:
  Youth is full of sport,
  Age's breath is short,   10
Youth is nimble, Age is lame:
  Youth is hot and bold,
  Age is weak and cold,
Youth is wild, and Age is tame:—
  Age, I do abhor thee,   15
  Youth, I do adore thee;
O! my Love, my Love is young!
  Age, I do defy thee—
  O sweet shepherd, hie thee,
For methinks thou stay'st too long.   20

W. SHAKESPEARE

7

Under the greenwood tree
Who loves to lie with me,
And turn his merry note
Unto the sweet bird's throat—
Come hither, come hither, come hither!   5
    Here shall he see
    No enemy
But winter and rough weather.

Who doth ambition shun
And loves to live i' the sun,   10
Seeking the food he eats
And pleased with what he gets—

Come hither, come hither, come hither!
    Here shall he see
    No enemy
But winter and rough weather.

W. SHAKESPEARE

8

It was a lover and his lass
    With a hey and a ho, and a hey-nonino!
That o'er the green cornfield did pass
In the spring time, the only pretty ring time,
When birds do sing hey ding a ding ding: 5
    Sweet lovers love the Spring.

Between the acres of the rye
These pretty country folks would lie:

This carol they began that hour,
How that a life was but a flower: 10

And therefore take the present time
    With a hey and a ho, and a hey-nonino!
For love is crownéd with the prime
In spring time, the only pretty ring time,
When birds do sing hey ding a ding ding:
    Sweet lovers love the Spring.   16

W. SHAKESPEARE

9

PRESENT IN ABSENCE

Absence, hear thou my protestation
    Against thy strength,
    Distance, and length;
Do what thou canst for alteration:
    For hearts of truest mettle   5
    Absence doth join, and Time doth settle.

Who loves a mistress of such quality,
    He soon hath found
    Affection's ground

Beyond time, place, and all mortality.   10
   To hearts that cannot vary
   Absence is Present, Time doth tarry.

By absence this good means I gain,
   That I can catch her,
      Where none can watch her,   15
In some close corner of my brain:
   There I embrace and kiss her;
   And so I both enjoy and miss her.

ANON

10

ABSENCE

Being your slave, what should I do but tend
   Upon the hours and times of your desire?
I have no precious time at all to spend
   Nor services to do, till you require:

Nor dare I chide the world-without-end hour   5
   Whilst I, my sovereign, watch the clock for you,
Nor think the bitterness of absence sour
   When you have bid your servant once adieu:

Nor dare I question with my jealous thought
   Where you may be, or your affairs suppose,   10
But like a sad slave, stay and think of nought
   Save, where you are, how happy you make those;—

So true a fool is love, that in your will,
Though you do anything, he thinks no ill.

W. SHAKESPEARE

11

How like a winter hath my absence been
   From Thee, the pleasure of the fleeting year!
What freezings have I felt, what dark days seen,
   What old December's bareness everywhere!

And yet this time removed was summer's time;   5
  The teeming autumn, big with rich increase,
Bearing the wanton burden of the prime
  Like widow'd wombs after their lords' decease:

Yet this abundant issue seem'd to me
  But hope of orphans, and unfather'd fruit;   10
For summer and his pleasures wait on thee,
  And, thou away, the very birds are mute;

Or if they sing, 'tis with so dull a cheer,
That leaves look pale, dreading the winter's near.

W. SHAKESPEARE

12

A CONSOLATION

When in disgrace with fortune and men's eyes
  I all alone beweep my outcast state,
And trouble deaf heaven with my bootless cries,
  And look upon myself, and curse my fate;

Wishing me like to one more rich in hope,   5
  Featured like him, like him with friends possest,
Desiring this man's art, and that man's scope,
  With what I most enjoy contented least;

Yet in these thoughts myself almost despising,
  Haply I think on Thee—and then my state,   10
Like to the lark at break of day arising
  From sullen earth, sings hymns at heaven's gate;

For thy sweet love remember'd such wealth brings,
That then I scorn to change my state with kings.

W. SHAKESPEARE

13

THE UNCHANGEABLE

O never say that I was false of heart,
  Though absence seem'd my flame to qualify:
As easy might I from myself depart
  As from my soul, which in thy breast doth lie;

That is my home of love; if I have ranged,   5
  Like him that travels, I return again,
Just to the time, not with the time exchanged,
  So that myself bring water for my stain.

Never believe, though in my nature reign'd
  All frailties that besiege all kinds of blood,   10
That it could so preposterously be stain'd
  To leave for nothing all thy sum of good:

For nothing this wide universe I call,
Save thou, my rose: in it thou art my all.

                                        W. SHAKESPEARE

14

To me, fair Friend, you never can be old,
  For as you were when first your eye I eyed
Such seems your beauty still. Three winters cold
  Have from the forests shook three summers' pride;

Three beauteous springs to yellow autumn turn'd   5
  In process of the seasons have I seen,
Three April perfumes in three hot Junes burn'd,
  Since first I saw you fresh, which yet are green.

Ah! yet doth beauty, like a dial-hand,
  Steal from his figure, and no pace perceived;   10
So your sweet hue, which methinks still doth stand,
  Hath motion, and mine eye may be deceived:

For fear of which, hear this, thou age unbred,—
Ere you were born, was beauty's summer dead.

                                        W. SHAKESPEARE

15

DIAPHENIA

Diaphenia like the daffadowndilly,
  White as the sun, fair as the lily,
Heigh ho, how I do love thee!
  I do love thee as my lambs
  Are belovéd of their dams;   5
How blest were I if thou would'st prove me.

Diaphenia like the spreading roses,
  That in thy sweets all sweets encloses,
Fair sweet, how I do love thee!
  I do love thee as each flower   10
  Loves the sun's life-giving power;
For dead, thy breath to life might move me.

Diaphenia like to all things blesséd
  When all thy praises are expresséd,
Dear joy, how I do love thee!   15
  As the birds do love the spring,
  Or the bees their careful king:
Then in requite, sweet virgin, love me!

H. CONSTABLE

16

ROSALYNDE

Like to the clear in highest sphere
  Where all imperial glory shines,
Of selfsame colour is her hair
    Whether unfolded, or in twines:
        Heigh ho, fair Rosalynde!   5
Her eyes are sapphires set in snow,
    Resembling heaven by every wink;
The Gods do fear whenas they glow,
    And I do tremble when I think
        Heigh ho, would she were mine!   10

Her cheeks are like the blushing cloud
    That beautifies Aurora's face,
Or like the silver crimson shroud

That Phoebus' smiling looks doth grace;
    Heigh ho, fair Rosalynde!   15
Her lips are like two budded roses
    Whom ranks of lilies neighbour nigh,
Within which bounds she balm encloses
    Apt to entice a deity:
        Heigh ho, would she were mine!   20

Her neck is like a stately tower
    Where Love himself imprison'd lies,
To watch for glances every hour
    From her divine and sacred eyes:
        Heigh ho, fair Rosalynde!   25
Her paps are centres of delight,
    Her breasts are orbs of heavenly frame,
Where Nature moulds the dew of light
    To feed perfection with the same:
        Heigh ho, would she were mine!   30

With orient pearl, with ruby red,
    With marble white, with sapphire blue
Her body every way is fed,
    Yet soft in touch and sweet in view:
        Heigh ho, fair Rosalynde!   35
Nature herself her shape admires;
    The Gods are wounded in her sight;
And Love forsakes his heavenly fires
    And at her eyes his brand doth light:
        Heigh ho, would she were mine!   40

Then muse not, Nymphs, though I bemoan
    The absence of fair Rosalynde,
Since for a fair there's fairer none,
    Nor for her virtues so divine:
        Heigh ho, fair Rosalynde;   45
Heigh ho, my heart! would God that she were mine!
                         T. LODGE

17

COLIN

Beauty sat bathing by a spring
  Where fairest shades did hide her;
The winds blew calm, the birds did sing,
  The cool streams ran beside her.
My wanton thoughts enticed mine eye   5
  To see what was forbidden:
But better memory said, fie!
  So vain desire was chidden:—
      Hey nonny nonny O!
      Hey nonny nonny!   10

Into a slumber then I fell,
  When fond imagination
Seem'd to see, but could not tell
  Her feature or her fashion.
But ev'n as babes in dreams do smile,   15
  And sometimes fall a-weeping,
So I awaked, as wise this while
  As when I fell a-sleeping:—
      Hey nonny nonny O!
      Hey nonny nonny!   20

THE SHEPHERD TONY

18

TO HIS LOVE

Shall I compare thee to a summer's day?
  Thou art more lovely and more temperate:
Rough winds do shake the darling buds of May,
  And summer's lease hath all too short a date:

Sometime too hot the eye of heaven shines,   5
  And often is his gold complexion dimm'd:
And every fair from fair sometime declines,
  By chance, or nature's changing course, untrimm'd.

But thy eternal summer shall not fade
  Nor lose possession of that fair thou owest;   10

Nor shall death brag thou wanderest in his shade,
   When in eternal lines to time thou growest:

So long as men can breathe, or eyes can see,
So long lives this, and this gives life to thee.

                                        W. SHAKESPEARE

19

TO HIS LOVE

When in the chronicle of wasted time
   I see descriptions of the fairest wights,
And beauty making beautiful old rhyme
   In praise of ladies dead, and lovely knights;

Then in the blazon of sweet beauty's best   5
   Of hand, of foot, of lip, of eye, of brow,
I see their antique pen would have exprest
   Ev'n such a beauty as you master now.

So all their praises are but prophecies
   Of this our time, all you prefiguring;   10
And, for they look'd but with divining eyes,
   They had not skill enough your worth to sing:

For we, which now behold these present days,
Have eyes to wonder but lack tongues to praise.

                                        W. SHAKESPEARE

20

LOVE'S PERJURIES

On a day, alack the day!
Love, whose month is ever May,
Spied a blossom passing fair
Playing in the wanton air:
Through the velvet leaves the wind,   5
All unseen, 'gan passage find;
That the lover, sick to death,
Wish'd himself the heaven's breath.
Air, quoth he, thy cheeks may blow;
Air, would I might triumph so!   10

But, alack, my hand is sworn
Ne'er to pluck thee from thy thorn:
Vow, alack, for youth unmeet;
Youth so apt to pluck a sweet.
Do not call it sin in me   15
That I am forsworn for thee:
Thou for whom Jove would swear
Juno but an Ethiope were,
And deny himself for Jove,
Turning mortal for thy love.   20

                              W. SHAKESPEARE

21

A SUPPLICATION

Forget not yet the tried intent
Of such a truth as I have meant;
My great travail so gladly spent,
                    Forget not yet!

Forget not yet when first began   5
The weary life ye know, since whan
The suit, the service none tell can;
                    Forget not yet!

Forget not yet the great assays,
Toe cruel wrong, the scornful ways,   10
The painful patience in delays,
                    Forget not yet!

Forget not! O, forget not this,
How long ago hath been, and is
The mind that never meant amiss—   15
                    Forget not yet!

Forget not then thine own approved
The which so long hath thee so loved,
Whose steadfast faith yet never moved—
                    Forget not this!   20

                              SIR T. WYATT

22

TO AURORA

O if thou knew'st how thou thyself dost harm,
  And dost prejudge thy bliss, and spoil my rest;
  Then thou would'st melt the ice out of thy breast
And thy relenting heart would kindly warm.

O if thy pride did not our joys controul, 5
  What world of loving wonders should'st thou see!
  For if I saw thee once transform'd in me,
Then in thy bosom I would pour my soul;

Then all my thoughts should in thy visage shine,
  And if that aught mischanced thou should'st not moan 10
  Nor bear the burthen of thy griefs alone;
No, I would have my share in what were thine:

And whilst we thus should make our sorrows one,
This happy harmony would make them none.

W. ALEXANDER, EARL OF STERLINE

23

TRUE LOVE

Let me not to the marriage of true minds
  Admit impediments. Love is not love
Which alters when it alteration finds,
  Or bends with the remover to remove:—

O no! it is an ever-fixéd mark 5
  That looks on tempests, and is never shaken;
It is the star to every wandering bark,
  Whose worth's unknown, although his height be taken.

Love's not Time's fool, though rosy lips and cheeks
  Within his bending sickle's compass come; 10
Love alters not with his brief hours and weeks,
  But bears it out ev'n to the edge of doom:—

If this be error, and upon me proved,
I never writ, nor no man ever loved.

W. SHAKESPEARE

24

A DITTY

My true-love hath my heart, and I have his,
  By just exchange one for another given:
I hold his dear, and mine he cannot miss,
  There never was a better bargain driven:
    My true-love hath my heart, and I have his.   5

His heart in me keeps him and me in one,
  My heart in him his thoughts and senses guides:
He loves my heart, for once it was his own,
  I cherish his because in me it bides:
    My true-love hath my heart, and I have his.   10

                SIR P. SIDNEY

25

LOVE'S OMNIPRESENCE

Were I as base as is the lowly plain,
  And you, my Love, as high as heaven above,
Yet should the thoughts of me your humble swain
  Ascend to heaven, in honour of my Love.

Were I as high as heaven above the plain,   5
  And you, my Love, as humble and as low
As are the deepest bottoms of the main,
  Whereso'er you were, with you my love should go.

Were you the earth, dear Love, and I the skies,
  My love should shine on you like to the sun,   10
And look upon you with ten thousand eyes
  Till heaven wax'd blind, and till the world were done.

Whereso'er I am, below, or else above you,
Whereso'er you are, my heart shall truly love you.

                J. SYLVESTER

26

CARPE DIEM

O Mistress mine, where are you roaming?
O stay and hear! your true-love's coming
    That can sing both high and low;
Trip no further, pretty sweeting,
Journeys end in lovers' meeting—   5
    Every wise man's son doth know.

What is love? 'tis not hereafter;
Present mirth hath present laughter;
    What's to come is still unsure:
In delay there lies no plenty,—   10
Then come kiss me, Sweet-and-twenty,
    Youth's a stuff will not endure.
W. SHAKESPEARE

27

WINTER

When icicles hang by the wall.
    And Dick the shepherd blows his nail,
And Tom bears logs into the hall,
    And milk comes frozen home in pail;
When blood is nipt, and ways be foul,   5
Then nightly sings the staring owl
        Tuwhoo!
Tuwhit! tuwhoo! A merry note!
While greasy Joan doth keel the pot.

When all aloud the wind doth blow,   10
    And coughing drowns the parson's saw.
And birds sit brooding in the snow,
    And Marian's nose looks red and raw;
When roasted crabs hiss in the bowl—
Then nightly sings the staring owl   15
        Tuwhoo!
Tuwhit! tuwhoo! A merry note!
While greasy Joan doth keel the pot.
W. SHAKESPEARE

28

That time of year thou may'st in me behold
　When yellow leaves, or none, or few, do hang
Upon those boughs which shake against the cold,
　Bare ruin'd choirs, where late the sweet birds sang.

In me thou see'st the twilight of such day　　　　　　5
　As after sunset fadeth in the west,
Which by and by black night doth take away,
　Death's second self, that seals up all in rest.

In me thou see'st the glowing of such fire,
　That on the ashes of his youth doth lie　　　　　　10
As the death-bed whereon it must expire,
　Consumed with that which it was nourish'd by:
—This thou perceiv'st, which makes thy love more strong.
To love that well which thou must leave ere long.

W. SHAKESPEARE

29

REMEMBRANCE

When to the sessions of sweet silent thought
　I summon up remembrance of things past,
I sigh the lack of many a thing I sought,
　And with old woes new wail my dear time's waste;

Then can I drown an eye, unused to flow,　　　　　5
　For precious friends hid in death's dateless night,
And weep afresh love's long-since-cancell'd woe,
　And moan the expense of many a vanish'd sight.

Then can I grieve at grievances foregone,
　And heavily from woe to woe tell o'er　　　　　　10
The sad account of fore-bemoanéd moan,
　Which I new pay as if not paid before:

—But if the while I think on thee, dear friend,
All losses are restored, and sorrows end.

W. SHAKESPEARE

30

REVOLUTIONS

Like as the waves make towards the pebbled shore,
  So do our minutes hasten to their end;
Each changing place with that which goes before,
  In sequent toil all forwards do contend.

Nativity, once in the main of light,   5
  Crawls to maturity, wherewith being crown'd,
Crooked eclipses 'gainst his glory fight,
  And Time that gave doth now his gift confound.

Time doth transfix the flourish set on youth,
  And delves the parallels in beauty's brow;   10
Feeds on the rarities of nature's truth,
  And nothing stands but for his scythe to mow:

And yet, to times in hope, my verse shall stand
Praising thy worth, despite his cruel hand.

W. SHAKESPEARE

31

Farewell! thou art too dear for my possessing
  And like enough thou know'st thy estimate:
The charter of thy worth gives thee releasing;
  My bonds in thee are all determinate.

For how do I hold thee but by thy granting?   5
  And for that riches where is my deserving?
The cause of this fair gift in me is wanting,
  And so my patent back again is swerving.

Thyself thou gav'st, thy own worth then not knowing,
  Or me, to whom thou gav'st it, else mistaking;   10
So thy great gift, upon misprision growing,
  Comes home again, on better judgement making.

Thus have I had thee as a dream doth flatter;
In sleep, a king; but waking, no such matter.

W. SHAKESPEARE

32

THE LIFE WITHOUT PASSION

They that have power to hurt, and will do none,
　That do not do the thing they most do show,
Who, moving others, are themselves as stone,
　Unmovéd, cold, and to temptation slow,—

They rightly do inherit Heaven's graces,　　　　　　5
　And husband nature's riches from expense;
They are the lords and owners of their faces,
　Others, but stewards of their excellence.

The summer's flower is to the summer sweet,
　Though to itself it only live and die;　　　　　　　10
But if that flower with base infection meet,
　The basest weed outbraves his dignity:

For sweetest things turn sourest by their deeds;
Lilies that fester smell far worse than weeds.

W. SHAKESPEARE

33

THE LOVER'S APPEAL

And wilt thou leave me thus?
　Say nay! say nay! for shame!
　To save thee from the blame
　Of all my grief and grame.
And wilt thou leave me thus?　　　　　　　　　5
　Say nay! say nay!

And wilt thou leave me thus,
　That hath loved thee so long
　In wealth and woe among?
　And is thy heart so strong　　　　　　　　　10
As for to leave me thus?
　Say nay! say nay!

And wilt thou leave me thus,
  That hath given thee my heart
  Never for to depart   15
  Neither for pain nor smart?
And wilt thou leave me thus?
    Say nay! say nay!

And wilt thou leave me thus,
  And have no more pity   20
  Of him that loveth thee?
  Alas! thy cruelty!
And wilt thou leave me thus?
    Say nay! say nay!

SIR T. WYATT

34

THE NIGHTINGALE

As it fell upon a day
In the merry month of May,
Sitting in a pleasant shade
Which a grove of myrtles made,
Beasts did leap and birds did sing,   5
Trees did grow and plants did spring,
Every thing did banish moan
Save the Nightingale alone.
She, poor bird, as all forlorn,
Lean'd her breast up-till a thorn,   10
And there sung the dolefull'st ditty
That to hear it was great pity.
Fie, fie, fie, now would she cry;
Tereu, tereu, by and by:
That to hear her so complain   15
Scarce I could from tears refrain;
For her griefs so lively shown
Made me think upon mine own.
—Ah, thought I, thou mourn'st in vain,
None takes pity on thy pain: 20
Senseless trees, they cannot hear thee,
Ruthless beasts, they will not cheer thee;
King Pandion, he is dead,
All thy friends are lapp'd in lead:

All thy fellow birds do sing   25
Careless of thy sorrowing:
Even so, poor bird, like thee
None alive will pity me.

R. BARNFIELD

35

Care-charmer Sleep, son of the sable Night,
    Brother to Death, in silent darkness born,
Relieve my anguish, and restore the light;
    With dark forgetting of my care return.

And let the day be time enough to mourn   5
The shipwreck of my ill-adventured youth:
    Let waking eyes suffice to wail their scorn,
Without the torment of the night's untruth.

Cease, dreams, the images of day-desires,
    To model forth the passions of the morrow;   10
Never let rising Sun approve you liars
    To add more grief to aggravate my sorrow:

Still let me sleep, embracing clouds in vain,
And never wake to feel the day's disdain.

S. DANIEL

36

MADRIGAL

Take, O take those lips away
    That so sweetly were forsworn,
And those eyes, the break of day,
    Lights that do mislead the morn:
But my kisses bring again,   5
            Bring again—
Seals of love, but seal'd in vain,
            Seal'd in vain!

W. SHAKESPEARE

37

LOVE'S FAREWELL

Since there's no help, come let us kiss and part,—
    Nay I have done, you get no more of me;
And I am glad, yea, glad with all my heart,
    That thus so cleanly I myself can free;

Shake hands for ever, cancel all our vows,   5
    And when we meet at any time again,
Be it not seen in either of our brows
    That we one jot of former love retain.

Now at the last gasp of love's latest breath,
    When, his pulse failing, passion speechless lies,   10
When faith is kneeling by his bed of death,
    And innocence is closing up his eyes,

—Now if thou would'st, when all have given him over,
From death to life thou might'st him yet recover!
                                                M. DRAYTON

38

TO HIS LUTE

My lute, be as thou wert when thou didst grow
    With thy green mother in some shady grove,
    When immelodious winds but made thee move,
And birds their ramage did on thee bestow.

Since that dear Voice which did thy sounds approve,   5
Which wont in such harmonious strains to flow,
    Is reft from Earth to tune those spheres above,
What art thou but a harbinger of woe?

Thy pleasing notes be pleasing notes no more,
    But orphans' wailings to the fainting ear;   10
    Each stroke a sigh, each sound draws forth a tear;
For which be silent as in woods before:

Or if that any hand to touch thee deign,
Like widow'd turtle still her loss complain.

W. DRUMMOND

39

BLIND LOVE

O me! what eyes hath love put in my head
  Which have no correspondence with true sight:
Or if they have, where is my judgement fled
  That censures falsely what they are aright?

If that be fair whereon my false eyes dote,   5
  What means the world to say it is not so?
If it be not, then love doth well denote
  Love's eye is not so true as all men's: No,

How can it? O how can love's eye be true,
  That is so vex'd with watching and with tears?   10
No marvel then though I mistake my view:
  The sun itself sees not till heaven clears.

O cunning Love! with tears thou keep'st me blind,
Lest eyes well-seeing thy foul faults should find!

W. SHAKESPEARE

40

THE UNFAITHFUL SHEPHERDESS

While that the sun with his beams hot
  Scorchéd the fruits in vale and mountain,
Philon the shepherd, late forgot,
  Sitting beside a crystal fountain,
    In shadow of a green oak tree   5
    Upon his pipe this song play'd he:
Adieu Love, adieu Love, untrue Love,
Untrue Love, untrue Love, adieu Love;
Your mind is light, soon lost for new love.

So long as I was in your sight 10
 I was your heart, your soul, and treasure;
And evermore you sobb'd and sigh'd
 Burning in flames beyond all measure:
  —Three days endured your love to me,
  And it was lost in other three! 15
Adieu Love, adieu Love, untrue Love,
Untrue Love, untrue Love, adieu Love;
Your mind is light, soon lost for new love.

Another Shepherd you did see
 To whom your heart was soon enchainéd; 20
Full soon your love was leapt from me,
 Full soon my place he had obtainéd.
  Soon came a third, your love to win,
  And we were out and he was in.
Adieu Love, adieu Love, untrue Love, 25
Untrue Love, untrue Love, adieu Love;
Your mind is light, soon lost for new love.

Sure you have made me passing glad
 That you your mind so soon removéd,
Before that I the leisure had 30
 To choose you for my best belovéd:
  For all your love was past and done
  Two days before it was begun:—
Adieu Love, adieu Love, untrue Love,
Untrue Love, untrue Love, adieu Love; 35
Your mind is light, soon lost for new love.

ANON

41

A RENUNCIATION

If women could be fair, and yet not fond,
 Or that their love were firm, not fickle still,
I would not marvel that they make men bond
 By service long to purchase their good will;
But when I see how frail those creatures are, 5
I muse that men forget themselves so far.

To mark the choice they make, and how they change,
 How oft from Phoebus they do flee to Pan;

Unsettled still, like haggards wild they range,
  These gentle birds that fly from man to man;   10
Who would not scorn and shake them from the fist,
And let them fly, fair fools, which way they list?

Yet for disport we fawn and flatter both,
  To pass the time when nothing else can please,
And train them to our lure with subtle oath,   15
  Till, weary of their wiles, ourselves we ease;
And then we say when we their fancy try,
To play with fools, O what a fool was I!

                                        E. VERE, EARL OF OXFORD

42

Blow, blow, thou winter wind
Thou art not so unkind
  As man's ingratitude;
Thy tooth is not so keen
Because thou art not seen,   5
  Although thy breath be rude.
Heigh ho! sing heigh ho! unto the green holly:
Most friendship is feigning, most loving mere folly:
  Then, heigh ho! the holly!
  This life is most jolly.   10

Freeze, freeze, thou bitter sky,
That dost not bite so nigh
  As benefits forgot:
Though thou the waters warp,
Thy sting is not so sharp   15
  As friend remember'd not.
Heigh ho! sing heigh ho! unto the green holly:
Most friendship is feigning, most loving mere folly:
  Then, heigh ho! the holly!
  This life is most jolly.   20

                            W. SHAKESPEARE

43

MADRIGAL

My thoughts hold mortal strife
I do detest my life,
And with lamenting cries,
Peace to my soul to bring,
Oft call that prince which here doth monarchize: 5
   —But he, grim grinning King,
Who caitiffs scorns, and doth the blest surprise,
Late having deck'd with beauty's rose his tomb,
Disdains to crop a weed, and will not come.

W. DRUMMOND

44

DIRGE OF LOVE

Come away, come away, Death,
And in sad cypres let me be laid;
   Fly away, fly away, breath;
I am slain by a fair cruel maid.
My shroud of white, stuck all with yew,   5
     O prepare it!
My part of death, no one so true
     Did share it.

Not a flower, not a flower sweet
On my black coffin let there be strown;   10
   Not a friend, not a friend greet
My poor corpse, where my bones shall be thrown:
A thousand thousand sighs to save,
     Lay me, O where
Sad true lover never find my grave,   15
     To weep there.

W. SHAKESPEARE

45

FIDELE

Fear no more the heat o' the sun
    Nor the furious winter's rages;
Thou thy worldly task hast done,
    Home art gone and ta'en thy wages:
Golden lads and girls all must,   5
As chimney-sweepers, come to dust.

Fear no more the frown o' the great,
    Thou art past the tyrant's stroke;
Care no more to clothe and eat;
    To thee the reed is as the oak: 10
The sceptre, learning, physic, must
All follow this, and come to dust.

Fear no more the lightning-flash
    Nor the all-dreaded thunder-stone;
Fear not slander, censure rash;   15
    Thou hast finish'd joy and moan:
All lovers young, all lovers must
Consign to thee, and come to dust.

W. SHAKESPEARE

46

A SEA DIRGE

Full fathom five thy father lies:
    Of his bones are coral made;
Those are pearls that were his eyes:
    Nothing of him that doth fade
But doth suffer a sea-change   5
Into something rich and strange.
Sea-nymphs hourly ring his knell:
Hark! now I hear them,—
    Ding, dong, bell.

W. SHAKESPEARE

47

A LAND DIRGE

Call for the robin-redbreast and the wren,
  Since o'er shady groves they hover
  And with leaves and flowers do cover
The friendless bodies of unburied men.
  Call unto his funeral dole   5
  The ant, the field-mouse, and the mole,
To rear him hillocks that shall keep him warm
And (when gay tombs are robb'd) sustain no harm;
But keep the wolf far thence, that's foe to men,
For with his nails he'll dig them up again.   10

J. WEBSTER

48

POST MORTEM

If thou survive my well-contented day
  When that churl Death my bones with dust shall cover,
And shalt by fortune once more re-survey
  These poor rude lines of thy deceaséd lover;
Compare them with the bettering of the time,   5
  And though they be outstripp'd by every pen,
Reserve them for my love, not for their rhyme
  Exceeded by the height of happier men.

O then vouchsafe me but this loving thought—
  ' Had my friend's muse grown with this growing age,   10
A dearer birth than this his love had brought,
  To march in ranks of better equipage:

But since he died, and poets better prove,
Theirs for their style I'll read, his for his love.'

W. SHAKESPEARE

49

THE TRIUMPH OF DEATH

No longer mourn for me when I am dead
  Than you shall hear the surly sullen bell
Give warning to the world, that I am fled
  From this vile world, with vilest worms to dwell;

Nay, if you read this line, remember not   5
  The hand that writ it; for I love you so,
That I in your sweet thoughts would be forgot
  If thinking on me then should make you woe.

O if, I say, you look upon this verse
  When I perhaps compounded am with clay,   10
Do not so much as my poor name rehearse,
  But let your love even with my life decay;

Lest the wise world should look into your moan,
And mock you with me after I am gone.

                           W. SHAKESPEARE

50

MADRIGAL

Tell me where is Fancy bred,
Or in the heart, or in the head?
How begot, how nourishéd?
    Reply, reply.
It is engender'd in the eyes,   5
With gazing fed; and Fancy dies
In the cradle where it lies:
  Let us all ring Fancy's knell;
  I'll begin it,—Ding, dong, bell.
    —Ding, dong, bell.   10

                     W. SHAKESPEARE

51

CUPID AND CAMPASPE

Cupid and my Campaspe play'd
At cards for kisses; Cupid paid:
He stakes his quiver, bow, and arrows,
His mother's doves, and team of sparrows;
Loses them too; then down he throws   5
The coral of his lip, the rose
Growing on 's cheek (but none knows how);
With these, the crystal of his brow,
And then the dimple of his chin;
All these did my Campaspe win: 10
At last he set her both his eyes—
She won, and Cupid blind did rise.
    O Love! has she done this to thee?
    What shall, alas! become of me?

J. LYLY

52

Pack, clouds, away, and welcome day,
  With night we banish sorrow;
Sweet air blow soft, mount lark aloft
  To give my Love good-morrow!
Wings from the wind to please her mind   5
  Notes from the lark I'll borrow;
Bird prune thy wing, nightingale sing,
  To give my Love good-morrow;
    To give my Love good-morrow
    Notes from them all I'll borrow.   10

Wake from thy nest, Robin-red-breast,
  Sing birds in every furrow;
And from each bill, let music shrill
  Give my fair Love good-morrow!
Blackbird and thrush in every bush,   15
  Stare, linnet, and cock-sparrow,
You pretty elves, amongst yourselves
  Sing my fair Love good-morrow!
    To give my Love good-morrow
    Sing birds in every furrow!   20

T. HEYWOOD

53

PROTHALAMION

Calm was the day, and through the trembling air
  Sweet-breathing Zephyrus did softly play—
  A gentle spirit, that lightly did delay
Hot Titan's beams, which then did glister fair;
    When I (whom sullen care,   5
Through discontent of my long fruitless stay
  In princes' court, and expectation vain
Of idle hopes, which still do fly away
  Like empty shadows, did afflict my brain)
    Walk'd forth to ease my pain   10
Along the shore of silver-streaming Thames;
Whose rutty bank, the which his river hems,
  Was painted all with variable flowers,
And all the meads adorn'd with dainty gems
    Fit to deck maidens' bowers,   15
    And crown their paramours
Against the bridal day, which is not long:
Sweet Thames! run softly, till I end my song.

There in a meadow by the river side
  A flock of nymphs I chancéd to espy,
  All lovely daughters of the flood thereby,
With goodly greenish locks all loose untied
    As each had been a bride;
And each one had a little wicker basket
  Made of fine twigs, entrailéd curiously,   20
In which they gather'd flowers to fill their flasket,
  And with fine fingers cropt full feateously
    The tender stalks on high.
Of every sort which in that meadow grew
They gather'd some; the violet, pallid blue,   30
  The little daisy that at evening closes,
The virgin lily and the primrose true,
    With store of vermeil roses,
    To deck their bridegrooms' posies
Against the bridal day, which was not long: 35
Sweet Thames! run softly, till I end my song.

With that I saw two swans of goodly hue
  Come softly swimming down along the lee;

Two fairer birds I yet did never see;
The snow which doth the top of Pindus strow   40
   Did never whiter show,
Nor Jove himself, when he a swan would be
   For love of Leda, whiter did appear;
Yet Leda was (they say) as white as he,
   Yet not so white as these, nor nothing near;   45
     So purely white they were,
That even the gentle stream, the which them bare,
Seem'd foul to them, and bade his billows spare
   To wet their silken feathers, lest they might
Soil their fair plumes with water not so fair,   50
     And mar their beauties bright,
     That shone as Heaven's light
Against their bridal day, which was not long:
Sweet Thames! run softly, till I end my song.

Eftsoons the nymphs, which now had flowers their fill, 55
   Ran all in haste to see that silver brood
   As they came floating on the crystal flood;
Whom when they saw, they stood amazéd still
   Their wondering eyes to fill;
Them seem'd they never saw a sight so fair   60
   Of fowls, so lovely, that they sure did deem
Them heavenly born, or to be that same pair
   Which through the sky draw Venus' silver team;
     For sure they did not seem
To be begot of any earthly seed,   65
But rather angels, or of angels' breed;
   Yet were they bred of summer's heat, they say,
In sweetest season, when each flower and weed
     The earth did fresh array;
     So fresh they seem'd as day,   70
Even as their bridal day, which was not long:
Sweet Thames! run softly, till I end my song.

Then forth they all out of their baskets drew
   Great store of flowers, the honour of the field,
   That to the sense did fragrant odours yield,   75
All which upon those goodly birds they threw
   And all the waves did strew,
That like old Peneus' waters they did seem
   When down along by pleasant Tempe's shore
Scatter'd with flowers, through Thessaly they stream,   80
That they appear, through lilies' plenteous store,

Like a bride's chamber-floor.
Two of those nymphs meanwhile two garlands bound
Of freshest flowers which in that mead they found,
   The which presenting all in trim array,   85
Their snowy foreheads therewithal they crown'd;
      Whilst one did sing this lay
      Prepared against that day,
Against their bridal day, which was not long:
Sweet Thames! run softly, till I end my song.   90

'Ye gentle birds! the world's fair ornament,
   And Heaven's glory, whom this happy hour
   Doth lead unto your lovers' blissful bower,
Joy may you have, and gentle heart's content
    Of your love's couplement;   95
And let fair Venus, that is queen of love,
   With her heart-quelling son upon you smile,
Whose smile, they say, hath virtue to remove
All love's dislike, and friendship's faulty guile
    For ever to assoil.   100
Let endless peace your steadfast hearts accord,
And blessed plenty wait upon your board;
   And let your bed with pleasures chaste abound,
That fruitful issue may to you afford
    Which may your foes confound,   105
    And make your joys redound
Upon your bridal day, which is not long:
Sweet Thames! run softly, till I end my song.'

So ended she; and all the rest around
   To her redoubled that her undersong,   110
   Which said their bridal day should not be long:
And gentle Echo from the neighbour ground
    Their accents did resound.
So forth those joyous birds did pass along
   Adown the lee that to them murmur'd low,   115
As he would speak but that he lack'd a tongue,
   Yet did by signs his glad affection show,
    Making his stream run slow.
And all the fowl which in his flood did dwell
'Gan flock about these twain, that did excel   120
   The rest, so far as Cynthia doth shend
The lesser stars. So they, enrangéd well,

Did on those two attend,
And their best service lend
Against their wedding day, which was not long;   125
Sweet Thames! run softly, till I end my song.

At length they all to merry London came,
   To merry London, my most kindly nurse,
   That to me gave this life's first native source,
Though from another place I take my name,   130
    An house of ancient fame:
There when they came whereas those bricky towers
   The which on Thames' broad aged back do ride,
Where now the studious lawyers have their bowers,
   There whilome wont the Templar-knights to bide, 135
    Till they decay'd through pride;
Next whereunto there stands a stately place,
   Where oft I gainéd gifts and goodly grace
   Of that great lord, which therein wont to dwell,
Whose want too well now feels my friendless case;   140
    But ah! here fits not well
    Old woes, but joys, to tell
Against the bridal day, which is not long:
Sweet Thames! run softly, till I end my song.

Yet therein now doth lodge a noble peer,   145
   Great England's glory and the world's wide wonder,
   Whose dreadful name late through all Spain did thunder,
And Hercules' two pillars standing near
    Did make to quake and fear:
   Fair branch of honour, flower of chivalry!   150
   That fillest England with thy triumphs' fame,
Joy have thou of thy noble victory,
   And endless happiness of thine own name
    That promiseth the same;
That through thy prowess and victorious arms   155
Thy country may be freed from foreign harms,
   And great Eliza's glorious name may ring
Through all the world, fill'd with thy wide alarms,
    Which some brave Muse may sing
    To ages following,   160
Upon the bridal day, which is not long:
Sweet Thames! run softly, till I end my song.

From those high towers this noble lord issúing
   Like radiant Hesper, when his golden hair

In th' ocean billows he hath bathéd fair,   165
Descended to the river's open viewing
    With a great train ensuing.
Above the rest were goodly to be seen
    Two gentle knights of lovely face and feature,
Beseeming well the bower of any queen,   170
    With gifts of wit and ornaments of nature,
      Fit for so goodly stature,
That like the twins of Jove they seem'd in sight
Which deck the baldric of the Heavens bright;
    They two, forth pacing to the river's side,   175
Received those two fair brides, their love's delight;
      Which, at th' appointed tide,
      Each one did make his bride
Against their bridal day, which is not long:
Sweet Thames! run softly, till I end my song.   180

                        E. SPENSER

54

THE HAPPY HEART

Art thou poor, yet hast thou golden slumbers?
      O sweet content!
Art thou rich, yet is thy mind perplexed?
      O punishment!
Dost thou laugh to see how fools are vexed   5
To add to golden numbers, golden numbers?
O sweet content! O sweet, O sweet content!
  Work apace, apace, apace, apace;
  Honest labour bears a lovely face;
Then hey nonny nonny, hey nonny nonny!   10

Canst drink the waters of the crispéd spring?
      O sweet content!
Swimm'st thou in wealth, yet sink'st in thine own tears?
      O punishment!
Then he that patiently want's burden bears   15
No burden bears, but is a king, a king!
O sweet content! O sweet, O sweet content!
  Work apace, apace, apace, apace;
  Honest labour bears a lovely face;
Then hey nonny nonny, hey nonny nonnny!   20

                        T. DEKKER

55

This Life, which seems so fair,
Is like a bubble blown up in the air
   By sporting children's breath,
   Who chase it everywhere
And strive who can most motion it bequeath.   5
And though it sometimes seem of its own might,

   Like to an eye of gold, to be fix'd there,
And firm to hover in that empty height,
That only is because it is so light.
   —But in that pomp it doth not long appear;   10
For, when 'tis most admired, in a thought,
Because it erst was nought, it turns to nought.

                          W. DRUMMOND

56

SOUL AND BODY

Poor Soul, the centre of my sinful earth,
   [Fool'd by] those rebel powers that thee array,
Why dost thou pine within, and suffer dearth,
   Painting thy outward walls so costly gay?

Why so large cost, having so short a lease,   5
   Dost thou upon thy fading mansion spend?
Shall worms, inheritors of this excess,
   Eat up thy charge? is this thy body's end?

Then, Soul, live thou upon thy servant's loss,
   And let that pine to aggravate thy store;   10
But terms divine in selling hours of dross;
   Within be fed, without be rich no more:—

So shalt thou feed on death, that feeds on men,
And death once dead, there's no more dying then.

                          W. SHAKESPEARE

57

LIFE

The World's a bubble, and the Life of Man
    Less than a span:
In his conception wretched, from the womb
    So to the tomb;
Curst from the cradle, and brought up to years   5
    With cares and fears.
Who then to frail mortality shall trust,
But limns the water, or but writes in dust.

Yet since with sorrow here we live opprest,
    What life is best?   10
Courts are but only superficial schools
    To dandle fools:
The rural parts are turn'd into a den
    Of savage men:
And where's a city from all vice so free,   15
But may be term'd the worst of all the three?

Domestic cares afflict the husband's bed,
    Or pains his head:
Those that live single, take it for a curse,
    Or do things worse: 20
Some would have children: those that have them moan
    Or wish them gone:
What is it, then, to have, or have no wife,
But single thraldom, or a double strife?

Our own affections still at home to please   25
    Is a disease:
To cross the sea to any foreign soil,
    Perils and toil:
Wars with their noise affright us; when they cease,
    We are worse in peace;—   30
What then remains, but that we still should cry
Not to be born, or, being born, to die?

                        LORD BACON

58

THE LESSONS OF NATURE

Of this fair volume which we World do name
   If we the sheets and leaves could turn with care,
Of Him who it corrects, and did it frame,
   We clear might read the art and wisdom rare:

Find out His power which wildest powers doth tame,   5
   His providence extending everywhere,
   His justice which proud rebels doth not spare,
In every page, no period of the same.

But silly we, like foolish children, rest
   Well pleased with colour'd vellum, leaves of gold,   10
Fair dangling ribbands, leaving what is best,
   On the great Writer's sense ne'er taking hold;

Or if by chance we stay our minds on aught,
It is some picture on the margin wrought.
W. DRUMMOND

59

Doth then the world go thus, doth all thus move?
   Is this the justice which on Earth we find?
   Is this that firm decree which all both bind?
Are these your influences, Powers above?

Those souls which vice's moody mists most blind,   5
Blind Fortune, blindly, most their friend doth prove;
And they who thee, poor idol, Virtue! love.
   Ply like a feather toss'd by storm and wind.

Ah! if a Providence doth sway this all,
   Why should best minds groan under most distress?   10
Or why should pride humility make thrall,
   And injuries the innocent oppress?

Heavens! hinder, stop this fate; or grant a time
When good may have, as well as bad, their prime.
W. DRUMMOND

60

THE WORLD'S WAY

Tired with all these, for restful death I cry—
  As, to behold desert a beggar born,
And needy nothing trimm'd in jollity,
  And purest faith unhappily forsworn,

And gilded honour shamefully misplaced,   5
  And maiden virtue rudely strumpeted,
And right perfection wrongfully disgraced,
  And strength by limping sway disabled,

And art made tongue-tied by authority,
  And folly, doctor-like, controlling skill,   10
And simple truth miscall'd simplicity,
  And captive Good attending captain Ill:—
—Tired with all these, from these would I be gone,
Save that, to die, I leave my Love alone.

W. SHAKESPEARE

61

SAINT JOHN BAPTIST

The last and greatest Herald of Heaven's King
  Girt with rough skins, hies to the deserts wild,
Among that savage brood the woods forth bring,
  Which he more harmless found than man, and mild.

His food was lucusts, and what there doth spring,   5
  With honey that from virgin hives distill'd;
Parch'd body, hollow eyes, some uncouth thing
  Made him appear, long since from earth exiled.

There burst he forth: ' All ye whose hopes rely
  On God, with me amidst these deserts mourn,   10
  Repent, repent, and from old errors turn! '
—Who listen'd to his voice, obey'd his cry?

Only the echoes, which he made relent,
Rung from their flinty caves, Repent! Repent!

W. DRUMMOND

THE GOLDEN TREASURY

BOOK SECOND

ODE ON THE
MORNING OF CHRIST'S NATIVITY

This is the month, and this the happy morn
  Wherein the Son of Heaven's Eternal King
Of wedded maid and virgin mother born,
  Our great redemption from above did bring;
  For so the holy sages once did sing   5
That He our deadly forfeit should release,
And with His Father work us a perpetual peace.

That glorious Form, that Light unsufferable,
  And that far-beaming blaze of Majesty
Wherewith He wont at Heaven's high council-table   10
  To sit the midst of Trinal Unity,
  He laid aside; and, here with us to be,
Forsook the courts of everlasting day,
And chose with us a darksome house of mortal clay.

Say, heavenly Muse, shall not thy sacred vein   15
  Afford a present to the Infant God?
Hast thou no verse, no hymn, or solemn strain
  To welcome Him to this His new abode,
  Now while the heaven, by the sun's team untrod,
Hath took no print of the approaching light,   20
And all the spangled host keep watch in squadrons bright?

See how from far, upon the eastern road,
  The star-led wizards haste with odours sweet:
O run, prevent them with thy humble ode
  And lay it lowly at His blessed feet;   25
  Have thou the honour first thy Lord to greet,
And join thy voice unto the angel quire
From out His secret altar touch'd with hallow'd fire.

THE HYMN

It was the winter wild
  While the heaven-born Child   30
All meanly wrapt in the rude manger lies;
  Nature in awe to Him
  Had doff'd her gaudy trim,
With her great Master so to sympathize:
  It was no season then for her   35
To wanton with the sun, her lusty paramour.

  Only with speeches fair
  She woos the gentle air
To hide her guilty front with innocent snow;
  And on her naked shame,   40
  Pollute with sinful blame,
The saintly veil of maiden white to throw;
  Confounded, that her Maker's eyes
Should look so near upon her foul deformities.

  But He, her fears to cease,   45
  Sent down the meek-eyed Peace;
She, crown'd with olive green, came softly sliding
  Down through the turning sphere,
  His ready harbinger,
With turtle wing the amorous clouds dividing;   50
  And waving wide her myrtle wand,
She strikes a universal peace through sea and land.

  No war, or battle's sound
  Was heard the world around:
The idle spear and shield were high uphung;   55
  The hookèd chariot stood
  Unstain'd with hostile blood;
The trumpet spake not to the armèd throng;
  And kings sat still with awful eye,
As if they surely knew their sovran Lord was by.   60

  But peaceful was the night
  Wherein the Prince of Light
His reign of peace upon the earth began:
  The winds, with wonder whist,
  Smoothly the waters kist,   65
Whispering new joys to the mild ocèan—
  Who now hath quite forgot to rave,
While birds of calm sit brooding on the charmèd wave.

The stars, with deep amaze,
    Stand fix'd in steadfast gaze,   70
Bending one way their precious influence;
    And will not take their flight
    For all the morning light,
Or Lucifer that often warn'd them thence;
    But in their glimmering orbs did glow   75
Until their Lord Himself bespake, and bid them go.

    And though the shady gloom
    Had given day her room,
The sun himself withheld his wonted speed,
    And hid his head for shame,   80
    As his inferior flame
The new-enlighten'd world no more should need:
    He saw a greater Sun appear
Than his bright throne or burning axletree could bear.

    The shepherds on the lawn   85
    Or ere the point of dawn
Sate simply chatting in a rustic row;
    Full little thought they than
    That the mighty Pan
Was kindly come to live with them below;   90
    Perhaps their loves, or else their sheep
Was all that did their silly thoughts so busy keep.

    When such music sweet
    Their hearts and ears did greet
As never was by mortal finger strook—   95
    Divinely-warbled voice
    Answering the stringéd noise,
As all their souls in blissful rapture took:
    The air, such pleasure loth to lose,
With thousand echoes still prolongs each heavenly close.   100

    Nature that heard such sound
    Beneath the hollow round
Of Cynthia's seat the airy region thrilling,
    Now was almost won
    To think her part was done,   105
And that her reign had here its last fulfilling;
    She knew such harmony alone
Could hold all heaven and earth in happier union.

At last surrounds their sight
A globe of circular light,   110
That with long beams the shamefaced night array'd;
The helméd Cherubim
And sworded Seraphim
Are seen in glittering ranks with wings display'd,
Harping in loud and solemn quire   115
With unexpressive notes, to Heaven's new-born Heir.

Such music (as 'tis said)
Before was never made
But when of old the sons of morning sung,
While the Creator great   120
His constellations set
And the well-balanced world on hinges hung;
And cast the dark foundations deep,
And bid the weltering waves their oozy channel keep.

Ring out, ye crystal spheres!   125
Once bless our human ears,
If ye have power to touch our senses so;
And let your silver chime
Move in melodious time;
And let the bass of heaven's deep organ blow,   130
And with your ninefold harmony
Make up full consort to the angelic symphony.

For if such holy song,
Enwrap our fancy long,
Time will run back, and fetch the age of gold;   135
And speckled vanity
Will sicken soon and die,
And leprous sin will melt from earthly mould;
And Hell itself will pass away,
And leave her dolorous mansions to the peering day.   140

Yea, Truth and Justice then
Will down return to men,
Orb'd in a rainbow; and, like glories wearing,
Mercy will sit between
Throned in celestial sheen,   145
With radiant feet the tissued clouds down steering;
And Heaven, as at some festival,
Will open wide the gates of her high palace hall.

But wisest Fate says No;
This must not yet be so; 150
The Babe yet lies in smiling infancy
That on the bitter cross
Must redeem our loss;
So both Himself and us to glorify:
Yet first, to those ychain'd in sleep 155
The wakeful trump of doom must thunder through the deep,

With such a horrid clang
As on mount Sinai rang
While the red fire and smouldering clouds outbrake:
The aged Earth aghast 160
With terror of that blast
Shall from the surface to the centre shake,
When, at the world's last sessión,
The dreadful Judge in middle air shall spread His throne.

And then at last our bliss 165
Full and perfect is,
But now begins; for from this happy day
The old Dragon under ground,
In straiter limits bound,
Not half so far casts his usurpéd sway; 170
And, wroth to see his kingdom fail,
Swinges the scaly horror of his folded tail.

The oracles are dumb;
No voice or hideous hum
Runs through the archéd roof in words deceiving: 175
Apollo from his shrine
Can no more divine,
With hollow shriek the steep of Delphos leaving:
No nightly trance or breathéd spell
Inspires the pale-eyed priest from the prophetic cell. 180

The lonely mountains o'er
And the resounding shore
A voice of weeping heard, and loud lament;
From haunted spring and dale
Edged with poplar pale 185
The parting Genius is with sighing sent;
With flower-inwoven tresses torn
The nymphs in twilight shade of tangled thickets mourn.

In consecrated earth
And on the holy hearth   190
The Lars and Lemures moan with midnight plaint;
    In urns, and altars round
    A drear and dying sound
Affrights the Flamens at their service quaint;
    And the chill marble seems to sweat,   195
While each peculiar Power forgoes his wonted seat.

    Peor and Baalim
    Forsake their temples dim,
With that twice-batter'd god of Palestine;
    And moonéd Ashtaroth   200
    Heaven's queen and mother both,
Now sits not girt with tapers' holy shine;
    The Lybic Hammon shrinks his horn,
In vain the Tyrian maids their wounded Thammuz mourn.

    And sullen Moloch, fled,   205
    Hath left in shadows dread
His burning idol all of blackest hue;
    In vain with cymbals' ring
    They call the grisly king,
In dismal dance about the furnace blue;   210
    The brutish gods of Nile as fast,
Isis, and Orus, and the dog Anubis, haste.

    Nor is Osiris seen
    In Memphian grove, or green,
Trampling the unshower'd grass with lowings loud: 215
    Nor can he be at rest
    Within his sacred chest;
Nought but profoundest hell can be his shroud;
    In vain with timbrell'd anthems dark
The sable-stoléd sorcerers bear his worshipt ark.   220

    He feels from Juda's land
    The dreaded infant's hand;
The rays of Bethlehem blind his dusky eyn;
    Nor all the gods beside
    Longer dare abide,   225
Not Typhon huge ending in snaky twine:
    Our Babe, to show his Godhead true,
Can in His swaddling bands control the damnéd crew.

So, when the sun in bed
  Curtain'd with cloudy red   230
Pillows his chin upon an orient wave,
    The flocking shadows pale
    Troop to the infernal jail,
Each fetter'd ghost slips to his several grave;
    And the yellow-skirted fays   235
Fly after the night-steeds, leaving their moon-loved maze.

    But see, the Virgin blest
    Hath laid her Babe to rest;
Time is, our tedious song should here have ending:
    Heaven's youngest-teeméd star   240
    Hath fix'd her polish'd car,
Her sleeping Lord with hand-maid lamp attending:
    And all about the courtly stable
Bright-harness'd angels sit in order serviceable.

                                   J. MILTON

63

SONG FOR SAINT CECILIA'S DAY, 1687

From Harmony, from heavenly Harmony
    This universal frame began:
  When Nature underneath a heap
    Of jarring atoms lay
  And could not heave her head,   5
The tuneful voice was heard from high
    Arise, ye more than dead!
Then cold, and hot, and moist, and dry
In order to their stations leap,
    And Music's power obey.   10
From harmony, from heavenly harmony
    This universal frame began:
    From harmony to harmony
Through all the compass of the notes it ran,
The diapason closing full in Man.   15

What passion cannot Music raise and quell?
    When Jubal struck the chorded shell
  His listening brethren stood around,
    And, wondering, on their faces fell
  To worship that celestial sound.   20

Less than a god they thought there could not dwell
　　Within the hollow of that shell
　　That spoke so sweetly and so well.
What passion cannot Music raise and quell?

　The trumpet's loud clangor   25
　　Excites us to arms,
　With shrill notes of anger
　　And mortal alarms.
　The double double double beat
　　Of the thundering drum   30
　　Cries ' Hark! the foes come;
Charge, charge, 'tis too late to retreat! '

The soft complaining flute
　In dying notes discovers
　The woes of hopeless lovers,   35
Whose dirge is whisper'd by the warbling lute.

　Sharp violins proclaim
Their jealous pangs and desperation,
Fury, frantic indignation,
Depth of pains, and height of passion   40
　For the fair disdainful dame.

But oh! what art can teach,
What human voice can reach
　The sacred organ's praise?
Notes inspiring holy love,   45
　Notes that wing their heavenly ways
To mend the choirs above.

Orpheus could lead the savage race,
And trees unrooted left their place
　Sequacious of the lyre: 50
But bright Cecilia raised the wonder higher:
When to her Organ vocal breath was given,
An Angel heard, and straight appear'd—
　Mistaking Earth for Heaven!

GRAND CHORUS

　As from the power of sacred lays   55
　　The spheres began to move,

And sung the great Creator's praise
  To all the blest above;
So when the last and dreadful hour
This crumbling pageant shall devour 60
The trumpet shall be heard on high,
The dead shall live, the living die,
And Music shall untune the sky.

J. DRYDEN

64

ON THE LATE MASSACRE IN PIEDMONT

Avenge, O Lord! Thy slaughter'd Saints, whose bones
  Lie scatter'd on the Alpine mountains cold;
  Even them who kept Thy truth so pure of old,
When all our fathers worshipt stocks and stones,

Forget not: in Thy book record their groans 5
  Who were Thy sheep, and in their ancient fold
  Slain by the bloody Piedmontese, that roll'd
Mother with infant down the rocks. Their moans

The vales redoubled to the hills, and they
  To Heaven. Their martyr'd blood and ashes sow 10
O'er all the Italian fields, where still doth sway

The triple tyrant: that from these may grow
A hundred-fold, who, having learnt Thy way,
  Early may fly the Babylonian woe.

J. MILTON

65

HORATIAN ODE UPON CROMWELL'S RETURN FROM IRELAND

The forward youth that would appear,
Must now forsake his Muses dear,
    Nor in the shadows sing
    His numbers languishing.

Tis time to leave the books in dust,   5
And oil th' unuséd armour's rust,
     Removing from the wall
     The corslet of the hall.

So restless Cromwell could not cease
In the inglorious arts of peace,   10
     But through adventurous war
     Urgéd his active star:

And like the three-fork'd lightning, first
Breaking the clouds where it was nurst,
     Did thorough his own side   15
     His fiery way divide:

(For 'tis all one to courage high
The emulous, or enemy;
     And with such, to enclose
     Is more than to oppose;)   20

Then burning through the air he went
And palaces and temples rent;
     And Caesar's head at last
     Did through his laurels blast.

'Tis madness to resist or blame   25
The face of angry heaven's flame;
     And if we would speak true,
     Much to the man is due

Who, from his private gardens, where
He lived reservéd and austere   30
     (As if his highest plot
     To plant the bergamot),

Could by industrious valour climb
To ruin the great work of Time,
     And cast the Kingdoms old   35
     Into another mould;

Though Justice against Fate complain,
And plead the ancient Rights in vain—
     But those do hold or break
     As men are strong or weak.   40

Nature, that hateth emptiness,
Allows of penetration less,
 And therefore must make room
 Where greater spirits come.

What field of all the Civil War   45
Where his were not the deepest scar?
 And Hampton shows what part
 He had of wiser art;

Where, twining subtle fears with hope,
He wove a net of such a scope   50
 That Charles himself might chase
 To Carisbrook's narrow case;

That thence the Royal actor borne
The tragic scaffold might adorn:
 While round the arméd bands   55
 Did clap their bloody hands;

He nothing common did or mean
Upon that memorable scene,
 But with his keener eye
 The axe's edge did try;   60

Nor call'd the Gods, with vulgar spite,
To vindicate his helpless right;
 But bow'd his comely head
 Down, as upon a bed.

—This was that memorable hour   65
Which first assured the forcéd power
 So when they did design
 The Capitol's first line,

A Bleeding Head, where they begun,
Did fright the architects to run;   70
 And yet in that the State
 Foresaw its happy fate!

And now the Irish are ashamed
To see themselves in one year tamed:
 So much one man can do   75
 That does both act and know.

They can affirm his praises best,
And have, though overcome, confest
    How good he is, how just
    And fit for highest trust;   80

Nor yet grown stiffer with command,
But still in the Republic's hand—
    How fit he is to sway
    That can so well obey!—

He to the Commons' feet presents   85
A Kingdom for his first year's rents,
    And (what he may) forbears
    His fame, to make it theirs:

And has his sword and spoils ungirt
To lay them at the Public's skirt.   90
    So when the falcon high
    Falls heavy from the sky,

She, having kill'd, no more does search
But on the next green bough to perch,
    Where, when he first does lure,   95
    The falconer has her sure.

—What may not then our Isle presume
While victory his crest does plume?
    What may not others fear
    If thus he crowns each year?   100

As Caesar he, ere long, to Gaul,
To Italy an Hannibal,
    And to all states not free
    Shall climacteric be.

The Pict no shelter now shall find   105
Within his parti-colour'd mind,
    But from this valour sad,
    Shrink underneath the plaid—

Happy, if in the tufted brake
The English hunter him mistake,   110
    Nor lay his hounds in near
    The Caledonian deer.

But thou, the War's and Fortune's son,
March indefatigably on;
    And for the last effect   115
    Still keep the sword erect:

Besides the force it has to fright
The spirits of the shady night,
    The same arts that did gain
    A power, must it maintain.   120

                  A. MARVELL

66

LYCIDAS

Elegy on a Friend drowned in the Irish Channel

Yet once more, O ye laurels, and once more
Ye myrtles brown, with ivy never sere,
I come to pluck your berries harsh and crude,
And with forced fingers rude
Shatter your leaves before the mellowing year.   5
Bitter constraint, and sad occasion dear
Compels me to disturb your season due:
For Lycidas is dead, dead ere his prime,
Young Lycidas, and hath not left his peer:
Who would not sing for Lycidas? he knew   10
Himself to sing, and build the lofty ryme.
He must not float upon his watery bier
Unwept, and welter to the parching wind,
Without the meed of some melodious tear.

Begin then, Sisters of the sacred well   15
That from beneath the seat of Jove doth spring,
Begin, and somewhat loudly sweep the string.
Hence with denial vain and coy excuse:
So may some gentle Muse
With lucky words favour my destined urn;   20
And as he passes, turn
And bid fair peace be to my sable shroud.

For we were nursed upon the self-same hill,
Fed the same flock by fountain, shade, and rill.
Together both, ere the high lawns appear'd   25

Under the opening eye-lids of the morn,
We drove a-field, and both together heard
What time the gray-fly winds her sultry horn,
Battening our flocks with the fresh dews of night,
Oft till the star, that rose at evening bright,   30
Toward heaven's descent had sloped his westering wheel.
Meanwhile the rural ditties were not mute,
Temper'd to the oaten flute;
Rough Satyrs danced, and Fauns with cloven heel
From the glad sound would not be absent long;   35
And old Damoetas loved to hear our song.

But O the heavy change, now thou art gone,
Now thou art gone, and never must return!
Thee, Shepherd, thee the woods, and desert caves
With wild thyme and the gadding vine o'ergrown,   40
And all their echoes, mourn:
The willows and the hazel copses green
Shall now no more be seen
Fanning their joyous leaves to thy soft lays.
As killing as the canker to the rose,   45
Or taint-worm to the weanling herds that graze,
Or frost to flowers, that their gay wardrobe wear
When first the white-thorn blows;
Such, Lycidas, thy loss to shepherd's ear.

Where were ye, Nymphs, when the remorseless deep   50
Closed o'er the head of your loved Lycidas?
For neither were ye playing on the steep
Where your old bards, the famous Druids, lie,
Nor on the shaggy top of Mona high,
Nor yet where Deva spreads her wizard stream: 55
Ay me! I fondly dream—
Had ye been there—for what could that have done?
What could the Muse herself that Orpheus bore,
The Muse herself, for her enchanting son,
Whom universal nature did lament,   60
When by the rout that made the hideous roar
His gory visage down the stream was sent,
Down the swift Hebrus to the Lesbian shore?

Alas! what boots it with uncessant care
To tend the homely, slighted, shepherd's trade   65
And strictly meditate the thankless Muse?
Were it not better done, as others use,

To sport with Amaryllis in the shade,
Or with the tangles of Neaera's hair?
Fame is the spur that the clear spirit doth raise   70
(That last infirmity of noble mind)
To scorn delights, and live laborious days;
But the fair guerdon when we hope to find,
And think to burst out into sudden blaze,
Comes the blind Fury with the abhorréd shears   75
And slits the thin-spun life. ' But not the praise '
Phoebus replied, and touch'd my trembling ears;
' Fame is no plant that grows on mortal soil,
Nor in the glistering foil
Set off to the world, nor in broad rumour lies: 80
But lives and spreads aloft by those pure eyes
And perfect witness of all-judging Jove;
As he pronounces lastly on each deed,
Of so much fame in heaven expect thy meed.'

O fountain Arethuse, and thou honour'd flood   85
Smooth-sliding Mincius, crown'd with vocal reeds,
That strain I heard was of a higher mood:
But now my oat proceeds,
And listens to the herald of the sea
That came in Neptune's plea;   90
He ask'd the waves, and ask'd the felon winds,
What hard mishap hath doom'd this gentle swain?
And question'd every gust of rugged wings
That blows from off each beakéd promontory;
They knew not of his story;   95
And sage Hippotades their answer brings,
That not a blast was from his dungeon stray'd;
The air was calm, and on the level brine
Sleek Panope with all her sisters play'd.
It was that fatal and perfidious bark   100
Built in the eclipse, and rigg'd with curses dark,
That sunk so low that sacred head of thine.

Next Camus, reverend sire, went footing slow,
His mantle hairy, and his bonnet sedge,
Inwrought with figures dim, and on the edge   105
Like to that sanguine flower inscribed with woe:
' Ah! who hath reft,' quoth he, ' my dearest pledge? '
Last came, and last did go
The pilot of the Galilean lake;
Two massy keys he bore of metals twain   110

(The golden opes, the iron shuts amain);
He shook his mitred locks, and stern bespake:
' How well could I have spared for thee, young swain,
Enow of such as for their bellies' sake
Creep and intrude and climb into the fold! 115
Of other care they little reckoning make
Than how to scramble at the shearers' feast,
And shove away the worthy bidden guest.
Blind mouths! that scarce themselves know how to hold
A sheep-hook, or have learn'd aught else the least 120
That to the faithful herdman's art belongs!
What recks it them? What need they? They are sped;
And when they list, their lean and flashy songs
Grate on their scrannel pipes of wretched straw;
The hungry sheep look up, and are not fed. 125
But swoln with wind and the rank mist they draw
Rot inwardly, and foul contagion spread:
Besides what the grim wolf with privy paw
Daily devours apace, and nothing said:
—But that two-handed engine at the door 130
Stands ready to smite once, and smite no more.'

    Return, Alpheus, the dread voice is past
That shrunk thy streams; return, Sicilian Muse,
And call the vales, and bid them hither cast
Their bells and flowerets of a thousand hues. 135
Ye valleys low, where the mild whispers use
Of shades, and wanton winds, and gushing brooks,
On whose fresh lap the swart star sparely looks,
Throw hither all your quaint enamell'd eyes
That on the green turf suck the honey'd showers 140
And purple all the ground with vernal flowers.
Bring the rathe primrose that forsaken dies;
The tufted crow-toe, and pale jessamine,
The white pink, and the pansy freak'd with jet,
The glowing violet, 145
The musk-rose, and the well-attired woodbine,
With cowslips wan that hang the pensive head,
And every flower that sad embroidery wears:
Bid amarantus all his beauty shed,
And daffadillies fill their cups with tears 150
To strew the laureat hearse where Lycid lies.
For, so to interpose a little ease,
Let our frail thoughts dally with false surmise;
Ay me! whilst thee the shores and sounding seas

Wash far away,—where'er thy bones are hurl'd,   155
Whether beyond the stormy Hebrides
Where thou perhaps, under the whelming tide,
Visitest the bottom of the monstrous world;
Or whether thou, to our moist vows denied,
Sleep'st by the fable of Bellerus old,   160
Where the great Vision of the guarded mount
Looks toward Namancos and Bayona's hold,
—Look homeward, Angel, now, and melt with ruth:
—And, O ye dolphins, waft the hapless youth!

   Weep no more, woeful shepherds, weep no more,   165
For Lycidas, your sorrow, is not dead,
Sunk though he be beneath the watery floor;
So sinks the day-star in the ocean-bed,
And yet anon repairs his drooping head
And tricks his beams, and with new-spangled ore   170
Flames in the forehead of the morning sky:
So Lycidas sunk low, but mounted high
Through the dear might of Him that walk'd the waves;
Where, other groves and other streams along,
With nectar pure his oozy locks he laves,   175
And hears the unexpressive nuptial song
In the blest kingdoms meek of joy and love.
There entertain him all the saints above
In solemn troops, and sweet societies,
That sing, and singing in their glory move,   180
And wipe the tears for ever from his eyes.
Now, Lycidas, the shepherds weep no more;
Henceforth thou art the Genius of the shore
In thy large recompense, and shalt be good
To all that wander in that perilous flood.   185

   Thus sang the uncouth swain to the oaks and rills,
While the still morn went out with sandals grey;
He touch'd the tender stops of various quills,
With eager thought warbling his Doric lay:
And now the sun had stretch'd out all the hills,   190
And now was dropt into the western bay:
At last he rose, and twitch'd his mantle blue:
To-morrow to fresh woods, and pastures new.

                            J. MILTON

67

ON THE TOMBS IN WESTMINSTER ABBEY

Mortality, behold and fear,
What a change of flesh is here!
Think how many royal bones
Sleep within these heaps of stones;
Here they lie, had realms and lands,   5
Who now want strength to stir their hands,
Where from their pulpits seal'd with dust
They preach, ' In greatness is no trust.'
Here's an acre sown indeed
With the richest royallest seed   10
That the earth did e'er suck in
Since the first man died for sin:
Here the bones of birth have cried
' Though gods they were, as men they died! '
Here are sands, ignoble things,   15
Dropt from the ruin'd sides of kings:
Here's a world of pomp and state
Buried in dust, once dead by fate.

                                        F. BEAUMONT

68

THE LAST CONQUEROR

Victorious men of earth, no more
    Proclaim how wide your empires are;
Though you bind-in every shore,
    And your triumphs reach as far
        As night or day,   5
    Yet you, proud monarchs, must obey
And mingle with forgotten ashes, when
Death calls ye to the crowd of common men.

Devouring Famine, Plague, and War,
    Each able to undo mankind,   10
Death's servile emissaries are;
    Nor to these alone confined,

He hath at will
More quaint and subtle ways to kill;
A smile or kiss, as he will use the art,   15
Shall have the cunning skill to break a heart.

J. SHIRLEY

69

DEATH THE LEVELLER

The glories of our blood and state
    Are shadows, not substantial things;
There is no armour against fate;
    Death lays his icy hand on kings:
        Sceptre and Crown   5
        Must tumble down,
And in the dust be equal made
With the poor crooked scythe and spade.

Some men with swords may reap the field,
    And plant fresh laurels where they kill;   10
But their strong nerves at last must yield;
    They tame but one another still:
        Early or late
        They stoop to fate,
And must give up their murmuring breath   15
When they, pale captives, creep to death.

The garlands wither on your brow;
    Then boast no more your mighty deeds;
Upon Death's purple altar now
    See where the victor-victim bleeds;   20
        Your heads must come
        To the cold tomb;
Only the actions of the just
Smell sweet, and blossom in their dust.

J. SHIRLEY

70

WHEN THE ASSAULT WAS INTENDED TO THE CITY

Captain, or Colonel, or Knight in arms,
   Whose chance on these defenceless doors may seize,
   If deed of honour did thee ever please,
Guard them, and him within protect from harms.

He can requite thee; for he knows the charms   5
   That call fame on such gentle acts as these,
   And he can spread thy name o'er lands and seas,
Whatever clime the sun's bright circle warms.

Lift not thy spear against the Muses' bower:
   The great Emathian conqueror bid spare   10
The house of Pindarus, when temple and tower

   Went to the ground: and the repeated air
Of sad Electra's poet had the power
   To save the Athenian walls from ruin bare.

J. MILTON

71

ON HIS BLINDNESS

When I consider how my light is spent
   Ere half my days, in this dark world and wide,
   And that one talent which is death to hide
Lodged with me useless, though my soul more bent

To serve therewith my Maker, and present   5
   My true account, lest He returning chide,—
   Doth God exact day-labour, light denied?
I fondly ask:—But Patience, to prevent

That murmur, soon replies; God doth not need   10
   Either man's work, or His own gifts: who best
   Bear His mild yoke, they serve Him best: His state

Is kingly; thousands at His bidding speed
  And post o'er land and ocean without rest:—
  They also serve who only stand and wait.

J. MILTON

72

CHARACTER OF A HAPPY LIFE

How happy is he born or taught
  That serveth not another's will;
Whose armour is his honest thought,
  And silly truth his highest skill!

Whose passions not his masters are,   5
  Whose soul is still prepared for death;
Untied unto the world with care
  Of princely love or vulgar breath;

Who hath his life from rumours freed,
  Whose conscience is his strong retreat   10
Whose state can neither flatterers feed,
  Nor ruin make accusers great;

Who envieth none whom chance doth raise
  Or vice; who never understood
How deepest wounds are given with praise;   15
  Nor rules of state, but rules of good:

Who God doth late and early pray
  More of his grace than gifts to lend;
Who entertains the harmless day
  With a well-chosen book or friend;   20

—This man is free from servile bands
  Of hope to rise, or fear to fall;
Lord of himself, though not of lands;
  And having nothing, he hath all.

SIR H. WOTTON

73

THE NOBLE NATURE

It is not growing like a tree
In bulk, doth make Man better be;
Or standing long an oak, three hundred year,
To fall a log at last, dry, bald, and sere:
    A lily of a day   5
    Is fairer far in May,
Although it fall and die that night;
It was the plant and flower of Light.
In small proportions we just beauties see;
And in short measures life may perfect be.   10

B. JONSON

74

THE GIFTS OF GOD

When God at first made Man,
Having a glass of blessings standing by;
Let us (said He) pour on him all we can:
Let the world's riches, which dispersèd lie,
    Contract into a span   5

    So strength first made a way;
Then beauty flow'd, then wisdom, honour, pleasure:
When almost all was out, God made a stay,
Perceiving that alone, of all His treasure,
    Rest in the bottom lay.   10

    For if I should (said He,
Bestow this jewel also on my creature,
He would adore my gifts instead of me,
And rest in Nature, not the God of Nature:
    So both should losers be.   15

    Yet let him keep the rest,
But keep them with repining restlessness;
Let him be rich and weary, that at least,
If goodness lead him not, yet weariness
    May toss him to my breast.   20

G. HERBERT

75

THE RETREAT

Happy those early days, when I
Shined in my Angel-infancy!
Before I understood this place
Appointed for my second race,
Or taught my soul to fancy aught   5
But a white, celestial thought;
When yet I had not walk'd above
A mile or two from my first Love,
And looking back, at that short space
Could see a glimpse of His bright face;   10
When on some gilded cloud or flower
My gazing soul would dwell an hour,
And in those weaker glories spy
Some shadows of eternity;
Before I taught my tongue to wound   15
My conscience with a sinful sound,
Or had the black art to dispense
A several sin to every sense,
But felt through all this fleshly dress
Bright shoots of everlastingness.   20

O how I long to travel back,
And tread again that ancient track!
That I might once more reach that plain,
Where first I left my glorious train;
From whence th' enlighten'd spirit sees   25
That shady City of Palm trees!
But ah! my soul with too much stay
Is drunk, and staggers in the way:—
Some men a forward motion love,
But I by backward steps would move;   30
And when this dust falls to the urn,
In that state I came, return.
                              H. VAUGHAN

76

TO MR. LAWRENCE

Lawrence, of virtuous father virtuous son,
　　Now that the fields are dank and ways are mire,
　　Where shall we sometimes meet, and by the fire
Help waste a sullen day, what may be won

From the hard season gaining? Time will run   5
　　On smoother, till Favonius re-inspire
　　The frozen earth, and clothe in fresh attire
The lily and rose, that neither sow'd nor spun.

What neat repast shall feast us, light and choice,
　　Of Attic taste, with wine, whence we may rise   10
To hear the lute well touch'd, or artful voice

　　Warble immortal notes and Tuscan air?
　　He who of those delights can judge, and spare
To interpose them oft, is not unwise.

　　　　　　　　　　　　　　　J. MILTON

77

TO CYRIACK SKINNER

Cyriack, whose grandsire, on the royal bench
　　Of British Themis, with no mean applause
　　Pronounced, and in his volumes taught, our laws,
Which others at their bar so often wrench;

To-day deep thoughts resolve with me to drench   5
　　In mirth, that after no repenting draws;
　　Let Euclid rest, and Archimedes pause,
And what the Swede intend, and what the French.

To measure life learn thou betimes, and know
　　Toward solid good what leads the nearest way;   10
　　For other things mild Heaven a time ordains,

And disapproves that care, though wise in show,
　　That with superfluous burden loads the day,
　　And, when God sends a cheerful hour, refrains.

　　　　　　　　　　　　　　　J. MILTON

78

HYMN TO DIANA

Queen and Huntress, chaste and fair,
    Now the sun is laid to sleep,
Seated in thy silver chair
    State in wonted manner keep:
        Hesperus entreats thy light,   5
        Goddess excellently bright.

Earth, let not thy envious shade
    Dare itself to interpose;
Cynthia's shining orb was made
    Heaven to clear when day did close: 10
        Bless us then with wishéd sight.
        Goddess excellently bright.

Lay thy bow of pearl apart
    And thy crystal-shining quiver;
Give unto the flying hart   15
    Space to breathe, how short soever:
        Thou that mak'st a day of night,
        Goddess excellently bright!

                  B. JONSON

79

WISHES FOR THE SUPPOSED MISTRESS

    Whoe'er she be,
  That not impossible She
That shall command my heart and me;

    Where'er she lie,
  Lock'd up from mortal eye   5
In shady leaves of destiny:

    Till that ripe birth
  Of studied Fate stand forth,
And teach her fair steps tread our earth;

    Till that divine   10
  Idea take a shrine
Of crystal flesh, through which to shine:

—Meet you her, my Wishes,
Bespeak her to my blisses,
And be ye call'd, my absent kisses.   15

I wish her beauty
That owes not all its duty
To gaudy tire, or glist'ring shoe-tie:

Something more than
Taffata or tissue can,   20
Or rampant feather, or rich fan.

A face that's best
By its own beauty drest,
And can alone commend the rest:

A face made up   25
Out of no other shop
Than what Nature's white hand sets ope.

Sidneian showers
Of sweet discourse, whose powers
Can crown old Winter's head with flowers.   30

Whate'er delight
Can make day's forehead bright
Or give down to the wings of night.

Soft silken hours,
Open suns, shady bowers;   35
'Bove all, nothing within that lowers.

Days, that need borrow
No part of their good morrow
From a fore-spent night of sorrow:

Days, that in spite   40
Of darkness, by the light
Of a clear mind are day all night.

Life, that dares send
A challenge to his end,
And when it comes, say, ' Welcome, friend.'   45

I wish her store
Of worth may leave her poor
Of wishes; and I wish——no more.

—Now, if Time knows
That Her, whose radiant brows   50
Weave them a garland of my vows;

Her that dares be
What these lines wish to see:
I seek no further, it is She.

'Tis She, and here   55
Lo! I unclothe and clear
My wishes' cloudy character.

Such worth as this is
Shall fix my flying wishes,
And determine them to kisses.   60

Let her full glory,
My fancies, fly before ye;
Be ye my fictions:—but her story.

R. CRASHAW

80

THE GREAT ADVENTURER

Over the mountains
  And over the waves,
Under the fountains
  And under the graves;
Under floods that are deepest,   5
  Which Neptune obey;
Over rocks that are steepest
  Love will find out the way.

Where there is no place
  For the glow-worm to lie;   10
Where there is no space
  For receipt of a fly;
Where the midge dares not venture
  Lest herself fast she lay;
If love come, he will enter   15
  And soon find out his way.

You may esteem him
  A child for his might;
Or you may deem him
  A coward from his flight;   20
But if she whom love doth honour
  Be conceal'd from the day,
Set a thousand guards upon her,
  Love will find out the way.

Some think to lose him   25
  By having him confined;
And some do suppose him,
  Poor thing, to be blind;
But if ne'er so close ye wall him,
  Do the best that you may,   30
Blind love, if so ye call him,
  Will find out his way.

You may train the eagle
  To stoop to your fist;
Or you may inveigle   35
  The phoenix of the east;
The lioness, ye may move her
  To give o'er her prey;
But you'll ne'er stop a lover:
  He will find out his way.   40

ANON

81

CHILD AND MAIDEN

Ah, Chloris! that I now could sit
  As unconcern'd as when
Your infant beauty could beget
  No pleasure, nor no pain!
When I the dawn used to admire,   5
  And praised the coming day,
I little thought the growing fire
  Must take my rest away.

Your charms in harmless childhood lay
  Like metals in the mine;   10

Age from no face took more away
    Than youth conceal'd in thine.
But as your charms insensibly
    To their perfection prest,
Fond love as unperceived did fly,   15
    And in my bosom rest.

My passion with your beauty grew,
    And Cupid at my heart,
Still as his mother favour'd you,
    Threw a new flaming dart: 20
Each gloried in their wanton part;
    To make a lover, he
Employ'd the utmost of his art—
    To make a beauty, she.

SIR C. SEDLEY

82

COUNSEL TO GIRLS

Gather ye rose-buds while ye may,
    Old Time is still a-flying:
And this same flower that smiles to-day,
    To-morrow will be dying.

The glorious Lamp of Heaven, the Sun,   5
    The higher he's a-getting
The sooner will his race be run,
    And nearer he's to setting.

That age is best which is the first,
    When youth and blood are warmer;   10
But being spent, the worse, and worst
    Times, still succeed the former.

Then be not coy, but use your time;
    And while ye may, go marry:
For having lost but once your prime,   15
    You may for ever tarry.

R. HERRICK

83

TO LUCASTA, ON GOING TO THE WARS

Tell me not, Sweet, I am unkind
    That from the nunnery
Of thy chaste breast and quiet mind
    To war and arms I fly.

True, a new mistress now I chase,   5
    The first foe in the field;
And with a stronger faith embrace
    A sword, a horse, a shield.

Yet this inconstancy is such
    As you too shall adore;   10
I could not love thee, Dear, so much,
    Loved I not Honour more.

                         COLONEL LOVELACE

84

ELIZABETH OF BOHEMIA

You meaner beauties of the night,
    That poorly satisfy our eyes
More by your number than your light,
    You common people of the skies,
What are you, when the Moon shall rise?   5

You curious chanters of the wood
    That warble forth dame Nature's lays,
Thinking your passions understood
    By your weak accents; what's your praise
When Philomel her voice shall raise?   10

You violets that first appear,
    By your pure purple mantles known
Like the proud virgins of the year,
    As if the spring were all your own,—
What are you, when the Rose is blown?   15

So when my Mistress shall be seen
    In form and beauty of her mind,

By virtue first, then choice, a Queen,
  Tell me, if she were not design'd
Th' eclipse and glory of her kind?   20

                    SIR H. WOTTON

85

TO THE LADY MARGARET LEY

Daughter to that good Earl, once President
  Of England's Council and her Treasury,
  Who lived in both, unstain'd with gold or fee,
And left them both, more in himself content,

Till the sad breaking of that Parliament   5
  Broke him, as that dishonest victory
  At Chaeronea, fatal to liberty,
Kill'd with report that old man eloquent;—

Though later born than to have known the days
  Wherein your father flourish'd, yet by you,   10
    Madam, methinks I see him living yet;

So well your words his noble virtues praise,
  That all both judge you to relate them true,
    And to possess them, honour'd Margaret.

                    J. MILTON

86

THE LOVELINESS OF LOVE

It is not Beauty I demand,
  A crystal brow, the moon's despair,
Nor the snow's daughter, a white hand,
  Nor mermaid's yellow pride of hair:

Tell me not of your starry eyes,   5
  Your lips that seem on roses fed,
Your breasts, where Cupid trembling lies
  Nor sleeps for kissing of his bed:—

A bloomy pair of vermeil cheeks
　　Like Hebe's in her ruddiest hours,
A breath that softer music speaks
　　Than summer winds a-wooing flowers,　　　　10

These are but gauds: nay, what are lips?
　　Coral beneath the ocean-stream,
Whose brink when your adventurer sips　　　　15
　　Full oft he perisheth on them.

And what are cheeks, but ensigns oft
　　That wave hot youth to fields of blood?
Did Helen's breast, though ne'er so soft,
　　Do Greece or Ilium any good?　　　　20

Eyes can with baleful ardour burn;
　　Poison can breath, that erst perfumed;
There's many a white hand holds an urn
　　With lovers' hearts to dust consumed.

For crystal brows—there's nought within;　　　　25
　　They are but empty cells for pride;
He who the Syren's hair would win
　　Is mostly strangled in the tide.

Give me, instead of Beauty's bust,
　　A tender heart, a loyal mind　　　　30
Which with temptation I could trust,
　　Yet never link'd with error find,—

One in whose gentle bosom I
　　Could pour my secret heart of woes,
Like the care-burthen'd honey-fly　　　　35
　　That hides his murmurs in the rose,—

My earthly Comforter! whose love
　　So indefeasible might be
That, when my spirit won above,
　　Hers could not stay, for sympathy.　　　　40

ANON[1]

1 When *The Golden Treasury* was first published, Palgrave was unaware of the identity of the author of this poem, the which was written by George Darley and would otherwise appear with the two poems on pages 349-350.

87

THE TRUE BEAUTY

He that loves a rosy cheek
   Or a coral lip admires,
Or from star-like eyes doth seek
   Fuel to maintain his fires;
As old Time makes these decay,   5
So his flames must waste away.

But a smooth and steadfast mind,
   Gentle thoughts, and calm desires,
Hearts with equal love combined,
   Kindle never-dying fires:—   10
Where these are not, I despise
Lovely cheeks or lips or eyes.

T. CAREW

88

TO DIANEME

Sweet, be not proud of those two eyes
Which starlike sparkle in their skies;
Nor be you proud, that you can see
All hearts your captives; yours yet free!
Be you not proud of that rich hair   5
Which wantons with the lovesick air;
Whenas that ruby which you wear,
Sunk from the tip of your soft ear,
Will last to be a precious stone
When all your world of beauty's gone.   10

R. HERRICK

89

Go, lovely Rose!
Tell her, that wastes her time and me,
   That now she knows,
When I resemble her to thee,
How sweet and fair she seems to be.   5

    Tell her that's young
And shuns to have her graces spied,
    That hadst thou sprung
In deserts, where no men abide,
Thou must have uncommended died.   10

    Small is the worth
Of beauty from the light retired:
    Bid her come forth,
Suffer herself to be desired,
And not blush so to be admired.   15

    Then die! that she
The common fate of all things rare
    May read in thee:
How small a part of time they share
That are so wondrous sweet and fair!   20

              E. WALLER

90

TO CELIA

Drink to me only with thine eyes,
    And I will pledge with mine;
Or leave a kiss but in the cup
    And I'll not look for wine.
The thirst that from the soul doth rise   5
    Doth ask a drink divine;
But might I of Jove's nectar sup,
    I would not change for thine.

I sent thee late a rosy wreath,
    Not so much honouring thee   10
As giving it a hope that there
    It could not wither'd be;
But thou thereon didst only breathe
    And sent'st it back to me;
Since when it grows, and smells, I swear,   15
    Not of itself but thee!

              B. JONSON

91

CHERRY-RIPE

There is a garden in her face
　Where roses and white lilies grow;
A heavenly paradise is that place,
　Wherein all pleasant fruits do flow;
There cherries grow which none may buy,   5
Till ' Cherry-Ripe ' themselves do cry.

Those cherries fairly do enclose
　Of orient pearl a double row,
Which when her lovely laughter shows,
　They look like rose-buds fill'd with snow: 10
Yet them nor peer nor prince can buy,
Till ' Cherry-Ripe ' themselves do cry.

Her eyes like angels watch them still;
　Her brows like bended bows to stand,
Threat'ning with piercing frowns to kill   15
　All that attempt with eye or hand
Those sacred cherries to come nigh,
—Till ' Cherry-Ripe ' themselves do cry!

T. CAMPION

92

THE POETRY OF DRESS

I

A sweet disorder in the dress
Kindles in clothes a wantonness:—
A lawn about the shoulders thrown
Into a fine distractión,—
An erring lace, which here and there   5
Enthrals the crimson stomacher—
A cuff neglectful, and thereby
Ribbands to flow confusedly,—
A winning wave, deserving note,
In the tempestuous petticoat,—   10
A careless shoe-string, in whose tie
I see a wild civility,—

Do more bewitch me, than when art
Is too precise in every part.

R. HERRICK

93

II

Whenas in silks my Julia goes
Then, then (methinks) how sweetly flows
That liquefaction of her clothes.

Next, when I cast mine eyes and see
That brave vibration each way free;　　　5
O how that glittering taketh me!

R. HERRICK

94

III

My Love in her attire doth shew her wit,
　　It doth so well become her:
For every season she hath dressings fit,
　　For Winter, Spring, and Summer.
　　No beauty she doth miss　　　5
　　　When all her robes are on:
　　But Beauty's self she is
　　　When all her robes are gone.

ANON

95

ON A GIRDLE

That which her slender waist confined
Shall now my joyful temples bind:
No monarch but would give his crown
His arms might do what this has done.

It was my Heaven's extremest sphere,　　　5
The pale which held that lovely deer:
My joy, my grief, my hope, my love
Did all within this circle move.

A narrow compass! and yet there
Dwelt all that's good, and all that's fair: 10
Give me but what this ribband bound,
Take all the rest the Sun goes round.

E. WALLER

96

TO ANTHEA WHO MAY COMMAND HIM
ANY THING

Bid me to live, and I will live
Thy Protestant to be:
Or bid me love, and I will give
A loving heart to thee.

A heart as soft, a heart as kind,   5
A heart as sound and free
As in the whole world thou canst find,
That heart I'll give to thee.

Bid that heart stay, and it will stay,
To honour thy decree: 10
Or bid it languish quite away,
And 't shall do so for thee.

Bid me to weep, and I will weep
While I have eyes to see:
And, having none, yet I will keep   15
A heart to weep for thee.

Bid me despair, and I'll despair
Under that cypress tree:
Or bid me die, and I will dare
E'en Death, to die for thee.   20

Thou art my life, my love, my heart,
The very eyes of me,
And hast command of every part,
To live and die for thee.

R. HERRICK

97

Love not me for comely grace,
For my pleasing eye or face,
Nor for any outward part,
No, nor for my constant heart,—
    For those may fail, or turn to ill,   5
      So thou and I shall sever:
Keep therefore a true woman's eye,
And love me still, but know not why—
    So hast thou the same reason still
      To doat upon me ever!   10

ANON

98

Not, Celia, that I juster am
    Or better than the rest;
For I would change each hour, like them,
    Were not my heart at rest.

But I am tied to very thee   5
    By every thought I have;
Thy face I only care to see,
    Thy heart I only crave.

All that in woman is adored
    In thy dear self I find—   10
For the whole sex can but afford
    The handsome and the kind.

Why then should I seek further store,
    And still make love anew?
When change itself can give no more,   15
    'Tis easy to be true.

SIR C. SEDLEY

99

TO ALTHEA FROM PRISON

When Love with unconfinéd wings
  Hovers within my gates,
And my divine Althea brings
  To whisper at the grates;
When I lie tangled in her hair   5
  And fetter'd to her eye,
The Gods that wanton in the air
  Know no such liberty.

When flowing cups run swiftly round
  With no allaying Thames,   10
Our careless heads with roses crown'd,
  Our hearts with loyal flames;
When thirsty grief in wine we steep,
  When healths and draughts go free—
Fishes that tipple in the deep   15
  Know no such liberty.

When, like committed linnets, I
  With shriller throat shall sing
The sweetest, mercy, majesty
  And glories of my King;   20
When I shall voice aloud how good
  He is, how great should be,
Enlargéd winds, that curl the flood,
  Know no such liberty.

Stone walls do not a prison make,   25
  Nor iron bars a cage;
Minds innocent and quiet take
  That for an hermitage:
If I have freedom in my love
  And in my soul am free,   30
Angels alone, that soar above,
  Enjoy such liberty.

COLONEL LOVELACE

100

TO LUCASTA, ON GOING BEYOND THE SEAS

IF to be absent were to be
      Away from thee;
   Or that when I am gone
   You or I were alone;
   Then, my Lucasta, might I crave   5
Pity from blustering wind, or swallowing wave.

   Though seas and land betwixt us both,
      Our faith and troth,
      Like separated souls,
      All time and space controls: 10
   Above the highest sphere we meet
Unseen, unknown, and greet as Angels greet.

   So then we do anticipate
      Our after-fate,
      And are alive i' the skies,   15
      If thus our lips and eyes
   Can speak like spirits unconfined
In Heaven, their earthy bodies left behind.

                          COLONEL LOVELACE

101

ENCOURAGEMENTS TO A LOVER

   Why so pale and wan, fond lover?
      Prythee, why so pale?
   Will, when looking well can't move her,
      Looking ill prevail?
      Prythee, why so pale?   5

   Why so dull and mute, young sinner?
      Prythee, why so mute?
   Will, when speaking well can't win her,
      Saying nothing do't?
      Prythee, why so mute?   10

Quit, quit, for shame! this will not move,
   This cannot take her;
If of herself she will not love,
   Nothing can make her:
   The devil take her!   15

          SIR J. SUCKLING

102

A SUPPLICATION

Awake, awake, my Lyre!
And tell thy silent master's humble tale
   In sounds that may prevail;
  Sounds that gentle thoughts inspire:
    Though so exalted she   5
    And I so lowly be,
Tell her, such different notes make all thy harmony.

    Hark! how the strings awake:
And, though the moving hand approach not near,
    Themselves with awful fear   10
  A kind of numerous trembling make.
    Now all thy forces try;
    Now all thy charms apply;
Revenge upon her ear the conquests of her eye.

    Weak Lyre! thy virtue sure   15
Is useless here, since thou art only found
    To cure, but not to wound,
  And she to wound, but not to cure.
    Too weak too wilt thou prove
    My passion to remove;   20
Physic to other ills, thou'rt nourishment to love.

    Sleep, sleep again, my Lyre!
For thou canst never tell my humble tale
    In sounds that will prevail,
  No gentle thoughts in her inspire;   25
    All thy vain mirth lay by,
    Bid thy strings silent lie,
Sleep, sleep again, my Lyre, and let thy master die.

          A. COWLEY

103

THE MANLY HEART

Shall I, wasting in despair,
Die because a woman's fair?
Or make pale my cheeks with care
'Cause another's rosy are?
Be she fairer than the day   5
Or the flowery meads in May—
    If she think not well of me,
    What care I how fair she be?

Shall my silly heart be pined
'Cause I see a woman kind;   10
Or a well disposéd nature
Joinéd with a lovely feature?
Be she meeker, kinder, than
Turtle-dove or pelican,
    If she be not so to me,   15
    What care I how kind she be?

Shall a woman's virtues move
Me to perish for her love?
Or her well-deservings known
Make me quite forget mine own?   20
Be she with that goodness blest
Which may merit name of Best;
    If she be not such to me,
    What care I how good she be?

'Cause her fortune seems too high,   25
Shall I play the fool and die?
She that bears a noble mind
If not outward helps she find,
Thinks what with them he would do
That without them dares her woo;   30
    And unless that mind I see,
    What care I how great she be?

Great or good, or kind or fair,
I will ne'er the more despair;
If she love me, this believe,   35
I will die ere she shall grieve;

If she slight me when I woo,
I can scorn and let her go;
 For if she be not for me,
 What care I for whom she be? 40

G. WITHER

104

MELANCHOLY

Hence, all you vain delights,
As short as are the nights
 Wherein you spend your folly:
There's nought in this life sweet,
If man were wise to see't, 5
But only melancholy,
O sweetest melancholy!
Welcome, folded arms, and fixéd eyes,
A sigh that piercing mortifies,
A look that's fasten'd to the ground, 10
A tongue chain'd up without a sound!
Fountain heads and pathless groves,
Places which pale passion loves!
Moonlight walks, when all the fowls
Are warmly housed, save bats and owls! 15
 A midnight bell, a parting groan—
 These are the sounds we feed upon;
Then stretch our bones in a still gloomy valley;
Nothing 's so dainty sweet as lovely melancholy.

J. FLETCHER

105

TO A LOCK OF HAIR

Thy hue, dear pledge, is pure and bright
As in that well-remember'd night
When first thy mystic braid was wove,
And first my Agnes whisper'd love.

Since then how often hast thou prest 5
The torrid zone of this wild breast,
Whose wrath and hate have sworn to dwell
With the first sin that peopled hell;

A breast whose blood 's a troubled ocean,
Each throb the earthquake's wild commotion!   10
O if such clime thou canst endure
Yet keep thy hue unstain'd and pure,
What conquest o'er each erring thought
Of that fierce realm had Agnes wrought!
I had not wander'd far and wide   15
With such an angel for my guide;
Nor heaven nor earth could then reprove me
If she had lived, and lived to love me.

Not then this world's wild joys had been
To me one savage hunting scene,   20
My sole delight the headlong race
And frantic hurry of the chase;
To start, pursue, and bring to bay,
Rush in, drag down, and rend my prey,
Then—from the carcass turn away!   25
Mine ireful mood had sweetness tamed,
And soothed each wound which pride inflamed:—
Yes, God, and man might now approve me
If thou hadst lived, and lived to love me!

SIR W. SCOTT

106

THE FORSAKEN BRIDE

O waly waly up the bank,
    And waly waly down the brae,
And waly waly yon burn-side
    Where I and my Love wont to gae!
I leant my back unto an aik,   5
    I thought it was a trusty tree;
But first it bow'd, and syne it brak,
    Sae my true Love did lichtly me.

O waly waly, but love be bonny
    A little time while it is new;   10
But when 'tis auld, it waxeth cauld
    And fades awa' like morning dew.
O wherefore should I busk my head?
    Or wherefore should I kame my hair?
For my true Love has me forsook,   15
    And says he'll never loe me mair.

Now Arthur-seat sall be my bed;
   The sheets shall ne'er be 'fil'd by me:
Saint Anton's well sall be my drink,
   Since my true Love has forsaken me.   20
Marti'mas wind, when wilt thou blaw
   And shake the green leaves aff the tree?
O gentle Death, when wilt thou come?
   For of my life I am wearie.

'Tis not the frost, that freezes fell,   25
   Nor blawing snaw's inclemencie;
'Tis not sic cauld that makes my cry,
   But my Love's heart grown cauld to me.
When we came in by Glasgow town
   We were a comely sight to see;   30
My Love was clad in the black velvét,
   And I myself in cramasie.

But had I wist, before I kist,
   That love had been sae ill to win;
I had lockt my heart in a case of gowd   35
   And pinn'd it with a siller pin.
And, O! if my young babe were born,
   And set upon the nurse's knee,
And I mysell were dead and gane,
   For a maid again I'll never be.   40

                ANON

107

FAIR HELEN

I wish I were where Helen lies;
Night and day on me she cries;
O that I were where Helen lies
   On fair Kirconnell lea!

Curst be the heart that thought the thought,   5
And curst the hand that fired the shot,
When in my arms burd Helen dropt,
   And died to succour me!

O think na but my heart was sair
When my Love dropt down and spak nae mair!   10
I laid her down wi' meikle care
   On fair Kirconnell lea.

As I went down the water-side,
None but my foe to be my guide,
None but my foe to be my guide,   15
    On fair Kirconnell lea;

I lighted down my sword to draw,
I hackéd him in pieces sma',
I hackéd him in pieces sma',
    For her sake that died for me.   20

O Helen fair, beyond compare!
I'll make a garland of thy hair
Shall bind my heart for evermair
    Until the day I die.

O that I were where Helen lies!   25
Night and day on me she cries;
Out of my bed she bids me rise,
    Says, ' Haste and come to me! '

O Helen fair! O Helen chaste!
If I were with thee, I were blest,   30
Where thou lies low and takes thy rest
    On fair Kirconnell lea.

I wish my grave were growing green,
A winding-sheet drawn ower my een,
And I in Helen's arms lying,   35
    On fair Kirconnell lea.

I wish I were where Helen lies;
Night and day on me she cries;
And I am weary of the skies,
    Since my Love died for me.   40

                      ANON

108

THE TWA CORBIES

As I was walking all alane
I heard twa corbies making a mane;
The tane unto the t'other say,
' Where sall we gang and dine to-day? '

'—In behint yon auld fail dyke,   5
I wot there lies a new-slain Knight;
And naebody kens that he lies there,
But his hawk, his hound, and lady fair.

' His hound is to the hunting gane,
His hawk to fetch the wild-fowl hame,   10
His lady's ta'en another mate,
So we may make our dinner sweet.

' Ye'll sit on his white hause-bane,
And I'll pick out his bonny blue een:
Wi' ae lock o' his gowden hair   15
We'll theek our nest when it grows bare.

' Mony a one for him makes mane,
But nane sall ken where he is gane;
O'er his white banes, when they are bare,
The wind sall blaw for evermair.'   20
                                           ANON

109

TO BLOSSOMS

Fair pledges of a fruitful tree,
    Why do ye fall so fast?
    Your date is not so past,
But you may stay yet here awhile
    To blush and gently smile,   5
    And go at last.

What, were ye born to be
    An hour or half's delight,

And so to bid good-night?
'Twas pity Nature brought ye forth   10
　　Merely to show your worth,
　　　　And lose you quite.

But you are lovely leaves, where we
　　May read how soon things have
　　Their end, though ne'er so brave: 15
And after they have shown their pride
　　Like you awhile, they glide
　　　　Into the grave.

R. HERRICK

110

TO DAFFODILS

Fair Daffodils, we weep to see
　　You haste away so soon:
As yet the early-rising Sun
　　Has not attain'd his noon.
　　　　Stay, stay,   5
　　Until the hasting day
　　　　Has run
　　But to the even-song;
And, having pray'd together, we
　　Will go with you along.   10

We have short time to stay, as you,
　　We have as short a Spring;
As quick a growth to meet decay
　　As you, or any thing.
　　　　We die,   15
　　As your hours do, and dry
　　　　Away
　　Like to the Summer's rain;
Or as the pearls of morning's dew,
　　Ne'er to be found again.   20

R. HERRICK

III

THOUGHTS IN A GARDEN

How vainly men themselves amaze
To win the palm, the oak, or bays,   5
And their uncessant labours see
Crown'd from some single herb or tree,
Whose short and narrow-vergéd shade
Does prudently their toils upbraid;
While all the flowers and trees do close
To weave the garlands of repose.

Fair Quiet, have I found thee here,   10
And Innocence thy sister dear!
Mistaken long, I sought you then
In busy companies of men:
Your sacred plants, if here below,
Only among the plants will grow:
Society is all but rude   15
To this delicious solitude.

No white nor red was ever seen
So amorous as this lovely green.
Fond lovers, cruel as their flame,
Cut in these trees their mistress' name: 20
Little, alas, they know or heed
How far these beauties hers exceed!
Fair trees! wheres'e'er your barks I wound,
No name shall but your own be found.

When we have run our passions' heat.   25
Love hither makes his best retreat:
The gods, that mortal beauty chase,
Still in a tree did end their race:
Apollo hunted Daphne so,
Only that she might laurel grow: 30
And Pan did after Syrinx speed
Not as a nymph, but for a reed.

What wondrous life in this I lead!
Ripe apples drop about my head;
The luscious clusters of the vine   35
Upon my mouth do crush their wine;

The nectarine and curious peach
Into my hands themselves do reach;
Stumbling on melons, as I pass,
Ensnared with flowers, I fall on grass.   40

Meanwhile the mind, from pleasure less,
Withdraws into its happiness;
The mind, that ocean where each kind
Does straight its own resemblance find;
Yet it creates, transcending these,   45
Far other worlds, and other seas;
Annihilating all that's made
To a green thought in a green shade.

Here at the fountain's sliding foot
Or at some fruit-tree's mossy root,   50
Casting the body's vest aside,
My soul into the boughs does glide;
There, like a bird, it sits and sings,
Then whets and combs its silver wings,
And, till prepared for longer flight,   55
Waves in its plumes the various light.

Such was that happy Garden-state
While man there walk'd without a mate:
After a place so pure and sweet,
What other help could yet be meet!   60
But 'twas beyond a mortal's share
To wander solitary there:
Two paradises 'twere in one,
To live in Paradise alone.

How well the skilful gardener drew   65
Of flowers and herbs this dial new!
Where, from above, the milder sun
Does through a fragrant zodiac run:
And, as it works, th' industrious bee
Computes its time as well as we.   70
How could such sweet and wholesome hours
Be reckon'd, but with herbs and flowers!

                                        A. MARVELL

112

L'ALLÉGRO

Hence, loathéd Melancholy,
Of Cerberus and blackest Midnight born
  In Stygian cave forlorn
'Mongst horrid shapes, and shrieks, and sights unholy!
  Find out some uncouth cell,   5
Where brooding Darkness spreads his jealous wings
  And the night-raven sings;
There, under ebon shades and low-brow'd rocks
  As ragged as thy locks,
In dark Cimmerian desert ever dwell.   10

    But come, thou Goddess fair and free,
    In heaven yclep'd Euphrosyne,
    And by men, heart-easing Mirth,
    Whom lovely Venus at a birth
    With two sister Graces more   15
    To ivy-crownéd Bacchus bore:
    Or whether (as some sager sing)
    The frolic wind that breathes the spring,
    Zephyr, with Aurora playing,
    As he met her once a-Maying—   20
    There on beds of violets blue
    And fresh-blown roses wash'd in dew
    Fill'd her with thee, a daughter fair,
    So buxom, blithe, and debonair.
      Haste thee, Nymph, and bring with thee   25
    Jest, and youthful jollity,
    Quips, and cranks, and wanton wiles,
    Nods, and becks, and wreathéd smiles,
    Such as hang on Hebe's cheek,
    And love to live in dimple sleek;   30
    Sport that wrinkled Care derides,
    And Laughter holding both his sides.
    Come, and trip it as you go
    On the light fantastic toe;
    And in thy right hand lead with thee   35
    The mountain nymph, sweet Liberty;
    And if I give thee honour due,
    Mirth, admit me of thy crew,
    To live with her, and live with thee

In unreprovéd pleasures free;   40
To hear the lark begin his flight
And singing startle the dull night
From his watch-tower in the skies,
Till the dappled dawn doth rise;
Then to come, in spite of sorrow,   45
And at my window bid good-morrow
Through the sweetbriar, or the vine,
Or the twisted eglantine:
While the cock with lively din
Scatters the rear of darkness thin,   50
And to the stack, or the barn-door,
Stoutly struts his dames before:
Oft listening how the hounds and horn
Cheerly rouse the slumbering morn,
From the side of some hoar hill,   55
Through the high wood echoing shrill.
Sometime walking, not unseen,
By hedge-row elms, on hillocks green,
Right against the eastern gate
Where the great Sun begins his state   60
Robed in flames and amber light,
The clouds in thousand liveries dight;
While the ploughman, near at hand,
Whistles o'er the furrow'd land,
And the milkmaid singeth blithe,   65
And the mower whets his scythe,
And every shepherd tells his tale
Under the hawthorn in the dale.
    Straight mine eye hath caught new pleasures
Whilst the landscape round it measures;   70
Russet lawns, and fallows grey,
Where the nibbling flocks do stray;
Mountains, on whose barren breast
The labouring clouds do often rest;
Meadows trim with daisies pied,   75
Shallow brooks, and rivers wide;
Towers and battlements it sees
Bosom'd high in tufted trees,
Where perhaps some Beauty lies,
The Cynosure of neighbouring eyes.   80
    Hard by, a cottage chimney smokes
From betwixt two aged oaks,
Where Corydon and Thyris, met,
Are at their savoury dinner set

Of herbs, and other country messes 85
Which the neat-handed Phillis dresses;
And then in haste her bower she leaves
With Thestylis to bind the sheaves;
Or, if the earlier season lead,
To the tann'd haycock in the mead. 90
  Sometimes with secure delight
The upland hamlets will invite,
When the merry bells ring round,
And the jocund rebecks sound
To many a youth and many a maid, 95
Dancing in the chequer'd shade;
And young and old come forth to play
On a sunshine holy-day,
Till the live-long daylight fail:
Then to the spicy nut-brown ale, 100
With stories told of many a feat,
How Faery Mab the junkets eat;
She was pinch'd, and pull'd, she said;
And he, by Friar's lantern led;
Tells how the drudging Goblin sweat 105
To earn his cream-bowl duly set,
When in one night, ere glimpse of morn,
His shadowy flail hath thresh'd the corn
That ten day-labourers could not end;
Then lies him down the lubber fiend, 110
And, stretch'd out all the chimney's length,
Basks at the fire his hairy strength;
And crop-full out of doors he flings,
Ere the first cock his matin rings.
Thus done the tales, to bed they creep, 115
By whispering winds soon lull'd asleep.
  Tower'd cities please us then
And the busy hum of men,
Where throngs of knights and barons bold,
In weeds of peace high triumphs hold, 120
With store of ladies, whose bright eyes
Rain influence, and judge the prize
Of wit or arms, while both contend
To win her grace, whom all commend.
There let Hymen oft appear 125
In saffron robe, with taper clear,
And pomp, and feast, and revelry,
With mask, and antique pageantry;
Such sights as youthful poets dream

On summer eves by haunted stream.   130
Then to the well-trod stage anon,
If Jonson's learned sock be on,
Or sweetest Shakespeare, Fancy's child,
Warble his native wood-notes wild.
  And ever against eating cares   135
Lap me in soft Lydian airs
Married to immortal verse,
Such as the meeting soul may pierce
In notes, with many a winding bout
Of linkéd sweetness long drawn out,   140
With wanton heed and giddy cunning,
The melting voice through mazes running,
Untwisting all the chains that tie
The hidden soul of harmony;
That Orpheus' self may heave his head   145
From golden slumber, on a bed
Of heap'd Elysian flowers, and hear
Such strains as would have won the ear
Of Pluto, to have quite set free
His half-regain'd Eurydice.   150

  These delights if thou canst give,
Mirth, with thee I mean to live.

J. MILTON

113

IL PENSEROSO

Hence vain deluding Joys,
The brood of Folly without father bred!
  How little you bestead
Or fill the fixéd mind with all your toys!
  Dwell in some idle brain,   5
And fancies fond with gaudy shapes possess
As thick and numberless
As the gay motes that people the sunbeams,
  Or likest hovering dreams
The fickle pensioners of Morpheus' train.   10

  But hail, thou goddess sage and holy,
Hail, divinest Melancholy!

Whose saintly visage is too bright
To hit the sense of human sight,
And therefore to our weaker view   15
O'erlaid with black, staid Wisdom's hue;
Black, but such as in esteem
Prince Memnon's sister might beseem,
Or that starr'd Ethiop queen that strove
To set her beauty's praise above   20
The sea-nymphs, and their powers offended:
Yet thou art higher far descended:
Thee bright-hair'd Vesta, long of yore,
To solitary Saturn bore;
His daughter she; in Saturn's reign   25
Such mixture was not held a stain:
Oft in glimmering bowers and glades
He met her, and in secret shades
Of woody Ida's inmost grove,
Whilst yet there was no fear of Jove.   30
   Come, pensive nun, devout and pure,
Sober, steadfast, and demure,
All in a robe of darkest grain
Flowing with majestic train,
And sable stole of cypres lawn   35
Over thy decent shoulders drawn
Come, but keep thy wonted state,
With even step, and musing gait,
And looks commercing with the skies,
Thy rapt soul sitting in thine eyes: 40
There, held in holy passion still,
Forget thyself to marble, till
With a sad leaden downward cast
Thou fix them on the earth as fast:
And join with thee calm Peace, and Quiet   45
Spare Fast, that oft with gods doth diet,
And hears the Muses in a ring
Ay round about Jove's altar sing:
And add to these retired Leisure
That in trim gardens takes his pleasure:—   50
But first, and chiefest, with thee bring
Him that yon soars on golden wing
Guiding the fiery-wheeléd throne,
The cherub Contemplatión;
And the mute Silence hist along,   55
'Less Philomel will deign a song
In her sweetest saddest plight,

Smoothing the rugged brow of Night,
While Cynthia checks her dragon yoke
Gently o'er the accustom'd oak.   60
—Sweet bird, that shunn'st the noise of folly,
Most musical, most melancholy!
Thee, chauntress, oft, the woods among
I woo, to hear thy even-song;
And missing thee, I walk unseen   65
On the dry smooth-shaven green,
To behold the wandering Moon
Riding near her highest noon,
Like one that had been led astray
Through the heaven's wide pathless way,   70
And oft, as if her head she bow'd,
Stooping through a fleecy cloud.
    Oft, on a plat of rising ground
I hear the far-off curfeu sound
Over some wide-water'd shore,   75
Swinging slow with sullen roar;
Or, if the air will not permit,
Some still removéd place will fit,
Where glowing embers through the room
Teach light to counterfeit a gloom;   80
Far from all resort of mirth,
Save the cricket on the hearth,
Or the bellman's drowsy charm
To bless the doors from nightly harm.
    Or let my lamp at midnight hour   85
Be seen in some high lonely tower,
Where I may oft out-watch the Bear
With thrice-great Hermes, or unsphere
The spirit of Plato, to unfold
What worlds or what vast regions hold   90
The immortal mind, that hath forsook
Her mansion in this fleshly nook:
And of those demons that are found
In fire, air, flood, or under ground,
Whose power hath a true consent   95
With planet, or with element.
Sometime let gorgeous Tragedy
In scepter'd pall come sweeping by,
Presenting Thebes, or Pelops' line,
Or the tale of Troy divine;   100
Or what (though rare) of later age
Ennobled hath the buskin'd stage.

But, O sad Virgin, that thy power
Might raise Musaeus from his bower,
Or bid the soul of Orpheus sing   105
Such notes as, warbled to the string,
Drew iron tears down Pluto's cheek
And made Hell grant what Love did seek!
Or call up him that left half-told
The story of Cambuscan bold,   110
Of Camball, and of Algarsife,
And who had Canacé to wife,
That own'd the virtuous ring and glass;
And of the wondrous horse of brass
On which the Tartar king did ride: 115
And if aught else great bards beside
In sage and solemn tunes have sung
Of tourneys, and of trophies hung,
Of forests, and enchantments drear,
Where more is meant than meets the ear.   120
    Thus, Night, oft see me in thy pale career,
Till civil-suited Morn appear,
Not trick'd and frounced as she was wont
With the Attic Boy to hunt,
But kercheft in a comely cloud   125
While rocking winds are piping loud,
Or usher'd with a shower still,
When the gust hath blown his fill,
Ending on the rustling leaves
With minute drops from off the eaves.   130
And when the sun begins to fling
His flaring beams, me, goddess, bring
To archéd walks of twilight groves,
And shadows brown, that Sylvan loves,
Of pine, or monumental oak,   135
Where the rude axe, with heavéd stroke,
Was never heard the nymphs to daunt
Or fright them from their hallow'd haunt.
There in close covert by some brook
Where no profaner eye may look,   140
Hide me from day's garish eye,
While the bee with honey'd thigh,
That at her flowery work doth sing,
And the waters murmuring,
With such consort as they keep   145
Entice the dewy-feather'd Sleep;
And let some strange mysterious dream

Wave at his wings in airy stream
Of lively portraiture display'd,
Softly on my eyelids laid: 150
And, as I wake, sweet music breathe
Above, about, or underneath,
Sent by some Spirit to mortals good,
Or the unseen Genius of the wood.
But let my due feet never fail 155
To walk the studious cloister's pale,
And love the high-embowéd roof,
With antique pillars massy-proof,
And storied windows richly dight
Casting a dim religious light: 160
There let the pealing organ blow
To the full-voiced quire below
In service high and anthems clear,
As may with sweetness, through mine ear,
Dissolve me into ecstasies, 165
And bring all Heaven before mine eyes.
    And may at last my weary age
Find out the peaceful hermitage,
The hairy gown and mossy cell
Where I may sit and rightly spell 170
Of every star that heaven doth show,
And every herb that sips the dew;
Till old experience do attain
To something like prophetic strain.

    These pleasures, Melancholy, give, 175
And I with thee will choose to live.

J. MILTON

114

SONG OF THE EMIGRANTS IN BERMUDA

Where the remote Bermudas ride
In the ocean's bosom unespied,
From a small boat that row'd along
The listening winds received this song:
' What should we do but sing His praise   5
That led us through the watery maze
Unto an isle so long unknown,
And yet far kinder than our own?
Where He the huge sea-monsters wracks,
That lift the deep upon their backs,   10
He lands us on a grassy stage,
Safe from the storms and prelate's rage:
He gave us this eternal spring
Which here enamels everything,
And sends the fowls to us in care   15
On daily visits through the air;
He hangs in shades the orange bright
Like golden lamps in a green night,
And does in the pomegranates close
Jewels more rich than Ormus shows: 20
He makes the figs our mouths to meet,
And throws the melons at our feet;
But apples plants of such a price,
No tree could ever bear them twice.
With cedars chosen by His hand   25
From Lebanon He stores the land;
And makes the hollow seas that roar
Proclaim the ambergris on shore.
He cast (of which we rather boast)
The Gospel's pearl upon our coast;   30
And in these rocks for us did frame.
A temple where to sound His name.
Oh! let our voice His praise exalt
Till it arrive at Heaven's vault,
Which thence (perhaps) rebounding may   35
Echo beyond the Mexique bay! '
Thus sung they in the English boat
An holy and a cheerful note:
And all the way, to guide their chime,
With falling oars they kept the time.   40

A. MARVELL

115

AT A SOLEMN MUSIC

Blest pair of Sirens, pledges of Heaven's joy,
    Sphere-born harmonious Sisters, Voice and Verse!
Wed your divine sounds, and mixt power employ
    Dead things with inbreathed sense able to pierce;
    And to our high-raised phantasy present   5
That undisturbéd Song of pure concent
Ay sung before the sapphire-colour'd throne
        To Him that sits thereon,
With saintly shout and solemn jubilee;
Where the bright Seraphim in burning row   10
    Their loud uplifted angel-trumpets blow;
And the Cherubic host in thousand quires
Touch their immortal harps of golden wires,
With those just Spirits that wear victorious palms,
        Hymns devout and holy psalms   15
        Singing everlastingly:
That we on earth, with undiscording voice
May rightly answer that melodious noise;
As once we did, till disproportion'd sin
Jarr'd against nature's chime, and with harsh din   20
Broke the fair music that all creatures made
To their great Lord, whose love their motion sway'd
In perfect diapason, whilst they stood
In first obedience, and their state of good.
    O may we soon again renew that Song,   25
    And keep in tune with Heaven, till God ere long
    To His celestial consort us unite,
To live with Him, and sing in endless morn of light.

                                               J. MILTON

116

ALEXANDER'S FEAST, OR, THE POWER OF MUSIC

'Twas at the royal feast for Persia won
    By Philip's warlike son—
    Aloft in awful state
    The godlike hero sate
    On his imperial throne;   5

His valiant peers were placed around,
Their brows with roses and with myrtles bound
   (So should desert in arms be crown'd);
   The lovely Thais by his side
   Sate like a blooming eastern bride   10
   In flower of youth and beauty's pride:—
      Happy, happy, happy pair!
        None but the brave
        None but the brave
    None but the brave deserves the fair!   15

   Timotheus placed on high
   Amid the tuneful quire
With flying fingers touch'd the lyre:
The trembling notes ascend the sky
   And heavenly joys inspire.   20
   The song began from Jove
Who left his blissful seats above—
Such is the power of mighty love!
A dragon's fiery form belied the god;
Sublime on radiant spires he rode   25
When he to fair Olympia prest,
And while he sought her snowy breast,
   Then round her slender waist he curl'd,
And stamp'd an image of himself, a sovereign of the world.
   —The listening crowd admire the lofty sound;   30
   A present deity! they shout around:
A present deity! the vaulted roofs rebound:
      With ravish'd ears
      The monarch hears,
      Assumes the god,   35
      Affects to nod
    And seems to shake the spheres.

The praise of Bacchus then the sweet musician sung,
   Of Bacchus ever fair and ever young:
      The jolly god in triumph comes!   40
      Sound the trumpets, beat the drums!
        Flush'd with a purple grace
        He shows his honest face:
Now give the hautboys breath; he comes, he comes!
      Bacchus, ever fair and young,   45
      Drinking joys did first ordain;
      Bacchus' blessings are a treasure,
      Drinking is the soldier's pleasure:

Rich the treasure,
Sweet the pleasure,
Sweet is pleasure after pain.   50

Soothed with the sound, the king grew vain;
Fought all his battles o'er again,
And thrice he routed all his foes, and thrice he slew the slain.
The master saw the madness rise,   55
His glowing cheeks, his ardent eyes;
And while he Heaven and Earth defied
Changed his hand and check'd his pride.
    He chose a mournful Muse
    Soft pity to infuse: 60
He sung Darius great and good,
    By too severe a fate
Fallen, fallen, fallen, fallen,
    Fallen from his high estate,
And weltering in his blood;   65
Deserted, at his utmost need,
By those his former bounty fed;
On the bare earth exposed he lies
With not a friend to close his eyes.
    —With downcast looks the joyless victor sate,   70
Revolving in his alter'd soul
    The various turns of Chance below;
And now and then a sigh he stole,
    And tears began to flow.

The mighty master smiled to see   75
That love was in the next degree;
'Twas but a kindred-sound to move,
For pity melts the mind to love.
Softly sweet, in Lydian measures
Soon he soothed his soul to pleasures.   80
War, he sung, is toil and trouble,
Honour but an empty bubble;
Never ending, still beginning,
    Fighting still, and still destroying;
If the world be worth thy winning,   85
    Think, O think, it worth enjoying:
Lovely Thais sits beside thee,
Take the good the gods provide thee!
—The many rend the skies with loud applause;
So Love was crown'd, but Music won the cause.   90

The prince, unable to conceal his pain,
    Gazed on the fair
    Who caused his care,
And sigh'd and look'd, sigh'd and look'd,
Sigh'd and look'd, and sigh'd again: 95
At length with love and wine at once opprest
The vanquish'd victor sunk upon her breast.

  Now strike the golden lyre again:
A louder yet, and yet a louder strain!
Break his bands of sleep asunder   100
And rouse him like a rattling peal of thunder.
Hark, hark! the horrid sound
  Has raised up his head:
  As awaked from the dead
And amazed he stares around.   105
Revenge, revenge, Timotheus cries,
See the Furies arise!
  See the snakes that they rear
  How they hiss in their hair,
And the sparkles that flash from their eyes!   110
    Behold a ghastly band,
    Each a torch in his hand!
Those are Grecian ghosts, that in battle were slain
    And unburied remain
    Inglorious on the plain: 115
    Give the vengeance due
    To the valiant crew!
Behold how they toss their torches on high,
How they point to the Persian abodes
And glittering temples of their hostile gods.   120
—The princes applaud with a furious joy:
And the King seized a flambeau with zeal to destroy;
    Thais led the way
    To light him to his prey,
And like another Helen, fired another Troy!   125

    —Thus, long ago,
Ere heaving bellows learn'd to blow,
  While organs yet were mute,
  Timotheus, to his breathing flute
    And sounding lyre,   130
Could swell the soul to rage, or kindle soft desire.
  At last divine Cecilia came,
  Inventress of the vocal frame;

The sweet enthusiast from her sacred store
   Enlarged the former narrow bounds,   135
   And added length to solemn sounds,
With Nature's mother-wit, and arts unknown before.
— Let old Timotheus yield the prize
   Or both divide the crown;
He raised a mortal to the skies;   140
   She drew an angel down!

J. DRYDEN

THE GOLDEN TREASURY

BOOK THIRD

ODE ON THE PLEASURE ARISING FROM VICISSITUDE

Now the golden Morn aloft
  Waves her dew-bespangled wing,
With vermeil cheek and whisper soft
  She woos the tardy Spring:
Till April starts, and calls around   5
The sleeping fragrance from the ground,
And lightly o'er the living scene
Scatters his freshest, tenderest green.

New-born flocks, in rustic dance,
  Frisking ply their feeble feet;   10
Forgetful of their wintry trance
  The birds his presence greet:
But chief, the sky-lark warbles high
His trembling thrilling ecstasy;
And lessening from the dazzled sight,   15
Melts into air and liquid light.

Yesterday the sullen year
  Saw the snowy whirlwind fly;
Mute was the music of the air,
  The herd stood drooping by;   20
Their raptures now that wildly flow
No yesterday nor morrow know;
'Tis Man alone that joy descries
With forward and reverted eyes.

Smiles on past Misfortune's brow   25
  Soft Reflection's hand can trace,
And o'er the cheek of Sorrow throw
  A melancholy grace;
While Hope prolongs our happier hour,
Or deepest shades, that dimly lour   30
And blacken round our weary way,
Gilds with a gleam of distant day.

Still, where rosy Pleasure leads,
  See a kindred Grief pursue;
Behind the steps that Misery treads   35
  Approaching Comfort view:
The hues of bliss more brightly glow
Chastised by sabler tints of woe,
And blended form, with artful strife,
The strength and harmony of life.   40

See the wretch that long has tost
  On the thorny bed of pain,
At length repair his vigour lost
  And breathe and walk again:
The meanest floweret of the vale,   45
The simplest note that swells the gale,
The common sun, the air, the skies,
To him are opening Paradise.

                              T. GRAY

118

THE QUIET LIFE

Happy the man, whose wish and care
  A few paternal acres bound,
Content to breathe his native air
                    In his own ground.

Whose herds with milk, whose fields with bread,   5
  Whose flocks supply him with attire;
Whose trees in summer yield him shade,
                    In winter fire.

Blest, who can unconcern'dly find
  Hours, days, and years slide soft away   10
In health of body, peace of mind,
                    Quiet by day,

Sound sleep by night; study and ease
  Together mix'd; sweet recreation,
And innocence, which most does please   15
                    With meditation.

Thus let me live, unseen, unknown;
  Thus unlamented let me die;
Steal from the world, and not a stone
          Tell where I lie.   20

A. POPE

119

THE BLIND BOY

O say what is that thing call'd Light,
  Which I must ne'er enjoy;
What are the blessings of the sight,
  O tell your poor blind boy!

You talk of wondrous things you see,   5
  You say the sun shines bright;
I feel him warm, but how can he
  Or make it day or night?

My day or night myself I make
  Whene'er I sleep or play;   10
And could I ever keep awake
  With me 'twere always day.

With heavy sighs I often hear
  You mourn my hapless woe;
But sure with patience I can bear   15
  A loss I ne'er can know.

Then let not what I cannot have
  My cheer of mind destroy:
Whilst thus I sing, I am a king,
  Although a poor blind boy.   20

C. CIBBER

120

ON A FAVOURITE CAT, DROWNED IN A TUB OF GOLDFISHES

'Twas on a lofty vase's side,
Where China's gayest art had dyed
 The azure flowers that blow,
Demurest of the tabby kind,
The pensive Selima, reclined,   5
 Gazed on the lake below.

Her conscious tail her joy declared:
The fair round face, the snowy beard,
 The velvet of her paws,
Her coat that with the tortoise vies,   10
Her ears of jet, and emerald eyes,
 She saw; and purr'd applause.

Still had she gazed, but 'midst the tide
Two angel forms were seen to glide,
 The Genii of the stream: 15
Their scaly armour's Tyrian hue
Through richest purple to the view
 Betray'd a golden gleam.

The hapless Nymph with wonder saw:
A whisker first, and then a claw   20
 With many an ardent wish
She stretch'd, in vain, to reach the prize—
What female heart can gold despise?
 What Cat's averse to Fish?

Presumptuous maid! with looks intent   25
Again she stretch'd, again she bent,
 Nor knew the gulf between—
Malignant Fate sat by and smiled—
The slippery verge her feet beguiled;
 She tumbled headlong in!   30

Eight times emerging from the flood
She mew'd to every watery God
 Some speedy aid to send:—
No Dolphin came, no Nereid stirr'd,
Nor cruel Tom nor Susan heard—   35
 A favourite has no friend!

From hence, ye Beauties, undeceived,
Know one false step is ne'er retrieved,
   And be with caution bold:
Not all that tempts your wandering eyes   40
And heedless hearts, is lawful prize,
   Nor all that glisters, gold!

T. GRAY

121

TO CHARLOTTE PULTENEY

Timely blossom, Infant fair,
Fondling of a happy pair,
Every morn and every night
Their solicitous delight,
Sleeping, waking, still at ease,   5
Pleasing, without skill to please;
Little gossip, blithe and hale,
Tattling many a broken tale,
Singing many a tuneless song,
Lavish of a heedless tongue;   10
Simple maiden, void of art,
Babbling out of the very heart,
Yet abandon'd to thy will,
Yet imagining no ill,
Yet too innocent to blush;   15
Like the linnet in the bush
To the mother-linnet's note
Moduling her slender throat;
Chirping forth thy petty joys,
Wanton in the change of toys,   20
Like the linnet green, in May
Flitting to each bloomy spray;
Wearied then and glad of rest,
Like the linnet in the nest:—
This thy present happy lot,   25
This, in time will be forgot:
Other pleasures, other cares,
Ever-busy Time prepares;
nd thou shalt in thy daughter see,
This picture, once, resembled thee.   30

A. PHILIPS

122

RULE, BRITANNIA

When Britain first at Heaven's command
  Arose from out the azure main,
This was the charter of the land,
  And guardian angels sung this strain:
Rule, Britannia! rule the waves!   5
  Britons never will be slaves.

The nations not so blest as thee
  Must in their turns to tyrants fall,
While thou shalt flourish great and free,
  The dread and envy of them all.   10

Still more majestic shalt thou rise,
  More dreadful from each foreign stroke;
As the loud blast that tears the skies
  Serves but to root thy native oak.

Thee haughty tyrants ne'er shall tame;   15
  All their attempts to bend thee down
Will but arouse thy generous flame,
  But work their woe and thy renown.

To thee belongs the rural reign;
  Thy cities shall with commerce shine;   20
All thine shall be the subject main,
  And every shore it circles thine!

The Muses, still with Freedom found,
  Shall to thy happy coast repair;
Blest Isle, with matchless beauty crown'd,   25
  And manly hearts to guard the fair:—
Rule, Britannia! rule the waves!
  Britons never will be slaves!

                            J. THOMSON

123

THE BARD

A Pindaric Ode

' Ruin seize thee, ruthless King!
  Confusion on thy banners wait!
Tho' fann'd by Conquest's crimson wing
  They mock the air with idle state.
Helm, nor hauberk's twisted mail,   5
Nor e'en thy virtues, tyrant, shall avail
To save thy secret soul from nightly fears,
From Cambria's curse, from Cambria's tears! '
—Such were the sounds that o'er the crested pride
  Of the first Edward scatter'd wild dismay,   10
As down the steep of Snowdon's shaggy side
  He wound with toilsome march his long array:—
Stout Glo'ster stood aghast in speechless trance;
' To arms! ' cried Mortimer, and couch'd his quivering lance.

  On a rock, whose haughty brow   15
Frowns o'er old Conway's foaming flood,
  Robbed in the sable garb of woe,
With haggard eyes the Poet stood;
  (Loose his beard and hoary hair
Stream'd like a meteor to the troubled air;)   20
And with a master's hand and prophet's fire
Struck the deep sorrows of his lyre:
' Hark, how each giant oak and desert cave
  Sighs to the torrent's awful voice beneath!
O'er thee, O King! their hundred arms they wave,   25
  Revenge on thee in hoarser murmurs breathe;
Vocal no more, since Cambria's fatal day,
To high-born Hoel's harp, or soft Llewellyn's lay.

' Cold is Cadwallo's tongue,
  That hush'd the stormy main: 30
Brave Urien sleeps upon his craggy bed:
  Mountains, ye mourn in vain
  Modred, whose magic song
Made huge Plinlimmon bow his cloud-topt head.
  On dreary Arvon's shore they lie   35

Smear'd with gore and ghastly pale:
Far, far aloof the affrighted ravens sail;
   The famish'd eagle screams, and passes by.
Dear lost companions of my tuneful art,
   Dear as the light that visits these sad eyes,   40
Dear as the ruddy drops that warm my heart,
   Ye died amidst your dying country's cries—
No more I weep. They do not sleep;
   On yonder cliffs, a griesly band,
I see them sit; they linger yet,   45
   Avengers of their native land:
With me in dreadful harmony they join,
And weave with bloody hands the tissue of thy line.

' Weave the warp and weave the woof,
   The winding-sheet of Edward's race: 50
Give ample room and verge enough
   The characters of hell to trace.
Mark the year and mark the night
When Severn shall re-echo with affright
The shrieks of death thro' Berkley's roofs that ring,   55
Shrieks of an agonizing king!
   She-wolf of France, with unrelenting fangs
That tear'st the bowels of thy mangled mate,
   From thee be born, who o'er thy country hangs
The scourge of Heaven! What terrors round him wait!   60
Amazement in his van, with Flight combined,
And Sorrow's faded form, and Solitude behind.

' Mighty victor, mighty lord,
   Low on his funeral couch he lies!
No pitying heart, no eye, afford   65
   A tear to grace his obsequies.
Is the sable warrior fled?
Thy son is gone. He rests among the dead.
The swarm that in thy noon-tide beam were born?
—Gone to salute the rising morn.   70
Fair laughs the Morn, and soft the zephyr blows,
   While proudly riding o'er the azure realm
In gallant trim the gilded Vessel goes:
   Youth on the prow, and Pleasure at the helm:
Regardless of the sweeping Whirlwind's sway,   75
That, hush'd in grim repose, expects his evening prey.

'Fill high the sparkling bowl,
The rich repast prepare;
  Reft of a crown, he yet may share the feast:
Close by the regal chair   80
  Fell Thirst and Famine scowl
  A baleful smile upon their baffled guest.
Heard ye the din of battle bray,
  Lance to lance, and horse to horse?
  Long years of havoc urge their destined course,   85
And thro' the kindred squadrons mow their way.
  Ye towers of Julius, London's lasting shame,
With many a foul and midnight murder fed,
  Revere his Consort's faith, his Father's fame,
And spare the meek usurper's holy head!   90
  Above, below, the rose of snow,
  Twined with her blushing foe, we spread:
  The bristled boar in infant-gore
  Wallows beneath the thorny shade.
Now, brothers, bending o'er the accurséd loom,   95
Stamp we our vengeance deep, and ratify his doom.

'Edward, lo! to sudden fate
  (Weave we the woof; The thread is spun;)
Half of thy heart we consecrate.
  (The web is wove; The work is done.)   100
Stay, O stay! nor thus forlorn
Leave me unbless'd, unpitied, here to mourn:
In yon bright track that fires the western skies
They melt, they vanish from my eyes.
But O! what solemn scenes on Snowdon's height   105
  Descending slow their glittering skirts unroll?
Visions of glory, spare my aching sight,
  Ye unborn ages, crowd not on my soul!
No more our long-lost Arthur we bewail:—
All hail, ye genuine kings! Britannia's issue, hail!   110

'Girt with many a baron bold
Sublime their starry fronts they rear;
  And gorgeous dames, and statesmen old
In bearded majesty, appear.
In the midst a form divine!   115
Her eye proclaims her of the Briton-Line:
Her lion-port, her awe-commanding face
Attemper'd sweet to virgin-grace.
What strings symphonious tremble in the air,

What strains of vocal transport round her play?   120
Hear from the grave, great Taliessin, hear;
　They breathe a soul to animate thy clay.
Bright Rapture calls, and soaring as she sings,
Waves in the eye of Heaven her many-colour'd wings.

' The verse adorn again   125
　Fierce War, and faithful Love,
And Truth severe, by fairy Fiction drest.
　In buskin'd measures move
Pale Grief, and pleasing Pain,
With Horror, tyrant of the throbbing breast.   130
A voice as of the cherub-choir
　Gales from blooming Eden bear,
　And distant warblings lessen on my ear,
That lost in long futurity expire.
Fond impious man, think'st thou yon sanguine cloud   135
　Raised by thy breath, has quench'd the orb of day?
To-morrow he repairs the golden flood
　And warms the nations with redoubled ray.
Enough for me: with joy I see
　The different doom our fates assign: 140
Be thine Despair and sceptred Care;
　To triumph and to die are mine.'
—He spoke, and headlong from the mountain's height
Deep in the roaring tide he plunged to endless night.

T. GRAY

124

ODE WRITTEN IN 1746

How sleep the Brave who sink to rest
By all their Country's wishes blest!
When Spring, with dewy fingers cold,
Returns to deck their hallow'd mould,
She there shall dress a sweeter sod   5
Than Fancy's feet have ever trod.

By fairy hands their knell is rung,
By forms unseen their dirge is sung:
There Honour comes, a pilgrim grey,
To bless the turf that wraps their clay;   10
And Freedom shall awhile repair
To dwell, a weeping hermit, there!

W. COLLINS

125

LAMENT FOR CULLODEN

The lovely lass o' Inverness,
  Nae joy nor pleasure can she see;
For e'en and morn she cries, Alas!
  And ay the saut tear blin's her ee:
Drumossie moor—Drumossie day—   5
  A waefu' day it was to me!
For there I lost my father dear,
  My father dear, and brethren three.

Their winding-sheet the bluidy clay,
  Their graves are growing green to see: 10
And by them lies the dearest lad
  That ever blest a woman's ee!
Now wae to thee, thou cruel lord,
  A bluidy man I trow thou be;
For mony a heart thou hast made sair   15
  That ne'er did wrang to thine or thee.

R. BURNS

126

LAMENT FOR FLODDEN

I've heard them lilting at the ewe-milking,
  Lasses a' lilting before dawn of day;
But now they are moaning on ilka green loaning—
  The Flowers of the Forest are a' wede away.

At bughts, in the morning, nae blythe lads are scorning,   5
  Lasses are lonely and dowie and wae;
Nae daffing, nae gabbing, but sighing and sabbing,
  Ilk ane lifts her leglin and hies her away.

In har'st, at the shearing, nae youths now are jeering,
  Bandsters are runkled, and lyart, or grey;   10
At fair or at preaching, nae wooing, nae fleeching—
  The Flowers of the Forest are a' wede away.

At e'en, in the gloaming, nae younkers are roaming
   'Bout stacks with the lasses at bogle to play;
But ilk maid sits dreary, lamenting her dearie—   15
   The Flowers of the Forest are weded away.

Dool and wae for the order, sent our lads to the Border!
   The English, for ance, by guile wan the day;
The Flowers of the Forest, that fought aye the foremost,
   The prime of our land, are cauld in the clay.   20

We'll hear nae mair lilting at the ewe-milking;
   Women and bairns are heartless and wae;
Sighing and moaning on ilka green loaning—
   The Flowers of the Forest are a' wede away.

J. ELLIOT

127

THE BRAES OF YARROW

' Thy braes were bonny, Yarrow stream,
   When first on them I met my lover;
Thy braes how dreary, Yarrow stream,
   When now thy waves his body cover!
For ever now, O Yarrow stream,
   Thou art to me a stream of sorrow;   5
For never on thy banks shall I
   Behold my love, the flower of Yarrow.

' He promised me a milk-white steed
   To bear me to his father's bowers;   10
He promised me a little page
   To squire me to his father's towers;
He promised me a wedding-ring,—
   The wedding-day was fix'd to-morrow;—
Now he is wedded to his grave,   15
   Alas, his watery grave, in Yarrow!

' Sweet were his words when last we met;
   My passion I as freely told him;
Clasp'd in his arms, I little thought
   That I should never more behold him!
Scarce was he gone, I saw his ghost;   20
   It vanish'd with a shriek of sorrow;

Thrice did the water-wraith ascend,
  And gave a doleful groan thro' Yarrow.

' His mother from the window look'd   25
  With all the longing of a mother;
His little sister weeping walk'd
  The green-wood path to meet her brother;
They sought him east, they sought him west,
  They sought him all the forest thorough;   30
They only saw the cloud of night,
  They only heard the roar of Yarrow.

' No longer from thy window look—
  Thou hast no son, thou tender mother!
No longer walk, thou lovely maid;   35
  Alas, thou hast no more a brother!
No longer seek him east or west
  And search no more the forest thorough;
For, wandering in the night so dark,
  He fell a lifeless corpse in Yarrow.   40

' The tear shall never leave my cheek,
  No other youth shall be my marrow—
I'll seek thy body in the stream,
  And then with thee I'll sleep in Yarrow.'
—The tear did never leave her cheek,   45
  No other youth became her marrow;
She found his body in the stream,
  And now with him she sleeps in Yarrow.

                                              J. LOGAN

                    128

        WILLY DROWNED IN YARROW

        Down in yon garden sweet and gay
          Where bonnie grows the lily,
        I heard a fair maid sighing say,
          ' My wish be wi' sweet Willie!

        ' Willie's rare, and Willie's fair,   5
          And Willie's wondrous bonny;
        And Willie hecht to marry me
          Gin e'er he married ony.

' O gentle wind, that bloweth south
   From where my Love repaireth,   10
Convey a kiss frae his dear mouth
   And tell me how he fareth!

' O tell sweet Willie to come doun
   And hear the mavis singing,
And see the birds on ilka bush   15
   And leaves around them hinging.

' The lav'rock there, wi' her white breast
   And gentle throat sae narrow;
There's sport eneuch for gentlemen
   On Leader haughs and Yarrow.   20

' O Leader haughs are wide and braid
   And Yarrow haughs are bonny;
There Willie hecht to marry me
   If e'er he married ony.

' But Willie's gone, whom I thought on,   25
   And does not hear me weeping;
Draws many a tear frae 's true love's e'e
   When other maids are sleeping.

' Yestreen I made my bed fu' braid,
   The night I'll mak' it narrow,   30
For a' the live-lang winter night
   I lie twined o' my marrow.

' O came ye by yon water-side?
   Pou'd you the rose or lily?
Or came you by yon meadow green,   35
   Or saw you my sweet Willie? '

She sought him up, she sought him down,
   She sought him braid and narrow;
Syne, in the cleaving of a craig,
   She found him drown'd in Yarrow!   40

ANON

129

LOSS OF THE ROYAL GEORGE

Toll for the Brave!
The brave that are no more!
All sunk beneath the wave
Fast by their native shore!

Eight hundred of the brave,   5
Whose courage well was tried,
Had made the vessel heel
And laid her on her side.

A land-breeze shook the shrouds
And she was overset;   10
Down went the Royal George,
With all her crew complete.

Toll for the brave!
Brave Kempenfelt is gone;
His last sea-fight is fought,   15
His work of glory done.

It was not in the battle;
No tempest gave the shock;
She sprang no fatal leak,
She ran upon no rock.   20

His sword was in the sheath,
His fingers held the pen,
When Kempenfelt went down
With twice four hundred men.

Weigh the vessel up   25
Once dreaded by our foes,
And mingle with your cup
The tears that England owes.

Her timbers yet are sound,
And she may float again   30
Full charged with England's thunder,
And plough the distant main:

But Kempenfelt is gone,
His victories are o'er;
And he and his eight hundred   35
Must plough the wave no more.

W. COWPER

130

BLACK-EYED SUSAN

All in the Downs the fleet was moor'd,
  The streamers waving in the wind,
When black-eyed Susan came aboard;
  ' O! where shall I my true-love find?
Tell me, ye jovial sailors, tell me true   5
If my sweet William sails among the crew.'

William, who high upon the yard
  Rock'd with the billow to and fro,
Soon as her well-known voice he heard,
  He sigh'd, and cast his eyes below: 10
The cord slides swiftly through his glowing hands,
And quick as lightning on the deck he stands.

So the sweet lark, high poised in air,
  Shuts close his pinions to his breast
If chance his mate's shrill call he hear,   15
  And drops at once into her nest:—
The noblest captain in the British fleet
Might envy William's lips those kisses sweet.

' O Susan, Susan, lovely dear,
  My vows shall ever true remain;   20
Let me kiss off that falling tear;
  We only part to meet again.
Change as ye list, ye winds; my heart shall be
The faithful compass that still points to thee.

' Believe not what the landmen say   25
  Who tempt with doubts thy constant mind:
They'll tell thee, sailors, when away,
  In every port a mistress find:
Yes, yes, believe them when they tell thee so,
For Thou art present wheresoe'er I go.   30

' If to far India's coast we sail,
  Thy eyes are seen in diamonds bright,
Thy breath is Afric's spicy gale,
  Thy skin is ivory so white.
Thus every beauteous object that I view   35
Wakes in my soul some charm of lovely Sue.

' Though battle call me from thy arms
  Let not my pretty Susan mourn;
Though cannons roar, yet safe from harms
  William shall to his Dear return.   40
Love turns aside the balls that round me fly,
Lest precious tears should drop from Susan's eye.'

The boatswain gave the dreadful word,
  The sails their swelling bosom spread;
No longer must she stay aboard;   45
  They kiss'd, she sigh'd, he hung his head.
Her lessening boat unwilling rows to land;
' Adieu! ' she cries; and waved her lily hand.

                       J. GAY

131

SALLY IN OUR ALLEY

Of all the girls that are so smart
  There's none like pretty Sally;
She is the darling of my heart,
  And she lives in our alley.
There is no lady in the land   5
  Is half so sweet as Sally;
She is the darling of my heart,
  And she lives in our alley.

Her father he makes cabbage-nets
  And through the streets does cry 'em;   10
Her mother she sells laces long
  To such as please to buy 'em:
But sure such folks could ne'er beget
  So sweet a girl as Sally!
She is the darling of my heart,   15
  And she lives in our alley.

When she is by, I leave my work,
  I love her so sincerely;
My master comes like any Turk,
  And bangs me most severely—   20
But let him bang his bellyful,
  I'll bear it all for Sally;
She is the darling of my heart,
  And she lives in our alley.

Of all the days that's in the week   25
  I dearly love but one day—
And that's the day that comes betwixt
  A Saturday and Monday;
For then I'm drest all in my best
  To walk abroad with Sally;   30
She is the darling of my heart,
  And she lives in our alley.

My master carries me to church,
  And often am I blamed
Because I leave him in the lurch   35
  As soon as text is named;
I leave the church in sermon-time
  And slink away to Sally;
She is the darling of my heart,
  And she lives in our alley.   40

When Christmas comes about again
  O then I shall have money;
I'll hoard it up, and box and all,
  I'll give it to my honey:
I would it were ten thousand pound,   45
  I'd give it all to Sally;
She is the darling of my heart,
  And she lives in our alley.

My master and the neighbours all
  Make game of me and Sally,   50
And, but for her, I'd better be
  A slave and row a galley;
But when my seven long years are out
  O then I'll marry Sally,—
O then we'll wed, and then we'll bed,   55
  But not in our alley!

H. CAREY

132

A FAREWELL

Go fetch to me a pint o' wine,
　An' fill it in a silver tassie;
That I may drink before I go
　A service to my bonnie lassie:
The boat rocks at the pier o' Leith,　　　5
　Fu' loud the wind blaws frae the Ferry,
The ship rides by the Berwick-law,
　And I maun leave my bonnie Mary.

The trumpets sound, the banners fly,
　The glittering spears are rankéd ready,　　10
The shouts o' war are heard afar,
　The battle closes thick and bloody;
But it's not the roar o' sea or shore
　Wad make me langer wish to tarry;
Nor shout o' war that's heard afar—　　　15
　It's leaving thee, my bonnie Mary.

                              R. BURNS

133

If doughty deeds my lady please
　Right soon I'll mount my steed;
And strong his arm, and fast his seat,
　That bears frae me the meed.
I'll wear thy colours in my cap,　　　5
　Thy picture in my heart;
And he that bends not to thine eye
　Shall rue it to his smart.
　　Then tell me how to woo thee, love;
　　　O tell me how to woo thee!　　10
　　For thy dear sake, nae care I'll take,
　　　Tho' ne'er another trow me.

If gay attire delight thine eye
　I'll dight me in array;
I'll tend thy chamber door all night,　　15
　And squire thee all the day.

If sweetest sounds can win thine ear,
  These sounds I'll strive to catch;
Thy voice I'll steal to woo thysell,
  That voice that nane can match.   20

But if fond love thy heart can gain,
  I never broke a vow;
Nae maiden lays her skaith to me,
  I never loved but you.
For you alone I ride the ring,   25
  For you I wear the blue;
For you alone I strive to sing,
  O tell me how to woo!
    Then tell me how to woo thee, love;
     O tell me how to woo thee!   30
    For thy dear sake, nae care I'll take,
     Tho' ne'er another trow me.

R. GRAHAM OF GARTMORE

134

TO A YOUNG LADY

Sweet stream, that winds through yonder glade,
Apt emblem of a virtuous maid—
Silent and chaste she steals along,
Far from the world's gay busy throng:
With gentle yet prevailing force,   5
Intent upon her destined course;
Graceful and useful all she does,
Blessing and blest where'er she goes;
Pure-bosom'd as that watery glass,
And Heaven reflected in her face.   10

W. COWPER

135

THE SLEEPING BEAUTY

Sleep on, and dream of Heaven awhile—
  Tho' shut so close thy laughing eyes,
Thy rosy lips still wear a smile
  And move, and breathe delicious sighs!

Ah, now soft blushes tinge her cheeks
  And mantle o'er her neck of snow:
Ah, now she murmurs, now she speaks
  What most I wish—and fear to know!

She starts, she trembles, and she weeps!
  Her fair hands folded on her breast:
—And now, how like a saint she sleeps!
  A seraph in the realms of rest!

Sleep on secure! Above control
  Thy thoughts belong to Heaven and thee:
And may the secret of thy soul
  Remain within its sanctuary!

S. ROGERS

136

For ever, Fortune, wilt thou prove
An unrelenting foe to Love,
And when we meet a mutual heart
Come in between, and bid us part?

Bid us sigh on from day to day,
And wish and wish the soul away;
Till youth and genial years are flown,
And all the life of life is gone?

But busy, busy, still art thou,
To bind the loveless joyless vow,
The heart from pleasure to delude,
And join the gentle to the rude.

For once, O Fortune, hear my prayer,
And I absolve thy future care;
All other blessings I resign,
Make but the dear Amanda mine.

J. THOMSON

137

The merchant, to secure his treasure,
　Conveys it in a borrow'd name:
Euphelia serves to grace my measure,
　But Cloe is my real flame.

My softest verse, my darling lyre   5
　Upon Euphelia's toilet lay—
When Cloe noted her desire
　That I should sing, that I should play.

My lyre I tune, my voice I raise,
　But with my numbers mix my sighs;   10
And whilst I sing Euphelia's praise,
　I fix my soul on Cloe's eyes.

Fair Cloe blush'd: Euphelia frown'd:
　I sung, and gazed; I play'd, and trembled:
And Venus to the Loves around   15
　Remark'd how ill we all dissembled.

M. PRIOR

138

When lovely woman stoops to folly
　And finds too late that men betray,—
What charm can soothe her melancholy,
　What art can wash her guilt away?

The only art her guilt to cover,   5
　To hide her shame from every eye,
To give repentance to her lover
　And wring his bosom, is—to die.

O. GOLDSMITH

139

Ye flowery banks o' bonie Doon,
　How can ye blume sae fair?
How can ye chant, ye little birds,
　And I sae fu' o' care?

Thou'll break my heart, thou bonie bird   5
　　That sings upon the bough;
Thou minds me o' the happy days
　　When my fause Luve was true.

Thou'll break my heart, thou bonie bird
　　That sings beside thy mate;   10
For sae I sat, and sae I sang,
　　And wist na o' my fate.

Aft hae I rov'd by bonie Doon
　　To see the woodbine twine;
And ilka bird sang o' its luve,   15
　　And sae did I o' mine.

Wi' lightsome heart I pu'd a rose,
　　Frae aff its thorny tree;
And my fause luver staw my rose,
　　But left the thorn wi' me.   20

R. BURNS

140

THE PROGRESS OF POESY

A Pindaric Ode

Awake, Aeolian lyre, awake,
And give to rapture all thy trembling strings.
From Helicon's harmonious springs
　　A thousand rills their mazy progress take:
The laughing flowers that round them blow   5
Drink life and fragrance as they flow.
Now the rich stream of Music winds along
Deep, majestic, smooth, and strong.
Through verdant vales and Ceres' golden reign;
Now rolling down the steep amain,   10
Headlong, impetuous, see it pour:
The rocks and nodding groves rebellow to the roar.

O Sovereign of the willing soul,
Parent of sweet and solemn-breathing airs,
Enchanting shell! the sullen Cares   15
　　And frantic Passions hear thy soft control.

On Thracia's hills the Lord of War
Has curb'd the fury of his car
And dropt his thirsty lance at thy command.
Perching on the sceptred hand   20
Of Jove, thy magic lulls the feather'd king
With ruffled plumes, and flagging wing:
Quench'd in dark clouds of slumber lie
The terror of his beak, and lightnings of his eye.

Thee the voice, the dance, obey   25
Temper'd to thy warbled lay.
    O'er Idalia's velvet green
    The rosy-crownéd Loves are seen
On Cytherea's day,
    With antic Sports, and blue-eyed Pleasures,   30
    Frisking light in frolic measures;
Now pursuing, now retreating,
    Now in circling troops they meet:
To brisk notes in cadence beating
    Glance their many-twinkling feet.   35
Slow melting strains their Queen's approach declare:
    Where'er she turns the Graces homage pay:
With arms sublime that float upon the air
    In gliding state she wins her easy way:
O'er her warm cheek and rising bosom move   40
The bloom of young Desire and purple light of Love.

    Man's feeble race what ills await!
Labour, and Penury, the racks of Pain,
Disease, and Sorrow's weeping train,
    And Death, sad refuge from the storms of Fate! 45
The fond complaint, my song, disprove,
And justify the laws of Jove.
Say, has he given in vain the heavenly Muse?
Night, and all her sickly dews,
Her spectres wan, and birds of boding cry   50
He gives to range the dreary sky:
Till down the eastern cliffs afar
Hyperion's march they spy, and glittering shafts of war.

    In climes beyond the solar road,
Where shaggy forms o'er ice-built mountains roam, 55
The Muse has broke the twilight gloom
    To cheer the shivering native's dull abode.

And oft, beneath the odorous shade
Of Chili's boundless forests laid,
She deigns to hear the savage youth repeat   60
In loose numbers wildly sweet
Their feather-cinctured chiefs, and dusky loves.
Her track, where'er the Goddess roves,
Glory pursue, and generous Shame,
Th' unconquerable Mind, and Freedom's holy flame.   65

Woods, that wave o'er Delphi's steep,
Isles, that crown th' Aegean deep,
    Fields that cool Ilissus laves,
    Or where Maeander's amber waves
In lingering lab'rinths creep,   70
    How do your tuneful echoes languish,
    Mute, but to the voice of anguish!
Where each old poetic mountain
    Inspiration breath'd around;
Every shade and hallow'd fountain   75
    Murmur'd deep a solemn sound:
Till the sad Nine, in Greece's evil hour,
    Left their Parnassus for the Latian plains.
Alike they scorn the pomp of tyrant Power,
    And coward Vice, that revels in her chains.   80
When Latium had her lofty spirit lost,
They sought, O Albion, next thy sea-encircled coast.

    Far from the sun and summer-gale
In thy green lap was Nature's Darling laid,
What time, where lucid Avon stray'd,   85
    To him the mighty Mother did unveil
Her awful face: the dauntless Child
Stretch'd forth his little arms, and smiled.
This pencil take (she said), whose colours clear
Richly paint the vernal year: 90
Thine, too, these golden keys, immortal Boy!
This can unlock the gates of Joy;
Of Horror that, and thrilling Fears,
Or ope the sacred source of sympathetic Tears.

    Nor second He, that rode sublime   95
Upon the seraph-wings of Ecstasy,
The secrets of the Abyss to spy:
    He pass'd the flaming bounds of Place and Time:

The living Throne, the sapphire-blaze,
Where Angels tremble while they gaze,   100
He saw; but blasted with excess of light,
Closed his eyes in endless night.
Behold where Dryden's less presumptuous car
Wide o'er the fields of Glory bear
Two coursers of ethereal race   105
With necks in thunderclothed, and long-resounding pace.

Hark, his hands the lyre explore!
Bright-eyed Fancy, hovering o'er,
   Scatters from her pictur'd urn
   Thoughts that breathe, and words that burn.   110
But ah! 'tis heard no more——
   O! Lyre divine, what daring Spirit
   Wakes thee now? Tho' he inherit
Nor the pride, nor ample pinion,
   That the Theban Eagle bear,   115
Sailing with supreme dominion
   Thro' the azure deep of air:
Yet oft before his infant eyes would run
   Such forms as glitter in the Muse's ray
With orient hues, unborrow'd of the sun: 120
   Yet shall he mount, and keep his distant way
Beyond the limits of a vulgar fate:
Beneath the Good how far—but far above the Great.

                                                    T. GRAY

141

THE PASSIONS

An Ode for Music

When Music, heavenly maid, was young,
While yet in early Greece she sung,
The Passions oft, to hear her shell,
Throng'd around her magic cell
Exulting, trembling, raging, fainting,   5
Possest beyond the Muse's painting;
By turns they felt the glowing mind
Disturb'd, delighted, rais'd, refin'd:
Till once, 'tis said, when all were fir'd,
Fill'd with fury, rapt, inspir'd,   10

From the supporting myrtles round
They snatch'd her instruments of sound,
And, as they oft had heard apart
Sweet lessons of her forceful art,
Each, for Madness ruled the hour,   15
Would prove his own expressive power.

First Fear his hand, its skill to try,
  Amid the chords bewilder'd laid,
And back recoil'd, he knew not why,
  E'en at the sound himself had made.   20

Next Anger rush'd, his eyes on fire,
  In lightnings own'd his secret stings;
In one rude clash he struck the lyre
  And swept with hurried hand the strings.

With woeful measures wan Despair,   25
  Low sullen sounds, his grief beguiled,
A solemn, strange, and mingled air,
  'Twas sad by fits, by starts 'twas wild.

But thou, O Hope, with eyes so fair,
  What was thy delightful measure?   30
Still it whisper'd promised pleasure
  And bade the lovely scenes at distance hail!
Still would her touch the strain prolong;
  And from the rocks, the woods, the vale,
She call'd on Echo still through all the song;   35
  And, where her sweetest theme she chose,
  A soft responsive voice was heard at every close;
And Hope enchanted smiled, and waved her golden hair.

And longer had she sung,—but with a frown
  Revenge impatient rose: 40
He threw his blood-stain'd sword in thunder down;
  And with a withering look
  The war-denouncing trumpet took,
And blew a blast so loud and dread,
Were ne'er prophetic sounds so full of woe.   45
  And ever and anon he beat
  The doubling drum with furious heat;
And, though sometimes, each dreary pause between,
  Dejected Pity at his side
  Her soul-subduing voice applied,   50

Yet still he kept his wild unalter'd mien,
While each strain'd ball of sight seem'd bursting from his head.

Thy numbers, Jealousy, to nought were fix'd:
   Sad proof of thy distressful state!
Of differing themes the veering song was mix'd;   55
   And now it courted Love, now raving call'd on Hate.

With eyes up-rais'd, as one inspir'd,
Pale Melancholy sat retir'd;
And from her wild sequester'd seat,
In notes by distance made more sweet,   60
Pour'd through the mellow horn her pensive soul:
   And dashing soft from rocks around
   Bubbling runnels join'd the sound;
Through glades and glooms the mingled measure stole,
   Or, o'er some haunted stream, with fond delay,   65
   Round an holy calm diffusing,
   Love of peace and lonely musing,
In hollow murmurs died away.
But O! how alter'd was its sprightlier tone,
When Cheerfulness, a nymph of healthiest hue,   70
   Her bow across her shoulder flung,
   Her buskins gemm'd with morning dew,
Blew an inspiring air, that dale and thicket rung,
   The hunter's call to Faun and Dryad known!
The oak-crown'd Sisters and their chaste-eyed Queen,   75
   Satyrs and Sylvan Boys, were seen
   Peeping from forth their alleys green:
Brown Exercise rejoic'd to hear;
   And Sport leap'd up, and seiz'd his beechen spear.

Last came Joy's ecstatic trial: 80
He, with viny crown advancing,
   First to the lively pipe his hand addrest:
But soon he saw the brisk awak'ning viol,
   Whose sweet entrancing voice he lov'd the best:
They would have thought who heard the strain   85
     They saw, in Temple's vale, her native maids
    Amidst the festal-sounding shades
To some unwearied minstrel dancing;
While, as his flying fingers kiss'd the strings,
   Love fram'd with Mirth a gay fantastic round: 90
   Loose were her tresses seen, her zone unbound;

And he, amidst his frolic play,
    As if he would the charming air repay,
Shook thousand odours from his dewy wings.

O Music! sphere-descended maid,   95
Friend of Pleasure, Wisdom's aid!
Why, goddess, why, to us denied,
Lay'st thou thy ancient lyre aside?
As in that lov'd Athenian bower
You learn'd an all-commanding power,   100
Thy mimic soul, O nymph endear'd,
Can well recall what then it heard.
Where is thy native simple heart
Devote to Virtue, Fancy, Art?
Arise, as in that elder time,   105
Warm, energic, chaste, sublime!
Thy wonders in that god-like age
Fill thy recording Sister's page;—
'Tis said, and I believe the tale,
Thy humblest reed could more prevail,   110
Had more of strength, diviner rage,
Than all which charms this laggard age,
E'en all at once together found,
Cecilia's mingled world of sound:—
O bid our vain endeavours cease: 115
Revive the just designs of Greece:
Return in all thy simple state!
Confirm the tales her sons relate!

                                              W. COLLINS

142

ODE ON THE SPRING

Lo! where the rosy-bosom'd Hours,
    Fair Venus' train, appear,
Disclose the long-expecting flowers
    And wake the purple year!
The Attic warbler pours her throat   5
Responsive to the cuckoo's note,
The untaught harmony of Spring:
    While, whispering pleasure as they fly,
    Cool Zephyrs through the clear blue sky
Their gather'd fragrance fling.   10

Where'er the oak's thick branches stretch
  A broader, browner shade,
Where'er the rude and moss-grown beech
O'er-canopies the glade,
Beside some water's rushy brink   15
With me the Muse shall sit, and think
(At ease reclined in rustic state)
    How vain the ardour of the Crowd,
How low, how little are the Proud,
How indigent the Great!   20

Still is the toiling hand of Care;
  The panting herds repose:
Yet hark, how through the peopled air
  The busy murmur glows!
The insect youth are on the wing,   25
Eager to taste the honied spring
And float amid the liquid noon:
    Some lightly o'er the current skim,
    Some show their gaily-gilded trim
Quick-glancing to the sun.   30

To Contemplation's sober eye
  Such is the race of Man:
And they that creep, and they that fly,
  Shall end where they began.
Alike the busy and the gay   35
But flutter through life's little day,
In Fortune's varying colours drest:
    Brush'd by the hand of rough Mischance.
    Or chill'd by Age, their airy dance
They leave, in dust to rest.   40

Methinks I hear in accents low
  The sportive kind reply:
Poor moralist! and what art thou?
  A solitary fly!
Thy joys no glittering female meets,   45
No hive hast thou of hoarded sweets,
No painted plumage to display:
    On hasty wings thy youth is flown;
    Thy sun is set, thy spring is gone—
We frolic while 'tis May.   50

                                    T. GRAY

143

THE POPLAR FIELD

The poplars are fell'd; farewell to the shade
And the whispering sound of the cool colonnade;
The winds play no longer and sing in the leaves,
Nor Ouse on his bosom their image receives.

Twelve years have elapsed since I first took a view   5
Of my favourite field, and the bank where they grew:
And now in the grass behold they are laid,
And the tree is my seat that once lent me a shade.

The blackbird has fled to another retreat,
Where the hazels afford him a screen from the heat;
And the scene where his melody charm'd me before
Resounds with his sweet-flowing ditty no more.

My fugitive years are all hasting away,
And I must ere long lie as lowly as they,
With a turf on my breast and a stone at my head,   15
Ere another such grove shall arise in its stead.

'Tis a sight to engage me, if anything can,
To muse on the perishing pleasures of man;
Though his life be a dream, his enjoyments, I see,
Have a being less durable even than he.   20

W. COWPER

144

TO A MOUSE

On turning her up in her nest with the plough, November 1785

Wee, sleekit, cow'rin', tim'rous beastie,
O what a panic 's in thy breastie!
Thou need na start awa sae hasty,
   Wi' bickering brattle!
I wad be laith to rin an' chase thee   5
   Wi' murd'ring pattle!

I'm truly sorry man's dominion
Has broken nature's social union,
An' justifies that ill opinion
   Which makes thee startle   10
At me, thy poor earth-born companion,
   An' fellow-mortal!

I doubt na, whiles, but thou may thieve;
What then? poor beastie, thou maun live!
A daimen-icker in a thrave   15
   'S a sma' request:
I'll get a blessin' wi' the lave,
   And never miss't!

Thy wee bit housie, too, in ruin!
Its silly wa's, the win's are strewin':   20
And naething, now, to big a new ane,
   O' foggage green!
An' bleak December's winds ensuin'
   Baith snell an' keen!

Thou saw the fields laid bare and waste   25
An' weary winter comin' fast,
An' cozie here, beneath the blast,
   Thou thought to dwell,
Till, crash! the cruel coulter past
   Out thro' thy cell.   30

That wee bit heap o' leaves an' stibble
Has cost thee mony a weary nibble!
Now thou's turn'd out, for a' thy trouble,
   But house or hald,
To thole the winter's sleety dribble   35
   An' cranreuch cauld!

But, Mousie, thou art no thy lane
In proving foresight may be vain:
The best laid schemes o' mice an' men
   Gang aft a-gley,   40
An' lea'e us nought but grief an' pain,
   For promised joy.

Still thou art blest, compared wi' me!
The present only toucheth thee:
But, och! I backward cast my e'e   45
  On prospects drear!
An' forward, tho' I canna see,
  I guess an' fear!

R. BURNS

145

A WISH

Mine be a cot beside the hill;
  A bee-hive's hum shall soothe my ear;
A willowy brook that turns a mill,
  With many a fall shall linger near.

The swallow, oft, beneath my thatch   5
  Shall twitter from her clay-built nest;
Oft shall the pilgrim lift the latch,
  And share my meal, a welcome guest.

Around my ivied porch shall spring
  Each fragrant flower that drinks the dew;   10
And Lucy, at her wheel, shall sing
  In russet gown and apron blue.

The village-church among the trees,
  Where first our marriage-vows were given,
With merry peals shall swell the breeze   15
  And point with taper spire to Heaven.

S. ROGERS

146

TO EVENING

If aught of oaten stop or pastoral song
May hope, O pensive Eve, to soothe thine ear,
  Like thy own brawling springs,
  Thy springs, and dying gales;

O Nymph reserved,—while now the bright-hair'd sun   5
Sits in yon western tent, whose cloudy skirts
    With brede ethereal wove
    O'erhang his wavy bed;

Now air is hush'd, save where the weak-ey'd bat
With short shrill shriek flits by on leathern wing,   10
    Or where the beetle winds
    His small but sullen horn,

As oft he rises 'midst the twilight path,
Against the pilgrim borne in heedless hum,—
    Now teach me, maid composed,   15
    To breathe some soften'd strain,

Whose numbers, stealing through thy dark'ning vale,
May not unseemly with its stillness suit;
    As musing slow I hail
    Thy genial loved return.   20

For when thy folding-star arising shows
His paly circlet, at his warning lamp
    The fragrant Hours, and Elves
    Who slept in buds the day,

And many a Nymph who wreathes her brows with sedge 25
And sheds the freshening dew, and lovelier still
    The pensive Pleasures sweet,
    Prepare thy shadowy car.

Then let me rove some wild and heathy scene;
Or find some ruin midst its dreary dells,   30
    Whose walls more awful nod
    By thy religious gleams.

Or if chill blustering winds or driving rain
Prevent my willing feet, be mine the hut
    That, from the mountain's side,   35
    Views wilds and swelling floods,

And hamlets brown, and dim-discover'd spires;
And hears their simple bell; and marks o'er all
    Thy dewy fingers draw
    The gradual dusky veil.   40

While Spring shall pour his showers, as oft he wont,
And bathe thy breathing tresses, meekest Eve!
    While Summer loves to sport
    Beneath thy lingering light;

While sallow Autumn fills thy lap with leaves;   45
Or Winter, yelling through the troublous air,
    Affrights thy shrinking train
    And rudely rends thy robes;

So long, regardful of thy quiet rule,
Shall Fancy, Friendship, Science, smiling Peace,   50
    Thy gentlest influence own,
    And love thy favourite name!

                                W. COLLINS

147

ELEGY
WRITTEN IN A COUNTRY CHURCH-YARD

The curfew tolls the knell of parting day,
    The lowing herd wind slowly o'er the lea,
The ploughman homeward plods his weary way,
    And leaves the world to darkness, and to me.

Now fades the glimmering landscape on the sight,   5
    And all the air a solemn stillness holds,
Save where the beetle wheels his droning flight,
    And drowsy tinklings lull the distant folds:

Save that from yonder ivy-mantled tower
    The moping owl does to the moon complain   10
Of such as, wandering near her secret bower,
    Molest her ancient solitary reign.

Beneath those rugged elms, that yew-tree's shade,
    Where heaves the turf in many a mouldering heap,
Each in his narrow cell for ever laid,   15
    The rude Forefathers of the hamlet sleep.

The breezy call of incense-breathing morn,
    The swallow twittering from the straw-built shed,
The cock's shrill clarion, or the echoing horn,
    No more shall rouse them from their lowly bed.   20

For them no more the blazing hearth shall burn,
　　Or busy housewife ply her evening care:
No children run to lisp their sire's return,
　　Or climb his knees the envied kiss to share.

Oft did the harvest to their sickle yield,　　　25
　　Their furrow oft the stubborn glebe has broke;
How jocund did they drive their team afield!
　　How bow'd the woods beneath their sturdy stroke!

Let not Ambition mock their useful toil,
　　Their homely joys, and destiny obscure;
Nor Grandeur hear with a disdainful smile　　30
　　The short and simple annals of the Poor.

The boast of heraldry, the pomp of power,
　　And all that beauty, all that wealth e'er gave,
Awaits alike th' inevitable hour:—　　　35
　　The paths of glory lead but to the grave.

Nor you, ye Proud, impute to these the fault
　　If Memory o'er their tomb no trophies raise,
Where through the long-drawn aisle and fretted vault
　　The pealing anthem swells the note of praise.　　40

Can storied urn or animated bust
　　Back to its mansion call the fleeting breath?
Can Honour's voice provoke the silent dust,
　　Or Flattery soothe the dull cold ear of Death?

Perhaps in this neglected spot is laid　　　45
　　Some heart once pregnant with celestial fire;
Hands, that the rod of empire might have sway'd,
　　Or waked to ecstasy the living lyre:

But Knowledge to their eyes her ample page
　　Rich with the spoils of time, did ne'er unroll;　　50
Chill Penury repress'd their noble rage,
　　And froze the genial current of the soul.

Full many a gem of purest ray serene
　　The dark unfathom'd caves of ocean bear:
Full many a flower is born to blush unseen,　　55
　　And waste its sweetness on the desert air.

Some village-Hampden, that with dauntless breast
   The little tyrant of his fields withstood,
Some mute inglorious Milton here may rest,
   Some Cromwell, guiltless of his country's blood.   60

Th' applause of list'ning senates to command,
   The threats of pain and ruin to despise,
To scatter plenty o'er a smiling land,
   And read their history in a nation's eyes,

Their lot forbad: nor circumscribed alone   65
   Their growing virtues, but their crimes confined;
Forbad to wade through slaughter to a throne,
   And shut the gates of mercy on mankind,

The struggling pangs of conscious truth to hide.
   To quench the blushes of ingenuous shame,   70
Or heap the shrine of Luxury and Pride
   With incense kindled at the Muse's flame.

Far from the madding crowd's ignoble strife,
   Their sober wishes never learn'd to stray;
Along the cool sequester'd vale of life   75
   They kept the noiseless tenour of their way.

Yet e'en these bones from insult to protect
   Some frail memorial still erected nigh,
With uncouth rhymes and shapeless sculpture deck'd,
   Implores the passing tribute of a sigh.   80

Their name, their years, spelt by th' unletter'd Muse,
   The place of fame and elegy supply:
And many a holy text around she strews,
   That teach the rustic moralist to die.

For who, to dumb forgetfulness a prey,   85
   This pleasing anxious being e'er resign'd,
Left the warm precincts of the cheerful day,
   Nor cast one longing lingering look behind?

On some fond breast the parting soul relies,
   Some pious drops the closing eye requires;   90
E'en from the tomb the voice of Nature cries,
   E'en in our ashes live their wonted fires.

For thee, who, mindful of th' unhonour'd dead,
    Dost in these lines their artless tale relate;
If chance, by lonely contemplation led,   95
    Some kindred spirit shall inquire thy fate,

Haply some hoary-headed swain may say,
    ' Oft have we seen him at the peep of dawn
Brushing with hasty steps the dews away,
    To meet the sun upon the upland lawn;   100

' There at the foot of yonder nodding beech
    That wreathes its old fantastic roots so high,
His listless length at noontide would he stretch,
    And pore upon the brook that babbles by.

' Hard by yon wood, now smiling as in scorn,   105
    Muttering his wayward fancies he would rove;
Now drooping, woeful wan, like one forlorn,
    Or crazed with care, or cross'd in hopeless love.

' One morn I miss'd him on the custom'd hill,
    Along the heath, and near his favourite tree; 110
Another came; nor yet beside the rill,
    Nor up the lawn, nor at the wood was he;

' The next with dirges due in sad array
    Slow through the church-way path we saw him borne,—
Approach and read (for thou canst read) the lay   115
    Graved on the stone beneath yon aged thorn.'

THE EPITAPH

Here rests his head upon the lap of Earth
    A Youth, to Fortune and to Fame unknown;
Fair Science frown'd not on his humble birth,
    And Melancholy mark'd him for her own.   120

Large was his bounty, and his soul sincere;
    Heaven did a recompense as largely send:
He gave to Misery all he had, a tear,
    He gain'd from Heaven, 'twas all he wish'd, a friend.

No farther seeks his merits to disclose, 125
  Or draw his frailties from their dread abode,
(There they alike in trembling hope repose,)
  The bosom of his Father and his God.

                                             T. GRAY

148

MARY MORISON

O Mary, at thy window be,
  It is the wish'd, the trysted hour!
Those smiles and glances let me see
  That make the miser's treasure poor:
  How blythely wad I bide the stoure, 5
A weary slave frae sun to sun,
  Could I the rich reward secure,
The lovely Mary Morison.

Yestreen when to the trembling string
  The dance gaed thro' the lighted ha', 10
To thee my fancy took its wing,—
  I sat, but neither heard nor saw:
  Tho' this was fair, and that was braw,
And yon the toast of a' the town,
  I sigh'd, and said amang them a', 15
'Ye arena Mary Morison.'

O Mary, canst thou wreck his peace
  Wha for thy sake wad gladly dee?
Or canst thou break that heart of his,
  Whase only faut is loving thee? 20
  If love for love thou wiltna gie,
At least be pity to me shown;
  A thought ungentle canna be
The thought o' Mary Morison.

                                             R. BURNS

149

BONNIE LESLEY

O saw ye bonnie Lesley
   As she gaed o'er the border?
She's gane, like Alexander,
   To spread her conquests farther.

To see her is to love her,   5
   And love but her for ever;
For nature made her what she is,
   And never made anither!

Thou art a queen, fair Lesley,
   Thy subjects we, before thee;
Thou art divine, fair Lesley,   10
   The hearts o' men adore thee.

The deil he couldna scaith thee,
   Or aught that wad belang thee;
He'd look into they bonnie face,   15
   And say ' I canna wrang thee! '

The Powers aboon will tent thee;
   Misfortune sha' na steer thee;
Thou'rt like themselves sae lovely,
   That ill they'll ne'er let near thee.   20

Return again, fair Lesley,
   Return to Caledonie!
That we may brag we hae a lass
   There 's nane again sae bonnie.

                  R. BURNS

150

O my Luve 's like a red, red rose
   That 's newly sprung in June:
O my Luve 's like the melodie
   That's sweetly play'd in tune.

As fair art thou, my bonnie lass,   5
   So deep in luve am I:

And I will luve thee still, my dear,
  Till a' the seas gang dry:

Till a' the seas gang dry, my dear,
  And the rocks melt wi' the sun;   10
I will luve thee still, my dear,
  While the sands o' life shall run.

And fare thee weel, my only Luve!
  And fare thee weel a while!
And I will come again, my Luve,   15
  Tho' it were ten thousand mile.

                      R. BURNS

151

HIGHLAND MARY

Ye banks and braes and streams around
  The castle o' Montgomery,
Green be your woods, and fair your flowers,
  Your waters never drumlie!
There simmer first unfauld her robes,   5
  And there the langest tarry;
For there I took the last fareweel
  O' my sweet Highland Mary.

How sweetly bloom'd the gay green birk,
  How rich the hawthorn's blossom,   10
As underneath their fragrant shade
  I clasp'd her to my bosom!
The golden hours on angel wings
  Flew o'er me and my dearie;
For dear to me as light and life   15
  Was my sweet Highland Mary.

Wi' mony a vow and lock'd embrace
  Our parting was fu' tender;
And pledging aft to meet again,
  We tore oursels asunder;   20
But, oh! fell Death's untimely frost,
  That nipt my flower sae early!
Now green 's the sod, and cauld 's the clay,
  That wraps my Highland Mary!

O pale, pale now, those rosy lips,   25
  I aft hae kiss'd sae fondly!
And closed for ay the sparkling glance
  That dwelt on me sae kindly;
And mouldering now in silent dust
  That heart that lo'ed me dearly!   30
But still within my bosom's core
  Shall live my Highland Mary.

R. BURNS

152

AULD ROBIN GRAY

When the sheep are in the fauld, and the kye at hame,
And a' the warld to rest are gane,
The waes o' my heart fa' in showers frae my e'e,
While my gudeman lies sound by me.

Young Jamie lo'ed me weel, and sought me for his bride;   5
But saving a croun he had naething else beside:
To make the croun a pund, young Jamie gaed to sea;
And the croun and the pund were baith for me.

He hadna been awa' a week but only twa,
When my father brak his arm, and the cow was stown awa;   10
My mother she fell sick, and my Jamie at the sea—
And auld Robin Gray came a-courtin' me.

My father couldna work, and my mother could na spin;
I toil'd day and night, but their bread I couldna win;
Auld Rob maintain'd them baith, and wi' tears in his e'e   15
Said, Jennie, for their sakes, O, marry me!

My heart it said nay; I look'd for Jamie back;
But the wind it blew high, and the ship it was a wrack;
His ship it was a wrack—why didna Jamie dee?
Or why do I live to cry, Wae's me?   20

My father urgit sair: my mother didna speak;
But she look'd in my face till my heart was like to break:
They gi'ed him my hand, but my heart was at the sea;
Sae auld Robin Gray he was gudeman to me.

I hadna been a wife a week but only four,   25
When mournfu' as I sat on the stane at the door,
I saw my Jamie's wraith, for I couldna think it he—
Till he said, I'm come hame to marry thee.

O sair, sair did we greet, and muckle did we say;
We took but ae kiss, and I bad him gang away: 30
I wish that I were dead, but I'm no like to dee;
And why was I born to say, Wae's me!

I gang like a ghaist, and I carena to spin;
I daurna think on Jamie, for that wad be a sin;
But I'll do my best a gude wife ay to be,   35
For auld Robin Gray he is kind unto me.

LADY A. LINDSAY

153

DUNCAN GRAY

Duncan Gray cam here to woo,
 Ha, ha, the wooing o't,
On blythe Yule night when we were fou,
 Ha, ha, the wooing o't:
Maggie coost her head fu' high,   5
Look'd asklent and unco skeigh,
Gart poor Duncan stand abeigh;
 Ha, ha, the wooing o't!

Duncan fleech'd, and Duncan pray'd;
Meg was deaf as Ailsa Craig;   10
Duncan sigh'd baith out and in,
Grat his een baith bleer't and blin',
Spak o' lowpin ower a linn!

Time and chance are but a tide,
Slighted love is sair to bide;   15
Shall I, like a fool, quoth he,
For a haughty hizzie dee?
She may gae to—France for me!

How it comes let doctors tell,
Meg grew sick—as he grew heal;   20
Something in her bosom wrings,
For relief a sigh she brings;
And O, her een, they spak sic things!

Duncan was a lad o' grace;
   Ha, ha, the wooing o't!   25
Maggie's was a piteous case;
   Ha, ha, the wooing o't!
Duncan couldna be her death,
Swelling pity smoor'd his wrath;
Now they're crouse and canty baith: 30
   Ha, ha, the wooing o't!

                  R. BURNS

154

THE SAILOR'S WIFE

And are ye sure the news is true?
   And are ye sure he 's weel?
Is this a time to think o' wark?
   Ye jades, lay by your wheel;
Is this the time to spin a thread,   5
   When Colin 's at the door?
Reach down my cloak, I'll to the quay,
   And see him come ashore.
For there 's nae luck about the house,
   There 's nae luck at a';   10
There's little pleasure in the house
   When our gudeman 's awa'.

And gie to me my bigonet,
   My bishop's satin gown;
For I maun tell the baillie's wife   15
   That Colin 's in the town.
My Turkey slippers maun gae on,
   My stockins pearly blue;
It 's a' to pleasure our gudeman,
   For he 's baith leal and true.   20

Rise, lass, and mak a clean fireside,
   Put on the muckle pot;
Gie little Kate her button gown
   And Jock his Sunday coat;
And mak their shoon as black as slaes,   25
   Their hose as white as snaw;
It 's a' to please my ain gudeman,
   For he 's been long awa'.

There 's twa fat hens upo' the coop
   Been fed this month and mair;   30
Mak haste and thraw their necks about,
   That Colin weel may fare;
And spread the table neat and clean,
   Gar ilka thing look braw,
For wha can tell how Colin fared   35
   When he was far awa'?

Sae true his heart, sae smooth his speech,
   His breath like caller air;
His very foot has music in't
   As he comes up the stair—   40
And will I see his face again?
   And will I hear him speak?
I'm downright dizzy wi' the thought,
   In troth I'm like to greet!

If Colin 's weel, and weel content,   45
   I hae nae mair to crave:
And gin I live to keep him sae,
   I'm blest aboon the lave:
And will I see his face again,
   And will I hear him speak?   50
I'm downright dizzy wi' the thought,
   In troth I'm like to greet.
For there 's nae luck about the house,
   There 's nae luck at a';
There 's little pleasure in the house   55
   When our gudeman 's awa'.

                        W. J. MICKLE

155

JEAN

Of a' the airts the wind can blaw
   I dearly like the West,
For there the bonnie lassie lives,
   The lassie I lo'e best:
There's wild woods grow, and rivers row,   5
   And mony a hill between;
But day and night my fancy's flight
   Is ever wi' my Jean.

I see her in the dewy flowers,
   I see her sweet and fair: 10
I hear her in the tunefu' birds,
   I hear her charm the air:
There 's not a bonnie flower that springs
   By fountain, shaw, or green,
There 's not a bonnie bird that sings   15
   But minds me o' my Jean.

O blaw ye westlin winds, blaw saft
   Amang the leafy trees;
Wi' balmy gale, frae hill and dale
   Bring hame the laden bees;   20
And bring the lassie back to me
   That 's ay sae neat and clean;
Ae smile o' her wad banish care,
   Sae charming is my Jean.

What sighs and vows amang the knowes   25
   Hae pass'd atween us twa!
How fond to meet, how wae to part
   That night she gaed awa!
The Powers aboon can only ken
   To whom the heart is seen,   30
That nane can be sae dear to me
   As my sweet lovely Jean!

                           R. BURNS

156

JOHN ANDERSON

John Anderson my jo, John,
   When we were first acquent
Your locks were like the raven,
   Your bonnie brow was brent;
But now your brow is beld, John,   5
   Your locks are like the snow;
But blessings on your frosty pow,
   John Anderson my jo.

John Anderson my jo, John,
   We clamb the hill thegither,   10
And mony a canty day, John,
   We've had wi' ane anither:

Now we maun totter down, John,
  But hand in hand we'll go,
And sleep thegither at the foot,   15
  John Anderson my jo.

                              R. BURNS

157

THE LAND O' THE LEAL

I'm wearing awa', Jean,
Like snaw when it's thaw, Jean,
I'm wearing awa'
  To the land o' the leal.
There's nae sorrow there, Jean,   5
There 's neither cauld nor care, Jean,
The day is ay fair
  In the land o' the leal.

Ye were ay leal and true, Jean,
Your task 's ended noo, Jean,   10
And I'll welcome you
  To the land o' the leal.
Our bonnie bairn's there, Jean,
She was baith guid and fair, Jean;
O we grudged her right sair   15
  To the land o' the leal!

Then dry that tearfu' e'e, Jean,
My soul langs to be free, Jean,
And angels wait on me
  To the land o' the leal.   20
Now fare ye weel, my ain Jean,
This warld's care is vain, Jean;
We'll meet and ay be fain
  In the land o' the leal.

                              LADY NAIRNE

158

ODE ON A DISTANT PROSPECT OF ETON COLLEGE

Ye distant spires, ye antique towers
   That crown the watery glade,
Where grateful Science still adores
   Her Henry's holy shade;
And ye, that from the stately brow   5
Of Windsor's heights th' expanse below
   Of grove, of lawn, of mead survey,
Whose turf, whose shade, whose flowers among
Wanders the hoary Thames along
   His silver-winding way: 10

Ah happy hills! ah pleasing shade!
   Ah fields beloved in vain!
Where once my careless childhood stray'd,
   A stranger yet to pain!
I feel the gales that from ye blow   15
A momentary bliss bestow,
   As waving fresh their gladsome wing
My weary soul they seem to soothe,
And, redolent of joy and youth,
   To breathe a second spring.   20

Say, Father Thames, for thou hast seen
   Full many a sprightly race
Disporting on thy margent green
   The paths of pleasure trace;
Who foremost now delight to cleave   25
With pliant arm, thy glassy wave?
   The captive linnet which enthral?
What idle progeny succeed
To chase the rolling circle's speed
   Or urge the flying ball?   30

While some on earnest business bent
   Their murmuring labours ply
'Gainst graver hours, that bring constraint
   To sweeten liberty:
Some bold adventurers disdain   35

The limits of their little reign
    And unknown regions dare descry:
Still as they run they look behind,
They hear a voice in every wind,
    And snatch a fearful joy.   40

Gay hope is theirs by fancy fed,
    Less pleasing when possest;
The tear forgot as soon as shed,
    The sunshine of the breast:
Theirs buxom health, of rosy hue,   45
Wild wit, invention ever new,
    And lively cheer, of vigour born;
The thoughtless day, the easy night,
The spirits pure, the slumbers light
    That fly th' approach of morn.   50

Alas! regardless of their doom
    The little victims play!
No sense have they of ills to come
    Nor care beyond to-day:
Yet see how all around them wait   55
The Ministers of human fate
    And black Misfortune's baleful train!
Ah show them where in ambush stand
To seize their prey, the murderous band!
    Ah, tell them they are men!   60

These shall the fury Passions tear,
    The vultures of the mind,
Disdainful Anger, pallid Fear,
    And Shame that skulks behind;
Or pining Love shall waste their youth,   65
Or Jealousy with rankling tooth
    That inly gnaws the secret heart,
And Envy wan, and faded Care,
Grim-visaged comfortless Despair,
    And Sorrow's piercing dart.   70

Ambition this shall tempt to rise,
    Then whirl the wretch from high,
To bitter Scorn a sacrifice
    And grinning Infamy.
The stings of Falsehood those shall try,   75
And hard Unkindness' alter'd eye,

That mocks the tear it forced to flow;
And keen Remorse with blood defiled,
And moody Madness laughing wild
   Amid severest woe.   80

Lo, in the vale of years beneath
   A griesly troop are seen,
The painful family of Death,
   More hideous than their Queen:
This racks the joints, this fires the veins,   85
That every labouring sinew strains,
   Those in the deeper vitals rage:
Lo, Poverty, to fill the band,
That numbs the soul with icy hand,
   And slow-consuming Age.   90

To each his sufferings: all are men,
   Condemn'd alike to groan;
The tender for another's pain,
   Th' unfeeling for his own.
Yet, ah! why should they know their fate,   95
Since sorrow never comes too late,
   And happiness too swiftly flies?
Thought would destroy their paradise.
No more;—where ignorance is bliss,
   'Tis folly to be wise.   100

                      T. GRAY

159

HYMN TO ADVERSITY

Daughter of Jove, relentless power,
   Thou tamer of the human breast,
Whose iron scourge and torturing hour
   The bad affright, afflict the best!
Bound in thy adamantine chain   5
The proud are taught to taste of pain,
   And purple tyrants vainly groan
With pangs unfelt before, unpitied and alone.

When first thy Sire to send on earth
   Virtue, his darling child, design'd,   10
To thee he gave the heavenly birth
   And bade to form her infant mind.

Stern, rugged Nurse! thy rigid lore
With patience many a year she bore:
What sorrow was, thou bad'st her know,   15
And from her own she learn'd to melt at others' woe.

Scared at thy frown terrific, fly
  Self-pleasing Folly's idle brood,
Wild Laughter, Noise, and thoughtless Joy,
  And leave us leisure to be good.   20
Light they disperse, and with them go
The summer Friend, and flattering Foe;
By vain Prosperity received,
To her they vow their truth, and are again believed.

Wisdom in sable garb array'd   25
  Immersed in rapturous thought profound,
And Melancholy, silent maid,
  With leaden eye, that loves the ground,
Still on thy solemn steps attend:
Warm Charity, the general friend,   30
With Justice, to herself severe,
And Pity dropping soft the sadly-pleasing tear.

O, gently on thy suppliant's head
  Dread Goddess, lay the chastening hand!
Not in thy Gorgon terrors clad,   35
  Nor circled with the vengeful band
(As by the impious thou art seen)
With thundering voice, and threatening mien,
With screaming Horror's funeral cry,
Despair, and fell Disease, and ghastly Poverty: 40

Thy form benign, O Goddess, wear,
  Thy milder influence impart,
Thy philosophic train be there
  To soften, not to wound my heart.
The generous spark extinct revive,   45
Teach me to love and to forgive,
Exact my own defects to scan,
What others are to feel, and know myself a Man.

                      T. GRAY

160

THE SOLITUDE OF ALEXANDER SELKIRK

I am monarch of all I survey,
  My right there is none to dispute;
From the centre all round to the sea
  I am lord of the fowl and the brute.
O solitude! where are the charms   5
  That sages have seen in thy face?
Better dwell in the midst of alarms
  Than reign in this horrible place.

I am out of humanity's reach.
  I must finish my journey alone,   10
Never hear the sweet music of speech;
  I start at the sound of my own.
The beasts that roam over the plain
  My form with indifference see;
They are so unacquainted with man,   15
  Their tameness is shocking to me.

Society, friendship, and love
  Divinely bestow'd upon man,
O had I the wings of a dove
  How soon would I taste you again!   20
My sorrows I then might assuage
  In the ways of religion and truth,
Might learn from the wisdom of age,
  And be cheer'd by the sallies of youth.

Ye winds that have made me your sport,   25
  Convey to this desolate shore
Some cordial endearing report
  Of a land I shall visit no more:
My friends, do they now and then send
  A wish or a thought after me?   30
O tell me I yet have a friend,
  Though a friend I am never to see.

How fleet is a glance of the mind!
  Compared with the speed of its flight,
The tempest itself lags behind,
  And the swift-wingéd arrows of light.   35

When I think of my own native land
    In a moment I seem to be there;
But, alas! recollection at hand
    Soon hurries me back to despair.   40

But the seafowl is gone to her nest,
    The beast is laid down in his lair;
Even here is a season of rest,
    And I to my cabin repair.
There is mercy in every place,   45
    And mercy, encouraging thought!
Gives even affliction a grace
    And reconciles man to his lot.

W. COWPER

161

TO MARY UNWIN

Mary! I want a lyre with other strings,
    Such aid from heaven as some have feign'd they drew,
    An eloquence scarce given to mortals, new
And undebased by praise of meaner things,

That ere through age or woe I shed my wings   5
    I may record thy worth with honour due,
    In verse as musical as thou art true,
Verse that immortalizes whom it sings:—

But thou hast little need. There is a Book
    By seraphs writ with beams of heavenly light,   10
On which the eyes of God not rarely look,
    A chronicle of actions just and bright—

There all thy deeds, my faithful Mary, shine;
And since thou own'st that praise, I spare thee mine.

W. COWPER

162

TO THE SAME

The twentieth year is well-nigh past
Since first our sky was overcast;
Ah, would that this might be the last!
    My Mary!

Thy spirits have a fainter flow,   5
I see thee daily weaker grow—
'Twas my distress that brought thee low,
    My Mary!

Thy needles, once a shining store,
For my sake restless heretofore,   10
Now rust disused, and shine no more;
    My Mary!

For though thou gladly wouldst fulfil
The same kind office for me still,
Thy sight now seconds not thy will,   15
    My Mary!

But well thou play'dst the housewife's part,
And all thy threads with magic art
Have wound themselves about this heart,
    My Mary!   20

Thy indistinct expressions seem
Like language utter'd in a dream;
Yet me they charm, whate'er the theme,
    My Mary!

Thy silver locks, once auburn bright,   25
Are still more lovely in my sight
Than golden beams of orient light,
    My Mary!

For could I view nor them nor thee,
What sight worth seeing could I see?   30
The sun would rise in vain for me,
    My Mary!

Partakers of thy sad decline
Thy hands their little force resign;
Yet, gently press'd, press gently mine,   35
    My Mary!

Such feebleness of limbs thou prov'st
That now at every step thou mov'st
Upheld by two; yet still thou lov'st,
    My Mary!   40

And still to love, though press'd with ill,
In wintry age to feel no chill,
With me is to be lovely still,
    My Mary!

But ah! by constant heed I know   45
How oft the sadness that I show
Transforms thy smiles to looks of woe,
    My Mary!

And should my future lot be cast
With much resemblance of the past,   50
Thy worn-out heart will break at last—
    My Mary!

                       W. COWPER

163

THE DYING MAN IN HIS GARDEN

Why, Damon, with the forward day
Dost thou thy little spot survey,
From tree to tree, with doubtful cheer,
Observe the progress of the year,
What winds arise, what rains descend,   5
When thou before that year shalt end?

What do thy noonday walks avail,
To clear the leaf, and pick the snail
Then wantonly to death decree
An insect usefuller than thee?   10
Thou and the worm are brother-kind,
As low, as earthly, and as blind.

Vain wretch! canst thou expect to see
The downy peach make court to thee?
Or that thy sense shall ever meet
The bean-flower's deep-embosom'd sweet   15
Exhaling with an evening's blast?
Thy evenings then will all be past!

Thy narrow pride, thy fancied green
(For vanity 's in little seen),
All must be left when Death appears

In spite of wishes, groans, and tears;
Nor one of all thy plants that grow
But Rosemary will with thee go.

G. SEWELL

164

TO-MORROW

In the downhill of life, when I find I'm declining,
   May my lot no less fortunate be
Than a snug elbow-chair can afford for reclining,
   And a cot that o'erlooks the wide sea;
With an ambling pad-pony to pace o'er the lawn,   5
   While I carol away idle sorrow,
And blithe as the lark that each day hails the dawn
   Look forward with hope for to-morrow.

With a porch at my door, both for shelter and shade too,
   As the sunshine or rain may prevail;   10
And a small spot of ground for the use of the spade too,
   With a barn for the use of the flail:
A cow for my dairy, a dog for my game,
   And a purse when a friend wants to borrow;
I'll envy no nabob his riches or fame,   15
   Nor what honours await him to-morrow.

From the black northern blast may my cot be completely
   Secured by a neighbouring hill;
And at night may repose steal upon me more sweetly
   By the sound of a murmuring rill: 20
And while peace and plenty I find at my board,
   With a heart free from sickness and sorrow,
With my friends may I share what to-day may afford,
   And let them spread the table to-morrow.

And when I at last must throw off this frail covering   25
   Which I've worn for three-score years and ten,
On the brink of the grave I'll not seek to keep hovering,
   Nor my thread wish to spin o'er again:
But my face in the glass I'll serenely survey,
   And with smiles count each wrinkle and furrow;   30
As this old worn-out stuff, which is threadbare to-day,
   May become everlasting to-morrow.

J. COLLINS

165

Life! I know not what thou art,
But know that thou and I must part;
And when, or how, or where we met
I own to me 's a secret yet.

  Life! we've been long together   5
Through pleasant and through cloudy weather;
'Tis hard to part when friends are dear—
Perhaps 'twill cost a sigh, a tear;
—Then steal away, give little warning,
  Choose thine own time;   10
Say not Good Night,—but in some brighter clime
  Bid me Good Morning.

A. L. BARBAULD

THE GOLDEN TREASURY
BOOK FOURTH

ON FIRST LOOKING INTO CHAPMAN'S HOMER

Much have I travell'd in the realms of gold
  And many goodly states and kingdoms seen;
  Round many western islands have I been
Which bards in fealty to Apollo hold.

Oft of one wide expanse had I been told   5
  That deep-brow'd Homer ruled as his demesne;
  Yet did I never breathe its pure serene
Till I heard Chapman speak out loud and bold:

Then felt I like some watcher of the skies
  When a new planet swims into his ken;   10
Or like stout Cortez, when with eagle eye

  He stared at the Pacific—and all his men
Look'd at each other with a wild surmise—
  Silent, upon a peak in Darien.

                    J. KEATS

ODE ON THE POETS

Bards of Passion and of Mirth
Ye have left your souls on earth!
Have ye souls in heaven too,
Double-lived in regions new?

  Yes, and those of heaven commune   5
With the spheres of sun and moon;
With the noise of fountains wond'rous
And the parle of voices thund'rous;
With the whisper of heaven's trees
And one another, in soft ease   10
Seated on Elysian lawns
Brows'd by none but Dian's fawns;

Underneath large blue-bells tented,
Where the daisies are rose-scented,
And the rose herself has got   15
Perfume which on earth is not;
Where the nightingale doth sing
Not a senseless, trancéd thing,
But divine melodious truth;
Philosophic numbers smooth;   20
Tales and golden histories
Of heaven and its mysteries.

Thus ye live on high, and then
On the earth ye live again;
And the souls ye left behind you   25
Teach us, here, the way to find you,
Where your other souls are joying,
Never slumber'd, never cloying.
Here, your earth-born souls still speak
To mortals, of their little week;   30
Of their sorrows and delights;
Of their passions and their spites;
Of their glory and their shame;
What doth strengthen and what maim:—
Thus ye teach us, every day,   35
Wisdom, though fled far away.

Bards of Passion and of Mirth
Ye have left your souls on earth!
Ye have souls in heaven too,
Double-lived in regions new!   40

J. KEATS

168

LOVE

All thoughts, all passions, all delights,
  Whatever stirs this mortal frame,
All are but ministers of Love,
    And feed his sacred flame.

Oft in my waking dreams do I   5
  Live o'er again that happy hour,
When midway on the mount I lay
    Beside the ruin'd tower.

The moonshine stealing o'er the scene
  Had blended with the lights of eve;   10
And she was there, my hope, my joy,
    My own dear Genevieve!

She lean'd against the arméd man,
  The statue of the arméd knight;
She stood and listen'd to my lay,   15
    Amid the lingering light.

Few sorrows hath she of her own,
  My hope! my joy! my Genevieve!
She loves me best whene'er I sing
    The songs that make her grieve.   20

I play'd a soft and doleful air,
  I sang an old and moving story—
An old rude song, that suited well
    That ruin wild and hoary.

She listen'd with a flitting blush,   25
  With downcast eyes and modest grace;
For well she knew I could not choose
    But gaze upon her face.

I told her of the Knight that wore
  Upon his shield a burning brand;   30
And that for ten long years he woo'd
    The Lady of the Land.

I told her how he pined; and ah!
  The deep, the low, the pleading tone
With which I sang another's love   35
    Interpreted my own.

She listen'd with a flitting blush,
  With downcast eyes and modest grace;
And she forgave me, that I gazed
    Too fondly on her face.   40

But when I told the cruel scorn
  That crazed that bold and lovely Knight,
And that he cross'd the mountain-woods,
    Nor rested day nor night;

That sometimes from the savage den,   45
    And sometimes from the darksome shade,
And sometimes starting up at once
        In green and sunny glade

There came and look'd him in the face
    An angel beautiful and bright;   50
And that he knew it was a Fiend,
        This miserable Knight!

And that, unknowing what he did,
    He leap'd amid a murderous band,
And saved from outrage worse than death   55
        The Lady of the Land;

And how she wept, and clasp'd his knees
    And how she tended him in vain;
And ever strove to expiate
        The scorn that crazed his brain;   60

And that she nursed him in a cave,
    And how his madness went away,
When on the yellow forest leaves
        A dying man he lay;

—His dying words—but when I reach'd   65
    That tenderest strain of all the ditty,
My faltering voice and pausing harp
        Disturb'd her soul with pity!

All impulses of soul and sense
    Had thrill'd my guileless Genevieve;   70
The music and the doleful tale,
        The rich and balmy eve;

And hopes, and fears that kindle hope,
    An undistinguishable throng,
And gentle wishes long subdued,   75
        Subdued and cherish'd long!

She wept with pity and delight,
    She blush'd with love and virgin shame;
And like the murmur of a dream,
        I heard her breathe my name.   80

Her bosom heaved—she stepp'd aside,
  As conscious of my look she stept—
Then suddenly, with timorous eye
    She fled to me and wept.

She half enclosed me with her arms,   85
  She press'd me with a meek embrace;
And bending back her head, look'd up,
    And gazed upon my face.

'Twas partly love, and partly fear,
  And partly 'twas a bashful art,   90
That I might rather feel, than see,
    The swelling of her heart.

I calm'd her fears, and she was calm,
  And told her love with virgin pride;
And so I won my Genevieve,   95
    My bright and beauteous Bride.

                              S. T. COLERIDGE

                    169

              ALL FOR LOVE

O talk not to me of a name great in story;
The days of our youth are the days of our glory;
And the myrtle and ivy of sweet two-and-twenty
Are worth all your laurels, though ever so plenty.

What are garlands and crowns to the brow that is wrinkled?   5
'Tis but as a dead flower with May-dew besprinkled:
Then away with all such from the head that is hoary—
What care I for the wreaths that can only give glory?

O Fame!—if I e'er took delight in thy praises,
'Twas less for the sake of thy high-sounding phrases,   10
Than to see the bright eyes of the dear one discover
She thought that I was not unworthy to love her.

There chiefly I sought thee, there only I found thee;
Her glance was the best of the rays that surround thee;
When it sparkled o'er aught that was bright in my story,   15
I knew it was love, and I felt it was glory.

                              LORD BYRON

170

THE OUTLAW

O Brignall banks are wild and fair,
   And Greta woods are green,
And you may gather garlands there
   Would grace a summer queen.
And as I rode by Dalton Hall   5
   Beneath the turrets high,
A Maiden on the castle-wall
   Was singing merrily:
' O Brignall banks are fresh and fair,
   And Greta woods are green;   10
I'd rather rove with Edmund there
   Than reign our English queen.'

' If, Maiden, thou wouldst wend with me,
   To leave both tower and town,
Thou first must guess what life lead we   15
   That dwell by dale and down.
And if thou canst that riddle read,
   As read full well you may,
Then to the greenwood shalt thou speed
   As blithe as Queen of May.'   20
Yet sung she, ' Brignall banks are fair
   And Greta woods are green;
I'd rather rove with Edmund there
   Than reign our English queen.

' I read you by your bugle-horn   25
   And by your palfrey good,
I read you for a ranger sworn
   To keep the king's greenwood.'
' A ranger, lady, winds his horn,
   And 'tis at peep of light;   30
His blast is heard at merry morn,
   And mine at dead of night.'
Yet sung she, ' Brignall banks are fair,
   And Greta woods are gay;
I would I were with Edmund there   35
   To reign his Queen of May!

' With burnish'd brand and musketoon
  So gallantly you come,
I read you for a bold Dragoon
  That lists the tuck of drum.'   40
' I list no more the tuck of drum,
  No more the trumpet hear;
But when the beetle sounds his hum
  My comrades take the spear.
And O! though Brignall banks be fair   45
  And Greta woods be gay,
Yet mickle must the maiden dare
  Would reign my Queen of May!

' Maiden! a nameless life I lead,
  A nameless death I'll die;   50
The fiend whose lantern lights the mead
  Were better mate than I!
And when I'm with my comrades met
  Beneath the greenwood bough,—
What once we were we all forget,   55
  Nor think what we are now.'

CHORUS

  Yet Brignall banks are fresh and fair,
    And Greta woods are green,
  And you may gather garlands there
    Would grace a summer queen.   60

SIR W. SCOTT

171

There be none of Beauty's daughters
  With a magic like thee;
And like music on the waters
  Is thy sweet voice to me:
When, as if its sound were causing   5
The charmèd ocean's pausing,
The waves lie still and gleaming,
And the lull'd winds seem dreaming:

And the midnight moon is weaving
  Her bright chain o'er the deep,   10
Whose breast is gently heaving
  As an infant's asleep:

So the spirit bows before thee
To listen and adore thee;
With a full but soft emotion,   15
Like the swell of Summer's ocean.

LORD BYRON

172

LINES TO AN INDIAN AIR

I arise from dreams of thee
In the first sweet sleep of night,
When the winds are breathing low
And the stars are shining bright:
I arise from dreams of thee,   5
And a spirit in my feet
Has led me—who knows how?
To thy chamber-window, sweet!

The wandering airs they faint
On the dark, the silent stream—   10
The champak odours fail
Like sweet thoughts in a dream;
The nightingale's complaint
It dies upon her heart,
As I must die on thine,   15
O belovéd as thou art!

O lift me from the grass!
I die, I faint, I fail!
Let thy love in kisses rain
On my lips and eyelids pale.   20
My cheek is cold and white, alas!
My heart beats loud and fast;
O! press it close to thine again
Where it will break at last.

P. B. SHELLEY

173

She walks in beauty, like the night
Of cloudless climes and starry skies,
And all that's best of dark and bright
Meet in her aspect and her eyes,

Thus mellow'd to that tender light 5
　　Which heaven to gaudy day denies.

One shade the more, one ray the less,
　　Had half impair'd the nameless grace
Which waves in every raven tress,
　　Or softly lightens o'er her face, 10
Where thoughts serenely sweet express
　　How pure, how dear their dwelling-place.

And on that cheek and o'er that brow
　　So soft, so calm, yet eloquent,
The smiles that win, the tints that glow 15
　　But tell of days in goodness spent,
A mind at peace with all below,
　　A heart whose love is innocent.

　　　　　　　　　　　　　　　　　LORD BYRON

174

She was a phantom of delight
When first she gleam'd upon my sight;
A lovely apparition, sent
To be a moment's ornament;
Her eyes as stars of Twilight fair; 5
Like Twilight's, too, her dusky hair;
But all things else about her drawn
From May-time and the cheerful dawn;
A dancing shape, an image gay,
To haunt, to startle, and waylay. 10

I saw her upon nearer view,
A spirit, yet a woman too!
Her household motions light and free,
And steps of virgin-liberty;
A countenance in which did meet 15
Sweet records, promises as sweet;
A creature not too bright or good
For human nature's daily food,
For transient sorrows, simple wiles,
Praise, blame, love, kisses, tears, and smiles. 20

And now I see with eye serene
The very pulse of the machine;

A being breathing thoughtful breath,
A traveller between life and death:
The reason firm, the temperate will,   25
Endurance, foresight, strength, and skill;
A perfect woman, nobly plann'd
To warn, to comfort, and command;
And yet a Spirit still, and bright
With something of angelic light.   30

                                        W. WORDSWORTH

175

She is not fair to outward view
    As many maidens be;
Her loveliness I never knew
    Until she smiled on me.
O then I saw her eye was bright,   5
A well of love, a spring of light.

But now her looks are coy and cold,
    To mine they ne'er reply,
And yet I cease not to behold
    The love-light in her eye: 10
Her very frowns are fairer far
Than smiles of other maidens are.

                                        H. COLERIDGE

176

I fear thy kisses, gentle maiden;
    Thou needest not fear mine;
My spirit is too deeply laden
    Ever to burthen thine.

I fear thy mien, thy tones, thy motion;   5
    Thou needest not fear mine;
Innocent is the heart's devotion
    With which I worship thine.

                                        P. B. SHELLEY

177

THE LOST LOVE

She dwelt among the untrodden ways
  Beside the springs of Dove;
A maid whom there were none to praise,
  And very few to love:

A violet by a mossy stone   5
  Half hidden from the eye!
—Fair as a star, when only one
  Is shining in the sky.

She lived unknown, and few could know
  When Lucy ceased to be;   10
But she is in her grave, and oh,
  The difference to me!

                                      W. WORDSWORTH

178

I travell'd among unknown men
  In lands beyond the sea;
Nor, England! did I know till then
  What love I bore to thee.

'Tis past, that melancholy dream!   5
  Nor will I quit thy shore
A second time; for still I seem
  To love thee more and more.

Among thy mountains did I feel
  The joy of my desire;   10
And she I cherish'd turn'd her wheel
  Beside an English fire.

Thy mornings show'd, thy nights conceal'd
  The bowers where Lucy play'd;
And thine too is the last green field   15
  That Lucy's eyes survey'd.

                                      W. WORDSWORTH

179

THE EDUCATION OF NATURE

Three years she grew in sun and shower;
Then Nature said, ' A lovelier flower
 On earth was never sown:
This child I to myself will take;
She shall be mine, and I will make   5
 A lady of my own.

' Myself will to my darling be
Both law and impulse: and with me
 The girl, in rock and plain,
In earth and heaven, in glade and bower, 10
Shall feel an overseeing power
 To kindle or restrain.

' She shall be sportive as the fawn
That wild with glee across the lawn
 Or up the mountains springs;   15
And hers shall be the breathing balm,
And hers the silence and the calm
 Of mute insensate things.

' The floating clouds their state shall lend
To her; for her the willow bend;   20
 Nor shall she fail to see
E'en in the motions of the storm
Grace that shall mould the maiden's form
 By silent sympathy.

' The stars of midnight shall be dear 25
To her; and she shall lean her ear
 In many a secret place
Where rivulets dance their wayward round,
And beauty born of murmuring sound
 Shall pass into her face.   30

' And vital feelings of delight
Shall rear her form to stately height,
 Her virgin bosom swell;
Such thoughts to Lucy I will give
While she and I together live   35
 Here in this happy dell.'

Thus Nature spake—The work was done—
How soon my Lucy's race was run!
  She died, and left to me
This heath, this calm and quiet scene;   40
The memory of what has been,
  And never more will be.

W. WORDSWORTH

180

A slumber did my spirit seal;
  I had no human fears:
She seem'd a thing that could not feel
  The touch of earthly years.

No motion has she now, no force;   5
  She neither hears nor sees;
Roll'd round in earth's diurnal course
  With rocks, and stones, and trees.

W. WORDSWORTH

181

LORD ULLIN'S DAUGHTER

A Chieftain to the Highlands bound
  Cries ' Boatman, do not tarry!
And I'll give thee a silver pound
  To row us o'er the ferry! '

' Now who be ye, would cross Lochgyle   5
  This dark and stormy water? '
' O I'm the chief of Ulva's isle,
  And this, Lord Ullin's daughter.

' And fast before her father's men
  Three days we've fled together,   10
For should he find us in the glen,
  My blood would stain the heather.

' His horsemen hard behind us ride—
  Should they our steps discover,
Then who will cheer my bonny bride   15
  When they have slain her lover? '

Out spoke the hardy Highland wight,
  ' I'll go, my chief, I'm ready:
It is not for your silver bright,
  But for your winsome lady:—   20

' And by my word! the bonny bird
  In danger shall not tarry;
So though the waves are raging white
  I'll row you o'er the ferry.'

By this the storm grew loud apace,   25
  The water-wraith was shrieking;
And in the scowl of heaven each face
  Grew dark as they were speaking.

But still as wilder blew the wind
  And as the night grew drearer,   30
Adown the glen rode arméd men,
  Their trampling sounded nearer.

' O haste thee haste! ' the lady cries,
  ' Though tempests round us gather;
I'll meet the raging of the skies,   35
  But not an angry father.'

The boat has left a stormy land,
  A stormy sea before her,—
When, oh! too strong for human hand
  The tempest gather'd o'er her.   40

And still they row'd amidst the roar
  Of waters fast prevailing:
Lord Ullin reach'd that fatal shore,—
  His wrath was changed to wailing.

For, sore dismay'd, through storm and shade   45
  His child he did discover:—
One lovely hand she stretch'd for aid,
  And one was round her lover.

' Come back! come back! ' he cried in grief
  ' Across this stormy water:
And I'll forgive your Highland chief,   50
  My daughter!—O my daughter! '

'Twas vain: the loud waves lash'd the shore,
  Return or aid preventing:
The waters wild went o'er his child,   52
  And he was left lamenting.

T. CAMPBELL

182

JOCK O' HAZELDEAN

' Why weep ye by the tide, ladie?
  Why weep ye by the tide?
I'll wed ye to my youngest son,
  And ye sall be his bride:
And ye sall be his bride, ladie,   5
  Sae comely to be seen '—
But aye she loot the tears down fa'
  For Jock o' Hazeldean.

' Now let this wilfu' grief be done,
  And dry that cheek so pale;   10
Young Frank is chief of Errington
  And lord of Langley-dale;
His step is first in peaceful ha',
  His sword in battle keen '—
But aye she loot the tears down fa'   15
  For Jock o' Hazeldean.

' A chain of gold ye sall not lack,
  Nor braid to bind your hair;
Nor mettled hound, nor managed hawk,
  Nor palfrey fresh and fair;   20
And you, the foremost o' them a',
  Shall ride our forest queen '—
But aye she loot the tears down fa'
  For Jock o' Hazeldean.

The kirk was deck'd at morning-tide,   25
  The tapers glimmer'd fair;
The priest and bridegroom wait the bride,
  And dame and knight are there.
They sought her baith by bower and ha';
  The ladie was not seen!   30
She 's o'er the Border, and awa'
  Wi' Jock o' Hazeldean.

SIR W. SCOTT

183

FREEDOM AND LOVE

How delicious is the winning
Of a kiss at love's beginning,
When two mutual hearts are sighing
For the knot there's no unty·ng!

Yet remember, 'midst your wooing,   5
Love has bliss, but Love has ruing;
Other smiles may make you fickle,
Tears for other charms may trickle.

Love he comes, and Love he tarries,
Just as fate or fancy carries;   10
Longest stays, when sorest chidden;
Laughs and flies, when press'd and bidden.

Bind the sea to slumber stilly,
Bind its odour to the lily,
Bind the aspen ne'er to quiver,   15
Then bind Love to last for ever.

Love's a fire that needs renewal
Of fresh beauty for its fuel:
Love's wing moults when caged and captured,
Only free, he soars enraptured.   20

Can you keep the bee from ranging
Or the ringdove's neck from changing?
No! nor fetter'd Love from dying
In the knot there's no untying.

                                    T. CAMPBELL

184

LOVE'S PHILOSOPHY

The fountains mingle with the river
  And the rivers with the ocean,
The winds of heaven mix for ever
  With a sweet emotion;

Nothing in the world is single,   5
  All things by a law divine
In one another's being mingle—
  Why not I with thine?

See the mountains kiss high heaven
  And the waves clasp one another;   10
No sister-flower would be forgiven
  If it disdain'd its brother:
And the sunlight clasps the earth,
  And the moonbeams kiss the sea—
What are all these kissings worth,   15
  If thou kiss not me?

                              P. B. SHELLEY

185

ECHOES

How sweet the answer Echo makes
  To Music at night,
When, roused by lute or horn, she wakes,
And far away o'er lawns and lakes
  Goes answering light!   5

Yet Love hath echoes truer far
  And far more sweet
Than e'er, beneath the moonlight's star,
Of horn or lute or soft guitar
  The songs repeat.   10

'Tis when the sigh,—in youth sincere
  And only then—
The sigh that's breathed for one to hear,
Is by that one, that only Dear
  Breathed back again.   15

                              T. MOORE

186

A SERENADE

Ah! County Guy, the hour is nigh,
   The sun has left the lea,
The orange flower perfumes the bower,
   The breeze is on the sea.
The lark, his lay who trill'd all day   5
   Sits hush'd his partner nigh;
Breeze, bird, and flower confess the hour,
   But where is County Guy?

The village maid steals through the shade
   Her shepherd's suit to hear;   10
To beauty shy, by lattice high,
   Sings high-born Cavalier.
The star of Love, all stars above,
   Now reigns o'er earth and sky,
And high and low the influence know—   15
   But where is County Guy?

SIR W. SCOTT

187

TO THE EVENING STAR

Gem of the crimson-colour'd Even,
   Companion of retiring day,
Why at the closing gates of heaven,
   Belovéd Star, dost thou delay?

So fair thy pensile beauty burns   5
   When soft the tear of twilight flows;
So due thy plighted love returns
   To chambers brighter than the rose;

To Peace, to Pleasure, and to Love
   So kind a star thou seem'st to be,   10
Sure some enamour'd orb above
   Descends and burns to meet with thee.

Thine is the breathing, blushing hour,
   When all unheavenly passions fly,
Chased by the soul-subduing power   15
   Of Love's delicious witchery.

O! sacred to the fall of day,
   Queen of propitious stars, appear,
And early rise, and long delay,
   When Caroline herself is here!   20

Shine on her chosen green resort,
   Whose trees the sunward summit crown,
And wanton flowers, that well may court
   An angel's feet to tread them down.

Shine on her sweetly-scented road,   25
   Thou star of evening's purple dome,
That lead'st the nightingale abroad,
   And guid'st the pilgrim to his home.

Shine where my charmer's sweeter breath
   Embalms the soft exhaling dew,   30
Where dying winds a sigh bequeath
   To kiss the cheek of rosy hue.

Where, winnow'd by the gentle air,
   Her silken tresses darkly flow,
And fall upon her brow so fair,   35
   Like shadows on the mountain snow.

Thus, ever thus, at day's decline
   In converse sweet to wander far—
O bring with thee my Caroline,
   And thou shalt be my Ruling Star!   40

T. CAMPBELL

188

TO THE NIGHT

Swiftly walk over the western wave
   Spirit of Night!
Out of the misty eastern cave,
 Where, all the long and lone daylight,
Thou wovest dreams of joy and fear   5
Which make thee terrible and dear,—
   Swift be thy flight!

Wrap thy form in a mantle grey
   Star-inwrought!
Blind with thine hair the eyes of Day,   10
 Kiss her until she be wearied out,
Then wander o'er city, and sea, and land,
Touching all with thine opiate wand—
   Come, long-sought!

When I arose and saw the dawn,   15
   I sigh'd for thee;
When light rode high, and the dew was gone,
 And noon lay heavy on flower and tree,
And the weary Day turn'd to his rest,
Lingering like an unloved guest,   20
   I sigh'd for thee.

Thy brother Death came, and cried,
   ' Wouldst thou me? '
Thy sweet child Sleep, the filmy-eyed,
 Murmur'd like a noontide bee,   25
' Shall I nestle near thy side?
Wouldst thou me? '—And I replied,
   ' No, not thee! '

Death will come when thou art dead,
   ' Soon, too soon—   30
Sleep will come when thou art fled;
 Of neither would I ask the boon
I ask of thee, belovéd Night—
Swift be thine approaching flight,
   Come soon, soon!   35

           P. B. SHELLEY

189

TO A DISTANT FRIEND

Why art thou silent? Is thy love a plant
  Of such weak fibre that the treacherous air
  Of absence withers what was once so fair?
Is there no debt to pay, no boon to grant?

Yet have my thoughts for thee been vigilant,   5
  Bound to thy service with unceasing care—
The mind's least generous wish a mendicant
  For nought but what thy happiness could spare.

Speak!—though this soft warm heart, once free to hold
  A thousand tender pleasures, thine and mine,   10
Be left more desolate, more dreary cold
Than a forsaken bird's-nest fill'd with snow
  'Mid its own bush of leafless eglantine—
Speak, that my torturing doubts their end may know!
                                        W. WORDSWORTH

190

When we two parted
    In silence and tears,
Half broken-hearted,
    To sever for years,
Pale grew thy cheek and cold,   5
    Colder thy kiss;
Truly that hour foretold
    Sorrow to this!

The dew of the morning,
    Sunk chill on my brow;   10
It felt like the warning
    Of what I feel now.
Thy vows are all broken,
    And light is thy fame:
I hear thy name spoken   15
    And share in its shame.

They name thee before me,
  A knell to mine ear;
A shudder comes o'er me—
  Why wert thou so dear?   20
They know not I knew thee
  Who knew thee too well:
Long, long shall I rue thee
  Too deeply to tell.

In secret we met: 25
  In silence I grieve
That thy heart could forget,
  Thy spirit deceive.
If I should meet thee
  After long years,   30
How should I greet thee?—
  With silence and tears.

                                        LORD BYRON

191

HAPPY INSENSIBILITY

In a drear-nighted December,
  Too happy, happy tree,
Thy branches ne'er remember
  Their green felicity:
The north cannot undo them   5
With a sleety whistle through them,
Nor frozen thawings glue them
  From budding at the prime.

In a drear-nighted December,
  Too happy, happy brook,   10
Thy bubblings ne'er remember
  Apollo's summer look;
But with a sweet forgetting
They stay their crystal fretting,
Never, never petting   15
  About the frozen time.

Ah, would 'twere so with many
  A gentle girl and boy!
But were there ever any
  Writhed not at passèd joy?   20

To know the change and feel it,
When there is none to heal it
Nor numbéd sense to steel it—
    Was never said in rhyme.

J. KEATS

192

Where shall the lover rest
    Whom the fates sever
From his true maiden's breast,
    Parted for ever?
Where, through groves deep and high,   5
    Sounds the far billow,
Where early violets die
    Under the willow.
        Eleu loro!
Soft shall be his pillow.   10

There, through the summer day,
    Cool streams are laving:
There, while the tempests sway,
    Scarce are boughs waving;
There thy rest shalt thou take,   15
    Parted for ever,
Never again to wake,
    Never, O never!
        Eleu loro!
    Never, O never!   20

Where shall the traitor rest,
    He, the deceiver,
Who could win maiden's breast,
    Ruin, and leave her?
In the lost battle,   25
    Borne down by the flying,
Where mingles war's rattle
    With groans of the dying;
        Eleu loro!
    There shall he be lying.   30

Her wing shall the eagle flap
    O'er the falsehearted;
His warm blood the wolf shall lap
    Ere life be parted:

Shame and dishonour sit   35
  By his grave ever;
Blessing shall hallow it
  Never, O never!
    Eleu loro!
  Never, O never!   40

SIR W. SCOTT

193

LA BELLE DAME SANS MERCI

' O what can ail thee, knight-at-arms,
  Alone and palely loitering?
The sedge has wither'd from the Lake,
  And no birds sing.

' O what can ail thee, knight-at-arms,   5
  So haggard and so woebegone?
The squirrel's granary is full,
  And the harvest's done.

' I see a lily on thy brow
  With anguish moist and fever dew,   10
And on thy cheeks a fading rose
  Fast withereth too.'

' I met a Lady in the Meads,
  Full beautiful—a faery's child,
Her hair was long, her foot was light,   15
  And her eyes were wild.

' I made a garland for her head,
  And bracelets too, and fragrant zone;
She look'd at me as she did love,
  And made sweet moan.   20

' I set her on my pacing steed
  And nothing else saw all day long,
For sidelong would she bend, and sing
  A faery's song.

'She found me roots of relish sweet,   25
   And honey wild and manna dew,
And sure in language strange she said
   " I love thee true."

'She took me to her elfin grot,
   And there she wept, and sigh'd full sore,   30
And there I shut her wild wild eyes
   With kisses four.

'And there she lulléd me asleep,
   And there I dream'd—Ah! woe betide!
The latest dream I ever dream'd   35
   On the cold hill's side.

'I saw pale Kings and Princes too,
   Pale warriors, death-pale were they all;
They cried—" La belle Dame sans Merci
   Hath thee in thrall! "   40

'I saw their starved lips in the gloam
   With horrid warning gapéd wide,
And I awoke and found me here
   On the cold hill's side.

'And this is why I sojourn here   45
   Alone and palely loitering,
Though the sedge is wither'd from the Lake
   And no birds sing.'

J. KEATS

194

THE ROVER

'A weary lot is thine, fair maid,
   A weary lot is thine!
To pull the thorn thy brow to braid,
   And press the rue for wine.
A lightsome eye, a soldier's mien,   5
   A feather of the blue,
A doublet of the Lincoln green—
   No more of me you knew
      My Love!
No more of me you knew.   10

'This morn is merry June, I trow,
  The rose is budding fain;
But she shall bloom in winter snow
  Ere we two meet again.'
He turn'd his charger as he spake   15
  Upon the river shore,
He gave his bridle-reins a shake,
  Said 'Adieu for evermore
            My Love!
And adieu for evermore.'   20

                              SIR W. SCOTT

195

THE FLIGHT OF LOVE

When the lamp is shattered,
  The light in the dust lies dead—
When the cloud is scattered,
  The rainbow's glory is shed.
When the lute is broken,   5
  Sweet tones are remembered not;
When the lips have spoken,
  Loved accents are soon forgot.

As music and splendour
  Survive not the lamp and the lute,   10
The heart's echoes render
  No song when the spirit is mute—
No song but sad dirges,
  Like the wind through a ruined cell,
Or the mournful surges   15
  That ring the dead seaman's knell.

When hearts have once mingled,
  Love first leaves the well-built nest;
The weak one is singled
  To endure what it once possest.   20
O Love! who bewailest
  The frailty of all things here,
Why choose you the frailest
  For your cradle, your home, and your bier?

Its passions will rock thee   25
  As the storms rock the ravens on high;
Bright reason will mock thee
  Like the sun from a wintry sky.
From thy nest every rafter
  Will rot, and thine eagle home   30
Leave thee naked to laughter,
  When leaves fall and cold winds come.

P. B. SHELLEY

196

THE MAID OF NEIDPATH

O lovers' eyes are sharp to see,
  And lovers' ears in hearing;
And love, in life's extremity,
  Can lend an hour of cheering.
Disease had been in Mary's bower   5
  And slow decay from mourning,
Though now she sits on Neidpath's tower
  To watch her love's returning.

All sunk and dim her eyes so bright,
  Her form decay'd by pining,   10
Till through her wasted hand, at night,
  You saw the taper shining.
By fits a sultry hectic hue
  Across her cheek was flying;
By fits so ashy pale she grew   15
  Her maidens thought her dying.

Yet keenest powers to see and hear
  Seem'd in her frame residing;
Before the watch-dog prick'd his ear
  She heard her lover's riding;   20
Ere scarce a distant form was kenn'd
  She knew and waved to greet him,
And o'er the battlement did bend
  As on the wing to meet him.

He came—he pass'd—an heedless gaze,   25
  As o'er some stranger glancing;

Her welcome, spoke in faltering phrase,
　　Lost in his courser's prancing—
The castle-arch, whose hollow tone
　　Returns each whisper spoken,
Could scarcely catch the feeble moan   30
　　Which told her heart was broken.

SIR W. SCOTT

197

THE MAID OF NEIDPATH

Earl March look'd on his dying child,
　　And, smit with grief to view her—
'The youth,' he cr'ed, ' whom I exiled
　　Shall be restored to woo her.'

She's at the window many an hour   5
　　His coming to discover:
And he look'd up to Ellen's bower
　　And she look'd on her lover—

But ah! so pale, he knew her not,
　　Though her smile on him was dwelling—   10
'And am I then forgot—forgot?'
　　It broke the heart of Ellen.

In vain he weeps, in vain he sighs,
　　Her cheek is cold as ashes;
Nor love's own kiss shall wake those eyes   15
　　To lift their silken lashes.

T. CAMPBELL

198

Bright Star, would I were steadfast as thou art—
　　Not in lone splendour hung aloft the night,
And watching, with eternal lids apart,
　　Like nature's patient sleepless Eremite,

The moving waters at their priestlike task   5
　　Of pure ablution round earth's human shores,
Or gazing on the new soft-fallen mask
　　Of snow upon the mountains and the moors—

No—yet still steadfast, still unchangeable,
  Pillow'd upon my fair love's ripening breast,   10
To feel for ever its soft fall and swell,
  Awake for ever in a sweet unrest;

Still, still to hear her tender-taken breath,
And so live ever,—or else swoon to death.

                                    J. KEATS

199

THE TERROR OF DEATH

When I have fears that I may cease to be
  Before my pen has glean'd my teeming brain,
Before high-piléd books, in charact'ry
  Hold like rich garners the full-ripen'd grain;

When I behold, upon the night's starr'd face,   5
  Huge cloudy symbols of a high romance,
And think that I may never live to trace
  Their shadows, with the magic hand of chance;

And when I feel, fair creature of an hour!
  That I shall never look upon thee more,   10
Never have relish in the fairy power
  Of unreflecting love—then on the shore

Of the wide world I stand alone, and think
Till love and fame to nothingness do sink.

                                    J. KEATS

200

DESIDERIA

Surprised by joy—impatient as the wind—
  I turn'd to share the transport—O with whom
But Thee—deep buried in the silent tomb,
That spot which no vicissitude can find?

Love, faithful love recall'd thee to my mind—   5
  But how could I forget thee? Through what power
Even for the least division of an hour
Have I been so beguiled as to be blind

To my most grievous loss?—That thought's return
  Was the worst pang that sorrow ever bore,   10
Save one, one only, when I stood forlorn,

  Knowing my heart's best treasure was no more;
That neither present time, nor years unborn
  Could to my sight that heavenly face restore.

W. WORDSWORTH

201

At the mid hour of night, when stars are weeping, I fly
To the lone vale we loved, when life shone warm in thine eye;
And I think oft, if spirits can steal from the regions of air
To revisit past scenes of delight, thou wilt come to me there
And tell me our love is remember'd, even in the sky!   5
Then I sing the wild song it once was rapture to hear,
When our voices, commingling, breathed like one on the ear;
And as Echo far off through the vale my sad orison rolls,
I think, O my Love! 'tis thy voice, from the Kingdom of Souls
Faintly answering still the notes that once were so dear.   10

T. MOORE

202

ELEGY ON THYRZA

And thou art dead, as young and fair
  As aught of mortal birth;
And form so soft and charms so rare
  Too soon return'd to Earth!
Though Earth received them in her bed,   5
And o'er the spot the crowd may tread
  In carelessness or mirth,
There is an eye which could not brook
A moment on that grave to look.

I will not ask where thou liest low,   10
  Nor gaze upon the spot;
There flowers or weeds at will may grow,
  So I behold them not:
It is enough for me to prove
That what I loved and long must love   15

Like common earth can rot;
To me there needs no stone to tell
'Tis Nothing that I loved so well.

Yet did I love thee to the last,
　　As fervently as thou,   20
Who didst not change through all the past
　　And canst not alter now.
The love where Death has set his seal
Nor age can chill, nor rival steal,
　　Nor falsehood disavow: 25
And, what were worse, thou canst not see
Or wrong, or change, or fault in me.

The better days of life were ours;
　　The worst can be but mine:
The sun that cheers, the storm that lours,   30
　　Shall never more be thine.
The silence of that dreamless sleep
I envy now too much to weep;
　　Nor need I to repine
That all those charms have pass'd away   35
I might have watch'd through long decay.

The flower in ripen'd bloom unmatch'd
　　Must fall the earliest prey;
Though by no hand untimely snatch'd,
　　The leaves must drop away.   40
And yet it were a greater grief
To watch it withering, leaf by leaf,
　　Than see it pluck'd to-day;
Since earthly eye but ill can bear
To trace the change to foul from fair.   45

I know not if I could have borne
　　To see thy beauties fade;
The night that follow'd such a morn
　　Had worn a deeper shade:
Thy day without a cloud hath past,   50
And thou wert lovely to the last,
　　Extinguish'd, not decay'd;
As stars that shoot along the sky
Shine brightest as they fall from high.

As once I wept, if I could weep,   55
  My tears might well be shed,
To think I was not near, to keep
  One vigil o'er thy bed:
To gaze, how fondly! on thy face,
To fold thee in a faint embrace,   60
  Uphold thy drooping head;
And show that love, however vain,
Nor thou nor I can feel again.

Yet how much less it were to gain,
  Though thou hast left me free,   65
The loveliest things that still remain
  Than thus remember thee!
The all of thine that cannot die
Through dark and dread Eternity
  Returns again to me,   70
And more thy buried love endears
Than aught except its living years.

                              LORD BYRON

                   203

    One word is too often profaned
      For me to profane it,
    One feeling too falsely disdain'd
      For thee to disdain it;
    One hope is too like despair   5
      For prudence to smother,
    And Pity from thee more dear
      Than that from another.

    I can give not what men call love:
      But wilt thou accept not   10
    The worship the heart lifts above
      And the Heavens reject not,—
    The desire of the moth for the star,
      Of the night for the morrow,
    The devotion to something afar   15
      From the sphere of our sorrow?

                              P. B. SHELLEY

204

GATHERING SONG OF DONALD THE BLACK

Pibroch of Donuil Dhu,
  Pibroch of Donuil,
Wake thy wild voice anew,
  Summon Clan Conuil.
Come away, come away,   5
  Hark to the summons!
Come in your war-array,
  Gentles and commons.

Come from deep glen, and
  From mountain so rocky;   10
The war-pipe and pennon
  Are at Inverlocky.
Come every hill-plaid, and
  True heart that wears one,
Come every steel blade, and   15
  Strong hand that bears one.

Leave untended the herd,
  The flock without shelter;
Leave the corpse uninterr'd,
  The bride at the altar;   20
Leave the deer, leave the steer,
  Leave nets and barges:
Come with your fighting gear
  Broadswords and targes.

Come as the winds come, when   25
  Forests are rended;
Come as the waves come, when
  Navies are stranded:
Faster come, faster come,
  Faster and faster,   30
Chief, vassal, page and groom,
  Tenant and master.

Fast they come, fast they come;
  See how they gather!
Wide waves the eagle plume,   35
  Blended with heather.

Cast your plaids, draw your blades,
  Forward each man set!
Pibroch of Donuil Dhu
  Knell for the onset!   40

SIR W. SCOTT

205

A wet sheet and a flowing sea,
  A wind that follows fast
And fills the white and rustling sail
  And bends the gallant mast;
And bends the gallant mast, my boys,   5
  While like the eagle free
Away the good ship flies, and leaves
  Old England on the lee.

O for a soft and gentle wind!
  I heard a fair one cry;   10
But give to me the snoring breeze
  And white waves heaving high;
And white waves heaving high, my lads,
  The good ship tight and free—
The world of waters is our home,   15
  And merry men are we.

There's tempest in yon hornéd moon,
  And lightning in yon cloud;
But hark the music, mariners!
  The wind is piping loud;   20
The wind is piping loud, my boys,
  The lightning flashes free—
While the hollow oak our palace is,
  Our heritage the sea.

A. CUNNINGHAM

206

Ye Mariners of England
  That guard our native seas,
Whose flag has braved, a thousand years,
  The battle and the breeze,
Your glorious standard launch again   5
  To match another foe:

And sweep through the deep,
   While the stormy winds do blow;
While the battle rages loud and long
   And the stormy winds do blow.   10

The spirits of your fathers
   Shall start from every wave—
For the deck it was their field of fame,
   And Ocean was their grave.
Where Blake and mighty Nelson fell   15
   Your manly hearts shall glow,
As ye sweep through the deep,
   While the stormy winds do blow;
While the battle rages loud and long
   And the stormy winds do blow.   20

Britannia needs no bulwarks,
   No towers along the steep;
Her march is o'er the mountain waves,
   Her home is on the deep.
With thunders from her native oak   25
   She quells the floods below—
As they roar on the shore,
   When the stormy winds do blow;
When the battle rages loud and long,
   And the stormy winds do blow.   30

The meteor flag of England
   Shall yet terrific burn;
Till danger's troubled night depart
   And the star of peace return.
Then, then, ye ocean warriors!   35
   Our song and feast shall flow
To the fame of your name,
   When the storm has ceased to blow;
When the fiery fight is heard no more,
   And the storm has ceased to blow.   40

T. CAMPBELL

207

BATTLE OF THE BALTIC

Of Nelson and the North
Sing the glorious day's renown,
When to battle fierce came forth
All the might of Denmark's crown,
And her arms along the deep proudly shone;   5
By each gun the lighted brand
In a bold determined hand,
And the Prince of all the land
   Led them on.

Like leviathans afloat   10
Lay their bulwarks on the brine;
While the sign of battle flew
On the lofty British line:
It was ten of April morn by the chime:
As they drifted on their path
There was silence deep as death;   15
And the boldest held his breath
   For a time.

But the might of England flush'd
To anticipate the scene;   20
And her van the fleeter rush'd
O'er the deadly space between.
'Hearts of oak!' our captains cried, when each gun
From its adamantine lips
Spread a death-shade round the ships,   25
Like the hurricane eclipse
   Of the sun.

Again! again! again!
And the havoc did not slack,
Till a feeble cheer the Dane   30
To our cheering sent us back;—
Their shots along the deep slowly boom:—
Then ceased—and all is wail,
As they strike the shatter'd sail;
Or in conflagration pale   35
   Light the gloom.

Out spoke the victor then
As he hail'd them o'er the wave,
  ' Ye are brothers! ye are men!
And we conquer but to save:—   40
So peace instead of death let us bring:
  But yield, proud foe, thy fleet
  With the crews, at England's feet,
  And make submission meet
    To our King.'   45

Then Denmark blest our chief
That he gave her wounds repose;
  And the sounds of joy and grief
From her people wildly rose,
As death withdrew his shades from the day: 50
  While the sun look'd smiling bright
  O'er a wide and woeful sight,
  Where the fires of funeral light
    Died away.

Now joy, old England, raise!   55
For the tidings of thy might,
  By the festal cities' blaze,
Whilst the wine cup shines in light;
And yet amidst that joy and uproar,
  Let us think of them that sleep   60
  Full many a fathom deep
  By thy wild and stormy steep,
    Elsinore!

Brave hearts! to Britain's pride
Once so faithful and so true,   65
  On the deck of fame that died
With the gallant good Riou:
Soft sigh the winds of heaven o'er their grave!
  While the billow mournful rolls
  And the mermaid's song condoles,   70
  Singing glory to the souls
    Of the brave!

T. CAMPBELL

208

ODE TO DUTY

Stern Daughter of the Voice of God!
  O Duty! if that name thou love
Who art a light to guide, a rod
  To check the erring, and reprove;
Thou, who art victory and law   5
When empty terrors overawe,
From vain temptations dost set free,
And calm'st the weary strife of frail humanity!

There are who ask not if thine eye
  Be on them; who, in love and truth   10
Where no misgiving is, rely
  Upon the genial sense of youth:
Glad hearts! without reproach or blot,
Who do thy work, and know it not:
O! if through confidence misplaced   15
They fail, thy saving arms, dread Power! around them cast.

Serene will be our days and bright,
  And happy will our nature be,
When love is an unerring light,
  And joy its own security.   20
And they a blissful course may hold
Ev'n now, who, not unwisely bold,
Live in the spirit of this creed,
Yet seek thy firm support, according to their need.

I, loving freedom, and untried,   25
  No sport of every random gust,
Yet being to myself a guide,
  Too blindly have reposed my trust:
And oft, when in my heart was heard
Thy timely mandate, I deferr'd   30
The task, in smoother walks to stray;
But thee I now would serve more strictly, if I may.

Through no disturbance of my soul
  Or strong compunction in me wrought,
I supplicate for thy control,   35
  But in the quietness of thought:

Me this uncharter'd freedom tires;
I feel the weight of chance desires:
My hopes no more must change their name;
I long for a repose that ever is the same.   40

Stern Lawgiver! yet thou dost wear
  The Godhead's most benignant grace;
Nor know we anything so fair
  As is the smile upon thy face:
Flowers laugh before thee on their beds,   45
And fragrance in thy footing treads;
Thou dost preserve the stars from wrong;
And the most ancient heavens, through thee, are fresh and
    strong.

To humbler functions, awful Power!
  I call thee: I myself commend   50
Unto thy guidance from this hour;
  O let my weakness have an end!
Give unto me, made lowly wise,
The spirit of self-sacrifice;
The confidence of reason give;   55
And in the light of Truth thy bondman let me live.
W. WORDSWORTH

209

ON THE CASTLE OF CHILLON

Eternal Spirit of the chainless Mind!
  Brightest in dungeons, Liberty, thou art—
  For there thy habitation is the heart—
The heart which love of Thee alone can bind;

And when thy sons to fetters are consign'd,   5
  To fetters, and the damp vault's dayless gloom,
  Their country conquers with their martyrdom,
And Freedom's fame finds wings on every wind.

Chillon! thy prison is a holy place
  And thy sad floor an altar, for 'twas trod,   10
Until his very steps have left a trace
  Worn, as if thy cold pavement were a sod,
By Bonnivard! May none those marks efface!
  For they appeal from tyranny to God.
LORD BYRON

210

ENGLAND AND SWITZERLAND
1802

Two Voices are there; one is of the Sea,
  One of the Mountains; each a mighty voice:
  In both from age to age thou didst rejoice,
They were thy chosen music, Liberty!

There came a tyrant, and with holy glee   5
  Thou fought'st against him,—but hast vainly striven:
  Thou from thy Alpine holds at length art driven,
Where not a torrent murmurs heard by thee.

Of one deep bliss thine ear hath been bereft;
Then cleave, O cleave to that which still is left;   10
  For, high-soul'd Maid, what sorrow would it be

    That Mountain floods should thunder as before,
    And Ocean bellow from his rocky shore,
  And neither awful Voice be heard by Thee!

                                   W. WORDSWORTH

211

ON THE EXTINCTION OF THE VENETIAN
REPUBLIC

Once did She hold the gorgeous East in fee,
  And was the safeguard of the West; the worth
  Of Venice did not fall below her birth,
Venice, the eldest child of liberty.

She was a maiden city, bright and free;   5
  No guile seduced, no force could violate;
  And when she took unto herself a mate,
She must espouse the everlasting Sea.

And what if she had seen those glories fade,
  Those titles vanish, and that strength decay,—   10
Yet shall some tribute of regret be paid

When her long life hath reach'd its final day:
Men are we, and must grieve when even the shade
  Of that which once was great is pass'd away.

W. WORDSWORTH

212

LONDON, 1802

O Friend! I know not which way I must look
  For comfort, being, as I am, opprest
  To think that now our life is only drest
For show; mean handiwork of craftsman, cook,

Or groom!—We must run glittering like a brook   5
  In the open sunshine, or we are unblest;
  The wealthiest man among us is the best;
No grandeur now in Nature or in book

  delights us. Rapine, avarice, expense,
  This is idolatry; and these we adore: 10
  Plain living and high thinking are no more!

  The homely beauty of the good old cause
Is gone; our peace, our faithful innocence,
  And pure religion breathing household laws.

W. WORDSWORTH

213

THE SAME

Milton! thou shouldst be living at this hour:
  England hath need of thee: she is a fen
  Of stagnant waters: altar, sword, and pen,
Fireside, the heroic wealth of hall and bower,

Have forfeited their ancient English dower   5
  Of inward happiness. We are selfish men!
  O! raise us up, return to us again;
And give us manners, virtue, freedom, power.

Thy soul was like a Star, and dwelt apart:
  Thou hadst a voice whose sound was like the sea, 10
  Pure as the naked heavens, majestic, free;

So didst thou travel on life's common way
In cheerful godliness; and yet thy heart
    The lowliest duties on herself did lay.

W. WORDSWORTH

214

When I have borne in memory what has tamed
    Great nations; how ennobling thoughts depart
    When men change swords for ledgers, and desert
The student's bower for gold,—some fears unnamed

I had, my Country!—am I to be blamed?   5
    Now, when I think of thee, and what thou art,
    Verily, in the bottom of my heart
Of those unfilial fears I am ashamed.

For dearly must we prize thee; we who find
    In thee a bulwark for the cause of men;   10
        And I by my affection was beguiled:

What wonder if a Poet now and then,
Among the many movements of his mind,
    Felt for thee as a lover or a child!

W. WORDSWORTH

215

HOHENLINDEN

On Linden, when the sun was low,
All bloodless lay the untrodden snow;
And dark as winter was the flow
    Of Iser, rolling rapidly.

But Linden saw another sight,   5
When the drum beat at dead of night,
Commanding fires of death to light
    The darkness of her scenery.

By torch and trumpet fast array'd
Each horseman drew his battle blade   10
And furious every charger neigh'd
    To join the dreadful revelry.

Then shook the hills with thunder riven,
Then rush'd the steed, to battle driven,
And louder than the bolts of Heaven   15
  Far flash'd the red artillery.

But redder yet that light shall glow
On Linden's hills of stainéd snow;
And bloodier yet the torrent flow
  Of Iser, rolling rapidly.   20

'Tis morn; but scarce yon level sun
Can pierce the war-clouds, rolling dun,
Where furious Frank and fiery Hun
  Shout in their sulphurous canopy.

The combat deepens. On, ye brave   25
Who rush to glory, or the grave!
Wave, Munich, all thy banners wave,
  And charge with all thy chivalry!

Few, few shall part, where many meet!
The snow shall be their winding-sheet,   30
And every turf beneath their feet
  Shall be a soldier's sepulchre.

        T. CAMPBELL

216

AFTER BLENHEIM

It was a summer evening,
 Old Kaspar's work was done,
And he before his cottage door
 Was sitting in the sun;
And by him sported on the green   5
His little grandchild Wilhelmine.

She saw her brother Peterkin
 Roll something large and round
Which he beside the rivulet
 In playing there had found;   10
He came to ask what he had found
That was so large and smooth and round.

Old Kaspar took it from the boy
  Who stood expectant by;
And then the old man shook his head,   15
  And with a natural sigh
' 'Tis some poor fellow's skull,' said he,
' Who fell in the great victory.

' I find them in the garden,
  For there's many here about;   20
And often when I go to plough
  The ploughshare turns them out.
For many thousand men,' said he,
' Were slain in that great victory.'

' Now tell us what 'twas all about,'   25
  Young Peterkin he cries;
And little Wilhelmine looks up
  With wonder-waiting eyes;
' Now tell us all about the war,
And what they fought each other for.'   30

' It was the English,' Kaspar cried,
  ' Who put the French to rout;
But what they fought each other for
  I could not well make out.
But everybody said,' quoth he,   35
' That 'twas a famous victory.

' My father lived at Blenheim then,
  Yon little stream hard by;
They burnt his dwelling to the ground,
  And he was forced to fly:
So with his wife and child he fled,   40
Nor had he where to rest his head.

' With fire and sword the country round
  Was wasted far and wide,
And many a childing mother then
  And new-born baby died: 45
But things like that, you know, must be
At every famous victory.

' They say it was a shocking sight
  After the field was won;   50

For many thousand bodies here
   Lay rotting in the sun:
But things like that, you know, must be
After a famous victory.

  ' Great praise the Duke of Marlbro' won   **55**
    And our good Prince Eugene;'
  ' Why, 'twas a very wicked thing!'
    Said little Wilhelmine;
  ' Nay .. nay ... my little girl,' quoth he,
  ' It was a famous victory.   **60**

  ' And everybody praised the Duke
    Who this great fight did win.'
  ' But what good came of it at last?'
    Quoth little Peterkin:—
  ' Why, that I cannot tell,' said he,   **65**
  ' But 'twas a famous victory.'

                          R. SOUTHEY

217

PRO PATRIA MORI

When he who adores thee has left but the name
  Of his fault and his sorrows behind,
O! say wilt thou weep, when they darken the fame
  Of a life that for thee was resign'd?
Yes, weep, and however my foes may condemn,   **5**
  Thy tears shall efface their decree;
For, Heaven can witness, though guilty to them,
  I have been but too faithful to thee.

With thee were the dreams of my earliest love,
  Every thought of my reason was thine: **10**
In my last humble prayer to the Spirit above
  Thy name shall be mingled with mine!
O! blest are the lovers and friends who shall live
  The days of thy glory to see;
But the next dearest blessing that Heaven can give   **15**
  Is the pride of thus dying for thee.

                          T. MOORE

218

THE BURIAL OF SIR JOHN MOORE AT CORUNNA

Not a drum was heard, not a funeral note,
  As his corpse to the rampart we hurried;
Not a soldier discharged his farewell shot
  O'er the grave where our Hero we buried.

We buried him darkly at dead of night,   5
  The sods with our bayonets turning;
By the struggling moonbeam's misty light
  And the lantern dimly burning.

No useless coffin enclosed his breast,
  Not in sheet or in shroud we wound him;   10
But he lay like a Warrior taking his rest
  With his martial cloak around him.

Few and short were the prayers we said,
  And we spoke not a word of sorrow;
But we steadfastly gaz'd on the face that was dead,   15
  And we bitterly thought of the morrow.

We thought, as we hollow'd his narrow bed
  And smooth'd down his lonely pillow,
That the Foe and the Stranger would tread o'er his head,
  And we far away on the billow!   20

Lightly they'll talk of the Spirit that's gone
  And o'er his cold ashes upbraid him,—
But little he'll reck, if they let him sleep on
  In the grave where a Briton has laid him.

But half of our heavy task was done   25
  When the clock struck the hour for retiring;
And we heard the distant and random gun
  That the foe was sullenly firing.

Slowly and sadly we laid him down,
  From the field of his fame fresh and gory;   30
We carved not a line, and we raised not a stone—
  But we left him alone with his glory.

C. WOLFE

219

SIMON LEE THE OLD HUNTSMAN

In the sweet shire of Cardigan,
    Not far from pleasant Ivor Hall,
An old man dwells, a little man,—
    'Tis said he once was tall.
Full five-and-thirty years he lived   5
    A running huntsman merry;
And still the centre of his cheek
    Is red as a ripe cherry.

No man like him the horn could sound,
    And hill and valley rang with glee   10
When Echo bandied round and round
    The halloo of Simon Lee.
In those proud days he little cared
    For husbandry or tillage;
To blither tasks did Simon rouse   15
    The sleepers of the village.

He all the country could outrun,
    Could leave both man and horse behind;
And often, ere the chase was done,
    He reeled and was stone-blind.   20
And still there 's something in the world
    At which his heart rejoices;
For when the chiming hounds are out,
    He dearly loves their voices!

But O the heavy change!—bereft   25
    Of health, strength, friends, and kindred, see!
Old Simon to the world is left
    In liveried poverty:
His master's dead, and no one now
    Dwells in the Hall of Ivor;   30
Men, dogs, and horses, all are dead;
    He is the sole survivor.

And he is lean and he is sick;
    His body, dwindled and awry,
Rests upon ankles swoln and thick;   35
    His legs are thin and dry.

One prop he has, and only one,
  His wife, an aged woman,
Lives with him, near the waterfall,
  Upon the village common.   40

Beside their moss-grown hut of clay,
  Not twenty paces from the door,
A scrap of land they have, but they
  Are poorest of the poor.
This scrap of land he from the heath   45
  Enclosed when he was stronger;
But what to them avails the land
  Which he can till no longer?

Oft, working by her husband's side,
  Ruth does what Simon cannot do;   50
For she, with scanty cause for pride,
  Is stouter of the two.
And, though you with your utmost skill
  From labour could not wean them,
'Tis little, very little, all   55
  That they can do between them.

Few months of life has he in store
  As he to you will tell,
For still, the more he works, the more
  Do his weak ankles swell.   60
My gentle reader, I perceive
  How patiently you've waited,
And now I fear that you expect
  Some tale will be related.

O reader! had you in your mind   65
  Such stores as silent thought can bring,
O gentle reader! you would find
  A tale in everything.
What more I have to say is short,
  And you must kindly take it: 70
It is no tale; but, should you think,
  Perhaps a tale you'll make it.

One summer-day I chanced to see
  This old man doing all he could
To unearth the root of an old tree,   75
  A stump of rotten wood.

The mattock totter'd in his hand;
  So vain was his endeavour
That at the root of the old tree
  He might have work'd for ever.   80

' You're overtask'd, good Simon Lee,
  Give me your tool,' to him I said;
And at the word right gladly he
  Received my proffer'd aid.
I struck, and with a single blow   85
  The tangled root I sever'd,
At which the poor old man so long
  And vainly had endeavour'd.

The tears into his eyes were brought,
  And thanks and praises seem'd to run   90
So fast out of his heart, I thought
  They never would have done.
—I've heard of hearts unkind, kind deeds
  With coldness still returning;
Alas! the gratitude of men   95
  Hath oftener left me mourning.

                              W. WORDSWORTH

220

THE OLD FAMILIAR FACES

I have had playmates, I have had companions
In my days of childhood, in my joyful school-days;
  All, all are gone, the old familiar faces.

I have been laughing, I have been carousing,
Drinking late, sitting late, with my bosom cronies;   5
  All, all are gone, the old familiar faces.

I loved a love once, fairest among women:
Closed are her doors on me, I must not see her—
  All, all are gone, the old familiar faces.

I have a friend, a kinder friend has no man: 10
Like an ingrate, I left my friend abruptly;
  Left him, to muse on the old familiar faces.

Ghost-like I paced round the haunts of my childhood;
Earth seem'd a desert I was bound to traverse,
  Seeking to find the old familiar faces.   15

Friend of my bosom, thou more than a brother,
Why wert not thou born in my father's dwelling?
  So might we talk of the old familiar faces,

How some they have died, and some they have left me,
And some are taken from me; all are departed;   20
  All, all are gone, the old familiar faces.

C. LAMB

221

THE JOURNEY ONWARDS

As slow our ship her foamy track
  Against the wind was cleaving,
Her trembling pennant still look'd back
  To that dear isle 'twas leaving.
So loth we part from all we love,   5
  From all the links that bind us;
So turn our hearts, as on we rove,
  To those we've left behind us!

When, round the bowl, of vanish'd years
  We talk with joyous seeming—   10
With smiles that might as well be tears,
  So faint, so sad their beaming;
While memory brings us back again
  Each early tie that twined us,
O, sweet's the cup that circles then   15
  To those we've left behind us!

And when in other climes we meet
  Some isle or vale enchanting,
Where all looks flowery, wild, and sweet,
  And nought but love is wanting;   20
We think how great had been our bliss
  If Heaven had but assign'd us
To live and die in scenes like this,
  With some we've left behind us!

As travellers oft look back at eve   25
   When eastward darkly going,
To gaze upon that light they leave
   Still faint behind them glowing,—
So, when the close of pleasure's day
   To gloom hath near consign'd us,   30
We turn to catch one fading ray
   Of joy that's left behind us.

                                        T. MOORE

222

YOUTH AND AGE

There's not a joy the world can give like that it takes away,
When the glow of early thought declines in feeling's dull decay;
'Tis not on youth's smooth cheek the blush alone which fades so
   fast,
But the tender bloom of heart is gone, ere youth itself be past.

Then the few whose spirits float above the wreck of happiness   5
Are driven o'er the shoals of guilt or ocean of excess:
The magnet of their course is gone, or only points in vain
The shore to which their shiver'd sail shall never stretch again.

Then the mortal coldness of the soul like death itself comes down;
It cannot feel for others' woes, it dare not dream its own;   10
That heavy chill has frozen o'er the fountain of our tears,
And though the eye may sparkle still, 'tis where the ice appears.

Though wit may flash from fluent lips, and mirth distract the
   breast,
Through midnight hours that yield no more their former hope of
   rest;
'Tis but as ivy-leaves around the ruin'd turret wreathe,   15
All green and wildly fresh without, but worn and grey beneath.

O could I feel as I have felt, or be what I have been,
Or weep as I could once have wept o'er many a vanish'd scene,—
As springs in deserts found seem sweet, all brackish though they
   be,   20
So midst the wither'd waste of life, those tears would flow to me!

                                        LORD BYRON

223

A LESSON

There is a flower, the Lesser Celandine,
   That shrinks like many more from cold and rain,
And, the first moment that the sun may shine,
   Bright as the sun himself, 'tis out again!

When hailstones have been falling, swarm on swarm,   5
   Or blasts the green field and the trees distrest,
Oft have I seen it muffled up from harm
   In close self-shelter, like a thing at rest.

But lately, one rough day, this flower I past,
   And recognized it, though an alter'd form,   10
Now standing forth an offering to the blast,
   And buffeted at will by rain and storm.

I stopp'd and said, with inly-mutter'd voice,
   ' It doth not love the shower, nor seek the cold;
This neither is its courage nor its choice,   15
   But its necessity in being old.

' The sunshine may not cheer it, nor the dew;
   It cannot help itself in its decay;
Stiff in its members, wither'd, changed of hue,'
   And, in my spleen, I smiled that it was grey.   20

To be a prodigal's favourite—then, worse truth,
   A miser's pensioner—behold our lot!
O Man! that from thy fair and shining youth
   Age might but take the things Youth needed not!

W. WORDSWORTH

224

PAST AND PRESENT

I remember, I remember
   The house where I was born,
The little window where the sun
   Came peeping in at morn;

He never came a wink too soon 5
  Nor brought too long a day;
But now, I often wish the night
  Had borne my breath away.

I remember, I remember
  The roses, red and white, 10
The violets, and the lily-cups—
  Those flowers made of light!
The lilacs where the robin built,
  And where my brother set
The laburnum on his birth-day,— 15
  The tree is living yet!

I remember, I remember
  Where I was used to swing,
And thought the air must rush as fresh
  To swallows on the wing; 20
My spirit flew in feathers then
  That is so heavy now,
And summer pools could hardly cool
  The fever on my brow.

I remember, I remember 25
  The fir trees dark and high;
I used to think their slender tops
  Were close against the sky:
It was a childish ignorance,
  But now 'tis little joy 30
To know I'm farther off from Heaven
  Than when I was a boy.

                  T. HOOD

225

THE LIGHT OF OTHER DAYS

Oft in the stilly night,
  Ere slumber's chain has bound me,
Fond Memory brings the light
  Of other days around me:
    The smiles, the tears 5
    Of boyhood's years,
  The words of love then spoken;

The eyes that shone,
Now dimm'd and gone,
The cheerful hearts now broken!   10
Thus in the stilly night,
Ere slumber's chain has bound me,
Sad Memory brings the light
Of other days around me.

When I remember all   15
The friends so link'd together
I've seen around me fall
Like leaves in wintry weather,
I feel like one
Who treads alone   20
Some banquet-hall deserted,
Whose lights are fled
Whose garlands dead,
And all but he departed!
Thus in the stilly night,   25
Ere slumber's chain has bound me,
Sad Memory brings the light
Of other days around me.

T. MOORE

226

INVOCATION

Rarely, rarely, comest thou,
Spirit of Delight!
Wherefore hast thou left me now
Many a day and night?
Many a weary night and day   5
'Tis since thou art fled away.

How shall ever one like me
Win thee back again?
With the joyous and the free
Thou wilt scoff at pain.   10
Spirit false! thou hast forgot
All but those who need thee not.

As a lizard with the shade
  Of a trembling leaf,
Thou with sorrow art dismay'd;   15
  Even the sighs of grief
Reproach thee, that thou art not near,
And reproach thou wilt not hear.

Let me set my mournful ditty
  To a merry measure;   20
Thou wilt never come for pity,
  Thou wilt come for pleasure;
Pity then will cut away
Those cruel wings, and thou wilt stay.

I love all that thou lovest,   25
  Spirit of Delight!
The fresh Earth in new leaves drest
  And the starry night;
Autumn evening, and the morn
When the golden mists are born.   30

I love snow and all the forms
  Of the radiant frost;
I love waves, and winds, and storms,
  Everything almost
Which is Nature's, and may be   35
Untainted by man's misery.

I love tranquil solitude,
  And such society
As is quiet, wise, and good;
  Between thee and me   40
What diff'rence? but thou dost possess
The things I seek, not love them less.

I love Love—though he has wings,
  And like light can flee,
But above all other things,   45
  Spirit, I love thee—
Thou art love and life! O come!
Make once more my heart thy home!
P. B. SHELLEY

227

STANZAS WRITTEN IN DEJECTION
NEAR NAPLES

The sun is warm, the sky is clear,
   The waves are dancing fast and bright,
Blue isles and snowy mountains wear
   The purple noon's transparent might:
   The breath of the moist earth is light   5
Around its unexpanded buds;
   Like many a voice of one delight—
The winds, the birds, the ocean-floods—
The City's voice itself is soft like Solitude's.

I see the Deep's untrampled floor   10
   With green and purple seaweeds strown;
I see the waves upon the shore,
   Like light dissolved in star-showers, thrown:
   I sit upon the sands alone;
The lightning of the noontide ocean   15
   Is flashing round me, and a tone
Arises from its measured motion—
How sweet! did any heart now share in my emotion.

Alas! I have nor hope nor health,
   Nor peace within nor calm around,   20
Nor that content, surpassing wealth,
   The sage in meditation found,
   And walked with inward glory crowned—
Nor fame, nor power, nor love, nor leisure;
   Others I see whom these surround—   25
Smiling they live, and call life pleasure;
To me that cup has been dealt in another measure.

Yet now despair itself is mild
   Even as the winds and waters are;
I could lie down like a tired child,   30
   And weep away the life of care
Which I have borne, and yet must bear,
Till death like sleep might steal on me,
   And I might feel in the warm air
My cheek grow cold, and hear the sea   35
Breathe o'er my dying brain its last monotony.

P. B. SHELLEY

228

THE SCHOLAR

My days among the Dead are past;
  Around me I behold,
Where'er these casual eyes are cast,
  The mighty minds of old:
My never-failing friends are they,
With whom I converse day by day.

With them I take delight in weal
  And seek relief in woe;
And while I understand and feel
  How much to them I owe,
My cheeks have often been bedew'd
With tears of thoughtful gratitude.

My thoughts are with the Dead; with them
  I live in long-past years,
Their virtues love, their faults condemn,
  Partake their hopes and fears,
And from their lessons seek and find
Instruction with an humble mind.

My hopes are with the Dead; anon
  My place with them will be,
And I with them shall travel on
  Through all Futurity;
Yet leaving here a name, I trust,
That will not perish in the dust.

R. SOUTHEY

229

THE MERMAID TAVERN

Souls of Poets dead and gone,
What Elysium have ye known,
Happy field or mossy cavern,
Choicer than the Mermaid Tavern?
Have ye tippled drink more fine
Than mine host's Canary wine?

Or are fruits of Paradise
Sweeter than those dainty pies
Of venison? O generous food!
Drest as though bold Robin Hood   10
Would, with his Maid Marian,
Sup and bowse from horn and can.

I have heard that on a day
Mine host's signboard flew away
Nobody knew whither, till   15
An astrologer's old quill
To a sheepskin gave the story—
Said he saw you in your glory
Underneath a new-old Sign
Sipping beverage divine,   20
And pledging with contented smack
The Mermaid in the Zodiac.

Souls of Poets dead and gone,
What Elysium have ye known—
Happy field or mossy cavern—
Choicer than the Mermaid Tavern?   25

J. KEATS

230

THE PRIDE OF YOUTH

Proud Maisie is in the wood,
  Walking so early;
Sweet Robin sits on the bush
  Singing so rarely.

'Tell me, thou bonny bird,
  When shall I marry me?'   5
—'When six braw gentlemen
  Kirkward shall carry ye.'

'Who makes the bridal bed,
  Birdie, say truly?'
—'The grey-headed sexton   10
  That delves the grave duly.

'The glow-worm o'er grave and stone
  Shall light thee steady;
The owl from the steeple sing   15
  Welcome, proud lady.'

                  SIR W. SCOTT

231

THE BRIDGE OF SIGHS

One more Unfortunate
  Weary of breath,
Rashly importunate,
  Gone to her death!

Take her up tenderly,   5
  Lift her with care;
Fashion'd so slenderly,
  Young, and so fair!

Look at her garments
Clinging like cerements,   10
Whilst the wave constantly
  Drips from her clothing;
Take her up instantly,
  Loving, not loathing.

Touch her not scornfully;   15
Think of her mournfully,
  Gently and humanly;
Not of the stains of her—
All that remains of her
  Now is pure womanly.   20

Make no deep scrutiny
Into her mutiny
  Rash and undutiful:
Past all dishonour,
Death has left on her   25
  Only the beautiful.

Still, for all slips of hers,
  One of Eve's family—
Wipe those poor lips of hers
  Oozing so clammily.   30

Loop up her tresses
　　Escaped from the comb,
Her fair auburn tresses;
Whilst wonderment guesses
　　Where was her home?   35

Who was her father?
　　Who was her mother?
Had she a sister?
　　Had she a brother?
Or was there a dearer one   40
Still, and a nearer one
　　Yet, than all other?

Alas! for the rarity
Of Christian charity
　　Under the sun!   45
O! it was pitiful!
Near a whole city full,
　　Home she had none.

Sisterly, brotherly,
Fatherly, motherly   50
　　Feelings had changed:
Love, by harsh evidence,
Thrown from its eminence,
Even God's providence
　　Seeming estranged.   55

Where the lamps quiver
So far in the river,
　　With many a light
From window and casement,
From garret to basement,   60
She stood, with amazement,
　　Houseless by night.

The bleak wind of March
　　Made her tremble and shiver;
But not the dark arch,   65
　　Or the black flowing river:
Mad from life's history,
Glad to death's mystery
　　Swift to be hurl'd—
Any where, any where   70
　　Out of the world!

In she plunged boldly,
No matter how coldly
  The rough river ran,
Over the brink of it,—   75
Picture it, think of it,
  Dissolute Man!
Lave in it, drink of it
  Then, if you can!

Take her up tenderly,   80
  Lift her with care;
Fashion'd so slenderly,
  Young, and so fair!

Ere her limbs frigidly
Stiffen too rigidly,   85
  Decently, kindly,
Smooth and compose them;
And her eyes, close them,
  Staring so blindly!

Dreadfully staring   90
  Thro' muddy impurity,
As when with the daring
Last look of despairing
  Fix'd on futurity

Perishing gloomily,   95
Spurr'd by contumely,
Cold inhumanity,
Burning insanity,
  Into her rest.
—Cross her hands humbly,   100
As if praying dumbly,
  Over her breast!

Owning her weakness,
  Her evil behaviour,
And leaving, with meekness,   105
  Her sins to her Saviour!

T. HOOD

232

ELEGY

O snatch'd away in beauty's bloom!
On thee shall press no ponderous tomb;
   But on thy turf shall roses rear
   Their leaves, the earliest of the year,
And the wild cypress wave in tender gloom:

                                  5

And oft by yon blue gushing stream
   Shall Sorrow lean her drooping head,
And feed deep thought with many a dream,
   And lingering pause and lightly tread;
Fond wretch! as if her step disturb'd the dead!   10

Away! we know that tears are vain,
   That Death nor heeds nor hears distress:
Will this unteach us to complain?
   Or make one mourner weep the less?
And thou, who tell'st me to forget,   15
Thy looks are wan, thine eyes are wet.

                             LORD BYRON

233

HESTER

When maidens such as Hester die,
Their place ye may not well supply,
Though ye among a thousand try
    With vain endeavour.
A month or more hath she been dead,   5
Yet cannot I by force be led
To think upon the wormy bed
    And her together.

A springy motion in her gait,
A rising step, did indicate   10
Of pride and joy no common rate
    That flush'd her spirit:
I know not by what name beside
I shall it call: if 'twas not pride,
It was a joy to that allied   15
    She did inherit.

Her parents held the Quaker rule,
Which doth the human feeling cool;
But she was train'd in Nature's school,
    Nature had blest her.   20
A waking eye, a prying mind,
A heart that stirs, is hard to bind;
A hawk's keen sight ye cannot blind,
    Ye could not Hester.

My sprightly neighbour! gone before   25
To that unknown and silent shore,
Shall we not meet, as heretofore
    Some summer morning—
When from thy cheerful eyes a ray
Hath a struck a bliss upon the day,   30
A bliss that would not go away,
    A sweet fore-warning?

                        C. LAMB

234

CORONACH

He is gone on the mountain,
    He is lost to the forest,
Like a summer-dried fountain,
    When our need was the sorest.
The font reappearing   5
    From the raindrops shall borrow,
But to us comes no cheering,
    To Duncan no morrow!

The hand of the reaper
    Takes the ears that are hoary,   10
But the voice of the weeper
    Wails manhood in glory.
The autumn winds rushing
    Waft the leaves that are serest,
But our flower was in flushing   15
    When blighting was nearest.

Fleet foot on the corrie,
    Sage counsel in cumber,
Red hand in the foray,
    How sound is thy slumber!   20

Like the dew on the mountain,
  Like the foam on the river,
Like the bubble on the fountain,
  Thou art gone, and for ever!

SIR W. SCOTT

235

THE DEATH-BED

We watch'd her breathing thro' the night,
  Her breathing soft and low,
As in her breast the wave of life
  Kept heaving to and fro.

But when the morn came dim and sad   5
  And chill with early showers,
Her quiet eyelids closed—she had
  Another morn than ours.

T. HOOD

236

ROSABELLE

O listen, listen, ladies gay!
  No haughty feat of arms I tell;
Soft is the note, and sad the lay
  That mourns the lovely Rosabelle.

' Moor, moor the barge, ye gallant crew!   5
  And, gentle ladye, deign to stay!
Rest thee in Castle Ravensheuch,
  Nor tempt the stormy firth to-day.

' The blackening wave is edged with white;
  To inch and rock the sea-mews fly;   10
The fishers have heard the Water-Sprite,
  Whose screams forebode that wreck is nigh.

' Last night the gifted Seer did view
  A wet shroud swathed round ladye gay;
Then stay thee, Fair, in Ravensheuch;   15
  Why cross the gloomy firth to-day? '

' 'Tis not because Lord Lindesay's heir
    To-night at Roslin leads the ball,
But that my ladye-mother there
    Sits lonely in her castle-hall. 20

' 'Tis not because the ring they ride,
    And Lindesay at the ring rides well,
But that my sire the wine will chide
    If 'tis not fill'd by Rosabelle.'

—O'er Roslin all that dreary night 25
    A wondrous blaze was seen to gleam;
'Twas broader than the watch-fire's light,
    And redder than the bright moonbeam.

It glared on Roslin's castle rock,
    It ruddied all the copse-wood glen; 30
'Twas seen from Dryden's groves of oak,
    And seen from cavern'd Hawthornden.

Seem'd all on fire that chapel proud.
    Where Roslin's chiefs uncoffin'd lie,
Each Baron, for a sable shroud, 35
    Sheath'd in his iron panoply.

Seem'd all on fire within, around,
    Deep sacristy and altar's pale;
Shone every pillar foliage-bound,
    And glimmer'd all the dead men's mail. 40

Blazed battlement and pinnet high,
    Blazed every rose-carved buttress fair—
So still they blaze, when fate is nigh
    The lordly line of high St. Clair.

There are twenty of Roslin's barons bold 45
    Lie buried within that proud chapelle;
Each one the holy vault doth hold,
    But the sea holds lovely Rosabelle!

And each St. Clair was buried there
    With candle, with book, and with knell; 50
But the sea-caves rung, and the wild winds sung
    The dirge of lovely Rosabelle.

SIR W. SCOTT

237

ON AN INFANT DYING AS SOON AS BORN

I saw where in the shroud did lurk
A curious frame of Nature's work;
A flow'ret crushéd in the bud,
A nameless piece of Babyhood,
Was in her cradle-coffin lying;   5
Extinct, with scarce the sense of dying:
So soon to exchange the imprisoning womb
For darker closets of the tomb!
She did but ope an eye, and put
A clear beam forth, then straight up shut   10
For the long dark: ne'er more to see
Through glasses of mortality.
Riddle of destiny, who can show
What thy short visit meant, or know
What thy errand here below?   15
Shall we say, that Nature blind
Check'd her hand, and changed her mind,
Just when she had exactly wrought
A finish'd pattern without fault?
Could she flag, or could she tire,   20
Or lack'd she the Promethean fire
(With her nine moons' long workings sicken'd)
That should thy little limbs have quicken'd?
Limbs so firm, they seem'd to assure
Life of health, and days mature;   25
Woman's self in miniature!
Limbs so fair, they might supply
(Themselves now but cold imagery)
The sculptor to make Beauty by.
Or did the stern-eyed Fate descry   30
That babe or mother, one must die;
So in mercy left the stock
And cut the branch; to save the shock
Of young years widow'd, and the pain
When Single State comes back again   35
To the lone man who, 'reft of wife,
Thenceforward drags a maiméd life?
The economy of Heaven is dark,
And wisest clerks have miss'd the mark,
Why human buds, like this, should fall   40

More brief than fly ephemeral
That has his day; while shrivell'd crones
Stiffen with age to stocks and stones;
And crabbéd use the conscience sears
In sinners of an hundred years.   45
—Mother's prattle, mother's kiss,
Baby fond, thou ne'er wilt miss:
Rites, which custom does impose,
Silver bells, and baby clothes;
Coral redder than those lips   50
Which pale death did late eclipse;
Music framed for infants' glee,
Whistle never tuned for thee;
Though thou want'st not, thou shalt have them,
Loving hearts were they which gave them.   55
Let not one be missing; nurse,
See them laid upon the hearse
Of infant slain by doom perverse.
Why should kings and nobles have
Pictured trophies to their grave,   60
And we, churls, to thee deny
Thy pretty toys with thee to lie—
A more harmless vanity?

                   C. LAMB

238

THE AFFLICTION OF MARGARET

Where art thou, my beloved Son,
    Where art thou, worse to me than dead?
O find me, prosperous or undone!
    Or, if the grave be now thy bed,
Why am I ignorant of the same   5
That I may rest; and neither blame
Nor sorrow may attend thy name?

Seven years, alas! to have received
    No tidings of an only child;
To have despaired, have hoped, believed,   10
    And been for evermore beguiled,—
Sometimes with thoughts of very bliss!
I catch at them, and then I miss;
Was ever darkness like to this?

He was among the prime in worth,   15
   An object beauteous to behold;
Well born, well bred; I sent him forth
   Ingenuous, innocent, and bold:
If things ensued that wanted grace,
As hath been said, they were not base;   20
And never blush was on my face.

Ah! little doth the young one dream,
   When full of play and childish cares,
What power is in his wildest scream
   Heard by his mother unawares!   25
He knows it not, he cannot guess:
Years to a mother bring distress;
But do not make her love the less.

Neglect me! no, I suffered long
   From that ill thought; and being blind   30
Said, ' Pride shall help me in my wrong:
   Kind mother have I been, as kind
As ever breathed: ' and that is true;
I've wet my path with tears like dew,
Weeping for him when no one knew.   35

My Son, if thou be humbled, poor,
   Hopeless of honour and of gain,
O! do not dread thy mother's door;
   Think not of me with grief and pain:
I now can see with better eyes;   40
And worldly grandeur I despise,
And fortune with her gifts and lies.

Alas! the fowls of heaven have wings,
   And blasts of heaven will aid their flight;
They mount—how short a voyage brings   45
   The wanderers back to their delight!
Chains tie us down by land and sea;
And wishes, vain as mine, may be
All that is left to comfort thee.

Perhaps some dungeon hears thee groan,   50
   Maim'd, mangled by inhuman men;
Or thou upon a desert thrown
   Inheritest the lion's den;

Or hast been summon'd to the deep,
Thou, thou, and all thy mates, to keep 55
An incommunicable sleep.

I look for ghosts; but none will force
  Their way to me: 'tis falsely said
That there was ever intercourse
  Between the living and the dead; 60
For surely then I should have sight
Of him I wait for day and night
With love and longings infinite.

My apprehensions come in crowds;
  I dread the rustling of the grass; 65
The very shadows of the clouds
  Have power to shake me as they pass:
I question things, and do not find
One that will answer to my mind;
And all the world appears unkind. 70

Beyond participation lie
  My troubles, and beyond relief:
If any chance to heave a sigh,
  They pity me, and not my grief.
Then come to me, my Son, or send 75
Some tidings, that my woes may end;
I have no other earthly friend.

W. WORDSWORTH

239

HUNTING SONG

Waken, lords and ladies gay!
On the mountain dawns the day;
All the jolly chase is here
With hawk and horse and hunting-spear;
Hounds are in their couples yelling, 5
Hawks are whistling, horns are knelling,
Merrily merrily mingle they,
' Waken, lords and ladies gay! '

Waken, lords and ladies gay!
The mist has left the mountain grey, 10

Springlets in the dawn are steaming,
Diamonds on the brake are gleaming;
And foresters have busy been
To track the buck in thicket green;
Now we come to chant our lay,   15
' Waken, lords and ladies gay! '

Waken, lords and ladies gay!
To the greenwood haste away;
We can show you where he lies,
Fleet of foot and tall of size;   20
We can show the marks he made
When 'gainst the oak his antlers fray'd;
You shall see him brought to bay;
' Waken, lords and ladies gay! '

Louder, louder chant the lay,   25
Waken, lords and ladies gay!
Tell them youth and mirth and glee
Run a course as well as we;
Time, stern huntsman! who can balk,
Stanch as hound and fleet as hawk;   30
Think of this, and rise with day,
Gentle lords and ladies gay!

SIR W. SCOTT

240

TO THE SKYLARK

Ethereal minstrel! pilgrim of the sky!
 Dost thou despise the earth where cares abound?
Or, while the wings aspire, are heart and eye
 Both with thy nest upon the dewy ground?
Thy nest which thou canst drop into at will,   5
Those quivering wings composed, that music still!

To the last point of vision, and beyond,
 Mount, daring warbler!—that love-prompted strain
('Twixt thee and thine a never-failing bond),
 Thrills not the less the bosom of the plain: 10
Yet might'st thou seem, proud privilege! to sing
All independent of the leafy Spring.

Leave to the nightingale her shady wood;
  A privacy of glorious light is thine,
Whence thou dost pour upon the world a flood   15
  Of harmony, with instinct more divine;
Type of the wise, who soar, but never roam
True to the kindred points of Heaven and Home!

                           W. WORDSWORTH

241

TO A SKYLARK

Hail to thee, blithe Spirit!
  Bird thou never wert,
That from heaven, or near it,
  Pourest thy full heart
In profuse strains of unpremeditated art.   5

Higher still and higher
  From the earth thou springest
Like a cloud of fire;
  The blue deep thou wingest,
And singing still dost soar, and soaring ever singest.   10

In the golden lightning
  Of the sunken sun,
O'er which clouds are brightening,
  Thou dost float and run,
Like an unbodied joy whose race is just begun.   15

The pale purple even
  Melts around thy flight;
Like a star of heaven
  In the broad daylight
Thou art unseen, but yet I hear thy shrill delight: 20

Keen as are the arrows
  Of that silver sphere,
Whose intense lamp narrows
  In the white dawn clear
Until we hardly see, we feel that it is there.   25

All the earth and air
  With thy voice is loud,
As, when night is bare,
  From one lonely cloud
The moon rains out her beams, and heaven is overflow'd.   30

What thou art we know not;
  What is most like thee?
From rainbow clouds there flow not
  Drops so bright to see
As from thy presence showers a rain of melody.   35

Like a poet hidden
  In the light of thought,
Singing hymns unbidden,
  Till the world is wrought
To sympathy with hopes and fears it heeded not: 40

Like a high-born maiden
  In a palace tower,
Soothing her love-laden
  Soul in secret hour
With music sweet as love, which overflows her bower: 45

Like a glow-worm golden
  In a dell of dew,
Scattering unbeholden
  Its aerial hue
Among the flowers and grass, which screen it from the view: 50

Like a rose embower'd
  In its own green leaves,
By warm winds deflower'd,
  Till the scent it gives
Makes faint with too much sweet these heavy-wingèd thieves. 55

Sound of vernal showers
  On the twinkling grass,
Rain-awaken'd flowers,
  All that ever was
Joyous, and clear, and fresh, thy music doth surpass.   60

Teach us, sprite or bird,
  What sweet thoughts are thine:
I have never heard
  Praise of love or wine
That panted forth a flood of rapture so divine.   65

Chorus hymeneal,
  Or triumphal chant,
Match'd with thine would be all

But an empty vaunt—
A thing wherein we feel there is some hidden want. 70

What objects are the fountains
Of thy happy strain?
What fields, or waves, or mountains?
What shapes of sky or plain?
What love of thine own kind? what ignorance of pain? 75

With thy clear keen joyance
Languor cannot be:
Shadow of annoyance
Never came near thee:
Thou lovest; but ne'er knew love's sad satiety. 80

Waking or asleep
Thou of death must deem
Things more true and deep
Than we mortals dream,
Or how could thy notes flow in such a crystal stream? 85

We look before and after,
And pine for what is not:
Our sincerest laughter
With some pain is fraught;
Our sweetest songs are those that tell of saddest thought. 90

Yet if we could scorn
Hate, and pride, and fear;
If we were things born
Not to shed a tear,
I know not how thy joy we ever should come near. 95

Better than all measures
Of delightful sound,
Better than all treasures
That in books are found,
Thy skill to poet were, thou scorner of the ground! 100

Teach me half the gladness
That thy brain must know,
Such harmonious madness
From my lips would flow
The world should listen then, as I am listening now! 105

P. B. SHELLEY

242

THE GREEN LINNET

Beneath these fruit-tree boughs that shed
Their snow-white blossoms on my head,
With brightest sunshine round me spread
   Of spring's unclouded weather,
In this sequestered nook how sweet   5
To sit upon my orchard-seat!
And birds and flowers once more to greet,
   My last year's friends together.

One have I marked, the happiest guest
In all this covert of the blest: 10
Hail to Thee, far above the rest
   In joy of voice and pinion!
Thou, Linnet! in thy green array,
Presiding Spirit here to-day,
Dost lead the revels of the May,   15
   And this is thy dominion.

While birds, and butterflies, and flowers,
Make all one band of paramours,
Thou, ranging up and down the bowers,
   Art sole in thy employment;   20
A Life, a Presence like the Air,
Scattering thy gladness without care,
Too blest with any one to pair,
   Thyself thy own enjoyment.

Amid yon tuft of hazel trees,   25
That twinkle to the gusty breeze,
Behold him perch'd in ecstasies,
   Yet seeming still to hover;
There! where the flutter of his wings
Upon his back and body flings   30
Shadows and sunny glimmerings,
   That cover him all over.

My dazzled sight he oft deceives—
A Brother of the dancing leaves;
Then flits, and from the cottage-eaves   35
   Pours forth his song in gushes;

As if by that exulting strain
He mocked and treated with disdain
The voiceless Form he chose to feign,
   While fluttering in the bushes.   40
                        W. WORDSWORTH

243

TO THE CUCKOO

O blithe new-comer! I have heard,
   I hear thee and rejoice:
O Cuckoo! shall I call thee Bird,
   Or but a wandering Voice?

While I am lying on the grass   5
   Thy twofold shout I hear;
From hill to hill it seems to pass,
   At once far off and near.

Though babbling only to the vale
   Of sunshine and of flowers,   10
Thou bringest unto me a tale
   Of visionary hours.

Thrice welcome, darling of the Spring!
   Even yet thou art to me
No bird, but an invisible thing,   15
   A voice, a mystery;

The same whom in my school-boy days
   I listen'd to; that Cry
Which made me look a thousand ways
   In bush, and tree, and sky.   20

To seek thee did I often rove
   Through woods and on the green;
And thou wert still a hope, a love;
   Still longed for, never seen.

And I can listen to thee yet;   25
   Can lie upon the plain
And listen, till I do beget
   That golden time again.

O blesséd Bird! the earth we pace
  Again appears to be   30
An unsubstantial, fairy place,
  That is fit home for Thee!

W. WORDSWORTH

244

ODE TO A NIGHTINGALE

My heart aches, and a drowsy numbness pains
  My sense, as though of hemlock I had drunk,
Or emptied some dull opiate to the drains
  One minute past, and Lethe-wards had sunk:
'Tis not through envy of thy happy lot,   5
  But being too happy in thine happiness,—
    That thou, light-wingéd Dryad of the trees,
        In some melodious plot
  Of beechen green, and shadows numberless,
    Singest of summer in full-throated ease.   10

O for a draught of vintage! that hath been
  Cool'd a long age in the deep-delvéd earth,
Tasting of Flora and the country green,
  Dance, and Provençal song, and sunburnt mirth!
O for a beaker full of the warm South,   15
  Full of the true, the blushful Hippocrene,
    With beaded bubbles winking at the brim,
        And purple-stainéd mouth;
  That I might drink, and leave the world unseen,
    And with thee fade away into the forest dim: 20

Fade far away, dissolve, and quite forget
  What thou among the leaves hast never known,
The weariness, the fever, and the fret
  Here, where men sit and hear each other groan;
Where palsy shakes a few, sad, last grey hairs,   25
  Where youth grows pale, and spectre-thin, and dies;
    Where but to think is to be full of sorrow
        And leaden-eyed despairs;
  Where Beauty cannot keep her lustrous eyes,
    Or new Love pine at them beyond to-morrow.   30

Away! away! for I will fly to thee,
 Not charioted by Bacchus and his pards,
But on the viewless wings of Poesy,
 Though the dull brain perplexes and retards:
Already with thee! tender is the night,   35
 And haply the Queen-Moon is on her throne,
  Cluster'd around by all her starry Fays;
   But here there is no light,
 Save what from heaven is with the breezes blown
  Through verdurous glooms and winding mossy ways. 40

I cannot see what flowers are at my feet,
 Nor what soft incense hangs upon the boughs,
But, in embalméd darkness, guess each sweet
 Wherewith the seasonable month endows
The grass, the thicket, and the fruit-tree wild;   45
 White hawthorn, and the pastoral eglantine;
  Fast-fading violets cover'd up in leaves;
   And mid-May's eldest child
 The coming musk-rose, full of dewy wine,
  The murmurous haunt of flies on summer eves. 50

Darkling I listen; and, for many a time
 I have been half in love with easeful Death,
Call'd him soft names in many a muséd rhyme,
 To take into the air my quiet breath;
Now more than ever seems it rich to die,   55
 To cease upon the midnight with no pain,
  While thou art pouring forth thy soul abroad
   In such an ecstasy!
 Still wouldst thou sing, and I have ears in vain—
  To thy high requiem become a sod.   60

Thou wast not born for death, immortal Bird!
 No hungry generations tread thee down;
The voice I hear this passing night was heard
 In ancient days by emperor and clown:
Perhaps the self-same song that found a path   65
 Through the sad heart of Ruth, when, sick for home,
  She stood in tears amid the alien corn;
   The same that oft-times hath
 Charm'd magic casements, opening on the foam
  Of perilous seas, in faery lands forlorn.   70

Forlorn! the very word is like a bell
  To toll me back from thee to my sole self!
Adieu! the fancy cannot cheat so well
  As she is famed to do, deceiving elf.
Adieu! adieu! thy plaintive anthem fades   75
    Past the near meadows, over the still stream,
      Up the hillside; and now 'tis buried deep
        In the next valley-glades:
    Was it a vision, or a waking dream?
      Fled is that music:—do I wake or sleep?   80

J. KEATS

245

UPON WESTMINSTER BRIDGE
Sept. 3, 1802

Earth has not anything to show more fair:
  Dull would he be of soul who could pass by
  A sight so touching in its majesty:
This City now doth like a garment wear

The beauty of the morning: silent, bare,   5
  Ships, towers, domes, theatres, and temples lie
  Open unto the fields, and to the sky,
All bright and glittering in the smokeless air.

Never did sun more beautifully steep
  In his first splendour valley, rock, or hill;   10
Ne'er saw I, never felt, a calm so deep!

  The river glideth at his own sweet will:
Dear God! the very houses seem asleep;
  And all that mighty heart is lying still!

W. WORDSWORTH

246

OZYMANDIAS OF EGYPT

I met a traveller from an antique land
  Who said: Two vast and trunkless legs of stone
Stand in the desert. Near them on the sand,
  Half sunk, a shatter'd visage lies, whose frown

And wrinkled lip and sneer of cold command
  Tell that its sculptor well those passions read
Which yet survive, stamp'd on these lifeless things,
  The hand that mock'd them and the heart that fed;

And on the pedestal these words appear:
'My name is Ozymandias, king of kings:
  Look on my works, ye Mighty, and despair!'

Nothing beside remains. Round the decay
  Of that colossal wreck, boundless and bare,
The lone and level sands stretch far away.

P. B. SHELLEY

247

COMPOSED AT NEIDPATH CASTLE, THE PROPERTY OF LORD QUEENSBERRY, 1803

Degenerate Douglas! O the unworthy lord!
  Whom mere despite of heart could so far please
  And love of havoc, (for with such disease
Fame taxes him,) that he could send forth word

To level with the dust a noble horde,
  A brotherhood of venerable trees,
  Leaving an ancient dome, and towers like these,
Beggar'd and outraged!—Many hearts deplored

The fate of those old trees; and oft with pain
  The traveller at this day will stop and gaze
    On wrongs, which Nature scarcely seems to heed:

For sheltered places, bosoms, nooks, and bays,
  And the pure mountains, and the gentle Tweed,
And the green silent pastures, yet remain.

W. WORDSWORTH

248

ADMONITION TO A TRAVELLER

Yes, there is holy pleasure in thine eye!
  The lovely cottage in the guardian nook
  Hath stirr'd thee deeply; with its own dear brook,
Its own small pasture, almost its own sky!

But covet not the abode; forbear to sigh   5
  As many do, repining while they look;
  Intruders who would tear from Nature's book
This precious leaf with harsh impiety:

Think what the home must be if it were thine,
  Even thine, though few thy wants!—Roof, window, door, 10
  The very flowers are sacred to the Poor,

The roses to the porch which they entwine:
  Yea, all that now enchants thee, from the day
  On which it should be touch'd, would melt away!

                              W. WORDSWORTH

249

TO THE HIGHLAND GIRL OF INVERSNEYDE

Sweet Highland Girl, a very shower
Of beauty is thy earthly dower!
Twice seven consenting years have shed
Their utmost bounty on thy head:
And these grey rocks; that household lawn;   5
Those trees—a veil just half withdrawn;
This fall of water that doth make
A murmur near the silent lake;
This little bay; a quiet road
That holds in shelter thy abode;   10
In truth together do ye seem
Like something fashion'd in a dream;
Such forms as from their covert peep
When earthly cares are laid asleep!
But O fair Creature! in the light   15
Of common day, so heavenly bright,
I bless Thee, Vision as thou art,
I bless thee with a human heart:

God shield thee to thy latest years!
Thee, neither know I, nor thy peers;　　　20
And yet my eyes are fill'd with tears.

With earnest feeling I shall pray
For thee when I am far away;
For never saw I mien or face
In which more plainly I could trace　　　25
Benignity and home-bred sense
Ripening in perfect innocence.
Here scattered like a random seed,
Remote from men, Thou dost not need
The embarrassed look of shy distress,　　　30
And maidenly shamefacedness:
Thou wear'st upon thy forehead clear
The freedom of a mountaineer:
A face with gladness overspread;
Soft smiles, by human kindness bred;　　　35
And seemliness complete, that sways
Thy courtesies, about thee plays;
With no restraint, but such as springs
From quick and eager visitings
Of thoughts that lie beyond the reach　　　40
Of thy few words of English speech:
A bondage sweetly brook'd, a strife
That gives thy gestures grace and life!
So have I, not unmoved in mind,
Seen birds of tempest-loving kind　　　45
Thus beating up against the wind.

What hand but would a garland cull
For thee who art so beautiful?
O happy pleasure! here to dwell
Beside thee in some heathy dell;　　　50
Adopt your homely ways and dress,
A shepherd, thou a shepherdess!
But I could frame a wish for thee
More like a grave reality:
Thou art to me but as a wave　　　55
Of the wild sea: and I would have
Some claim upon thee, if I could,
Though but of common neighbourhood,
What joy to hear thee, and to see!
Thy elder brother I would be,　　　60
Thy father—anything to thee!

Now thanks to Heaven! that of its grace
Hath led me to this lonely place.
Joy have I had; and going hence
I bear away my recompense.   65
In spots like these it is we prize
Our memory, feel that she hath eyes:
Then why should I be loth to stir?
I feel this place was made for her;
To give new pleasure like the past,   70
Continued long as life shall last.
Nor am I loth, though pleased at heart,
Sweet Highland Girl! from thee to part;
For I, methinks, till I grow old,
As fair before me shall behold   75
As I do now, the cabin small,
    The lake, the bay, the waterfall;
And Thee, the Spirit of them all!

                                    W. WORDSWORTH

                    250

                THE REAPER

Behold her, single in the field,
    Yon solitary Highland Lass!
Reaping and singing by herself;
    Stop here, or gently pass!
Alone she cuts and binds the grain,   5
And sings a melancholy strain;
O listen! for the vale profound
Is overflowing with the sound.

No nightingale did ever chaunt
    More welcome notes to weary bands   10
Of travellers in some shady haunt,
    Among Arabian sands:
A voice so thrilling ne'er was heard
In spring-time from the cuckoo-bird,
Breaking the silence of the seas   15
Among the farthest Hebrides.

Will no one tell me what she sings?
    Perhaps the plaintive numbers flow
For old, unhappy, far-off things,
    And battles long ago: 20

Or is it some more humble lay,
Familiar matter of to-day?
Some natural sorrow, loss, or pain,
That has been, and may be again?

Whate'er the theme, the maiden sang   25
    As if her song could have no ending;
I saw her singing at her work,
    And o'er the sickle bending;
I listen'd, motionless and still;
And, as I mounted up the hill,   30
The music in my heart I bore,
Long after it was heard no more.

W. WORDSWORTH

251

THE REVERIE OF POOR SUSAN

At the corner of Wood Street, when daylight appears,
Hangs a Thrush that sings loud, it has sung for three years:
Poor Susan has pass'd by the spot, and has heard
In the silence of morning the song of the bird.

'Tis a note of enchantment; what ails her? She sees   5
A mountain ascending, a vision of trees;
Bright volumes of vapour through Lothbury glide,
And a river flows on through the vale of Cheapside.

Green pastures she views in the midst of the dale,
Down which she so often has tripp'd with her pail;   10
And a single small cottage, a nest like a dove's,
The one only dwelling on earth that she loves.

She looks, and her heart is in heaven: but they fade,
The mist and the river, the hill and the shade;
The stream will not flow, and the hill will not rise,   15
And the colours have all pass'd away from her eyes!

W. WORDSWORTH

TO A LADY, WITH A GUITAR

Ariel to Miranda:—Take
This slave of Music, for the sake
Of him who is the slave of thee;
And teach it all the harmony
In which thou canst, and only thou,   5
Make the delighted spirit glow,
Till joy denies itself again
And, too intense, is turn'd to pain.
For by permission and command
Of thine own Prince Ferdinand,   10
Poor Ariel sends this silent token
Of more than ever can be spoken;
Your guardian spirit, Ariel, who
From life to life must still pursue
Your happiness; for thus alone   15
Can Ariel ever find his own.
From Prospero's enchanted cell,
As the mighty verses tell,
To the throne of Naples he
Lit you o'er the trackless sea,   20
Flitting on, your prow before,
Like a living meteor.
When you die, the silent Moon
In her interlunar swoon
Is not sadder in her cell   25
Than deserted Ariel.
When you live again on earth,
Like an unseen star of birth
Ariel guides you o'er the sea
Of life from your nativity.   30
Many changes have been run
Since Ferdinand and you begun
Your course of love, and Ariel still
Has tracked your steps and served your will.
Now in humbler, happier lot,   35
This is all remember'd not;
And now, alas! the poor sprite is
Imprisoned for some fault of his
In a body like a grave;—
From you he only dares to crave,   40

For his service and his sorrow,
A smile to-day, a song to-morrow.

The artist who this idol wrought
To echo all harmonious thought,
Felled a tree, while on the steep   45
The woods were in their winter sleep,
Rocked in that repose divine
On the wind-swept Apennine;
And dreaming, some of Autumn past,
And some of Spring approaching fast,   50
And some of April buds and showers,
And some of songs in July bowers,
And all of love; and so this tree,—
O that such our death may be!—
Died in sleep, and felt no pain,   55
To live in happier form again:
From which, beneath Heaven's fairest star,
The artist wrought this loved Guitar;
And taught it justly to reply
To all who question skilfully   60
In language gentle as thine own;
Whispering in enamoured tone
Sweet oracles of woods and dells,
And summer winds in sylvan cells;
—For it had learnt all harmonies   65
Of the plains and of the skies,
Of the forests and the mountains,
And the many-voicéd fountains;
The clearest echoes of the hills,
The softest notes of falling rills,   70
The melodies of birds and bees,
The murmuring of summer seas,
And pattering rain, and breathing dew,
And airs of evening; and it knew
That seldom-heard mysterious sound   75
Which, driven on its diurnal round,
As it floats through boundless day,
Our world enkindles on its way:
—All this it knows, but will not tell
To those who cannot question well   80
The Spirit that inhabits it;
It talks according to the wit
Of its companions; and no more
Is heard than has been felt before

By those who tempt it to betray   85
These secrets of an elder day.
But, sweetly as its answers will
Flatter hands of perfect skill,
It keeps its highest holiest tone
For our belovéd friend alone.   90

P. B. SHELLEY

253

THE DAFFODILS

I wandered lonely as a cloud
    That floats on high o'er vales and hills,
When all at once I saw a crowd,
    A host, of golden daffodils,
Beside the lake, beneath the trees,   5
Fluttering and dancing in the breeze.

Continuous as the stars that shine
    And twinkle on the milky way,
They stretched in never-ending line
    Along the margin of a bay: 10
Ten thousand saw I at a glance
Tossing their heads in sprightly dance.

The waves beside them danced, but they
    Out-did the sparkling waves in glee:
A Poet could not but be gay   15
    In such a jocund company!
I gazed—and gazed—but little thought
What wealth the show to me had brought:

For oft, when on my couch I lie
    In vacant or in pensive mood,   20
They flash upon that inward eye
    Which is the bliss of solitude;
And then my heart with pleasure fills,
And dances with the daffodils.

W. WORDSWORTH

254

TO THE DAISY

With little here to do or see
Of things that in the great world be,
Daisy! again I talk to thee,
 For thou art worthy,
Thou unassuming Commonplace   5
Of Nature, with that homely face,
And yet with something of a grace
 Which love makes for thee!

Oft on the dappled turf at ease
I sit and play with similes,   10
Loose types of things through all degrees,
 Thoughts of thy raising;
And many a fond and idle name
I give to thee, for praise or blame,
As is the humour of the game,   15
 While I am gazing.

A nun demure, of lowly port;
Or sprightly maiden, of Love's court,
In thy simplicity the sport
 Of all temptations;   20
A queen in crown of rubies drest;
A starveling in a scanty vest;
Are all, as seems to suit thee best,
 Thy appellations.

A little Cyclops, with one eye   25
Staring to threaten and defy,
That thought comes next—and instantly
 The freak is over.
The shape will vanish, and behold!
A silver shield with boss of gold   30
That spreads itself, some fairy bold
 In fight to cover.

I see thee glittering from afar—
And then thou art a pretty star,
Not quite so fair as many are   35
 In heaven above thee!

Yet like a star, with glittering crest,
Self-poised in air thou seem'st to rest;—
May peace come never to his nest
    Who shall reprove thee!   40

Sweet Flower! for by that name at last
When all my reveries are past
I call thee, and to that cleave fast,
    Sweet silent creature!
That breath'st with me in sun and air,   45
Do thou, as thou art wont, repair
My heart with gladness, and a share
    Of thy meek nature!

                  W. WORDSWORTH

255

ODE TO AUTUMN

Season of mists and mellow fruitfulness,
  Close bosom-friend of the maturing sun;
Conspiring with him how to load and bless
  With fruit the vines that round the thatch-eaves run;
To bend with apples the moss'd cottage-trees,   5
  And fill all fruit with ripeness to the core;
    To swell the gourd, and plump the hazel shells
  With a sweet kernel; to set budding more,
And still more, later flowers for the bees,
Until they think warm days will never cease;   10
    For summer has o'erbrimm'd their clammy cells.

Who hath not seen thee oft amid thy store?
  Sometimes whoever seeks abroad may find
Thee sitting careless on a granary floor,
  Thy hair soft-lifted by the winnowing wind;   15
Or on a half-reap'd furrow sound asleep,
  Drows'd with the fume of poppies, while thy hook
    Spares the next swath and all its twinéd flowers;
And sometimes like a gleaner thou dost keep
  Steady thy laden head across a brook;   20
  Or by a cider-press, with patient look,
    Thou watchest the last oozings, hours by hours.

Where are the songs of Spring? Aye, where are they?
   Think not of them,—thou hast thy music too,
  While barréd clouds bloom the soft-dying day   **25**
   And touch the stubble-plains with rosy hue;
Then in a wailful choir the small gnats mourn
Among the river sallows, borne aloft
   Or sinking as the light wind lives or dies;
And full-grown lambs loud bleat from hilly bourn;   **30**
  Hedge-crickets sing, and now with treble soft
  The redbreast whistles from a garden-croft,
   And gathering swallows twitter in the skies.

                         J. KEATS

256

ODE TO WINTER

Germany, December 1800

When first the fiery-mantled Sun
His heavenly race began to run,
Round the earth and ocean blue
His children four the Seasons flew:—
  First, in green apparel dancing,   **5**
The young Spring smiled with angel-grace;
  Rosy Summer, next advancing,
Rush'd into her sire's embrace—
Her bright-hair'd sire, who bade her keep
  For ever nearest to his smiles.   10
On Calpe's olive-shaded steep
  Or India's citron-cover'd isles.
More remote, and buxom-brown,
  The Queen of vintage bow'd before his throne;
A rich pomegranate gemm'd her crown,   15
  A ripe sheaf bound her zone.

But howling Winter fled afar
To hills that prop the polar star;
And loves on deer-borne car to ride
With barren darkness at his side,   20
Round the shore where loud Lofoden
  Whirls to death the roaring whale,
Round the hall where Runic Odin
  Howls his war-song to the gale—

Save when adown the ravaged globe   25
  He travels on his native storm,
Deflowering Nature's grassy robe
  And trampling on her faded form;
Till light's returning lord assume
  The shaft that drives him to his polar field,   30
Of power to pierce his raven plume
  And crystal-cover'd shield.

O sire of storms! whose savage ear
That Lapland drum delights to hear,
When Frenzy with her bloodshot eye   35
Implores thy dreadful deity—
Archangel! power of desolation!
  Fast descending as thou art,
Say, hath mortal invocation
  Spells to touch thy stony heart?   40
Then, sullen Winter! hear my prayer
  And gently rule the ruin'd year;
Nor chill the wanderer's bosom bare,
  Nor freeze the wretch's falling tear:
To shuddering Want's unmantled bed   45
  Thy horror-breathing agues cease to lend,
And gently on the orphan head
  Of innocence descend.

But chiefly spare, O king of clouds!
The sailor on his airy shrouds,
When wrecks and beacons strew the steep   50
And spectres walk along the deep.
Milder yet thy snowy breezes
  Pour on yonder tented shores,
Where the Rhine's broad billow freezes,   55
  Or the dark-brown Danube roars.
O winds of Winter! list ye there
  To many a deep and dying groan?
Or start, ye demons of the midnight air,
  At shrieks and thunders louder than your own?   60
Alas! e'en your unhallow'd breath
  May spare the victim fallen low;
But man will ask no truce to death,
  No bounds to human woe.

                                        T. CAMPBELL

257

YARROW UNVISITED

1803

From Stirling Castle we had seen
  The mazy Forth unravell'd,
Had trod the banks of Clyde and Tay,
  And with the Tweed had travell'd;
And when we came to Clovenford,   5
  Then said my ' winsome Marrow,'
' Whate'er betide, we'll turn aside,
  And see the Braes of Yarrow.'

' Let Yarrow folk, frae Selkirk town,
  Who have been buying, selling,   10
Go back to Yarrow, 'tis their own,
  Each maiden to her dwelling!
On Yarrow's banks let herons feed,
  Hares couch, and rabbits burrow,
But we will downward with the Tweed,   15
  Nor turn aside to Yarrow.

' There's Galla Water, Leader Haughs,
  Both lying right before us;
And Dryburgh, where with chiming Tweed
  The lintwhites sing in chorus;   20
There's pleasant Tiviot-dale, a land
  Made blithe with plough and harrow:
Why throw away a needful day
  To go in search of Yarrow?

' What's Yarrow but a river bare   25
  That glides the dark hills under?
There are a thousand such elsewhere
  As worthy of your wonder.'
—Strange words they seem'd of slight and scorn;
  My True-love sigh'd for sorrow,   30
And look'd me in the face, to think
  I thus could speak of Yarrow!

' O green,' said I, ' are Yarrow's holms,
  And sweet is Yarrow flowing!
Fair hangs the apple frae the rock,   35
  But we will leave it growing.
O'er hilly path and open Strath
  We'll wander Scotland thorough;
But, though so near, we will not turn
  Into the dale of Yarrow.   40

' Let beeves and home-bred kine partake
  The sweets of Burn-mill meadow;
The swan on still St. Mary's Lake
  Float double, swan and shadow!
We will not see them; will not go   45
  To-day, nor yet to-morrow;
Enough if in our hearts we know
  There's such a place as Yarrow.

' Be Yarrow stream unseen, unknown!
  It must, or we shall rue it: 50
We have a vision of our own,
  Ah! why should we undo it?
The treasured dreams of times long past,
  We'll keep them, winsome Marrow!
For when we're there, although 'tis fair,   55
  'Twill be another Yarrow!

' If Care with freezing years should come,
  And wandering seem but folly,—
Should we be loth to stir from home,
  And yet be melancholy;   60
Should life be dull, and spirits low,
  'Twill soothe us in our sorrow
That earth has something yet to show,
  The bonny holms of Yarrow! '

                                  W. WORDSWORTH

258

YARROW VISITED
September 1814

And is this—Yarrow?—*This* the Stream
  Of which my fancy cherish'd
So faithfully, a waking dream,
  An image that hath perish'd?
O that some Minstrel's harp were near   5
  To utter notes of gladness
And chase this silence from the air,
  That fills my heart with sadness!

Yet why?—a silvery current flows
  With uncontroll'd meanderings;   10
Nor have these eyes by greener hills
  Been soothed, in all my wanderings.
And, through her depths, St. Mary's Lake
  Is visibly delighted;
For not a feature of those hills   15
  Is in the mirror slighted.

A blue sky bends o'er Yarrow Vale,
  Save where that pearly whiteness
Is round the rising sun diffused,
  A tender hazy brightness;   20
Mild dawn of promise! that excludes
  All profitless dejection;
Though not unwilling here to admit
  A pensive recollection.

Where was it that the famous Flower   25
  Of Yarrow Vale lay bleeding?
His bed perchance was yon smooth mound
  On which the herd is feeding:
And haply from this crystal pool,
  Now peaceful as the morning,   30
The Water-wraith ascended thrice,
  And gave his doleful warning.

Delicious is the Lay that sings
 The haunts of happy lovers,
The path that leads them to the grove,   35
 The leafy grove that covers:
And pity sanctifies the verse
 That paints, by strength of sorrow,
The unconquerable strength of love;
 Bear witness, rueful Yarrow!   40

But thou, that didst appear so fair
 To fond imagination,
Dost rival in the light of day
 Her delicate creation:
Meek loveliness is round thee spread,   5
 A softness still and holy:
The grace of forest charms decay'd,
 And pastoral melancholy.

That region left, the vale unfolds
 Rich groves of lofty stature,   50
With Yarrow winding through the pomp
 Of cultivated nature;
And, rising from those lofty groves,
 Behold a ruin hoary,
The shatter'd front of Newark's Towers,   55
 Renown'd in Border story.

Fair scenes for childhood's opening bloom,
 For sportive youth to stray in,
For manhood to enjoy his strength,
 And age to wear away in!   60
Yon cottage seems a bower of bliss,
 A covert for protection
Of tender thoughts, that nestle there—
 The brood of chaste affection.

How sweet on this autumnal day   65
 The wild-wood fruits to gather,
And on my True-love's forehead plant
 A crest of blooming heather!
And what if I enwreathed my own?
 'Twere no offence to reason;   70
The sober hills thus deck their brows
 To meet the wintry season.

I see—but not by sight alone,
  Loved Yarrow, have I won thee;
A ray of Fancy still survives— 75
  Her sunshine plays upon thee!
Thy ever-youthful waters keep
  A course of lively pleasure;
And gladsome notes my lips can breathe
  Accordant to the measure. 80

The vapours linger round the heights,
  They melt, and soon must vanish;
One hour is theirs, nor more is mine—
  Sad thought! which I would banish,
But that I know, where'er I go, 85
  Thy genuine image, Yarrow!
Will dwell with me—to heighten joy,
  And cheer my mind in sorrow.

                    W. WORDSWORTH

259

THE INVITATION

Best and brightest, come away,
Fairer far than this fair Day,
Which, like thee to those in sorrow,
Comes to bid a sweet good-morrow
To the rough Year just awake 5
In its cradle on the brake.
The brightest hour of unborn Spring
Through the winter wandering,
Found, it seems, the halcyon Morn
To hoar February born; 10
Bending from Heaven, in azure mirth,
It kiss'd the forehead of the Earth,
And smiled upon the silent sea,
And bade the frozen streams be free,
And waked to music all their fountains, 15
And breathed upon the frozen mountains,
And like a prophetess of May
Strew'd flowers upon the barren way,
Making the wintry world appear
Like one on whom thou smilest, dear. 20

Away, away, from men and towns,
To the wild wood and the downs—
To the silent wilderness
Where the soul need not repress
Its music, lest it should not find   25
An echo in another's mind,
While the touch of Nature's art
Harmonizes heart to heart.

Radiant Sister of the Day
Awake! arise! and come away!   30
To the wild woods and the plains,
And the pools where winter rains
Image all their roof of leaves,
Where the pine its garland weaves
Of sapless green and ivy dun   35
Round stems that never kiss the sun;
Where the lawns and pastures be
And the sandhills of the sea;
Where the melting hoar-frost wets
The daisy-star that never sets,   40
And wind-flowers and violets,
Which yet join not scent to hue,
Crown the pale year weak and new;
When the night is left behind
In the deep east, dun and blind,   45
And the blue noon is over us,
And the multitudinous
Billows murmur at our feet,
Where the earth and ocean meet,
And all things seem only one   50
In the universal sun.

P. B. SHELLEY

260

THE RECOLLECTION

Now the last day of many days,
    All beautiful and bright as thou,
        The loveliest and the last, is dead,
Rise, Memory, and write its praise!
Up,—to thy wonted work! come, trace   5
    The epitaph of glory fled,

For now the Earth has changed its face,
  A frown is on the Heaven's brow.

We wander'd to the Pine Forest
  That skirts the Ocean's foam;   10
The light wind was in its nest,
  The tempest in its home.
The whispering waves were half asleep,
  The clouds were gone to play,
And on the bosom of the deep   15
  The smile of Heaven lay;
It seem'd as if the hour were one
  Sent from beyond the skies
Which scatter'd from above the sun
  A light of Paradise.   20

We paused amid the pines that stood
  The giants of the waste,
Tortured by storms to shapes as rude
  As serpents interlaced,
And soothed by every azure breath   25
  That under Heaven is blown
To harmonies and hues beneath,
  As tender as its own:
Now all the tree-tops lay asleep
  Like green waves on the sea,   30
As still as in the silent deep
  The ocean woods may be.

How calm it was!—the silence there
  By such a chain was bound,
That even the busy woodpecker   35
  Made stiller by her sound
The inviolable quietness;
  The breath of peace we drew
With its soft motion made not less
  The calm that round us grew.   40
There seem'd from the remotest seat
  Of the white mountain waste,
To the soft flower beneath our feet
  A magic circle traced,—
A spirit interfused around,   45
  A thrilling silent life;
To momentary peace it bound
  Our mortal nature's strife;—

And still I felt the centre of
    The magic circle there   50
Was one fair form that fill'd with love
    The lifeless atmosphere.

We paused beside the pools that lie
    Under the forest bough;
Each seem'd as 'twere a little sky   55
    Gulf'd in a world below;
A firmament of purple light
    Which in the dark earth lay,
More boundless than the depth of night,
    And purer than the day—   60
In which the lovely forests grew
    As in the upper air,
More perfect both in shape and hue
    Than any spreading there.
There lay the glade and neighbouring lawn,   65
    And through the dark green wood
The white sun twinkling like the dawn
    Out of a speckled cloud.
Sweet views which in our world above
    Can never well be seen   70
Were imaged by the water's love
    Of that fair forest green:
And all was interfused beneath
    With an Elysian glow,
An atmosphere without a breath,   75
    A softer day below.
Like one beloved, the scene had lent
    To the dark water's breast
Its every leaf and lineament
    With more than truth exprest;   80
Until an envious wind crept by,
    Like an unwelcome thought
Which from the mind's too faithful eye
    Blots one dear image out.
Though thou art ever fair and kind,   85
    The forests ever green,
Less oft is peace in Shelley's mind
    Than calm in waters seen.

P. B. SHELLEY

261

BY THE SEA

It is a beauteous evening, calm and free;
  The holy time is quiet as a Nun
  Breathless with adoration; the broad sun
Is sinking down in its tranquillity;

The gentleness of heaven broods o'er the Sea: 5
  Listen! the mighty Being is awake,
  And doth with his eternal motion make
A sound like thunder—everlastingly.

Dear child! dear girl! that walkest with me here,
  If thou appear untouch'd by solemn thought   10
    Thy nature is not therefore less divine:

Thou liest in Abraham's bosom all the year,
  And worshipp'st at the Temple's inner shrine,
God being with thee when we knew it not.

                              W. WORDSWORTH

262

TO THE EVENING STAR

Star that bringest home the bee,
And sett'st the weary labourer free!
  If any star shed peace, 'tis thou,
    That send'st it from above,
  Appearing when Heaven's breath and brow   5
    Are sweet as hers we love.

Come to the luxuriant skies,
Whilst the landscape's odours rise,
  Whilst far-off lowing herds are heard,
    And songs when toil is done,   10
  From cottages whose smoke unstirr'd
    Curls yellow in the sun.

Star of love's soft interviews,
Parted lovers on thee muse;
 Their remembrancer in Heaven   15
  Of thrilling vows thou art,
 Too delicious to be riven
  By absence from the heart.

T. CAMPBELL

263

DATUR HORA QUIETI

The sun upon the lake is low,
 The wild birds hush their song,
The hills have evening's deepest glow,
 Yet Leonard tarries long.
Now all whom varied toil and care   5
 From home and love divide,
In the calm sunset may repair
 Each to the loved one's side.

The noble dame on turret high,
 Who waits her gallant knight,   10
Looks to the western beam to spy
 The flash of armour bright.
The village maid, with hand on brow
 The level ray to shade,
Upon the footpath watches now   15
 For Colin's darkening plaid.

Now to their mates the wild swans row,
 By day they swam apart,
And to the thicket wanders slow
 The hind beside the hart.   20
The woodlark at his partner's side
 Twitters his closing song—
All meet whom day and care divide,
 But Leonard tarries long!

SIR W. SCOTT

264

TO THE MOON

Art thou pale for weariness
Of climbing heaven, and gazing on the earth,
    Wandering companionless
Among the stars that have a different birth,—
And ever-changing, like a joyless eye   5
That finds no object worth its constancy?

                                        P. B. SHELLEY

265

A widow bird sate mourning for her love
    Upon a wintry bough;
The frozen wind crept on above,
    The freezing stream below.

There was no leaf upon the forest bare,   5
    No flower upon the ground,
And little motion in the air
    Except the mill-wheel's sound.

                                        P. B. SHELLEY

266

TO SLEEP

A flock of sheep that leisurely pass by,
    One after one; the sound of rain, and bees
    Murmuring; the fall of rivers, winds and seas,
Smooth fields, white sheets of water, and pure sky;

I have thought of all by turns, and yet do lie   5
    Sleepless; and soon the small birds' melodies
    Must hear, first uttered from my orchard trees,
And the first cuckoo's melancholy cry.

Even thus last night, and two nights more, I lay,
    And could not win thee, Sleep! by any stealth: 10
So do not let me wear to-night away:

> Without Thee what is all the morning's wealth?
> Come, blessèd barrier between day and day,
>   Dear mother of fresh thoughts and joyous health!

W. WORDSWORTH

267

THE SOLDIER'S DREAM

Our bugles sang truce, for the night-cloud had lower'd,
  And the sentinel stars set their watch in the sky;
And thousands had sunk on the ground overpower'd,
  The weary to sleep, and the wounded to die.

When reposing that night on my pallet of straw   5
  By the wolf-scaring faggot that guarded the slain,
At the dead of the night a sweet vision I saw;
  And thrice ere the morning I dreamt it again.

Methought from the battle-field's dreadful array
  Far, far I had roam'd on a desolate track: 10
'Twas autumn,—and sunshine arose on the way
  To the home of my fathers, that welcomed me back.

I flew to the pleasant fields traversed so oft
  In life's morning march, when my bosom was young;
I heard my own mountain-goats bleating aloft,   15
  And knew the sweet strain that the corn-reapers sung.

Then pledged we the wine-cup, and fondly I swore
  From my home and my weeping friends never to part;
My little ones kiss'd me a thousand times o'er,
  And my wife sobb'd aloud in her fullness of heart.   20

' Stay—stay with us!—rest!—thou art weary and worn! '—
  And fain was their war-broken soldier to stay:—
But sorrow return'd with the dawning of morn,
  And the voice in my dreaming ear melted away.

T. CAMPBELL

268

A DREAM OF THE UNKNOWN

I dream'd that as I wander'd by the way
   Bare Winter suddenly was changed to Spring,
And gentle odours led my steps astray,
   Mix'd with a sound of waters murmuring
Along a shelving bank of turf, which lay   5
   Under a copse, and hardly dared to fling
Its green arms round the bosom of the stream,
But kiss'd it and then fled, as thou mightest in dream.

There grew pied wind-flowers and violets,
   Daisies, those pearl'd Arcturi of the earth,   10
The constellated flower that never sets;
   Faint oxlips; tender blue-bells, at whose birth
The sod scarce heaved; and that tall flower that wets—
   Like a child, half in tenderness and mirth—
Its mother's face with heaven's collected tears,   15
When the low wind, its playmate's voice, it hears.

And in the warm hedge grew lush eglantine,
   Green cow-bind and the moonlight-colour'd may,
And cherry-blossoms, and white cups, whose wine
   Was the bright dew yet drain'd not by the day;   20
And wild roses, and ivy serpentine
   With its dark buds and leaves, wandering astray;
And flowers azure, black, and streak'd with gold,
Fairer than any waken'd eyes behold.

And nearer to the river's trembling edge   25
   There grew broad flag-flowers, purple prank with white,
And starry river buds among the sedge,
   And floating water-lilies, broad and bright,
Which lit the oak that overhung the hedge
   With moonlight beams of their own watery light;   30
And bulrushes, and reeds of such deep green
As soothed the dazzled eye with sober sheen.

Methought that of these visionary flowers
   I made a nosegay, bound in such a way
That the same hues, which in their natural bowers   35
   Were mingled or opposed, the like array

Kept these imprison'd children of the Hours
   Within my hand,—and then, elate and gay,
I hasten'd to the spot whence I had come,
That I might there present it—O! to Whom?

P. B. SHELLEY

269

THE INNER VISION

Most sweet it is with unuplifted eyes
   To pace the ground, if path be there or none,
While a fair region round the traveller lies
   Which he forbears again to look upon;

Pleased rather with some soft ideal scene,   5
   The work of Fancy, or some happy tone
Of meditation, slipping in between
   The beauty coming and the beauty gone.

If Thought and Love desert us, from that day
   Let us break off all commerce with the Muse: 10
With Thought and Love companions of our way—

   Whate'er the senses take or may refuse,—
   The Mind's internal heaven shall shed her dews
Of inspiration on the humblest lay.

W. WORDSWORTH

270

THE REALM OF FANCY

Ever let the Fancy roam!
Pleasure never is at home:
At a touch sweet Pleasure melteth,
Like to bubbles when rain pelteth;
Then let wingéd Fancy wander   5
Through the thought still spread beyond her:
Open wide the mind's cage-door,
She'll dart forth, and cloudward soar.
O sweet Fancy! let her loose;
Summer's joys are spoilt by use,   10

And the enjoying of the Spring
Fades as does its blossoming:
Autumn's red-lipp'd fruitage too,
Blushing through the mist and dew,
Cloys with tasting: What do then?   15
Sit thee by the ingle, when
The sear faggot blazes bright,
Spirit of a winter's night;
When the soundless earth is muffled,
And the cakéd snow is shuffled   20
From the ploughboy's heavy shoon;
When the Night doth meet the Noon
In a dark conspiracy
To banish Even from her sky.
—Sit thee there, and send abroad,   25
With a mind self-overawed,
Fancy, high-commission'd:—send her!
She has vassals to attend her;
She will bring, in spite of frost,
Beauties that the earth hath lost;   30
She will bring thee, all together,
All delights of summer weather;
All the buds and bells of May
From dewy sward or thorny spray;
All the heapéd Autumn's wealth,   35
With a still, mysterious stealth;
She will mix these pleasures up
Like three fit wines in a cup,
And thou shalt quaff it;—thou shalt hear
Distant harvest-carols clear;   40
Rustle of the reapéd corn;
Sweet birds antheming the morn:
And in the same moment—hark!
'Tis the early April lark,
Or the rooks, with busy caw,   45
Foraging for sticks and straw.
Thou shalt, at one glance, behold
The daisy and the marigold;
White-plumed lilies, and the first
Hedge-grown primrose that hath burst;   50
Shaded hyacinth, alway
Sapphire queen of the mid-May
And every leaf, and every flower
Pearléd with the self-same shower.
Thou shalt see the field-mouse peep   55

Meagre from its celléd sleep;
And the snake all winter-thin
Cast on sunny bank its skin;
Freckled nest-eggs thou shalt see
Hatching in the hawthorn-tree,   60
When the hen-bird's wing doth rest
Quiet on her mossy nest;
Then the hurry and alarm
When the bee-hive casts its swarm;
Acorns ripe down-pattering   65
While the autumn breezes sing.

   O sweet Fancy! let her loose;
Everything is spoilt by use:
Where 's the cheek that doth not fade,
Too much gazed at? Where 's the maid   70
Whose lip mature is ever new?
Where's the eye, however blue,
Doth not weary? Where's the face
One would meet in every place?
Where 's the voice, however soft,   75
One would hear so very oft?
At a touch sweet Pleasure melteth
Like to bubbles when rain pelteth.
Let then wingéd Fancy find
Thee a mistress to thy mind: 80
Dulcet-eyed as Ceres' daughter,
Ere the God of Torment taught her
How to frown and how to chide;
With a waist and with a side
White as Hebe's, when her zone   85
Slipt its golden clasp, and down
Fell her kirtle to her feet,
While she held the goblet sweet,
And Jove grew languid.—Break the mesh
Of the Fancy's silken leash;   90
Quickly break her prison-string,
And such joys as these she'll bring.
—Let the wingéd Fancy roam!
Pleasure never is at home.

                              J. KEATS

271

HYMN TO THE SPIRIT OF NATURE

Life of Life! thy lips enkindle
  With their love the breath between them;
And thy smiles before they dwindle
  Make the cold air fire; then screen them
In those looks, where whoso gazes   5
Faints, entangled in their mazes.

Child of Light! thy limbs are burning
  Through the vest which seems to hide them,
As the radiant lines of morning
  Through the clouds, ere they divide them;   10
And this atmosphere divinest
Shrouds thee wheresoe'er thou shinest.

Fair are others: none beholds thee;
  But thy voice sounds low and tender
Like the fairest, for it folds thee   15
  From the sight, that liquid splendour;
And all feel, yet see thee never,—
As I feel now, lost for ever!

Lamp of Earth! where'er thou movest
  Its dim shapes are clad with brightness.   20
And the souls of whom thou lovest
  Walk upon the winds with lightness
Till they fail, as I am failing,
Dizzy, lost, yet unbewailing!

                      P. B. SHELLEY

272

WRITTEN IN EARLY SPRING

I heard a thousand blended notes
  While in a grove I sat reclined,
In that sweet mood when pleasant thoughts
  Bring sad thoughts to the mind.

To her fair works did Nature link   5
  The human soul that through me ran;
And much it grieved my heart to think
  What man has made of man.

Through primrose tufts, in that green bower,
  The periwinkle trail'd its wreaths;   10
And 'tis my faith that every flower
  Enjoys the air it breathes.

The birds around me hopp'd and play'd,
  Their thoughts I cannot measure—
But the least motion which they made   15
  It seem'd a thrill of pleasure.

The budding twigs spread out their fan
  To catch the breezy air;
And I must think, do all I can,
  That there was pleasure there.   20

If this belief from heaven be sent,
  If such be Nature's holy plan,
Have I not reason to lament
  What man has made of man?

W. WORDSWORTH

273

RUTH: OR THE INFLUENCES OF NATURE

When Ruth was left half desolate
Her father took another mate;
 And Ruth, not seven years old,
A slighted child, at her own will
Went wandering over dale and hill,   5
 In thoughtless freedom, bold.

And she had made a pipe of straw,
And music from that pipe could draw
 Like sounds of winds and floods;
Had built a bower upon the green,   10
As if she from her birth had been
 An infant of the woods.

Beneath her father's roof, alone
She seem'd to live; her thoughts her own;
 Herself her own delight: 15
Pleased with herself, nor sad nor gay.
And, passing thus the live-long day,
 She grew to woman's height.

There came a youth from Georgia's shore—
A military casque he wore   20
 With splendid feathers drest;
He brought them from the Cherokees;
The feathers nodded in the breeze
 And made a gallant crest.

From Indian blood you deem him sprung: 25
But no! he spake the English tongue
 And bore a soldier's name;
And, when America was free
From battle and from jeopardy,
 He 'cross the ocean came.   30

With hues of genius on his cheek,
In finest tones the youth could speak:
 —While he was yet a boy
The moon, the glory of the sun,
And streams that murmur as they run, 35
 Had been his dearest joy.

He was a lovely youth! I guess
The panther in the wilderness
   Was not so fair as he;
And when he chose to sport and play,   40
No dolphin ever was so gay
   Upon the tropic sea.

Among the Indians he had fought;
And with him many tales he brought
   Of pleasure and of fear;
Such tales as, told to any maid   45
By such a youth, in the green shade,
   Were perilous to hear.

He told of girls, a happy rout!
Who quit their fold with dance and shout,   50
   Their pleasant Indian town,
To gather strawberries all day long;
Returning with a choral song
   When daylight is gone down.

He spake of plants that hourly change   55
Their blossoms, through a boundless range
   Of intermingling hues;
With budding, fading, faded flowers,
They stand the wonder of the bowers
   From morn to evening dews.   60

He told of the magnolia, spread
High as a cloud, high over head!
   The cypress and her spire;
—Of flowers that with one scarlet gleam
Cover a hundred leagues, and seem   65
   To set the hills on fire.

The youth of green savannahs spake,
And many an endless, endless lake
   With all its fairy crowds
Of islands, that together lie   70
As quietly as spots of sky
   Among the evening clouds.

'How pleasant,' then he said, 'it were
A fisher or a hunter there,
   In sunshine or in shade   75

To wander with an easy mind,
And build a household fire, and find
   A home in every glade!

'What days and what bright years! Ah me!
Our life were life indeed, with thee   80
   So pass'd in quiet bliss;
And all the while,' said he, ' to know
That we were in a world of woe,
   On such an earth as this!'

And then he sometimes interwove   85
Fond thoughts about a father's love,
   ' For there,' said he, ' are spun
Around the heart such tender ties,
That our own children to our eyes
   Are dearer than the sun.   90

' Sweet Ruth! and could you go with me
My helpmate in the woods to be,
   Our shed at night to rear;
Or run, my own adopted bride,
A sylvan huntress at my side,   95
   And drive the flying deer!

' Beloved Ruth! '—No more he said.
The wakeful Ruth at midnight shed
   A solitary tear:
She thought again—and did agree   100
With him to sail across the sea,
   And drive the flying deer.

' And now, as fitting is and right,
We in the church our faith will plight,
   A husband and a wife.'   105
Even so they did; and I may say
That to sweet Ruth that happy day
   Was more than human life.

Through dream and vision did she sink,
Delighted all the while to think   110
   That, on those lonesome floods
And green savannahs, she should share
His board with lawful joy, and bear
   His name in the wild woods.

But, as you have before been told,   115
This Stripling, sportive, gay, and bold,
   And with his dancing crest
So beautiful, through savage lands
Had roam'd about, with vagrant bands
   Of Indians in the West.   120

The wind, the tempest roaring high,
The tumult of a tropic sky
   Might well be dangerous food
For him, a youth to whom was given
So much of earth—so much of heaven,   125
   And such impetuous blood.

Whatever in those climes he found
Irregular in sight or sound
   Did to his mind impart
A kindred impulse, seem'd allied   130
To his own powers, and justified
   The workings of his heart.

Nor less, to feed voluptuous thought,
The beauteous forms of Nature wrought,—
   Fair trees and gorgeous flowers;
The breezes their own languor lent;   135
The stars had feelings, which they sent
   Into those favour'd bowers.

Yet, in his worst pursuits, I ween
That sometimes there did intervene
   Pure hopes of high intent: 140
For passions, link'd to forms so fair
And stately, needs must have their share
   Of noble sentiment.

But ill he lived, much evil saw,   145
With men to whom no better law
   Nor better life was known;
Deliberately and undeceived
Those wild men's vices he received,
   And gave them back his own.   150

His genius and his moral frame
Were thus impair'd, and he became
   The slave of low desires:
A man who without self-control

Would seek what the degraded soul
  Unworthily admires.

And yet he with no feign'd delight
Had woo'd the maiden, day and night
  Had loved her, night and morn:
What could he less than love a maid   160
Whose heart with so much nature play'd—
  So kind and so forlorn?

Sometimes most earnestly he said,
'O Ruth! I have been worse than dead;
  False thoughts, thoughts bold and vain   165
Encompass'd me on every side
When I, in confidence and pride,
  Had cross'd the Atlantic main.

'Before me shone a glorious world
Fresh as a banner bright, unfurl'd   170
  To music suddenly:
I look'd upon those hills and plains,
And seem'd as if let loose from chains
  To live at liberty.

'No more of this—for now, by thee,   175
Dear Ruth! more happily set free,
  With nobler zeal I burn;
My soul from darkness is released
Like the whole sky when to the east
  The morning doth return.'   180

Full soon that better mind was gone;
No hope, no wish remain'd, not one,—
  They stirr'd him now no more;
New objects did new pleasure give,
And once again he wish'd to live   185
  As lawless as before.

Meanwhile, as thus with him it fared,
They for the voyage were prepared,
  And went to the sea-shore:
But, when they thither came, the youth   190
Deserted his poor bride, and Ruth
  Could never find him more.

God help thee, Ruth!—Such pains she had,
That she in half a year was mad,
   And in a prison housed;   195
And there, with many a doleful song
Made of wild words, her cup of wrong
   She fearfully caroused.

Yet sometimes milder hours she knew,
Nor wanted sun, nor rain, nor dew,   200
   Nor pastimes of the May,
—They all were with her in her cell;
And a clear brook with cheerful knell
   Did o'er the pebbles play.

When Ruth three seasons thus had lain,   205
There came a respite to her pain;
   She from her prison fled;
But of the Vagrant none took thought;
And where it liked her best she sought
   Her shelter and her bread.   210

Among the fields she breathed again
The master-current of her brain
   Ran permanent and free;
And, coming to the banks of Tone,
There did she rest; and dwell alone   215
   Under the greenwood tree.

The engines of her pain, the tools
That shaped her sorrow, rocks and pools,
   And airs that gently stir
The vernal leaves—she loved them still,   220
Nor ever tax'd them with the ill
   Which had been done to her.

A barn her winter bed supplies;
But, till the warmth of summer skies
   And summer days is gone,
(And all do in this tale agree)   225
She sleeps beneath the greenwood tree,
   And other home hath none.

An innocent life, yet far astray!
And Ruth will, long before her day,   230

Be broken down and old.
Sore aches she needs must have! but less
Of mind, than body's wretchedness,
   From the damp, and rain, and cold.

If she is prest by want of food   235
She from her dwelling in the wood
   Repairs to a road-side;
And there she begs at one steep place,
Where up and down with easy pace
   The horsemen-travellers ride.   240

That oaten pipe of hers is mute
Or thrown away: but with a flute
   Her loneliness she cheers;
This flute, made of a hemlock stalk,
At evening in his homeward walk   245
   The Quantock woodman hears.

I, too, have pass'd her on the hills
Setting her little water-mills
   By spouts and fountains wild—
Such small machinery as she turn'd   250
Ere she had wept, ere she had mourn'd,
   A young and happy child!

Farewell! and when thy days are told,
Ill-fated Ruth! in hallow'd mould
   Thy corpse shall buried be;   255
For thee a funeral bell shall ring,
And all the congregation sing
   A Christian psalm for thee.

                   W. WORDSWORTH

274

WRITTEN IN THE EUGANEAN HILLS, NORTH ITALY

Many a green isle needs must be
In the deep wide sea of misery,
Or the mariner, worn and wan,
Never thus could voyage on
Day and night, and night and day,   5
Drifting on his dreary way,
With the solid darkness black
Closing round his vessel's track;
Whilst above, the sunless sky,
Big with clouds, hangs heavily,   10
And behind, the tempest fleet
Hurries on with lightning feet,
Riving sail, and cord, and plank,
Till the ship has almost drank
Death from the o'er-brimming deep;   15
And sinks down, down, like that sleep
When the dreamer seems to be
Weltering through eternity;
And the dim low line before
Of a dark and distant shore   20
Still recedes, as ever still
Longing with divided will,
But no power to seek or shun,
He is ever drifted on
O'er the unreposing wave,   25
To the haven of the grave.

Aye, many flowering islands lie
In the waters of wide Agony:
To such a one this morn was led
My bark, by soft winds piloted.   30
—'Mid the mountains Euganean
I stood listening to the pæan
With which the legion'd rooks did hail
The sun's uprise majestical:
Gathering round with wings all hoar,   35
Through the dewy mist they soar
Like gray shades, till the eastern heaven
Bursts, and then,—as clouds of even,

Fleck'd with fire and azure, lie
In the unfathomable sky,—   40
So their plumes of purple grain
Starr'd with drops of golden rain
Gleam above the sunlight woods,
As in silent multitudes
On the morning's fitful gale   45
Through the broken mist they sail;
And the vapours cloven and gleaming
Follow down the dark steep streaming,
Till all is bright, and clear, and still
Round the solitary hill.   50

Beneath is spread like a green sea
The waveless plain of Lombardy,
Bounded by the vaporous air,
Islanded by cities fair;
Underneath Day's azure eyes,   55
Ocean's nursling, Venice lies,—
A peopled labyrinth of walls,
Amphitrite's destined halls,
Which her hoary sire now paves
With his blue and beaming waves.   60
Lo! the sun upsprings behind,
Broad, red, radiant, half-reclined
On the level quivering line
Of the waters crystalline;
And before that chasm of light,   65
As within a furnace bright,
Column, tower, and dome, and spire,
Shine like obelisks of fire,
Pointing with inconstant motion
From the altar of dark ocean   70
To the sapphire-tinted skies;
As the flames of sacrifice
From the marble shrines did rise,
As to pierce the dome of gold
Where Apollo spoke of old.   75

Sun-girt City! thou hast been
Ocean's child, and then his queen;
Now is come a darker day,
And thou soon must be his prey,
If the power that raised thee here   80
Hallow so thy watery bier.

A less drear ruin then than now,
With thy conquest-branded brow
Stooping to the slave of slaves
From thy throne, among the waves   85
Wilt thou be,—when the sea-mew
Flies, as once before it flew,
O'er thine isles depopulate,
And all is in its ancient state,
Save where many a palace gate,   90
With green sea-flowers overgrown
Like a rock of ocean's own,
Topples o'er the abandon'd sea
As the tides change sullenly.
The fisher on his watery way   95
Wandering at the close of day,
Will spread his sail and seize his oar
Till he pass the gloomy shore,
Lest thy dead should, from their sleep
Bursting o'er the starlight deep,   100
Lead a rapid masque of death
O'er the waters of his path.

Noon descends around me now:
'Tis the noon of autumn's glow,
When a soft and purple mist   105
Like a vaporous amethyst,
Or an air-dissolvéd star
Mingling light and fragrance, far
From the curved horizon's bound
To the point of Heaven's profound,   110
Fills the overflowing sky;
And the plains that silent lie
Underneath; the leaves unsodden
Where the infant Frost has trodden
With his morning-wingéd feet   115
Whose bright print is gleaming yet;
And the red and golden vines
Piercing with their trellised lines
The rough, dark-skirted wilderness;
The dun and bladed grass no less,   120
Pointing from this hoary tower
In the windless air; the flower
Glimmering at my feet; the line
Of the olive-sandall'd Apennine
In the south dimly islanded;   125

And the Alps, whose snows are spread
High between the clouds and sun;
And of living things each one;
And my spirit, which so long
Darken'd this swift stream of song,—   120
Interpenetrated lie
By the glory of the sky;
Be it love, light, harmony,
Odour, or the soul of all
Which from Heaven like dew doth fall,   125
Or the mind which feeds this verse
Peopling the lone universe.

Noon descends, and after noon
Autumn's evening meets me soon.
Leading the infantine moon   140
And that one star, which to her
Almost seems to minister
Half the crimson light she brings
From the sunset's radiant springs:
And the soft dreams of the morn   145
(Which like wingéd winds had borne
To that silent isle, which lies
'Mid remember'd agonies,
The frail bark of this lone being),
Pass, to other sufferers fleeing,   150
And its ancient pilot, Pain,
Sits beside the helm again.

Other flowering isles must be
In the sea of Life and Agony:
Other spirits float and flee   155
O'er that gulf: even now, perhaps,
On some rock the wild wave wraps,
With folding wings they waiting sit
For my bark, to pilot it
To some calm and blooming cove,   160
Where for me, and those I love,
May a windless bower be built,
Far from passion, pain, and guilt,
In a dell 'mid lawny hills
Which the wild sea-murmur fills,   165
And soft sunshine, and the sound
Of old forests echoing round,
And the light and smell divine,

Of all flowers that breathe and shine.
—We may live so happy there, 170
That the Spirits of the Air
Envying us, may even entice
To our healing Paradise
The polluting multitude;
But their rage would be subdued 175
By that clime divine and calm,
And the winds whose wings rain balm
On the uplifted soul, and leaves
Under which the bright sea heaves;
While each breathless interval 180
In their whisperings musical
The inspired soul supplies
With its own deep melodies;
And the love which heals all strife
Circling, like the breath of life, 185
All things in that sweet abode
With its own mild brotherhood.
They, not it, would change; and soon
Every sprite beneath the moon
Would repent its envy vain, 190
And the earth grow young again.

P. B. SHELLEY

275

ODE TO THE WEST WIND

(1)

O wild West Wind, thou breath of Autumn's being,
   Thou, from whose unseen presence the leaves dead
Are driven, like ghosts from an enchanter fleeing,

Yellow, and black, and pale, and hectic red,
   Pestilence-stricken multitudes: O thou
Who chariotest to their dark wintry bed   5

The wingéd seeds, where they lie cold and low,
   Each like a corpse within its grave, until
Thine azure sister of the Spring shall blow

Her clarion o'er the dreaming earth, and fill 10
   (Driving sweet buds like flocks to feed in air)
With living hues and odours plain and hill:

Wild Spirit, which art moving everywhere;
Destroyer and Preserver; hear, oh, hear!

(2)

Thou on whose stream, mid the steep sky's commotion, 15
   Loose clouds like earth's decaying leaves are shed,
Shook from the tangled boughs of Heaven and Ocean,

Angels of rain and lightning: there are spread
   On the blue surface of thine airy surge,
Like the bright hair uplifted from the head 20

Of some fierce Maenad, even from the dim verge
   Of the horizon to the zenith's height,
The locks of the approaching storm. Thou dirge

Of the dying year, to which this closing night
   Will be the dome of a vast sepulchre, 25
Vaulted with all thy congregated might

Of vapours, from whose solid atmosphere
Black rain, and fire, and hail, will burst: oh, hear

(3)

Thou who didst waken from his summer dreams
   The blue Mediterranean, where he lay, 30
Lull'd by the coil of his crystalline streams,

Beside a pumice isle in Baiae's bay,
   And saw in sleep old palaces and towers
Quivering within the wave's intenser day,

All overgrown with azure moss and flowers 35
   So sweet, the sense faints picturing them! Thou
For whose path the Atlantic's level powers

Cleave themselves into chasms, while far below
   The sea-blooms and the oozy woods which wear
The sapless foliage of the ocean, know 40

Thy voice, and suddenly grow grey with fear,
And tremble and despoil themselves: oh, hear!

(4)

If I were a dead leaf thou mightest bear;
　　If I were a swift cloud to fly with thee;
A wave to pant beneath thy power, and share   45

The impulse of thy strength, only less free
　　Than thou, O uncontrollable! If even
I were as in my boyhood, and could be

The comrade of thy wanderings over Heaven,
　　As then, when to outstrip thy skyey speed   50
Scarce seemed a vision, I would ne'er have striven

As thus with thee in prayer in my sore need.
　　Oh, lift me as a wave, a leaf, a cloud!
I fall upon the thorns of life! I bleed!

A heavy weight of hours has chained and bowed   55
One too like thee: tameless, and swift, and proud.

(5)

Make me thy lyre, even as the forest is!
　　What if my leaves are falling like its own!
The tumult of thy mighty harmonies

Will take from both a deep, autumnal tone,   60
　　Sweet though in sadness. Be thou, Spirit fierce,
My spirit! Be thou me, impetuous one!

Drive my dead thoughts over the universe
　　Like withered leaves to quicken a new birth!
And, by the incantation of this verse,   65

Scatter, as from an unextinguished hearth
　　Ashes and sparks, my words among mankind!
Be through my lips to unawakened earth

The trumpet of a prophecy! O Wind,
If Winter comes, can Spring be far behind?   70

P. B. SHELLEY

276

NATURE AND THE POET

Suggested by a Picture of Peele Castle in a Storm, painted by Sir George Beaumont

I was thy neighbour once, thou rugged Pile!
    Four summer weeks I dwelt in sight of thee:
I saw thee every day; and all the while
    Thy Form was sleeping on a glassy sea.

So pure the sky, so quiet was the air!   5
    So like, so very like, was day to day!
Whene'er I look'd, thy image still was there;
    It trembled, but it never pass'd away.

How perfect was the calm! It seem'd no sleep,
    No mood, which season takes away, or brings: 10
I could have fancied that the mighty Deep
    Was even the gentlest of all gentle things.

Ah! then if mine had been the Painter's hand
    To express what then I saw; and add the gleam,
The light that never was on sea or land,   15
    The consecration, and the Poet's dream —

I would have planted thee, thou hoary Pile,
    Amid a world how different from this!
Beside a sea that could not cease to smile;
    On tranquil land, beneath a sky of bliss.   20

A picture had it been of lasting ease,
    Elysian quiet, without toil or strife;
No motion but the moving tide, a breeze,
    Or merely silent Nature's breathing life.

Such, in the fond illusion of my heart,   25
    Such picture would I at that time have made;
And seen the soul of truth in every part,
    A steadfast peace that might not be betray'd.

So once it would have been,—'tis so no more;
  I have submitted to a new control: 30
A power is gone, which nothing can restore;
  A deep distress hath humanized my soul.

Not for a moment could I now behold
  A smiling sea, and be what I have been
The feeling of my loss will ne'er be old;   35
  This, which I know, I speak with mind serene.

Then, Beaumont, Friend! who would have been the
    Friend
  If he had lived, of him whom I deplore,
This work of thine I blame not, but commend;
  This sea in anger, and that dismal shore.   40

O 'tis a passionate work!—yet wise and well,
  Well chosen is the spirit that is here;
That hulk which labours in the deadly swell,
  This rueful sky, this pageantry of fear!

And this huge Castle, standing here sublime,   45
  I love to see the look with which it braves,
—Cased in the unfeeling armour of old time—
  The lightning, the fierce wind, and trampling waves.

Farewell, farewell the heart that lives alone,
  Housed in a dream, at distance from the Kind!   50
Such happiness, wherever it be known,
  Is to be pitied; for 'tis surely blind.

But welcome fortitude, and patient cheer,
  And frequent sights of what is to be borne!
Such sights, or worse, as are before me here:—   55
  Not without hope we suffer and we mourn.

                      W. WORDSWORTH

277

THE POET'S DREAM

On a poet's lips I slept
Dreaming like a love-adept
In the sound his breathing kept;
Nor seeks nor finds he mortal blisses,
But feeds on the aerial kisses   5
Of shapes that haunt thought's wildernesses.
He will watch from dawn to gloom
The lake-reflected sun illume
The yellow bees in the ivy-bloom,
   Nor heed nor see what things they be;   10
But from these create he can
Forms more real than living man,
   Nurslings of immortality!

P. B. SHELLEY

278

The world is too much with us; late and soon,
  Getting and spending, we lay waste our powers
  Little we see in Nature that is ours;
We have given our hearts away, a sordid boon!

This Sea that bares her bosom to the moon,   5
  The winds that will be howling at all hours
  And are up-gather'd now like sleeping flowers,
For this, for everything, we are out of tune;

It moves us not.—Great God! I'd rather be
  A Pagan suckled in a creed outworn,   10
So might I, standing on this pleasant lea,

  Have glimpses that would make me less forlorn;
Have sight of Proteus rising from the sea;
  Or hear old Triton blow his wreathèd horn.

W. WORDSWORTH

279

WITHIN KING'S COLLEGE CHAPEL, CAMBRIDGE

Tax not the royal Saint with vain expense,
  With ill-match'd aims the Architect who plann'd
  (Albeit labouring for a scanty band
Of white-robed Scholars only) this immense

And glorious work of fine intelligence!   5
  Give all thou canst; high Heaven rejects the lore
  Of nicely-calculated less or more:
So deem'd the man who fashion'd for the sense

These lofty pillars, spread that branching roof
  Self-poised, and scoop'd into ten thousand cells,   10
  Where light and shade repose, where music dwells

  Lingering—and wandering on as loth to die;
Like thoughts whose very sweetness yieldeth proof
  That they were born for immortality.

                    W. WORDSWORTH

280

YOUTH AND AGE

  Verse, a breeze 'mid blossoms straying,
    Where Hope clung feeding, like a bee—
  Both were mine! Life went a-maying
      With Nature, Hope, and Poesy,
        When I was young!   5

  When I was young?—Ah, woeful When!
  Ah! for the change 'twixt Now and Then!
  This breathing house not built with hands,
    This body that does me grievous wrong,
  O'er aery cliffs and glittering sands   10
    How lightly then it flash'd along:
  Like those trim skiffs, unknown of yore,

On wind ng lakes and rivers wide,
That ask no aid of sail or oar,
   That fear no spite of wind or tide!   15
Nought cared this body for wind or weather
When Youth and I lived in't together.

Flowers are lovely; Love is flower-like;
   Friendship is a sheltering tree;
O! the joys, that came down shower-like,   20
   Of Friendship, Love, and Liberty,
      Ere I was old!

Ere I was old? Ah woeful Ere,
Which tells me, Youth's no longer here!
O Youth! for years so many and sweet   25
   'Tis known that Thou and I were one,
I'll think it but a fond conceit—
   It cannot be that thou art gone!
Thy vesper bell hath not yet toll'd:—
And thou wert ay a masker bold!   30
What strange disguise hast now put on
To make believe that thou art gone?
I see these locks in silvery slips,
   This drooping gait, this alter'd size:
But Springtide blossoms on thy lips,   35
   And tears take sunshine from thine eyes!
Life is but thought: so think I will
That Youth and I are housemates still.

Dew-drops are the gems of morning,
   But the tears of mournful eve!   40
Where no hope is, life's a warning
   That only serves to make us grieve,
      When we are old:

—That only serves to make us grieve
With oft and tedious taking-leave,   45
Like some poor nigh-related guest
That may not rudely be dismist,
Yet hath outstay'd his welcome while,
And tells the jest without the smile.
          S. T. COLERIDGE

281

THE TWO APRIL MORNINGS

We walk'd along, while bright and red
  Uprose the morning sun;
And Matthew stopp'd, he look'd, and said,
  ' The will of God be done! '

A village schoolmaster was he,   5
  With hair of glittering grey;
As blithe a man as you could see
  On a spring holiday.

And on that morning, through the grass
  And by the steaming rills   10
We travell'd merrily, to pass
  A day among the hills.

' Our work,' said I, ' was well begun;
  Then, from thy breast what thought,
Beneath so beautiful a sun,   15
  So sad a sigh has brought? '

A second time did Matthew stop;
  And fixing still his eye
Upon the eastern mountain-top
  To me he made reply: 20

' Yon cloud with that long purple cleft
  Brings fresh into my mind
A day like this, which I have left
  Full thirty years behind

' And just above yon slope of corn   25
  Such colours, and no other,
Were in the sky, that April morn,
  Of this the very brother.

' With rod and line I sued the sport
  Which that sweet season gave,
And, to the churchyard come, stopp'd short   30
  Beside my daughter's grave.

'Nine summers had she scarcely seen,
  The pride of all the vale;
And then she sang;—she would have been   35
  A very nightingale.

'Six feet in earth my Emma lay;
  And yet I loved her more—
For so it seem'd,—than till that day
  I e'er had loved before,   40

'And turning from her grave, I met
  Beside the churchyard yew
A blooming Girl, whose hair was wet
  With points of morning dew.

'A basket on her head she bare;   45
  Her brow was smooth and white:
To see a child so very fair,
  It was a pure delight!

'No fountain from its rocky cave
  E'er tripp'd with foot so free;   50
She seem'd as happy as a wave
  That dances on the sea.

'There came from me a sigh of pain
  Which I could ill confine;
I looked at her, and looked again: 55
  And did not wish her mine!'

Matthew is in his grave, yet now
  Methinks I see him stand
As at that moment, with a bough
  Of wilding in his hand.   60

W. WORDSWORTH

282

THE FOUNTAIN

A Conversation

We talk'd with open heart, and tongue
  Affectionate and true,
A pair of friends, though I was young,
  And Matthew seventy-two.

We lay beneath a spreading oak,   5
  Beside a mossy seat;
And from the turf a fountain broke
  And gurgled at our feet.

' Now, Matthew ! ' said I, ' let us match
  This water's pleasant tune   10
With some old border-song, or catch
  That suits a summer's noon;

' Or of the church-clock and the chimes
  Sing here beneath the shade
That half-mad thing of witty rhymes   15
  Which you last April made ! '

In silence Matthew lay, and eyed
  The spring beneath the tree:
And thus the dear old man replied,
  The grey-hair'd man of glee: 20

' No check, no stay, this Streamlet fears,
  How merrily it goes!
'Twill murmur on a thousand years
  And flow as now it flows.

' And here, on this delightful day,   25
  I cannot choose but think
How oft, a vigorous man, I lay
  Beside this fountain's brink.

'My eyes are dim with childish tears,
   My heart is idly stirr'd,   30
For the same sound is in my ears
   Which in those days I heard.

'Thus fares it still in our decay:
   And yet the wiser mind
Mourns less for what age takes away,   35
   Than what it leaves behind.

'The blackbird amid leafy trees,
   The lark above the hill,
Let loose their carols when they please,
   Are quiet when they will.   40

'With Nature never do they wage
   A foolish strife; they see
A happy youth, and their old age
   Is beautiful and free:

'But we are press'd by heavy laws;   45
   And often, glad no more,
We wear a face of joy, because
   We have been glad of yore.

'If there be one who need bemoan
   His kindred laid in earth,   50
The household hearts that were his own,—
   It is the man of mirth.

'My days, my friend, are almost gone,
   My life has been approved,
And many love me; but by none   55
   Am I enough beloved.'

'Now both himself and me he wrongs,
   The man who thus complains!
I live and sing my idle songs
   Upon these happy plains: 60

'And, Matthew, for thy children dead
   I'll be a son to thee!'
At this he grasp'd my hand and said,
   'Alas! that cannot be.'

We rose up from the fountain-side;   65
    And down the smooth descent
Of the green sheep-track did we glide;
    And through the wood we went;

And, ere we came to Leonard's rock,
    He sang those witty rhymes   70
About the crazy old church-clock
    And the bewilder'd chimes.

                                    W. WORDSWORTH

283

THE RIVER OF LIFE

The more we live, more brief appear
    Our life's succeeding stages:
A day to childhood seems a year,
    And years like passing ages.

The gladsome current of our youth,   5
    Ere passion yet disorders,
Steals lingering like a river smooth
    Along its grassy borders.

But as the careworn cheek grows wan,
    And sorrow's shafts fly thicker,
Ye stars, that measure life to man,   10
    Why seem your courses quicker?

When joys have lost their bloom and breath,
    And life itself is vapid,
Why, as we reach the Falls of death,   15
    Feel we its tide more rapid?

It may be strange—yet who would change
    Time's course to slower speeding,
When one by one our friends have gone
    And left our bosoms bleeding?   20

Heaven gives our years of fading strength
    Indemnifying fleetness;
And those of youth, a seeming length,
    Proportion'd to their sweetness.

                                        T. CAMPBELL

284

THE HUMAN SEASONS

Four seasons fill the measure of the year;
　There are four seasons in the mind of man:
He has his lusty Spring, when fancy clear
　Takes in all beauty with an easy span:

He has his Summer, when luxuriously   5
　Spring's honey'd cud of youthful thought he loves
To ruminate, and by such dreaming nigh
　His nearest unto heaven: quiet coves

His soul has in its Autumn, when his wings
　He furleth close; contented so to look   10
On mists in idleness—to let fair things
　Pass by unheeded as a threshold brook:

He has his Winter too of pale misfeature,
Or else he would forgo his mortal nature.

J. KEATS

285

A LAMENT

O World! O Life! O Time!
On whose last steps I climb,
　Trembling at that where I had stood before;
When will return the glory of your prime?
　No more—Oh, never more!   5

Out of the day and night
A joy has taken flight:
　Fresh spring, and summer, and winter hoar
Move my faint heart with grief, but with delight
　No more—Oh, never more!   10

P. B. SHELLEY

286

My heart leaps up when I behold
  A rainbow in the sky:
So was it when my life began,
So is it now I am a man,
So be it when I shall grow old,   5
    Or let me die!
The Child is father of the Man:
  And I could wish my days to be
Bound each to each by natural piety.

W. WORDSWORTH

287

ODE ON INTIMATIONS OF IMMORTALITY FROM RECOLLECTIONS OF EARLY CHILDHOOD

There was a time when meadow, grove, and stream,
  The earth, and every common sight,
    To me did seem
    Apparell'd in celestial light,
The glory and the freshness of a dream.   5
It is not now as it hath been of yore;—
    Turn wheresoe'er I may,
      By night or day,
The things which I have seen I now can see no more.

    The rainbow comes and goes,   10
    And lovely is the rose;
    The moon doth with delight
Look round her when the heavens are bare;
    Waters on a starry night
    Are beautiful and fair;   15
  The sunshine is a glorious birth;
  But yet I know, where'er I go,
That there hath pass'd away a glory from the earth.

Now, while the birds thus sing a joyous song,
  And while the young lambs bound   20
    As to the tabor's sound,
To me alone there came a thought of grief:
A timely utterance gave that thought relief,

And I again am strong.
The cataracts blow their trumpets from the steep,—   25
No more shall grief of mine the season wrong:
I hear the echoes through the mountains throng,
The winds come to me from the fields of sleep,
          And all the earth is gay;
              Land and sea   30
      Give themselves up to jollity,
            And with the heart of May
      Doth every beast keep holiday;–
            Thou child of joy,
Shout round me, let me hear thy shouts, thou happy
      Shepherd-boy!   35

Ye blessèd Creatures, I have heard the call
      Ye to each other make; I see
The heavens laugh with you in your jubilee;
      My heart is at your festival,
      My head hath its coronal,   40
The fulness of your bliss, I feel—I feel it all.
          O evil day! if I were sullen
            While Earth herself is adorning
                This sweet May-morning;
            And the children are culling   45
                On every side
      In a thousand valleys far and wide
      Fresh flowers; while the sun shines warm,
And the babe leaps up on his mother's arm:—
          I hear, I hear, with joy I hear!   50
      —But there 's a tree, of many, one,
A single field which I have look'd upon,
Both of them speak of something that is gone:
            The pansy at my feet
            Doth the same tale repeat: 55
Whither is fled the visionary gleam?
Where is it now, the glory and the dream?

Our birth is but a sleep and a forgetting;
The Soul that rises with us, our life's Star,
          Hath had elsewhere its setting,   60
            And cometh from afar;
          Not in entire forgetfulness,
          And not in utter nakedness,

But trailing clouds of glory do we come
           From God, who is our home: 65
Heaven lies about us in our infancy!
Shades of the prison-house begin to close
           Upon the growing Boy,
But he beholds the light, and whence it flows,
           He sees it in his joy;   70
The Youth, who daily farther from the east
      Must travel, still is Nature's priest,
        And by the vision splendid
        Is on his way attended;
At length the Man perceives it die away,   75
And fade into the light of common day.

Earth fills her lap with pleasures of her own;
Yearnings she hath in her own natural kind,
And, even with something of a mother's mind
           And no unworthy aim,   80
         The homely nurse doth all she can
To make her foster-child, her inmate, Man,
        Forget the glories he hath known,
And that imperial palace whence he came.

Behold the Child among his new-born blisses,   85
    A six years' darling of a pigmy size!
      See, where 'mid work of his own hand he lies,
Fretted by sallies of his mother's kisses,
    With light upon him from his father's eyes!
See, at his feet, some little plan or chart,   90
Some fragment from his dream of human life,
Shaped by himself with newly-learnèd art;
        A wedding or a festival,
        A mourning or a funeral;
          And this hath now his heart,   95
        And unto this he frames his song:
        Then will he fit his tongue
To dialogues of business, love, or strife;
        But it will not be long
        Ere this be thrown aside,   100
        And with new joy and pride
The little actor cons another part;
Filling from time to time his ' humorous stage '
With all the Persons, down to palsied Age,
That life brings with her in her equipage;   105
        As if his whole vocation
        Were endless imitation.

Thou, whose exterior semblance doth belie
    Thy soul's immensity;
Thou best Philosopher, who yet dost keep   **110**
Thy heritage, thou Eye among the blind,
That, deaf and silent, read'st the eternal deep,
Haunted for ever by the eternal Mind,—
    Mighty Prophet! Seer blest!
    On whom those truths do rest   **115**
Which we are toiling all our lives to find,
In darkness lost, the darkness of the grave;
Thou, over whom thy Immortality
Broods like the Day, a Master o'er a Slave,
A Presence which is not to be put by;   **120**
Thou little Child, yet glorious in the might
Of heaven-born freedom on thy being's height,
Why with such earnest pains dost thou provoke
The years to bring the inevitable yoke,
Thus blindly with thy blessedness at strife?   **125**
Full soon thy Soul shall have her earthly freight,
And custom lie upon thee with a weight
Heavy as frost, and deep almost as life!

    O joy! that in our embers
      Is something that doth live,   **130**
    That Nature yet remembers
      What was so fugitive!
The thought of our past years in me doth breed
Perpetual benediction: not indeed
For that which is most worthy to be blest,   **135**
Delight and liberty, the simple creed
Of Childhood, whether busy or at rest,
With new-fledged hope still fluttering in his breast:
    —Not for these I raise
    The song of thanks and praise;   **140**
  But for those obstinate questionings
  Of sense and outward things,
  Fallings from us, vanishings,
  Blank misgivings of a creature
Moving about in worlds not realized,   **145**
High instincts, before which our mortal nature
Did tremble like a guilty thing surprised:
    But for those first affections,
    Those shadowy recollections,
      Which, be they what they may,   **150**
Are yet the fountain-light of all our day,

Are yet a master-light of all our seeing;
    Uphold us, cherish and have power to make
Our noisy years seem moments in the being
    Of the eternal silence: truths that wake,   155
        To perish never;
Which neither listlessness, nor mad endeavour,
        Nor man nor boy
Nor all that is at enmity with joy,
Can utterly abolish or destroy!   160
  Hence in a season of calm weather
    Though inland far we be,
Our souls have sight of that immortal sea
    Which brought us hither;
    Can in a moment travel thither—   165
And see the children sport upon the shore,
And hear the mighty waters rolling evermore.

Then, sing ye birds, sing, sing a joyous song!
    And let the young lambs bound
    As to the tabor's sound!   170
  We, in thought, will join your throng
    Ye that pipe and ye that play,
    Ye that through your hearts to-day
    Feel the gladness of the May!
What though the radiance which was once so bright   175
Be now for ever taken from my sight,
  Though nothing can bring back the hour
Of splendour in the grass, of glory in the flower;
    We will grieve not, rather find
    Strength in what remains behind;   180
    In the primal sympathy
    Which having been must ever be;
    In the soothing thoughts that spring
    Out of human suffering;
    In the faith that looks through death,   185
  In years that bring the philosophic mind.

And O, ye Fountains, Meadows, Hills, and Groves,
Forbode not any severing of our loves!
Yet in my heart of hearts I feel your might;
I only have relinquish'd one delight   190
To live beneath your more habitual away;
I love the brooks which down their channels fret,
Even more than when I tripp'd lightly as they;

The innocent brightness of a new-born day
    Is lovely yet;   195
The clouds that gather round the setting sun
Do take a sober colouring from an eye
That hath kept watch o'er man's mortality;
Another race hath been, and other palms are won.
Thanks to the human heart by which we live,   200
Thanks to its tenderness, its joys, and fears,
To me the meanest flower that blows can give
Thoughts that do often lie too deep for tears.
                      W. WORDSWORTH

288

Music, when soft voices die,
Vibrates in the memory—
Odours, when sweet violets sicken,
Live within the sense they quicken.

Rose leaves, when the rose is dead,   5
Are heaped for the beloved's bed;
And so thy thoughts, when thou art gone,
Love itself shall slumber on.
                    P. B. SHELLEY

ADDITIONAL POEMS

289

SONG

My silks and fine array,
My smiles and languish'd air,
By Love are driv'n away;
And mournful lean Despair
Brings me yew to deck my grave: 5
Such end true lovers have.

His face is fair as heav'n
When springing buds unfold;
O why to him was't giv'n
Whose heart is wintry cold?   10
His breast is Love's all-worship'd tomb,
Where all Love's pilgrims come.

Bring me an axe and spade,
Bring me a winding-sheet;
When I my grave have made   15
Let winds and tempests beat:
Then down I'll lie as cold as clay.
True love doth pass away!

WILLIAM BLAKE

290

SONG

How sweet I roam'd from field to field
   And tasted all the summer's pride,
Till I the prince of love beheld
   Who in the sunny beams did glide!

He shew'd me lilies for my hair,   5
   And blushing roses for my brow;
He led me through his gardens fair
   Where all his golden pleasures grow.

337

With sweet May dews my wings were wet,
 And Phœbus fir'd my vocal rage;   10
He caught me in his silken net,
 And shut me in his golden cage.

He loves to sit and hear me sing,
 Then, laughing, sports and plays with me;
Then stretches out my golden wing,   15
 And mocks my loss of liberty.

WILLIAM BLAKE

291

NIGHT

The sun descending in the west,
The evening star does shine;
The birds are silent in their nest,
And I must seek for mine.
The moon, like a flower,   5
In heaven's high bower,
With silent delight
Sits and smiles on the night.

Farewell, green fields and happy groves,
Where flocks have took delight.   10
Where lambs have nibbled, silent moves
The feet of angels bright;
Unseen they pour blessing,
And joy without ceasing,
On each bud and blossom,   15
And each sleeping bosom.

They look in every thoughtless nest,
Where birds are cover'd warm;
They visit caves of every beast,
To keep them all from harm.   20
If they see any weeping
That should have been sleeping,
They pour sleep on their head,
And sit down by their bed.

When wolves and tygers howl for prey,   25
They pitying stand and weep,
Seeking to drive their thirst away,
And keep them from the sheep.

But if they rush dreadful,
The angels, most heedful,   30
Receive each mild spirit,
New worlds to inherit.

And there the lion's ruddy eyes
Shall flow with tears of gold,
And pitying the tender cries,   35
And walking round the fold,
Saying ' Wrath, by his meekness,
And, by his health, sickness
Is driven away
From our immortal day.   40

' And now beside thee, bleating lamb,
I can lie down and sleep;
Or think on Him who bore thy name,
Graze after thee and weep.
For, wash'd in life's river,   45
My bright mane for ever
Shall shine like the gold,
As I guard o'er the fold.'

                                    WILLIAM BLAKE

292

Hear the voice of the Bard!
Who Present, Past, and Future, sees;
Whose ears have heard
The Holy Word
That walk'd among the ancient trees,   5

Calling the lapsèd Soul,
And weeping in the evening dew;
That might controll
The starry pole,
And fallen, fallen light renew!   10

' O Earth, O Earth, return!
Arise from out the dewy grass;
Night is worn,
And the morn
Rises from the slumberous mass.   15

' Turn away no more;
Why wilt thou turn away?
The starry floor,
The wat'ry shore,
Is giv'n thee till the break of day.'   20

WILLIAM BLAKE

293

THE SICK ROSE

O Rose, thou art sick!
The invisible worm,
That flies in the night,
In the howling storm,

Has found out thy bed   5
Of crimson joy;
And his dark secret love
Does thy life destroy.

WILLIAM BLAKE

294

THE TYGER

Tyger! Tyger! burning bright
In the forests of the night,
What immortal hand or eye
Could frame thy fearful symmetry?

In what distant deeps or skies   5
Burnt the fire of thine eyes?
On what wings dare he aspire?
What the hand dare seize the fire?

And what shoulder, and what art,
Could twist the sinews of thy heart?   10
And when thy heart began to beat,
What dread hand? and what dread feet?

What the hammer? what the chain?
In what furnace was thy brain?

What the anvil? what dread grasp   15
Dare its deadly terrors clasp?

When the stars threw down their spears,
And water'd heaven with their tears,
Did he smile his work to see?
Did He who made the Lamb make thee?   20

Tyger! Tyger! burning bright
In the forests of the night,
What immortal hand or eye,
Dare frame thy fearful symmetry?

WILLIAM BLAKE

295

AH! SUNFLOWER

Ah, Sunflower! weary of time,
Who countest the steps of the Sun;
Seeking after that sweet golden clime,
Where the traveller's journey is done;

Where the Youth pined away with desire,   5
And the pale Virgin shrouded in snow,
Arise from their graves, and aspire
Where my Sunflower wishes to go.

WILLIAM BLAKE

296

THE SCHOOLBOY

I love to rise in a summer morn
When the birds sing on every tree;
The distant huntsman winds his horn,
And the skylark sings with me.
O! what sweet company.   5

But to go to school in a summer morn,
O! it drives all joy away;
Under a cruel eye outworn,
The little ones spend the day
In sighing and dismay.   10

Ah! then at times I drooping sit,
And spend many an anxious hour,
Nor in my book can I take delight,
Nor sit in learning's bower,
Worn thro' with the dreary shower.   15

How can the bird that is born for joy
Sit in a cage and sing?
How can a child, when fears annoy,
But droop his tender wing,
And forget his youthful spring?   20

O! father and mother, if buds are nip'd
And blossoms blown away,
And if the tender plants are strip'd
Of their joy in the springing day,
By sorrow and care's dismay,   25

How shall the summer arise in joy,
Or the summer fruits appear?
Or how shall we gather what griefs destroy,
Or bless the mellowing year,
When the blasts of winter appear?   30

WILLIAM BLAKE

297

Never seek to tell thy love,
Love that never told can be;
For the gentle wind does move
Silently, invisibly.

I told my love, I told my love,   5
I told her all my heart;
Trembling, cold, in ghastly fears,
Ah! she doth depart.

Soon as she was gone from me,
A traveller came by,   10
Silently, invisibly:
He took her with a sigh.

298

Stand close around, ye Stygian set,
  With Dirce in one boat conveyed!
Or Charon, seeing, may forget
  That he is old and she a shade.

WALTER SAVAGE LANDOR

299

Past ruin'd Ilion Helen lives,
  Alcestis rises from the shades;
Verse calls them forth; 'tis verse that gives
  Immortal youth to mortal maids.

Soon shall Oblivion's deepening veil   5
  Hide all the peopled hills you see,
The gay, the proud, while lovers hail
  In distant ages you and me.

The tear for fading beauty check,
  For passing glory cease to sigh;   10
One form shall rise above the wreck,
  One name, Ianthe, shall not die.

WALTER SAVAGE LANDOR

300

' Do you remember me? or are you proud? '
Lightly advancing thro' her star-trimm'd crowd,
Ianthe said, and look'd into my eyes.
' A *yes*, a *yes* to both: for Memory
Where you but once have been must ever be,   5
  And at your voice Pride from his throne must rise.'

WALTER SAVAGE LANDOR

301

ROSE AYLMER

Ah what avails the sceptred race,
  Ah what the form divine!
What every virtue, every grace!
  Rose Aylmer, all were thine.

Rose Aylmer. whom these wakeful eyes   5
  May weep, but never see,
A night of memories and of sighs
  I consecrate to thee.

WALTER SAVAGE LANDOR

302

THREE MEN OF GOTHAM

Seamen three! What men be ye?
  Gotham's three wise men we be.
Whither in your bowl so free?
  To rake the moon from out the sea.
The bowl goes trim. The moon doth shine.   5
And our ballast is old wine.
And your ballast is old wine.

Who art thou, so fast adrift?
  I am he they call Old Care.
Here on board we will thee lift.   10
  No: I may not enter there.
Wherefore so? 'Tis Jove's decree,
In a bowl Care may not be.
In a bowl Care may not be.

Fear ye not the waves that roll?   15
  No: in charméd bowl we swim.
What the charm that floats the bowl?
  Water may not pass the brim.
The bowl goes trim. The moon doth shine.
And our ballast is old wine.   20
And your ballast is old wine.

T. L. PEACOCK

303

THE GRAVE OF LOVE

I dug, beneath the cypress shade,
  What well might seem an elfin's grave;
And every pledge in earth I laid,
  That erst thy false affection gave.

I pressed them down the sod beneath;   5
 I placed one mossy stone above;
And twined the rose's fading wreath
 Around the sepulchre of love.

Frail as thy love, the flowers were dead,
 Ere yet the evening sun was set: 10
But years shall see the cypress spread,
 Immutable as my regret.

T. L. PEACOCK

304

 Love lives beyond
The tomb, the earth, which fades like dew!
 I love the fond,
The faithful, and the true.

 Love lives in sleep,   5
The happiness of healthy dreams:
 Eve's dews may weep,
But love delightful seems.

 'Tis seen in flowers,
And in the morning's pearly dew;   10
 In earth's green hours,
And in the heaven's eternal blue.

 'Tis heard in spring
When light and sunbeams, warm and kind,
 On angel's wing   15
Bring love and music to the mind.

 And where is voice,
So young, so beautiful, and sweet
 As nature's choice,
Where spring and lovers meet?   20

 Love lives beyond
The tomb, the earth, the flowers, and dew.
 I love the fond,
The faithful, young, and true.

JOHN CLARE

305

MEET ME IN THE GREEN GLEN

Love, meet me in the green glen,
  Beside the tall elm-tree,
Where the sweetbrier smells so sweet agen;
  There come with me,
    Meet me in the green glen.   5

Meet me at the sunset
  Down in the green glen,
Where we've often met
  By hawthorn-tree and foxes' den,
    Meet me in the green glen.   10

Meet me in the green glen,
  By sweetbrier bushes there;
Meet me by your own sen,
  Where the wild thyme blossoms fair.
    Meet me in the green glen.   15

Meet me by the sweetbrier,
  By the mole-hill swelling there;
When the west glows like a fire
  God's crimson bed is there.
    Meet me in the green glen.   20

JOHN CLARE

306

AUTUMN

I love the fitful gust that shakes
  The casement all the day,
And from the mossy elm-tree takes
  The faded leaves away,
Twirling them by the window pane   5
With thousand others down the lane.

I love to see the shaking twig
  Dance till the shut of eve,
The sparrow on the cottage rig,
  Whose chirp would make believe   10

That spring was just now flirting by
In summer's lap with flowers to lie.

I love to see the cottage smoke
  Curl upwards through the trees,
The pigeons nestled round the cote   15
  On November days like these;
The cock upon the dunghill crowing,
The mill-sails on the heath a-going.

The feather from the raven's breast
  Falls on the stubble lea,   20
The acorns near the old crow's nest
  Drop pattering down the tree;
The grunting pigs, that wait for all,
Scramble and hurry where they fall.

JOHN CLARE

307

from THE SHEPHERD'S CALENDAR

The shepherd-boy, that hastens now and then
From hail and snow beneath his sheltering den
Of flags, or file-leaved sedges tied in sheaves,
Or stubble shocks, oft as his eye perceives
Sun-threads shrink out in momentary smiles,   5
With fairy thoughts his loneliness beguiles;
Thinking the struggling winter howling by,
As down the edges of the distant sky
The hail-storm sweeps; and while he stops to strip
The stooping hedgebrier of its lingering hip,   10
He hears the wild geese gabble o'er his head;
Then, pleased with fancies in his musings bred,
He marks the figured forms in which they fly,
And pausing, follows with a wondering eye,
Likening their curious march, in curves or rows,   15
To every letter which his memory knows;
While, far above, the solitary crane
Swings lonely to unfrozen dykes again,
Cranking a jarring melancholy cry
Through the wild journey of the cheerless sky.   20

JOHN CLARE

308

I LOST THE LOVE OF HEAVEN

I lost the love of heaven above,
  I spurned the lust of earth below,
I felt the sweets of fancied love,
  And hell itself my only foe.

I lost earth's joys, but felt the glow   5
  Of heaven's flame abound in me,
Till loveliness and I did grow
  The bard of immortality.

I loved, but woman fell away;
  I hid me from her faded flame.   10
I snatched the sun's eternal ray
  And wrote till earth was but a name.

In every language upon earth,
  On every shore, o'er every sea,
I gave my name immortal birth   15
  And kept my spirit with the free.

JOHN CLARE

309

TO A WATERFOWL

Whither, midst falling dew,
While glow the heavens with the last steps of day,
Far, through their rosy depths, dost thou pursue
  Thy solitary way?

Vainly the fowler's eye   5
Might mark thy distant flight to do thee wrong,
As, darkly seen against the crimson sky,
  Thy figure floats along.

Seek'st thou the plashy brink
Of weedy lake, or marge of river wide,
Or where the rocking billows rise and sink   10
  On the chafed ocean side?

There is a Power whose care
Teaches thy way along that pathless coast,—
The desert and illimitable air,—   15
  Lone wandering, but not lost.

All day thy wings have fanned,
At that far height, the cold thin atmosphere;
Yet stoop not, weary, to the welcome land,
  Though the dark night is near.   20

And soon that toil shall end;
Soon shalt thou find a summer home and rest,
And scream among thy fellows; reeds shall bend,
  Soon, o'er thy sheltered nest.

Thou'rt gone, the abyss of heaven   25
Hath swallowed up thy form; yet on my heart
Deeply hath sunk the lesson thou hast given,
  And shall not soon depart.

He who, from zone to zone,
Guides through the boundless sky thy certain flight,   30
In the long way that I must tread alone,
  Will lead my steps aright.

                              W. C. BRYANT

310

from NEPENTHE

O blest unfabled Incense Tree,
That burns in glorious Araby,
With red scent chalicing the air,
Till earth-life grow Elysian there!

Half buried to her flaming breast   5
In this bright tree, she makes her nest,
Hundred-sunned Phœnix! when she must
Crumble at length to hoary dust!

Her gorgeous death-bed! her rich pyre
Burnt up with aromatic fire!   10
Her urn, sight high from spoiler men!
Her birthplace when self-born again!

The mountainless green wilds among,
Here ends she her unechoing song!
With amber tears and odorous sighs   15
Mourned by the desert where she dies! ...

O, fast her amber blood doth flow
   From the heart-wounded Incense Tree,
Fast as earth's deep-embosomed woe
   In silent rivulets to the sea!   20

Beauty may weep her fair first-born,
   Perchance in as resplendent tears,
Such golden dewdrops bow the corn
   When the stern sickleman appears.

But oh! such perfume to a bower   25
   Never allured sweet-seeking bee,
As to sip fast that nectarous shower
   A thirstier minstrel drew in me!

                                  GEORGE DARLEY

                    311

                    SONG

Sweet in her green dell the flower of beauty slumbers,
   Lull'd by the faint breezes sighing through her hair;
Sleeps she and hears not the melancholy numbers
   Breathed to my sad lute 'mid the lonely air.

Down from the high cliffs the rivulet is teeming   5
   To wind round the willow banks that lure him from above:
O that in tears, from my rocky prison streaming,
   I too could glide to the bower of my love!

Ah! where the woodbines with sleepy arms have wound her,
   Opes she her eyelids at the dream of my lay,   10
Listening, like the dove, while the fountains echo round her,
   To her lost mate's call in the forests far away.

Come then, my bird! For the peace thou ever bearest,
   Still Heaven's messenger of comfort to me—
Come—this fond bosom, O faithfullest and fairest,   15
   Bleeds with its death-wound, its wound of love for thee!

                                  GEORGE DARLEY

312

THE WOODLANDS

O spread ageän leaves an' flow'rs,
 Lwonesome woodlands! zunny woodlands
Here underneath the dewy show'rs
 O' warm-air'd spring-time, zunny woodlands!
As when, in drong or open ground,   5
Wi' happy bwoyish heart I vound
The twitt'rèn birds a-buildèn round
 Your high-bough'd hedges, zunny woodlands!

You gie'd me life, you gie'd me jaÿ,
 Lwonesome woodlands! zunny woodlands   10
You gie'd me health, as in my plaÿ
 I rambled through ye, zunny woodlands!
You gie'd me freedom, vor to rove
In airy meäd or sheädy grove;
You gie'd me smilèn Fannèy's love,   15
 The best ov all o't zunny woodlands!

My vu'st shill skylark whiver'd high,
 Lwonesome woodlands! zunny woodlands!
To zing below your deep-blue sky
 An' white spring-clouds, O zunny woodlands!   20
An' boughs o' trees that woonce stood here,
Wer glossy green the happy year
That gie'd me woone I lov'd so dear,
 An' now ha' lost, O zunny woodlands!

O let me rove ageän unspied,   25
 Lwonesome woodlands! zunny woodlands!
Along your green-bough'd hedges' zide,
 As then I rambled, zunny woodlands!
An' where the missèn trees woonce stood,
Or tongues woonce rung among the wood,   30
My memory shall meäke em good,
 Though you've a-lost em, zunny woodlands!

          WILLIAM BARNES

313

MAY

Come out o' door, 'tis Spring! 'tis Maÿ
The trees be green, the vields be gaÿ;
The weather's warm, the winter blast,
Wi' all his traïn o' clouds, is past;
The zun do rise while vo'k do sleep,   5
To teäke a higher daily zweep,
Wi' cloudless feäce a-flingèn down
His sparklèn light upon the groun'.

The aïr's a-streamèn soft,—come drow
The windor open; let it blow
In drough the house, where vire, an' door   10
A-shut, kept out the cwold avore.
Come, let the vew dull embers die,
An' come below the open sky;
An' wear your best, vor fear the groun'   15
In colours gaÿ mid sheäme your gown:
An' goo an' rig wi' me a mile
Or two up over geäte an' stile,
Drough zunny parrocks that do leäd,
Wi' crooked hedges, to the meäd,   20
Where elems high, in steätely ranks,
Do rise vrom yoller cowslip-banks,
An' birds do twitter vrom the spraÿ
O' bushes deck'd wi' snow-white maÿ;
An' gil' cups, wi' the deäisy bed,   25
Be under ev'ry step you tread.

We'll wind up roun' the hill, an' look
All down the thickly-timber'd nòok,
Out where the squier's house do show
His grey-wall'd peaks up drough the row   30
O' sheädy elems, where the rook
Do build her nest; an' where the brook
Do creep along the meäds, an' lie
To catch the brightness o' the sky;
An' cows, in water to their knees,   35
Do stan' a-whiskèn off the vlees.

Mother o' blossoms, and ov all
That's feäir a-vield vrom Spring till Fall,
The gookoo over white-weäv'd seas
Do come to zing in thy green trees,   40
An' buttervlees, in giddy flight,
Do gleäm the mwost by thy gaÿ light.
Oh! when, at last, my fleshly eyes
Shall shut upon the vields an' skies,
Mid zummer's zunny days be gone,   45
An' winter's clouds be comèn on:
Nor mid I draw upon the e'th,
O' thy sweet aïr my leätest breath;
Alassen I mid want to staÿ
Behine' for thee, O flow'ry Maÿ!   50

WILLIAM BARNES

314

THE CLOTE

O zummer clote! when the brook's a-slidèn
    So slow an' smooth down his zedgy bed,
Upon thy broad leaves so seäfe a-ridèn
    The water's top wi' thy yoller head.
        By black rin'd allers,
        An' weedy shallers   5
Thee then dost float, goolden zummer clote!

The grey-bough'd withy's a-leänèn lowly
    Above the water thy leaves do hide;
The bendèn bulrush, a-swaÿèn slowly,   10
    Do skirt in zummer thy river's zide;
        An' perch in shoals, O,
        Do vill the holes, O,
Where thee dost float, goolden zummer clote!

Oh, when thy brook-drinkèn flow'r 's a-blowèn,   15
    The burnèn zummer's a-zettèn in;
The time o' greenness, the time o' mowèn,
    When in the haÿ-vield, wi' zunburnt skin,
        The vo'k do drink, O,
        Upon the brink, O,   20
Where thee dost float, goolden zummer clote!

Wi' eārms a-spreadèn, an' cheäks a-blowèn,
  How proud wer I when I vu'st could zwim
Athirt the deep pleäce where thou bist growèn,
  Wi' thy long more vrom the bottom dim;   25
    While cows, knee-high, O,
      In brook, wer nigh, O,
Where thee dost float, goolden zummer clote!

Ov all the brooks drough the meäds a-windèn,
  Ov all the meäds by a river's brim,   30
There's nwone so feäir o' my own heart's vindèn,
  As where the maïdens do zee thee swim,
    An' stan' to teäke, O,
      Wi' long-stemm'd reäke, O,
Thy flow'r afloat, goolden zummer clote!   35

WILLIAM BARNES

315

THE WIFE A-LOST

Since I noo mwore do zee your feäce,
  Up steäirs or down below,
I'll zit me in the lwonesome pleäce,
  Where flat-bough'd beech do grow:
Below the beeches' bough, my love,   5
  Where you did never come,
An' I don't look to meet ye now,
  As I do look at hwome.

Since you noo mwore be at my zide,
  In walks in zummer het,   10
I'll goo alwone where mist do ride,
  Drough trees a-drippèn wet:
Below the raïn-wet bough, my love,
  Where you did never come,
An' I don't grieve to miss ye now,   15
  As I do grieve at home.

Since now bezide my dinner-bwoard
  Your vaïce do never sound,
I'll eat the bit I can avword,
  A-vield upon the ground;   20

Below the darksome bough, my love,
  Where you did never dine,
An' I don't grieve to miss ye now,
  As I at hwome do pine.

Since I do miss your vaïce an' feäce   25
  In praÿer at eventide,
I'll praÿ wi' woone sad vaïce vor greäce
  To goo where you do bide;
Above the tree an' bough, my love,
  Where you be gone avore,   30
An' be a-waïtèn vor me now,
  To come vor evermwore.

WILLIAM BARNES

316

SIBYLLA'S DIRGE

We do lie beneath the grass
  In the moonlight, in the shade
Of the yew-tree. They that pass
  Hear us not. We are afraid
    They would envy our delight,   5
    In our graves by glow-worm night.
Come follow us, and smile as we;
  We sail to the rock in the ancient waves,
Where the snow falls by thousands into the sea,
  And the drowned and the shipwrecked have happy graves.

THOMAS LOVELL BEDDOES

317

WOLFRAM'S SONG

Old Adam, the carrion crow,
  The old crow of Cairo;
He sat in the shower, and let it flow
  Under his tail and over his crest;
    And through every feather   5
    Leaked the wet weather;
And the bough swung under his nest;
  For his beak it was heavy with marrow.

Is that the wind dying? O no;
It's only two devils, that blow   10
Through a murderer's bones, to and fro,
  In the ghosts' moonshine.

Ho! Eve, my grey carrion wife,
  When we have supped on kings' marrow,
Where shall we drink and make merry our life?   15
  Our nest it is queen Cleopatra's scull,
    'Tis cloven and cracked,
    And battered and hacked,
  But with tears of blue eyes it is full:
Let us drink then, my raven of Cairo.   20
  Is that the wind dying? O no;
  It's only two devils, that blow
    Through a murderer's bones, to and fro,
      In the ghosts' moonshine.

                      THOMAS LOVELL BEDDOES

318

How many times do I love thee, dear?
  Tell me how many thoughts there be
    In the atmosphere
    Of a new-fall'n year,
Whose white and sable hours appear   5
  The latest flake of Eternity:
So many times do I love thee, dear.

How many times do I love again?
  Tell me how many beads there are
    In a silver chain
    Of evening rain,   10
Unravelled from the tumbling main
  And threading the eye of a yellow star:
So many times do I love again.

                      THOMAS LOVELL BEDDOES

319

SONG FROM THE SHIP

To sea, to sea! the calm is o'er;
 The wanton water leaps in sport,
And rattles down the pebbly shore;
 The dolphin wheels, the sea-cows snort.
And unseen Mermaids' pearly song   5
Comes bubbling up, the weeds among.
 Fling broad the sail, dip deep the oar:
 To sea, to sea! the calm is o'er.

To sea, to sea! our wide-winged bark
 Shall billowy cleave its sunny way,   10
And with its shadow, fleet and dark,
 Break the caved Tritons' azure ray,
Like mighty eagle soaring light
O'er antelopes on Alpine height.
 The anchor heaves, the ship swings free, 15
 The sails swell full. To sea, to sea!

THOMAS LOVELL BEDDOES

320

BRAHMA

If the red slayer think he slays,
 Or if the slain think he is slain,
They know not well the subtle ways
 I keep, and pass, and turn again.

Far or forgot to me is near;   5
 Shadow and sunlight are the same;
The vanished gods to me appear;
 And one to me are shame and fame.

They reckon ill who leave me out;
 When me they fly, I am the wings; 10
I am the doubter and the doubt,
 And I the hymn the Brahmin sings.

The strong gods pine for my abode,
    And pine in vain the sacred Seven;
But thou, meek lover of the good!   15
    Find me, and turn thy back on heaven.

RALPH WALDO EMERSON

321

THE SNOW-STORM

Announced by all the trumpets of the sky,
Arrives the snow, and, driving o'er the fields,
Seems nowhere to alight: the whited air
Hides hills and woods, the river, and the heaven,
And veils the farm-house at the garden's end.   5
The sled and traveller stopped, the courier's feet
Delayed, all friends shut out, the housemates sit
Around the radiant fireplace, enclosed
In a tumultuous privacy of storm.

    Come see the north wind's masonry.   10
Out of an unseen quarry evermore
Furnished with tile, the fierce artificer
Curves his white bastions with projected roof
Round every windward stake, or tree, or door.
Speeding, the myriad-handed, his wild work   15
So fanciful, so savage, nought cares he
For number or proportion. Mockingly,
On coop or kennel he hangs Parian wreaths;
A swan-like form invests the hidden thorn;
Fills up the farmer's lane from wall to wall,   20
Maugre the farmer's sighs; and at the gate
A tapering turret overtops the work.
And when his hours are numbered, and the world
Is all his own, retiring, as he were not,
Leaves, when the sun appears, astonished Art   25
To mimic in slow structures, stone by stone,
Built in an age, the mad wind's night-work,
The frolic architecture of the snow

RALPH WALDO EMERSON

322

GRIEF

I TELL you, hopeless grief is passionless;
That only men incredulous of despair,
  Half-taught in anguish, through the midnight air
Beat upward to God's throne in loud access
Of shrieking and reproach. Full desertness   5
  In souls as countries lieth silent-bare
  Under the blanching, vertical eye-glare
Of the absolute Heavens. Deep-hearted man, express
Grief for thy Dead in silence like to Death—
  Most like a monumental statue set   10
In everlasting watch and moveless woe
Till itself crumble to the dust beneath.
  Touch it; the marble eyelids are not wet:
If it could weep, it could arise and go.

                        ELIZABETH BARRETT BROWNING

323

I thought once how Theocritus had sung
Of the sweet years, the dear and wish'd-for years,
  Who each one in a gracious hand appears
To bear a gift for mortals old or young:
And, as I mused it in his antique tongue,   5
  I saw in gradual vision through my tears
  The sweet, sad years, the melancholy years—
Those of my own life, who by turns had flung
A shadow across me. Straightway I was 'ware,
  So weeping, how a mystic Shape did move   10
Behind me, and drew me backward by the hair;
  And a voice said in mastery, while I strove,
' Guess now who holds thee? '—' Death,' I said. But there
  The silver answer rang—' Not Death, but Love.'

                        ELIZABETH BARRETT BROWNING

324

MY LOST YOUTH

Often I think of the beautiful town
 That is seated by the sea;
Often in thought go up and down
The pleasant streets of that dear old town,
  And my youth comes back to me.   5
   And a verse of a Lapland song
   Is haunting my memory still:
   ' A boy's will is the wind's will,
And the thoughts of youth are long, long thoughts.'

I can see the shadowy lines of its trees,   10
 And catch, in sudden gleams,
The sheen of the far-surrounding seas,
And islands that were the Hesperides
  Of all my boyish dreams.
   And the burden of that old song,   15
   It murmurs and whispers still:
   ' A boy's will is the wind's will,
And the thoughts of youth are long, long thoughts.'

I remember the black wharves and the slips,
 And the sea-tides tossing free;   20
And Spanish sailors with bearded lips,
And the beauty and mystery of the ships,
  And the magic of the sea.
   And the voice of that wayward song
   Is singing and saying still: 25
   ' A boy's will is the wind's will,
And the thoughts of youth are long, long thoughts.'

I remember the bulwarks by the shore,
 And the fort upon the hill;
The sunrise gun, with its hollow roar,
The drum-beat repeated o'er and o'er,   30
  And the bugle wild and shrill.
   And the music of that old song
   Throbs in my memory still:
   ' A boy's will is the wind's will,
And the thoughts of youth are long, long thoughts.'   35

I remember the sea-fight far away,
    How it thundered o'er the tide!
And the dead captains, as they lay
In their graves, o'erlooking the tranquil bay   40
    Where they in battle died.
        And the sound of that mournful song
        Goes through me with a thrill:
        ' A boy's will is the wind's will,
And the thoughts of youth are long, long thoughts.'   45

I can see the breezy dome of groves,
    The shadows of Deering's Woods;
And the friendships old and the early loves
Come back with a Sabbath sound, as of doves
    In quiet neighbourhoods.   50
        And the verse of that sweet old song,
        It flutters and murmurs still:
        ' A boy's will is the wind's will,
And the thoughts of youth are long, long thoughts.'

I remember the gleams and glooms that dart   55
    Across the school-boy's brain;
The song and the silence in the heart,
That in part are prophecies, and in part
    Are longings wild and vain.
        And the voice of that fitful song   60
        Sings on, and is never still:
        ' A boy's will is the wind's will,
And the thoughts of youth are long, long thoughts.'

There are things of which I may not speak;
    There are dreams that cannot die;   65
There are thoughts that make the strong heart weak,
And bring a pallor into the cheek,
    And a mist before the eye.
        And the words of that fatal song
        Come over me like a chill: 70
        ' A boy's will is the wind's will,
And the thoughts of youth are long, long thoughts.'

Strange to me now are the forms I meet
    When I visit the dear old town;
But the native air is pure and sweet,   75
And the trees that o'ershadow each well-known street,
    As they balance up and down,

Are singing the beautiful song,
Are sighing and whispering still:
   ' A boy's will is the wind's will,
And the thoughts of youth are long, long thoughts.'   80

And Deering's Woods are fresh and fair,
   And with joy that is almost pain
My heart goes back to wander there,
And among the dreams of the days that were,   85
   I find my lost youth again.
     And the strange and beautiful song,
     The groves are repeating it still:
   ' A boy's will is the wind's will,
And the thoughts of youth are long, long thoughts.'   90

H. W. LONGFELLOW

325

from THE RUBÀIYÀT OF OMAR KHAYYÀM

Awake! for Morning in the Bowl of Night
Has flung the Stone that puts the Stars to Flight:
   And Lo! the Hunter of the East has caught
The Sultán's Turret in a Noose of Light.

Dreaming when Dawn's Left Hand was in the Sky,   5
I heard a Voice within the Tavern cry,
   ' Awake, my Little ones, and fill the Cup
Before Life's Liquor in its Cup be dry.'

And as the Cock crew, those who stood before
The Tavern shouted—' Open then the Door!   10
   You know how little while we have to stay,
And, once departed, may return no more.'

Now the New Year reviving old Desires,
The thoughtful Soul to Solitude retires,
   Where the WHITE HAND OF MOSES on the Bough   15
Puts out, and Jesus from the Ground suspires. . . .

     •   •   •   •   •   •   •

Think, in this batter'd Caravanserai
Whose Doorways are alternate Night and Day,
　　How Sultán after Sultán with his Pomp
Abode his Hour or two, and went his way.　　　　　20

They say the Lion and the Lizard keep
The Courts where Jamshýd gloried and drank deep:
　　And Bahrám, that great Hunter—the Wild Ass
Stamps o'er his Head, and he lies fast asleep.

I sometimes think that never blows so red　　　　　25
The Rose as where some buried Cæsar bled;
　　That every Hyacinth the Garden wears
Dropt in its Lap from some once lovely Head.

And this delightful Herb whose tender Green
Fledges the River's Lip on which we lean—　　　　　30
　　Ah, lean upon it lightly! for who knows
From what once Lovely Lip it springs unseen!

　　　　　.　　.　　.　　.　　.　　.

Alas, that Spring should vanish with the Rose!
That Youth's sweet-scented Manuscript should close!
　　The Nightingale that in the Branches sang,　　　　35
Ah, whence, and whither flown again, who knows!

Ah, Love! could thou and I with Fate conspire
To grasp this sorry Scheme of Things entire,
　　Would not we shatter it to bits—and then
Re-mould it nearer to the Heart's Desire!　　　　　40

Ah, Moon of my Delight who know'st no wane,
The Moon of Heaven is rising once again:
　　How oft hereafter rising shall she look
Through this same Garden after me—in vain!

And when Thyself with shining Foot shall pass　　　45
Among the Guests Star-scatter'd on the Grass,
　　And in thy joyous Errand reach the Spot
Where I made one—turn down an empty Glass!
                                        EDWARD FITZGERALD

326

TO HELEN

Helen, thy beauty is to me
　　Like those Nicéan barks of yore,
That gently, o'er a perfumed sea,
　　The weary, way-worn wanderer bore
　　　To his own native shore.　　　　　　　　5

On desperate seas long wont to roam,
　　Thy hyacinth hair, thy classic face,
Thy Naiad airs have brought me home
　　To the glory that was Greece
And the grandeur that was Rome.　　　　　10

Lo! in yon brilliant window-niche
　　How statue-like I see thee stand,
　　The agate lamp within thy hand!
Ah, Psyche, from the regions which
　　Are Holy Land!　　　　　　　　　　15

　　　　　　　　　　EDGAR ALLAN POE

327

TO ONE IN PARADISE

Thou wast that all to me, love,
　　For which my soul did pine—
A green isle in the sea, love,
　　A fountain and a shrine,
All wreathed with fairy fruits and flowers,　　5
　　And all the flowers were mine.

Ah, dream too bright to last!
　　Ah, starry Hope! that didst arise
But to be overcast!
　　A voice from out the Future cries,　　　　10
'On! on!'—but o'er the Past
　　(Dim gulf!) my spirit hovering lies
Mute, motionless, aghast!

For, alas! alas! with me
　　The light of Life is o'er!　　　　　　15

No more—no more—no more—
  (Such language holds the solemn sea
To the sands upon the shore)
  Shall bloom the thunder-blasted tree,
Or the stricken eagle soar!   20

And all my days are trances,
  And all my nightly dreams
Are where thy grey eye glances,
  And where thy footstep gleams—
In what ethereal dances,   25
  By what eternal streams.

EDGAR ALLAN POE

328

THE CITY IN THE SEA

Lo! Death has reared himself a throne
In a strange city lying alone
Far down within the dim West,
Where the good and the bad and the worst and the best
Have gone to their eternal rest.   5
There shrines and palaces and towers
(Time-eaten towers that tremble not!)
Resemble nothing that is ours.
Around, by lifting winds forgot,
Resignedly beneath the sky   10
The melancholy waters lie.

No rays from the holy heaven come down
On the long night-time of that town;
But light from out the lurid sea
Streams up the turrets silently—   15
Gleams up the pinnacles far and free—
Up domes—up spires—up kingly halls—

Up fanes—up Babylon-like walls—
Up shadowy long-forgotten bowers
Of sculptured ivy and stone flowers—   20
Up many and many a marvellous shrine
Whose wreathéd friezes intertwine
The viol, the violet, and the vine.

Resignedly beneath the sky
The melancholy waters lie.
So blend the turrets and shadows there   25
That all seem pendulous in air,
While from a proud tower in the town
Death looks gigantically down.
There open fanes and gaping graves   30
Yawn level with the luminous waves;
But not the riches there that lie
In each idol's diamond eye—
Not the gaily-jewelled dead
Tempt the waters from their bed;   35
For no ripples curl, alas!
Along that wilderness of glass—
No swellings tell that winds may be
Upon some far-off happier sea—
No heavings hint that winds have been   40
On seas less hideously serene.

But lo, a stir is in the air!
The wave—there is a movement there!
As if the towers had thrust aside,
In slightly sinking, the dull tide—   45
As if their tops had feebly given
A void within the filmy Heaven.
The waves have now a redder glow—
The hours are breathing faint and low—
And when, amid no earthly moans,   50
Down, down that town shall settle hence,
Hell, rising from a thousand thrones,
Shall do it reverence.

EDGAR ALLAN POE

329

THE KRAKEN

Below the thunders of the upper deep;
Far far beneath in the abysmal sea,
His ancient, dreamless, uninvaded sleep
The Kraken sleepeth: faintest sunlights flee
About his shadowy sides: above him swell   5
Huge sponges of millennial growth and height;
And far away into the sickly light,

From many a wondrous grot and secret cell
Unnumber'd and enormous polypi
Winnow with giant fins the slumbering green.   10
There hath he lain for ages and will lie
Battening upon huge seaworms in his sleep,
Until the latter fire shall heat the deep;
Then once by men and angels to be seen,
In roaring he shall rise and on the surface die.   15

ALFRED TENNYSON

330

THE EAGLE

He clasps the crag with crooked hands;
Close to the sun in lonely lands,
Ring'd with the azure world, he stands.

The wrinkled sea beneath him crawls;
He watches from his mountain walls,   5
And like a thunderbolt he falls.

ALFRED TENNYSON

331

Now sleeps the crimson petal, now the white;
Nor waves the cypress in the palace walk;
Nor winks the gold fin in the porphyry font:
The fire-fly wakens: waken thou with me.

Now droops the milkwhite peacock like a ghost,   5
And like a ghost she glimmers on to me.

Now lies the earth all Danaë to the stars,
And all thy heart lies open unto me.

Now slides the silent meteor on, and leaves
A shining furrow, as thy thoughts in me.   10

Now folds the lily all her sweetness up,
And slips into the bosom of the lake:
So fold thyself, my dearest, thou, and slip
Into my bosom and be lost in me.

ALFRED TENNYSON

332

The splendour falls on castle walls
    And snowy summits old in story:
The long light shakes across the lakes,
    And the wild cataract leaps in glory.
Blow, bugle, blow, set the wild echoes flying,   5
Blow, bugle; answer, echoes, dying, dying, dying.

O hark, O hark! how thin and clear,
    And thinner, clearer, farther going!
O sweet and far from cliff and scar
    The horns of Elfland faintly blowing!   10
Blow, let us hear the purple glens replying:
Blow, bugle; answer, echoes, dying, dying, dying.

O love, they die in yon rich sky,
    They faint on hill or field or river:
Our echoes roll from soul to soul,   15
    And grow for ever and for ever.
Blow, bugle, blow, set the wild echoes flying,
And answer, echoes, answer, dying, dying, dying.

                      ALFRED TENNYSON

333

TITHONUS

The woods decay, the woods decay and fall,
The vapours weep their burthen to the ground,
Man comes and tills the field and lies beneath,
And after many a summer dies the swan.
Me only cruel immortality   5
Consumes: I wither slowly in thine arms,
Here at the quiet limit of the world,
A white-hair'd shadow roaming like a dream
The ever silent spaces of the East,
Far-folded mists, and gleaming halls of morn.   10

Alas! for this grey shadow, once a man—
So glorious in his beauty and thy choice,
Who madest him thy chosen, that he seem'd
To his great heart none other than a God!

I ask'd thee, ' Give me immortality.'   **15**
Then didst thou grant mine asking with a smile,
Like wealthy men who care not how they give.
But thy strong Hours indignant work'd their wills,
And beat me down and marr'd and wasted me,
And tho' they could not end me, left me maim'd   **20**
To dwell in presence of immortal youth,
Immortal age beside immortal youth,
And all I was, in ashes. Can thy love,
Thy beauty, make amends, tho' even now,
Close over us, the silver star, thy guide,   **25**
Shines in those tremulous eyes that fill with tears
To hear me? Let me go: take back thy gift:
Why should a man desire in any way
To vary from the kindly race of men,
Or pass beyond the goal of ordinance   **30**
Where all should pause, as is most meet for all?

A soft air fans the cloud apart; there comes
A glimpse of that dark world where I was born.
Once more the old mysterious glimmer steals
From thy pure brows, and from thy shoulders pure,   **35**
And bosom beating with a heart renew'd.
Thy cheek begins to redden thro' the gloom,
Thy sweet eyes brighten slowly close to mine,
Ere yet they blind the stars, and the wild team
Which love thee, yearning for thy yoke, arise,   **40**
And shake the darkness from their loosen'd manes,
And beat the twilight into flakes of fire.

Lo! ever thus thou growest beautiful
In silence, then before thine answer given
Departest, and thy tears are on my cheek.   **45**
Why wilt thou ever scare me with thy tears,
And make me tremble lest a saying learnt,
In days far-off, on that dark earth, be true?
' The Gods themselves cannot recall their gifts.'

Ay me! ay me! with what another heart   **50**
In days far-off, and with what other eyes
I used to watch—if I be he that watch'd—
The lucid outline forming round thee; saw
The dim curls kindle into sunny rings;
Changed with thy mystic change, and felt my blood   **55**
Glow with the glow that slowly crimson'd all

Thy presence and thy portals, while I lay,
Mouth, forehead, eyelids, growing dewy-warm
With kisses balmier than half-opening buds
Of April, and could hear the lips that kiss'd   60
Whispering I knew not what of wild and sweet,
Like that strange song I heard Apollo sing,
While Ilion like a mist rose into towers.

    Yet hold me not for ever in thine East:
How can my nature longer mix with thine?   65
Coldly thy rosy shadows bathe me, cold
Are all thy lights, and cold my wrinkled feet
Upon thy glimmering thresholds, when the steam
Floats up from those dim fields about the homes
Of happy men that have the power to die,   70
And grassy barrows of the happier dead.
Release me, and restore me to the ground;
Thou seëst all things, thou wilt see my grave:
Thou wilt renew thy beauty morn by morn;
I earth in earth forget these empty courts,   75
And thee returning on thy silver wheels.

                     ALFRED TENNYSON

334

from IN MEMORIAM

II

Old Yew, which graspest at the stones
    That name the under-lying dead,
    Thy fibres net the dreamless head,
Thy roots are wrapt about the bones.

The seasons bring the flower again,   5
    And bring the firstling to the flock;
    And in the dusk of thee, the clock
Beats out the little lives of men.

O not for thee the glow, the bloom,
    Who changest not in any gale,   10
    Nor branding summer suns avail
To touch thy thousand years of gloom:

And gazing on thee, sullen tree,
    Sick for thy stubborn hardihood,
    I seem to fail from out my blood 15
And grow incorporate into thee.

XI

Calm is the morn without a sound,
    Calm as to suit a calmer grief,
    And only thro' the faded leaf
The chestnut pattering to the ground:

Calm and deep peace on this high wold, 5
    And on these dews that drench the furze,
    And all the silvery gossamers
That twinkle into green and gold:

Calm and still light on yon great plain
    That sweeps with all its autumn bowers, 10
    And crowded farms and lessening towers,
To mingle with the bounding main:

Calm and deep peace in this wide air,
    These leaves that redden to the fall;
    And in my heart, if calm at all, 15
If any calm, a calm despair:

Calm on the seas, and silver sleep,
    And waves that sway themselves in rest,
    And dead calm in that noble breast
Which heaves but with the heaving deep. 20

XV

To-night the winds begin to rise
    And roar from yonder dropping day:
    The last red leaf is whirl'd away,
The rooks are blown about the skies;

The forest crack'd, the waters curl'd, 5
    The cattle huddled on the lea;
    And wildly dash'd on tower and tree
The sunbeam strikes along the world:

And but for fancies, which aver
    That all thy motions gently pass 10

Athwart a plane of molten glass,
I scarce could brook the strain and stir

That makes the barren branches loud;
    And but for fear it is not so,
    The wild unrest that lives in woe   15
Would dote and pore on yonder cloud

That rises upward always higher,
    And onward drags a labouring breast,
    And topples round the dreary west,
A looming bastion fringed with fire.   20

LXXII

Risest thou thus, dim dawn, again,
    And howlest, issuing out of night,
    With blasts that blow the poplar white
And lash with storm the streaming pane?

Day, when my crown'd estate begun   5
    To pine in that reverse of doom,
    Which sicken'd every living bloom,
And blurr'd the splendour of the sun;

Who usherest in the dolorous hour
    With thy quick tears that make the rose   10
    Pull sideways, and the daisy close
Her crimson fringes to the shower;

Who might'st have heaved a windless flame
    Up the deep East, or, whispering, play'd
    A chequer-work of beam and shade   15
Along the hills, yet look'd the same,

As wan, as chill, as wild as now;
    Day, mark'd as with some hideous crime,
    When the dark hand struck down thro' time,
And cancell'd nature's best: but thou,   20

Lift as thou may'st thy burthen'd brows
    Thro' clouds that drench the morning star,
    And whirl the ungarner'd sheaf afar,
And sow the sky with flying boughs,

And up thy vault with roaring sound 25
    Climb thy thick noon, disastrous day;
    Touch thy dull goal of joyless grey,
And hide thy shame beneath the ground.

CI

Unwatch'd, the garden bough shall sway,
    The tender blossom flutter down,
    Unloved, that beech will gather brown,
This maple burn itself away;

Unloved, the sun-flower, shining fair, 5
    Ray round with flames her disk of seed,
    And many a rose-carnation feed
With summer spice the humming air;

Unloved, by many a sandy bar,
    The brook shall babble down the plain, 10
    At noon or when the lesser wain
Is twisting round the polar star;

Uncared for, gird the windy grove,
    And flood the haunts of hern and crake;
    Or into silver arrows break 15
The sailing moon in creek and cove;

Till from the garden and the wild
    A fresh association blow,
    And year by year the landscape grow
Familiar to the stranger's child; 20

As year by year the labourer tills
    His wonted glebe, or lops the glades;
    And year by year our memory fades
From all the circle of the hills.

CXV

Now fades the last long streak of snow,
    Now burgeons every maze of quick
    About the flowering squares, and thick
By ashen roots the violets blow.

Now rings the woodland loud and long,   5
    The distance takes a lovelier hue,
    And drown'd in yonder living blue
The lark becomes a sightless song.

Now dance the lights on lawn and lea,
    The flocks are whiter down the vale,   10
    And milkier every milky sail
On winding stream or distant sea;

Where now the seamew pipes, or dives
    In yonder greening gleam, and fly
    The happy birds, that change their sky   15
To build and brood; that live their lives

From land to land; and in my breast
    Spring wakens too; and my regret
    Becomes an April violet,
And buds and blossoms like the rest.   20

ALFRED TENNYSON

335

from MAUD

I have led her home, my love, my only friend.
There is none like her, none.
And never yet so warmly ran my blood
And sweetly, on and on
Calming itself to the long-wish'd-for end,   5
Full to the banks, close on the promised good.

None like her, none.
Just now the dry-tongued laurels' pattering talk
Seem'd her light foot along the garden walk,
And shook my heart to think she comes once more;   10
But even then I heard her close the door,
The gates of Heaven are closed, and she is gone.

There is none like her, none.
Nor will be when our summers have deceased.
O, art thou sighing for Lebanon
In the long breeze that streams to thy delicious East,   15
Sighing for Lebanon,

Dark cedar, tho' thy limbs have here increased,
Upon a pastoral slope as fair,
And looking to the South, and fed   20
With honey'd rain and delicate air,
And haunted by the starry head
Of her whose gentle will has changed my fate,
And made my life a perfumed altar-flame;
And over whom thy darkness must have spread   25
With such delight as theirs of old, thy great
Forefathers of the thornless garden, there
Shadowing the snow-limb'd Eve from whom she came.

ALFRED TENNYSON

336

MEETING AT NIGHT

The grey sea and the long black land;
And the yellow half-moon large and low;
And the startled little waves that leap
In fiery ringlets from their sleep,
As I gain the cove with pushing prow,   5
And quench its speed i' the slushy sand.

Then a mile of warm sea-scented beach;
Three fields to cross till a farm appears;
A tap at the pane, the quick sharp scratch
And blue spurt of a lighted match,   10
And a voice less loud, thro' its joys and fears,
Than the two hearts beating each to each!

ROBERT BROWNING

337

TWO IN THE CAMPAGNA

I wonder do you feel to-day
   As I have felt since, hand in hand,
We sat down on the grass, to stray
   In spirit better through the land,
This morn of Rome and May?

For me, I touched a thought, I know,
  Has tantalized me many times,
(Like turns of thread the spiders throw
  Mocking across our path) for rhymes
To catch at and let go.   10

Help me to hold it! First it left
  The yellowing fennel, run to seed
There, branching from the brickwork's cleft,
  Some old tomb's ruin: yonder weed
Took up the floating weft,   15

Where one small orange cup amassed
  Five beetles,—blind and green they grope
Among the honey-meal: and last,
  Everywhere on the grassy slope
I traced it. Hold it fast!   20

The champaign with its endless fleece
  Of feathery grasses everywhere!
Silence and passion, joy and peace,
  An everlasting wash of air—
Rome's ghost since her decease.   25

Such life here, through such lengths of hours,
  Such miracles performed in play,
Such primal naked forms of flowers,
  Such letting nature have her way
While heaven looks from its towers!   30

How say you? Let us, O my dove,
  Let us be unashamed of soul,
As earth lies bare to heaven above!
  How is it under our control
To love or not to love?   35

I would that you were all to me,
  You that are just so much, no more.
Nor yours nor mine, nor slave nor free!
  Where does the fault lie? What the core
O' the wound, since wound must be?   40

I would I could adopt your will,
  See with your eyes, and set my heart

Beating by yours, and drink my fill
    At your soul's springs,—your part my part
In life, for good and ill.   45

No. I yearn upward, touch you close,
    Then stand away. I kiss your cheek,
Catch your soul's warmth,—I pluck the rose
    And love it more than tongue can speak—
Then the good minute goes.   50

Already how am I so far
    Out of that minute? Must I go
Still like the thistle-ball, no bar,
    Onward, whenever light winds blow,
Fixed by no friendly star?   55

Just when I seemed about to learn!
    Where is the thread now? Off again!
The old trick! Only I discern—
    Infinite passion, and the pain
Of finite hearts that yearn.   60

ROBERT BROWNING

338

THE LOST LEADER

Just for a handful of silver he left us,
    Just for a riband to stick in his coat—
Found the one gift of which fortune bereft us,
    Lost all the others she lets us devote;
They, with the gold to give, doled him out silver,   5
    So much was theirs who so little allowed:
How all our copper had gone for his service!
    Rags—were they purple, his heart had been proud!
We that had loved him so, followed him, honoured him,
    Lived in his mild and magnificent eye,   10
Learned his great language, caught his clear accents,
    Made him our pattern to live and to die!
Shakespeare was of us, Milton was for us,
    Burns, Shelley, were with us,—they watch from their graves!
He alone breaks from the van and the freemen,   15
    —He alone sinks to the rear and the slaves!

We shall march prospering,—not thro' his presence;
  Songs may inspirit us,—not from his lyre;
Deeds will be done,—while he boasts his quiescence,
  Still bidding crouch whom the rest bade aspire: 20
Blot out his name, then, record one lost soul more,
  One task more declined, one more footpath untrod,
One more devils'-triumph and sorrow for angels,
  One wrong more to man, one more insult to God!
Life's night begins: let him never come back to us!   25
  There would be doubt, hesitation and pain,
Forced praise on our part—the glimmer of twilight,
  Never glad confident morning again!
Best fight on well, for we taught him—strike gallantly,
  Menace our heart ere we master his own;   30
Then let him receive the new knowledge and wait us,
  Pardoned in heaven, the first by the throne!

                                             ROBERT BROWNING

339

THE FLOWER'S NAME

Here's the garden she walked across,
  Arm in my arm, such a short while since:
Hark, now I push its wicket, the moss
  Hinders the hinges and makes them wince!
She must have reached this shrub ere she turned,   5
  As back with that murmur the wicket swung;
For she laid the poor snail, my chance foot spurned,
  To feed and forget it the leaves among.

Down this side of the gravel-walk
  She went while her robe's edge brushed the box: 10
And here she paused in her gracious talk
  To point me a moth on the milk-white phlox.
Roses, ranged in valiant row,
  I will never think that she passed you by!
She loves you noble roses, I know;   15
  But yonder, see, where the rock-plants lie!

This flower she stopped at, finger on lip,
  Stooped over, in doubt, as settling its claim;
Till she gave me, with pride to make no slip,
  Its soft meandering Spanish name: 20

What a name! Was it love or praise?
   Speech half-asleep or song half-awake?
I must learn Spanish, one of these days,
   Only for that slow sweet name's sake.

Roses, if I live and do well,   25
   I may bring her, one of these days,
To fix you fast with as fine a spell,
   Fit you each with his Spanish phrase;
But do not detain me now; for she lingers
   There, like sunshine over the ground,   30
And ever I see her soft white fingers
   Searching after the bud she found.

Flower, you Spaniard, look that you grow not,
   Stay as you are and be loved for ever!
Bud, if I kiss you 'tis that you blow not: 35
   Mind, the shut pink mouth opens never!
For while it pouts, her fingers wrestle,
   Twinkling the audacious leaves between,
Till round they turn and down they nestle—
   Is not the dear mark still to be seen?   40

Where I find her not, beauties vanish;
   Whither I follow her, beauties flee;
Is there no method to tell her in Spanish
   June's twice June since she breathed it with me?
Come, bud, show me the least of her traces,   45
   Treasure my lady's lightest footfall!
—Ah, you may flout and turn up your faces—
   Roses, you are not so fair after all!

ROBERT BROWNING

340

A WOMAN'S LAST WORD

   Let's contend no more, Love,
      Strive nor weep:
   All be as before, Love,
      —Only sleep!

   What so wild as words are?   5
      I and thou
   In debate, as birds are,
      Hawk on bough!

See the creature stalking
 While we speak!
Hush and hide the talking,
 Cheek on cheek!

What so false as truth is,
 False to thee?
Where the serpent's tooth is
 Shun the tree—

Where the apple reddens
 Never pry—
Lest we lose our Edens,
 Eve and I.

Be a god and hold me
 With a charm!
Be a man and fold me
 With thine arm!

Teach me, only teach, Love!
 As I ought
I will speak thy speech, Love,
 Think thy thought—

Meet, if thou require it,
 Both demands,
Laying flesh and spirit
 In thy hands.

That shall be to-morrow
 Not to-night:
I must bury sorrow
 Out of sight:

—Must a little weep, Love,
 (Foolish me!)
And so fall asleep, Love,
 Loved by thee.

ROBERT BROWNING

341

THE PATRIOT

It was roses, roses, all the way,
    With myrtle mixed in my path like mad:
The house-roofs seemed to heave and sway,
    The church-spires flamed, such flags they had,
A year ago on this very day.   5

The air broke into a mist with bells,
    The old walls rocked with the crowd and cries.
Had I said, ' Good folk, mere noise repels—
    But give me your sun from yonder skies! '
They had answered, ' And afterward, what else? '   10

Alack, it was I who leaped at the sun
    To give it my loving friends to keep!
Nought man could do, have I left undone:
    And you see my harvest, what I reap
This very day, now a year is run.   15

There's nobody on the house-tops now—
    Just a palsied few at the windows set;
For the best of the sight is, all allow,
    At the Shambles' Gate—or, better yet,
By the very scaffold's foot, I trow.   20

I go in the rain, and, more than needs,
    A rope cuts both my wrists behind;
And I think, by the feel, my forehead bleeds,
    For they fling, whoever has a mind,
Stones at me for my year's misdeeds.   25

Thus I entered, and thus I go!
    In triumphs, people have dropped down dead.
' Paid by the world, what dost thou owe
    Me? '—God might question; now instead,
'Tis God shall repay: I am safer so.   30

                                        ROBERT BROWNING

342

CONFESSIONS

What is he buzzing in my ears?
   ' Now that I come to die,
Do I view the world as a vale of tears?'.
   Ah, reverend sir, not I!

What I viewed there once, what I view again   5
   Where the physic bottles stand
On the table's edge,—is a suburb lane,
   With a wall to my bedside hand.

That lane sloped, much as the bottles do,
   From a house you could descry
O'er the garden-wall: is the curtain blue   10
   Or green to a healthy eye?

To mine, it serves for the old June weather
   Blue above lane and wall;
And the farthest bottle labelled ' Ether'.   15
   Is the house o'ertopping all.

At a terrace, somewhere near the stopper,
   There watched for me, one June,
A girl: I know, sir, it's improper,
   My poor mind's out of tune.   20

Only, there was a way . . . you crept
   Close by the side, to dodge
Eyes in the house, two eyes except:
   They styled their house ' The Lodge.'

What right had a lounger up their lane?   25
   But, by creeping very close,
With the good wall's help,—their eyes might strain
   And stretch themselves to Oes,

Yet never catch her and me together,
   As she left the attic, there,
By the rim of the bottle labelled ' Ether,'   30
   And stole from stair to stair,

And stood by the rose-wreathed gate. Alas,
We loved, sir—used to meet:
How sad and bad and mad it was—
But then, how it was sweet!　　　　　　　　　35

ROBERT BROWNING

343

SONG

When I was young, I said to Sorrow,
' Come I will play with thee '—
He is near me now all day;
And at night returns to say,
' I will come again to-morrow,　　　　　　　5
I will come and stay with thee.'

Through the woods we walk together;
His soft footsteps rustle nigh me.
To shield an unregarded head,
He hath built a wintry shed;　　　　　　　10
And all night in rainy weather,
I hear his gentle breathings by me.

AUBREY DE VERE

344

A GIRL'S SONG

Unkind was he, the first who sang
The spring-tide shamed, the flower's decay!
What woman yet without a pang
Could hear of Beauty's fleeting May?
O Beauty! with me bide, and I　　　　　　　5
A maid will live, a maid will die.

Could I be always fair as now,
And hear, as now, the Poets sing
' The long-lashed eyes, the virgin brow,
The hand well worthy kiss and ring,'　　　　　10
Then, then some casual grace were all
That e'er from me on man should fall!

I sailed last night Ina's stream:
Warm 'mid the wave my fingers lay;
The cold-lipped Naiad in my dream　　　　　　15

Kissed them, and sighed, and slipped away—
Ah me! down life's descending tide
Best things, they say, the swiftliest glide.

AUBREY DE VERE

345

REMEMBRANCE

Cold in the earth and the deep snow piled above thee!
Far, far removed, cold in the dreary grave!
Have I forgot, my Only Love, to love thee,
Severed at last by Time's all-wearing wave?

Now, when alone, do my thoughts no longer hover   5
Over the mountains on Angora's shore;
Resting their wings where heath and fern-leaves cover
That noble heart for ever, ever more?

Cold in the earth, and fifteen wild Decembers
From those brown hills have melted into spring—   10
Faithful indeed is the spirit that remembers
After such years of change and suffering!

Sweet Love of youth, forgive if I forget thee
While the World's tide is bearing me along:
Sterner desires and darker hopes beset me,   15
Hopes which obscure but cannot do thee wrong.

No other Sun has lightened up my heaven;
No other Star has ever shone for me:
All my life's bliss from thy dear life was given—
All my life's bliss is in the grave with thee.   20

But when the days of golden dreams had perished
And even Despair was powerless to destroy,
Then did I learn how existence could be cherished,
Strengthened and fed without the aid of joy.

Then did I check the tears of useless passion,   25
Weaned my young soul from yearning after thine;
Sternly denied its burning wish to hasten
Down to that tomb already more than mine!

And even yet, I dare not let it languish,
Dare not indulge in Memory's rapturous pain: 30
Once drinking deep of that divinest anguish,
How could I seek the empty world again?

EMILY BRONTË

346

Shall Earth no more inspire thee,
Thou lonely dreamer now?
Since passion may not fire thee
Shall Nature cease to bow?

Thy mind is ever moving   5
In regions dark to thee;
Recall its useless roving—
Come back and dwell with me.

I know my mountain-breezes
Enchant and soothe thee still—   10
I know my sunshine pleases
Despite thy wayward will.

When day with evening blending
Sinks from the summer sky,
I've seen thy spirit bending   15
In fond idolatry.

I've watched thee every hour—
I know my mighty sway—
I know my magic power
To drive thy griefs away.   20

Few hearts to mortals given
On earth so wildly pine
Yet none would ask a Heaven
More like the Earth than thine.

Then let my winds caress thee—   25
Thy comrade let me be—
Since nought beside can bless thee
Return and dwell with me.

EMILY BRONTË

347

LOVE AND FRIENDSHIP

Love is like the wild rose-briar,
Friendship like the holly-tree—
The holly is dark when the rose-briar blooms
But which will bloom most constantly?

The wild rose-briar is sweet in spring,   5
Its summer blossoms scent the air;
Yet wait till winter comes again
And who will call the wild-briar fair?

Then scorn the silly rose-wreath now
And deck thee with the holly's sheen,   10
That when December blights thy brow
He still may leave thy garland green.

                                        EMILY BRONTË

348

THE VISIONARY

Silent is the House—all are laid asleep;
One, alone, looks out o'er the snow-wreaths deep;
Watching every cloud, dreading every breeze
That whirls the 'wildering drifts and bends the groaning trees.

Cheerful is the hearth, soft the matted floor;   5
Not one shivering gust creeps through pane or door;
The little lamp burns straight, its rays shoot strong and far:
I trim it well to be the Wanderer's guiding-star.

Frown my haughty sire; chide my angry dame,
Set your slaves to spy, threaten me with shame: 10
But neither sire nor dame, nor prying serf shall know
What angel nightly tracks that waste of winter snow.

What I love shall come like visitant of air,
Safe in secret power from lurking human snare;
Who loves me, no word of mine shall e'er betray,   15
Though for faith unstained my life must forfeit pay.

Burn, then, little lamp; glimmer straight and clear—
Hush! a rustling wing stirs, methinks, the air:
He for whom I wait, thus ever comes to me;
Strange Power! I trust thy might; trust thou my constancy. 20

EMILY BRONTË

349

from THE PRISONER

' He comes with western winds, with evening's wandering airs,
With that clear dusk of heaven that brings the thickest stars;
Winds take a pensive tone and stars a tender fire
And visions rise and change which kill me with desire—

' Desire for nothing known in my maturer years   5
When joy grew mad with awe at counting future tears;
When, if my spirit's sky was full of flashes warm,
I knew not whence they came, from sun or thunder-storm;

' But first a hush of peace, a soundless calm descends;
The struggle of distress and fierce impatience ends;   10
Mute music soothes my breast—unuttered harmony
That I could never dream till earth was lost to me.

' Then dawns the Invisible, the Unseen its truth reveals;
My outward sense is gone, my inward essence feels—
Its wings are almost free, its home, its harbour found;   15
Measuring the gulf it stoops and dares the final bound!

' Oh dreadful is the check—intense the agony
When the ear begins to hear and the eye begins to see;
When the pulse begins to throb, the brain to think again;
The soul to feel the flesh and the flesh to feel the chain!   20

' Yet I would lose no sting, would wish no torture less;
The more that anguish racks the earlier it will bless;
And robed in fires of Hell, or bright with heavenly shine
If it but herald Death, the vision is divine! '

EMILY BRONTË

350

Fall, leaves, fall; die, flowers, away;
Lengthen night and shorten day;
Every leaf speaks bliss to me
Fluttering from the autumn tree.
I shall smile when wreaths of snow   5
Blossom where the rose should grow;
I shall sing when night's decay
Ushers in a drearier day.

EMILY BRONTË

351

How often sit I, poring o'er
  My strange distorted youth,
Seeking in vain, in all my store,
  One feeling based on truth;
Amid the maze of petty life   5
  A clue whereby to move,
A spot whereon in toil and strife
  To dare to rest and love.
So constant as my heart would be,
  So fickle as it must,   10
'Twere well for others and for me
  'Twere dry as summer dust.
Excitements come, and act and speech
  Flow freely forth;—but no,
Nor they, nor aught beside can reach   15
  The buried world below.

A. H. CLOUGH

352

Where lies the land to which the ship would go?
Far, far ahead, is all her seamen know.
And where the land she travels from? Away,
Far, far behind, is all that they can say.

On sunny noons upon the deck's smooth face,   5
Linked arm in arm, how pleasant here to pace;
Or, o'er the stern reclining, watch below
The foaming wake far widening as we go.

On stormy nights when wild north-westers rave,
How proud a thing to fight with wind and wave!   10
The dripping sailor on the reeling mast
Exults to bear, and scorns to wish it past.

Where lies the land to which the ship would go
Far, far ahead, is all her seamen know.
And where the land she travels from? Away,   15
Far, far behind, is all that they can say.

                                    A. H. CLOUGH

353

Say not, the struggle nought availeth,
    The labour and the wounds are vain,
The enemy faints not, nor faileth,
    And as things have been they remain.

If hopes were dupes, fears may be liars;   5
    It may be, in yon smoke concealed,
Your comrades chase e'en now the fliers,
    And, but for you, possess the field.

For while the tired waves, vainly breaking,
    Seem here no painful inch to gain,   10
Far back, through creeks and inlets making,
    Comes silent, flooding in, the main.

And not by eastern windows only,
    When daylight comes, comes in the light,
In front, the sun climbs slow, how slowly,   15
    But westward, look, the land is bright.

                                    A. H. CLOUGH

354

from AMOURS DE VOYAGE

Yes, as I walk, I behold, in a luminous, large intuition,
That I can be and become anything that I meet with or look at:
I am the ox in the dray, the ass with the garden-stuff panniers;
I am the dog in the doorway, the kitten that plays in the window,
On sunny slab of the ruin the furtive and fugitive lizard,

Swallow above me that twitters, and fly that is buzzing about me;
Yea, and detect, as I go, by a faint, but a faithful assurance,
E'en from the stones of the street, as from rocks or trees of the
    forest,
Something of kindred, a common, though latent vitality, greets me;
And, to escape from our strivings, mistakings, misgrowths, and
    perversions,   10
Fain could demand to return to that perfect and primitive silence,
Fain be enfolded and fixed, as of old, in their rigid embraces.

And as I walk on my way, I behold them consorting and coupling;
Faithful it seemeth, and fond, very fond, very probably faithful,
All as I go on my way, with a pleasure sincere and unmingled. 15
  Life is beautiful, Eustace, entrancing, enchanting to look at;
As are the streets of a city we pace while the carriage is changing,
As a chamber filled-in with harmonious, exquisite pictures,
Even so beautiful Earth; and could we eliminate only
This vile hungering impulse, this demon within us of craving, 20
Life were beatitude, living a perfect divine satisfaction.

                                                    A. H. CLOUGH

                            355

                  THE SANDS OF DEE

    ' O Mary, go and call the cattle home,
            And call the cattle home,
            And call the cattle home
        Across the sands of Dee; '
    The western wind was wild and dank with foam,   5
        And all alone went she.

    The western tide crept up along the sand,
            And o'er and o'er the sand,
            And round and round the sand,
        As far as eye could see.   10
    The rolling mist came down and hid the land:
        And never home came she.

    ' Oh! is it weed, or fish, or floating hair—
            A tress of golden hair,
            A drownèd maiden's hair
        Above the nets at sea?   15
    Was never salmon yet that shone so fair
        Among the stakes on Dee.'

They rowed her in across the rolling foam,
    The cruel crawling foam,   20
    The cruel hungry foam,
  To her grave beside the sea:
But still the boatmen hear her call the cattle home
  Across the sands of Dee.

CHARLES KINGSLEY

356

THE RAVAGED VILLA

In shards the sylvan vases lie,
    Their links of dance undone,
And brambles wither by thy brim,
    Choked fountain of the sun!
The spider in the laurel spins,   5
    The weed exiles the flower;
And, flung to kiln, Apollo's bust
    Makes lime for Mammon's tower.

HERMAN MELVILLE

357

MISGIVINGS

When ocean-clouds over inland hills
  Sweep storming in late autumn brown,
And horror the sodden valley fills,
  And the spire falls crashing in the town,
I muse upon my country's ills—   5
The tempest bursting from the waste of Time
On the world's fairest hope linked with man's foulest crime.

Nature's dark side is heeded now—
  (Ah! optimist-cheer disheartened flown)—
A child may read the moody brow   10
  Of yon black mountain lone.
With shouts the torrents down the gorges go,
  And storms are formed behind the storm we feel:
The hemlock shakes in the rafter, the oak in the driving keel.

HERMAN MELVILLE

358

A REQUIEM

WHEN, after storms that woodlands rue,
  To valleys comes atoning dawn,
The robins blithe their orchard-sports renew;
  And meadow-larks, no more withdrawn,
Carolling fly in the languid blue;   5
The while, from many a hid recess,
Alert to partake the blessedness,
The pouring mites their airy dance pursue.
  So, after ocean's ghastly gales,
When laughing light of hoyden morning breaks,   10
      Every finny hider wakes—
From vaults profound swims up with glittering scales;
  Through the delightsome sea he sails,
With shoals of shining tiny things
Frolic on every wave that flings   15
  Against the prow its showery spray;
All creatures joying in the morn,
Save them forever from joyance torn,
  Whose bark was lost where now the dolphins play;
Save them that by the fabled shore,   20
  Down the pale stream are washed away,
Far to the reef of bones are borne;
  And never revisits them the light,
Nor sight of long-sought land and pilot more;
  Nor heed they now the lone bird's flight   25
Round the lone spar where mid-sea surges pour.

HERMAN MELVILLE

359

ETHIOPIA SALUTING THE COLOURS

Who are you dusky woman, so ancient hardly human,
With your woolly-white and turban'd head, and bare bony feet?
Why rising by the roadside here, do you the colours greet?

('Tis while our army lines Carolina's sands and pines,
Forth from thy hovel door thou Ethiopia com'st to me,   5
As under doughty Sherman I march toward the sea.)

Me master years a hundred since from my parents sunder'd,
A little child, they caught me as the savage beast is caught,
Then hither me across the sea the cruel slaver brought.

No further does she say, but lingering all the day,   10
Her high-borne turban'd head she wags, and rolls her darkling
    eye,
And courtesies to the regiments, the guidons moving by.

What is it fateful woman, so blear, hardly human?
Why wag your head with turban bound, yellow, red and green?
Are the things so strange and marvellous you see or have seen? 15

                                    WALT WHITMAN

360

1

When lilacs last in the dooryard bloom'd,
And the great star early droop'd in the western sky in the night,
I mourn'd, and yet shall mourn with ever-returning spring.

Ever-returning spring, trinity sure to me you bring,
Lilac blooming perennial and drooping star in the west,   5
And thought of him I love.

2

O powerful western fallen star!
O shades of night—O moody, tearful night!
O great star disappear'd—O the black murk that hides the star!
O cruel hands that hold me powerless—O helpless soul of me! 10
O harsh surrounding cloud that will not free my soul.

3

In the dooryard fronting an old farm-house near the white-wash'd
    palings,
Stands the lilac-bush tall-growing with heart-shaped leaves of rich
    green,
With many a pointed blossom rising delicate, with the perfume
    strong I love,
With every leaf a miracle—and from this bush in the door-yard, 15
With delicate-colour'd blossoms and heart-shaped leaves of rich
    green,
A sprig with its flower I break.

4

In the swamp in secluded recesses,
A shy and hidden bird is warbling a song.

Solitary the thrush,   20
The hermit withdrawn to himself, avoiding the settlements,
Sings by himself a song.

Song of the bleeding throat,
Death's outlet song of life, (for well dear brother I know,
If thou wast not granted to sing thou would'st surely die).   25

5

Over the breast of the spring, the land, amid cities,
Amid lanes and through old woods, where lately the violets
        peep'd from the ground, spotting the gray debris,
Amid the grass in the fields each side of the lanes, passing the
        endless grass,
Passing the yellow-spear'd wheat, every grain from its shroud in
        the dark-brown fields uprisen,
Passing the apple-tree blows of white and pink in the orchards, 30
Carrying a corpse to where it shall rest in the grave,
Night and day journeys a coffin.

6

Coffin that passes through lanes and streets,
Through day and night with the great cloud darkening the land,
With the pomp of the inloop'd flags with the cities draped in
        black,   35
With the show of the States themselves as of crêpe-veil'd women
        standing,
With processions long and winding and the flambeaus of the
        night,
With the countless torches lit, with the silent sea of faces and the
        unbared heads,
With the waiting depot, the arriving coffin, and the sombre faces,
With dirges through the night, with the thousand voices rising
        strong and solemn,   40
With all the mournful voices of the dirges pour'd around the
        coffin,
The dim-lit churches and the shuddering organs—where amid
        these you journey,
With the tolling tolling bells' perpetual clang,
Here, coffin that slowly passes,
I give you my sprig of lilac.   45

WALT WHITMAN

361

RECONCILIATION

Word over all, beautiful as the sky,
Beautiful that war and all its deeds of carnage must in time be
    utterly lost,
That the hands of the sisters Death and Night incessantly softly
    wash again, and ever again, this soil'd world;
For my enemy is dead, a man divine as myself is dead,
I look where he lies white-faced and still in the coffin—I draw
    near,   5
Bend down and touch lightly with my lips the white face in the
    coffin.

WALT WHITMAN

362

THE LAST INVOCATION

At the last, tenderly,
From the walls of the powerful fortress'd house,
From the clasp of the knitted locks, from the keep of the well-
    closed doors,
Let me be wafted.

Let me glide noiselessly forth;   5
With the key of softness unlock the locks—with a whisper,
Set ope the doors O soul.

Tenderly—be not impatient,
(Strong is your hold O mortal flesh,
Strong is your hold O love.)   10

WALT WHITMAN

363

THE HIGH TIDE ON THE COAST OF
LINCOLNSHIRE

The old mayor climbed the belfry tower,
    The ringers ran by two, by three;
' Pull, if ye never pulled before;

Good ringers, pull your best,' quoth he.
' Play uppe, play uppe, O Boston bells!   5
Ply all your changes, all your swells,
 Play uppe " The Brides of Enderby." '

Men say it was a stolen tyde—
 The Lord that sent it, He knows all;
But in myne ears doth still abide   10
 The message that the bells let fall:
And there was naught of strange, beside
The flight of mews and peewits pied
 By millions crouched on the old sea wall.

I sat and spun within the doore,   15
 My thread brake off, I raised myne eyes;
The level sun, like ruddy ore,
 Lay sinking in the barren skies;
And dark against day's golden death.
She moved where Lindis wandereth,   20
My sonne's faire wife, Elizabeth.

' Cusha! Cusha! Cusha! ' calling,
Ere the early dews were falling,
Farre away I heard her song,
' Cusha! Cusha! ' all along;   25
Where the ready Lindis floweth,
  Floweth, floweth,
From the meads where melick groweth
Faintly came her milking song.

' Cusha! Cusha! Cusha! ' calling,   30
' For the dews will soone be falling;
Leave your meadow grasses mellow,
  Mellow, mellow;
Quit your cowslips, cowslips yellow;
Come uppe Whitefoot, come uppe Lightfoot,   35
Quit the stalks of parsley hollow,
  Hollow, hollow;
Come uppe Jetty, rise and follow
 From the clovers lift your head;
Come uppe Whitefoot, come uppe Lightfoot,   40
Come uppe Jetty, rise and follow,
 Jetty, to the milking shed.'

If it be long, aye, long ago,
   When I beginne to think howe long,
Againe I hear the Lindis flow,   45
   Swift as an arrowe, sharp and strong;
And all the aire, it seemeth mee,
Bin full of floating bells (sayth shee),
That ring the tune of Enderby.

Alle fresh the level pasture lay,   50
   And not a shadowe mote be seene,
Save where full fyve good miles away
   The steeple towered from out the greene;
And lo! the great bell farre and wide
Was heard in all the country side   55
That Saturday at eventide.

The swanherds where their sedges are
   Moved on in sunset's golden breath,
The shepherde lads I heard afarre,
   And my sonne's wife, Elizabeth;   60
Till floating o'er the grassy sea
Came downe that kyndly message free,
The ' Brides of Mavis Enderby.'

Then some looked uppe into the sky,
   And all along where Lindis flows   65
To where the goodly vessels lie,
   And where the lordly steeple shows.
They sayde, ' And why should this thing be?
What danger lowers by land or sea?
They ring the tune of Enderby!   70

' For evil news from Mablethorpe,
   Of pyrate galleys warping down;
For shippes ashore beyond the scorpe,
   They have not spared to wake the towne:
But while the west bin red to see,   75
And storms be none, and pyrates flee,
Why ring " The Brides of Enderby "? '

I looked without, and lo! my sonne
   Came riding downe with might and main:
He raised a shout as he drew on,   80
   Till all the welkin rang again,

'Elizabeth! Elizabeth!'
(A sweeter woman ne'er drew breath
Than my sonne's wife, Elizabeth.)

'The olde sea wall (he cried) is downe,   85
   The rising tide comes on apace,
And boats adrift in yonder towne
   Go sailing uppe the market-place.'
He shook as one that looks on death:
'God save you, mother!' straight he saith;   90
'Where is my wife, Elizabeth?'

'Good sonne, where Lindis winds away,
   With her two bairns I marked her long;
And ere yon bells beganne to play
   Afar I heard her milking song.'   95
He looked across the grassy lea,
To right, to left, 'Ho Enderby!'
They rang 'The Brides of Enderby!'

With that he cried and beat his breast;
   For, lo! along the river's bed   100
A mighty eygre reared his crest,
   And uppe the Lindis raging sped.
It swept with thunderous noises loud;
Shaped like a curling snow-white cloud,
Or like a demon in a shroud.   105

And rearing Lindis backward pressed
   Shook all her trembling bankes amaine;
Then madly at the eygre's breast
   Flung uppe her weltering walls again.
Then bankes came downe with ruin and rout—   110
Then beaten foam flew round about—
Then all the mighty floods were out.

So farre, so fast the eygre drave,
   The heart had hardly time to beat,
Before a shallow seething wave   115
   Sobbed in the grasses at oure feet:
The feet had hardly time to flee
Before it brake against the knee,
And all the world was in the sea.

Upon the roofe we sate that night,   120
   The noise of bells went sweeping by:

I marked the lofty beacon light
   Stream from the church tower, red and high—
A lurid mark and dread to see;
And awesome bells they were to mee,   125
That in the dark rang ' Enderby.'

They rang the sailor lads to guide
   From roofe to roofe who fearless rowed;
And I—my sonne was at my side,
   And yet the ruddy beacon glowed: 130
And yet he moaned beneath his breath,
' O come in life, or come in death!
O lost! my love, Elizabeth.'

And didst thou visit him no more?
   Thou didst, thou didst, my daughter deare;   135
The waters laid thee at his doore,
   Ere yet the early dawn was clear.
Thy pretty bairns in fast embrace,
The lifted sun shone on thy face,
Downe drifted to thy dwelling-place.   140

That flow strewed wrecks about the grass,
   That ebbe swept out the flocks to sea;
A fatal ebbe and flow, alas!
   To manye more than myne and mee:
But each will mourn his own (she saith),   145
And sweeter woman ne'er drew breath
Than my sonne ɔ wife, Elizabeth.

I shall never hear her more
By the reedy Lindis shore,
' Cusha! Cusha! Cusha! ' calling,   150
Ere the early dews be falling;
I shall never hear her song,
' Cusha! Cusha! ' all along
Where the sunny Lindis floweth,
   Goeth, floweth;   155
From the meads where melick groweth,
When the water winding down,
Onward floweth to the town.
I shall never see her more
Where the reeds and rushes quiver,   160
   Shiver, quiver;
Stand beside the sobbing river,
Sobbing, throbbing, in its falling

To the sandy lonesome shore;
I shall never hear her calling, 165
' Leave your meadow grasses mellow,
 Mellow, mellow;
Quit your cowslips, cowslips yellow;
Come uppe Whitefoot, come uppe Lightfoot ;
Quit your pipes of parsley hollow, 170
 Hollow, hollow;
Come uppe Lightfoot, rise and follow;
 Lightfoot, Whitefoot,
 From your clovers lift the head;
Come uppe Jetty, follow, follow, 175
 Jetty, to the milking shed.'

JEAN INGELOW

364

REQUIESCAT

Strew on her roses, roses,
 And never a spray of yew!
In quiet she reposes;
 Ah, would that I did too!

Her mirth the world required; 5
 She bathed it in smiles of glee.
But her heart was tired, tired,
 And now they let her be.

Her life was turning, turning,
 In mazes of heat and sound. 10
But for peace her soul was yearning,
 And now peace laps her round.

Her cabin'd, ample spirit,
 It flutter'd and fail'd for breath.
To-night it doth inherit 15
 The vasty hall of death.

MATTHEW ARNOLD

365

THE FORSAKEN MERMAN

Come, dear children, let us away;
Down and away below!
Now my brothers call from the bay,
Now the great winds shoreward blow,
Now the salt tides seaward flow;   5
Now the wild white horses play,
Champ and chafe and toss in the spray.
Children dear, let us away!
This way, this way!

Call her once before you go—   10
Call once yet!
In a voice that she will know:
'Margaret! Margaret!'
Children's voices should be dear
(Call once more) to a mother's ear;   15
Children's voices, wild with pain—
Surely she will come again!
Call her once and come away;
This way, this way!
'Mother dear, we cannot stay!   20
The wild white horses foam and fret.'
Margaret! Margaret!

Come, dear children, come away down;
Call no more!
One last look at the white-wall'd town,   25
And the little grey church on the windy shore,
Then come down!
She will not come though you call all day;
Come away, come away!

Children dear, was it yesterday   30
We heard the sweet bells over the bay?
In the caverns where we lay,
Through the surf and through the swell,
The far-off sound of a silver bell?
Sand-strewn caverns, cool and deep,   35
Where the winds are all asleep;
Where the spent lights quiver and gleam,

Where the salt weed sways in the stream,
Where the sea-beasts, ranged all round,
Feed in the ooze of their pasture-ground;   40
Where the sea-snakes coil and twine,
Dry their mail and bask in the brine;
Where great whales come sailing by,
Sail and sail, with unshut eye,
Round the world for ever and aye?   45
When did music come this way?
Children dear, was it yesterday?

Children dear, was it yesterday
(Call yet once) that she went away?
Once she sate with you and me,   50
On a red gold throne in the heart of the sea,
And the youngest sate on her knee.
She comb'd its bright hair, and she tended it well,
When down swung the sound of a far-off bell.
She sigh'd, she look'd up through the clear green sea;   55
She said: ' I must go, for my kinsfolk pray
In the little grey church on the shore to-day.
'Twill be Easter-time in the world—ah me!
And I lose my poor soul, Merman! here with thee.'
I said: ' Go up, dear heart, through the waves;   60
Say thy prayer, and come back to the kind sea-caves! '
She smiled, she went up through the surf in the bay.
Children dear, was it yesterday?

Children dear, were we long alone?
' The sea grows stormy, the little ones moan;   65
Long prayers,' I said, ' in the world they say;
Come! ' I said; and we rose through the surf in the bay.
We went up the beach, by the sandy down
Where the sea-stocks bloom, to the white-wall'd town;
Through the narrow paved streets, where all was still,   70
To the little grey church on the windy hill.
From the church came a murmur of folk at their prayers,
But we stood without in the cold blowing airs.
We climb'd on the graves, on the stones worn with rains,
And we gazed up the aisle through the small leaded panes.   75
She sate by the pillar; we saw her clear:
' Margaret, hist! come quick, we are here!
Dear heart,' I said, ' we are long alone;
The sea grows stormy, the little ones moan.'
But, ah, she gave me never a look,   80

For her eyes were seal'd to the holy book!
Loud prays the priest; shut stands the door.
Come away, children, call no more!
Come away, come down, call no more!

Down, down, down!   85
Down to the depths of the sea!
She sits at her wheel in the humming town,
Singing most joyfully.
Hark what she sings: ' O joy, O joy,
For the humming street, and the child with its toy!   90
For the priest, and the bell, and the holy well;
For the wheel where I spun,
And the blessed light of the sun!'
And so she sings her fill,
Singing most joyfully,   95
Till the spindle drops from her hand,
And the whizzing wheel stands still.
She steals to the window, and looks at the sand,
And over the sand at the sea;
And her eyes are set in a stare;   100
And anon there breaks a sigh,
And anon there drops a tear,
From a sorrow-clouded eye,
And a heart sorrow-laden,
A long, long sigh;   105
For the cold strange eyes of a little Mermaiden
And the gleam of her golden hair.

Come away, away children;
Come children, come down!
The hoarse wind blows coldly;   110
Lights shine in the town.
She will start from her slumber
When gusts shake the door;
She will hear the winds howling,
Will hear the waves roar.   115
We shall see, while above us
The waves roar and whirl,
A ceiling of amber,
A pavement of pearl,
Singing: ' Here came a mortal,   120
But faithless was she!
And alone dwell for ever
The kings of the sea.'

But, children, at midnight,
When soft the winds blow,   125
When clear falls the moonlight,
When spring-tides are low;
When sweet airs come seaward
From heaths starr'd with broom,
And high rocks throw mildly   130
On the blanch'd sands a gloom;
Up the still, glistening beaches,
Up the creeks we will hie,
Over banks of bright seaweed
The ebb-tide leaves dry.   135
We will gaze, from the sand-hills,
At the white, sleeping town;
At the church on the hill-side—
And then come back down.
Singing: ' There dwells a loved one,   140
But cruel is she!
She left lonely for ever
The kings of the sea.'

MATTHEW ARNOLD

366

PHILOMELA

Hark! ah, the nightingale—
The tawny-throated!
Hark, from that moonlit cedar what a burst!
What triumph! hark!—what pain!

O wanderer from a Grecian shore,   5
Still, after many years, in distant lands,
Still nourishing in thy bewilder'd brain
That wild, unquench'd, deep-sunken, old-world pain—
Say, will it never heal?
And can this fragrant lawn   10
With its cool trees, and night,
And the sweet, tranquil Thames,
And moonshine, and the dew.
To thy rack'd heart and brain
Afford no balm?   15

Dost thou to-night behold,
Here, through the moonlight on this English grass,
The unfriendly palace in the Thracian wild?
Dost thou again peruse
With hot cheeks and sear'd eyes 20
The too clear web, and thy dumb sister's shame?
Dost thou once more assay
Thy flight, and feel come over thee,
Poor fugitive, the feathery change
Once more, and once more seem to make resound 25
With love and hate, triumph and agony,
Lone Daulis, and the high Cephissian vale?
Listen, Eugenia—
How thick the bursts come crowding through the leaves!
Again—thou hearest? 30
Eternal passion!
Eternal pain!

MATTHEW ARNOLD

367

TO MARGUERITE

Yes! in the sea of life enisled,
With echoing straits between us thrown,
Dotting the shoreless watery wild,
We mortal millions live *alone*.
The islands feel the enclasping flow, 5
And then their endless bounds they know.

But when the moon their hollows lights,
And they are swept by balms of spring,
And in their glens, on starry nights,
The nightingales divinely sing; 10
And lovely notes, from shore to shore,
Across the sounds and channels pour—

Oh! then a longing like despair
Is to their farthest caverns sent;
For surely once, they feel, we were 15
Parts of a single continent!
Now round us spreads the watery plain—
Oh might our marges meet again!

Who order'd, that their longing's fire
Should be, as soon as kindled, cool'd?   20
Who renders vain their deep desire?—
A God, a God their severance ruled!
And bade betwixt their shores to be
The unplumb'd, salt, estranging sea.

MATTHEW ARNOLD

368

DOVER BEACH

The sea is calm to-night.
The tide is full, the moon lies fair
Upon the straits;—on the French coast the light
Gleams and is gone; the cliffs of England stand,
Glimmering and vast, out in the tranquil bay.   5
Come to the window, sweet is the night-air!
Only, from the long line of spray
Where the sea meets the moon-blanch'd land,
Listen! you hear the grating roar
Of pebbles which the waves draw back, and fling,   10
At their return, up the high strand,
Begin, and cease, and then again begin,
With tremulous cadence slow, and bring
The eternal note of sadness in.

Sophocles long ago   15
Heard it on the Ægæan, and it brought
Into his mind the turbid ebb and flow
Of human misery; we
Find also in the sound a thought,
Hearing it by this distant northern sea.   20

The Sea of Faith
Was once, too, at the full, and round earth's shore
Lay like the folds of a bright girdle furl'd.
But now I only hear
Its melancholy, long, withdrawing roar,   25
Retreating, to the breath
Of the night-wind, down the vast edges drear
And naked shingles of the world.

Ah, love, let us be true
To one another! for the world, which seems   30
To lie before us like a land of dreams,
So various, so beautiful, so new,
Hath really neither joy, nor love, nor light,
Nor certitude, nor peace, nor help for pain;
And we are here as on a darkling plain   35
Swept with confused alarms of struggle and flight,
Where ignorant armies clash by night.

                                    MATTHEW ARNOLD

369

THE LAST WORD

Creep into thy narrow bed,
Creep, and let no more be said!
Vain thy onset! all stands fast.
Thou thyself must break at last.

Let the long contention cease!   5
Geese are swans, and swans are geese.
Let them have it how they will!
Thou art tired; best be still.

They out-talk'd thee, hiss'd thee, tore thee?
Better men fared thus before thee;   10
Fired their ringing shot and pass'd,
Hotly charged—and sank at last.

Charge once more, then, and be dumb!
Let the victors, when they come,
When the forts of folly fall,   15
Find thy body by the wall!

                                    MATTHEW ARNOLD

370

HERACLITUS

They told me, Heraclitus, they told me you were dead,
They brought me bitter news to hear and bitter tears to shed.
I wept as I remember'd how often you and I
Had tired the sun with talking and sent him down the sky.

And now that thou art lying, my dear old Carian guest,   5
A handful of grey ashes, long, long ago at rest,
Still are thy pleasant voices, thy nightingales, awake;
For Death, he taketh all away, but them he cannot take.

WILLIAM CORY

371

DEPARTURE

It was not like your great and gracious ways!
Do you, that have naught other to lament,
Never, my Love, repent
Of how, that July afternoon,
You went,   5
With sudden, unintelligible phrase,
And frighten'd eye,
Upon your journey of so many days
Without a single kiss, or a good-bye?
I knew, indeed, that you were parting soon;   10
And so we sate, within the low sun's rays,
You whispering to me, for your voice was weak,
Your harrowing praise.
Well, it was well
To hear you such things speak,   15
And I could tell
What made your eyes a growing gloom of love,
As a warm South-wind sombres a March grove.
And it was like your great and gracious ways
To turn your talk on daily things, my Dear,   20
Lifting the luminous, pathetic lash
To let the laughter flash,
Whilst I drew near,
Because you spoke so low that I could scarcely hear.
But all at once to leave me at the last,   25
More at the wonder than the loss aghast,
With huddled, unintelligible phrase,
And frighten'd eye,
And go your journey of all days
With not one kiss, or a good-bye,   30
And the only loveless look the look with which you pass'd:
'Twas all unlike your great and gracious ways.

COVENTRY PATMORE

372

THE FAIRIES

Up the airy mountain,
  Down the rushy glen,
We daren't go a-hunting
  For fear of little men;
Wee folk, good folk,   5
  Trooping all together;
Green jacket, red cap,
  And white owl's feather!

Down along the rocky shore
  Some make their home,   10
They live on crispy pancakes
  Of yellow tide-foam;
Some in the reeds
  Of the black mountain lake,
With frogs for their watch-dogs,   15
  All night awake.

High on the hill-top
  The old King sits;
He is now so old and gray
  He's nigh lost his wits.   20
With a bridge of white mist
  Columbkill he crosses,
On his stately journeys
  From Slieveleague to Rosses;

Or going up with music   25
  On cold starry nights
To sup with the Queen
  Of the gay Northern Lights.
They stole little Bridget
  For seven years long;   30
When she came down again
  Her friends were all gone.

They took her lightly back,
  Between the night and morrow,
They thought that she was fast asleep,   35
  But she was dead with sorrow.

They have kept her ever since
  Deep within the lake,
On a bed of flag-leaves,
  Watching till she wake.   40

By the craggy hill-side,
  Through the mosses bare,
They have planted thorn-trees
  For pleasure here and there.
If any man so daring   45
  As dig them up in spite,
He shall find their sharpest thorns
  In his bed at night.

Up the airy mountain,
  Down the rushy glen,   50
We daren't go a-hunting
  For fear of little men;
Wee folk, good folk,
  Trooping all together;
Green jacket, red cap,   55
  And white owl's feather!

                  WILLIAM ALLINGHAM

373

THE ORPHAN'S SONG

I had a little bird,
I took it from the nest;
I prest it, and blest it,
And nursed it in my breast.

I set it on the ground,   5
I danced round and round,
And sang about it so cheerly,
With ' Hey my little bird, and ho my little bird,
And oh but I love thee dearly! '

I make a little feast   10
Of food soft and sweet,
I hold it in my breast,
And coax it to eat;

I pit, and I pat,
I call it this and that,   15

And sing about it so cheerly,
With ' Hey my little bird, and ho my little bird,
And ho but I love thee dearly! '

I may kiss, I may sing,
But I can't make it feed,   20
It taketh no heed
Of any pleasant thing.

I scolded, and I socked,
But it minded not a whit,
Its little mouth was locked,   25
And I could not open it.

Tho' with pit, and with pat,
And with this, and with that,
I sang about it so cheerly,
And ' Hey my little bird, and ho my little bird,   30
And ho but I love thee dearly.'

But when the day was done,
And the room was at rest,
And I sat all alone
With my birdie in my breast,   35

And the light had fled,
And not a sound was heard,
Then my little bird
Lifted up its head,

And the little mouth   40
Loosed its sullen pride,
And it opened, it opened,
With a yearning strong and wide.

Swifter than I speak
I brought it food once more,   45
But the poor little beak
Was locked as before.

I sat down again,
And not a creature stirred,
I laid the little bird   50
Again where it had lain;

And again when nothing stirred,
And not a word I said,
Then my little bird

Lifted up its head,   55
And the little beak
Loosed its stubborn pride,
And it opened, it opened,
With a yearning strong and wide.

It lay in my breast,   60
It uttered no cry,
'Twas famished, 'twas famished,
And I couldn't tell why.

I couldn't tell why,
But I saw that it would die,   65
For all that I kept dancing round and round,
And singing above it so cheerly,
With ' Hey my little bird, and ho my little bird,
And ho but I love thee dearly! '

I never look sad,   70
I hear what people say,
I laugh when they are gay
And they think I am glad.

My tears never start,
I never say a word,   75
But I think that my heart
Is like that little bird.

Every day I read,
And I sing, and I play,
But thro' the long day   80
It taketh no heed.

It taketh no heed
Of any pleasant thing,
I know it doth not read,
I know it doth not sing.   85

With my mouth I read,
With my hands I play,
My shut heart is shut,
Coax it how you may.

You may coax it how you may   90
While the day is broad and bright,
But in the dead night
When the guests are gone away,

And no more the music sweet
Up the house doth pass,   95

Nor the dancing feet
Shake the nursery glass;

And I've heard my aunt
Along the corridor,
And my uncle gaunt   100
Lock his chamber door;

And upon the stair
All is hushed and still,
And the last wheel
Is silent in the square;   105

And the nurses snore,
And the dim sheets rise and fall,
And the lamplight's on the wall,
And the mouse is on the floor;

And the curtains of my bed   110
Are like a heavy cloud,
And the clock ticks loud,
And sounds are in my head;

And little Lizzie sleeps
Softly at my side,   115
It opens, it opens,
With a yearning strong and wide!

It yearns in my breast,
It utters no cry,
'Tis famished, 'tis famished,   120
And I feel that I shall die.
I feel that I shall die,
And none will know why,
Tho' the pleasant life is dancing round and round
And singing about me so cheerly,   125
With ' Hey my little bird, and ho my little bird,
And ho but I love thee dearly! '

SYDNEY DOBELL

374

Should thy love die;
O bury it not under ice-blue eyes!
And lips that deny,
With a scornful surprise,
The life it once lived in thy breast when it wore no disguise. 5

      Should thy love die;
  O bury it where the sweet wild-flowers blow!
    And breezes go by,
  With no whisper of woe;
And strange feet cannot guess of the anguish that slumbers below. 10

      Should thy love die;
  O wander once more to the haunt of the bee!
    Where the foliaged sky
  Is most sacred to see,
And thy being first felt its wild birth like a wind-wakened tree. 15

      Should thy love die;
  O dissemble it! smile! let the rose hide the thorn!
    While the lark sings on high,
  And no thing looks forlorn,
Bury it, bury it, bury it where it was born.   20

GEORGE MEREDITH

375

from LOVE IN THE VALLEY

Under yonder beech-tree single on the green-sward,
  Couched with her arms behind her golden head,
Knees and tresses folded to slip and ripple idly,
  Lies my young love sleeping in the shade.
Had I the heart to slide an arm beneath her,   5
  Press her parting lips as her waist I gather slow,
Waking in amazement she could not but embrace me:
  Then would she hold me and never let me go?

Shy as the squirrel and wayward as the swallow,
  Swift as the swallow along the river's light   10
Circleting the surface to meet his mirrored winglets,
  Fleeter she seems in her stay than in her flight.
Shy as the squirrel that leaps among the pine-tops,
  Wayward as the swallow overhead at set of sun,
She whom I love is hard to catch and conquer,   15
  Hard, but O the glory of the winning were she won!

When her mother tends her before the laughing mirror,
  Tying up her laces, looping up her hair,
Often she thinks, were this wild thing wedded,
  More love should I have, and much less care.   20

When her mother tends her before the lighted mirror,
  Loosening her laces, combing down her curls,
Often she thinks, were this wild thing wedded,
  I should miss but one for many boys and girls.

Heartless she is as the shadow in the meadows   25
  Flying to the hills on a blue and breezy noon.
No, she is athirst and drinking up her wonder:
  Earth to her is young as the slip of the new moon.
Deals she an unkindness, 'tis but her rapid measure,
  Even as in a dance; and her smile can heal no less: 30
Like the swinging May-cloud that pelts the flowers with hailstones
  Off a sunny border, she was made to bruise and bless.

Lovely are the curves of the white owl sweeping
  Wavy in the dusk lit by one large star.
Lone on the fir-branch, his rattle-note unvaried,   35
  Brooding o'er the gloom, spins the brown eve-jar.
Darker grows the valley, more and more forgetting:
  So were it with me if forgetting could be willed.
Tell the grassy hollow that holds the bubbling well-spring,
  Tell it to forget the source that keeps it filled.   40

Stepping down the hill with her fair companions,
  Arm in arm, all against the raying West,
Boldly she sings, to the merry tune she marches,
  Brave in her shape, and sweeter unpossessed.
Sweeter, for she is what my heart first awaking   45
  Whispered the world was; morning light is she.
Love that so desires would fain keep her changeless;
  Fain would fling the net, and fain have her free.

Happy happy time, when the white star hovers
  Low over dim fields fresh with bloomy dew,   50
Near the face of dawn, that draws athwart the darkness,
  Threading it with colour, like yewberries the yew.
Thicker crowd the shades as the grave East deepens
  Glowing, and with crimson a long cloud swells.
Maiden still the morn is; and strange she is, and secret;   55
  Strange her eyes; her cheeks are cold as cold sea-shells. . . .

                              GEORGE MEREDITH

376

from MODERN LOVE

iv

All other joys of life he strove to warm,
And magnify, and catch them to his lip:
But they had suffered shipwreck with the ship,
And gazed upon him sallow from the storm.
Or if Delusion came, 'twas but to show   5
The coming minute mock the one that went.
Cold as a mountain in its star-pitched tent,
Stood high Philosophy, less friend than foe:
Whom self-caged Passion, from its prison-bars,
Is always watching with a wondering hate.   10
Not till the fire is dying in the grate,
Look we for any kinship with the stars.
Oh, wisdom never comes when it is gold,
And the great price we pay for it full worth:
We have it only when we are half earth.   15
Little avails that coinage to the old!

viii

Yet it was plain she struggled, and that salt
Of righteous feeling made her pitiful.
Poor twisting worm, so queenly beautiful!
Where came the cleft between us? whose the fault?   20
My tears are on thee, that have rarely dropped
As balm for any bitter wound of mine:
My breast will open for thee at a sign!
But, no: we are two reed-pipes, coarsely stopped:
The God once filled them with his mellow breath;   25
And they were music till he flung them down,
Used! used! Hear now the discord-loving clown
Puff his gross spirit in them, worse than death!
I do not know myself without thee more:
In this unholy battle I grow base: 30
If the same soul be under the same face,
Speak, and a taste of that old time restore!

xvi

In our old shipwrecked days there was an hour,
When in the firelight steadily aglow,

Joined slackly, we beheld the red chasm grow   35
Among the clicking coals. Our library-bower
That eve was left to us: and hushed we sat
As lovers to whom Time is whispering.
From sudden-opened doors we heard them sing:
The nodding elders mixed good wine with chat.   40
Well knew we that Life's greatest treasure lay
With us, and of it was our talk. ' Ah, yes!
Love dies! ' I said: I never thought it less.
She yearned to me that sentence to unsay.
Then when the fire domed blackening, I found   45
Her cheek was salt against my kiss, and swift
Up the sharp scale of sobs her breast did lift:—
Now am I haunted by that taste! that sound!

xliii

Mark where the pressing wind shoots javelin-like
Its skeleton shadow on the broad-backed wave!   50
Here is a fitting spot to dig Love's grave;
Here where the ponderous breakers plunge and strike,
And dart their hissing tongues high up the sand:
In hearing of the ocean, and in sight
Of those ribbed wind-streaks running into white.   55
If I the death of Love had deeply planned,
I never could have made it half so sure,
As by the unblest kisses which upbraid
The full-waked sense; or failing that, degrade!
'Tis morning: but no morning can restore   60
What we have forfeited. I see no sin:
The wrong is mixed. In tragic life, God wot,
No villain need be! Passions spin the plot:
We are betrayed by what is false within.

xlvii

We saw the swallows gathering in the sky,   65
And in the osier-isle we heard their noise.
We had not to look back on summer joys,
Or forward to a summer of bright dye:
But in the largeness of the evening earth
Our spirits grew as we went side by side.   70
The hour became her husband and my bride.
Love, that had robbed us so, thus blessed our dearth!
The pilgrims of the year waxed very loud
In multitudinous chatterings, as the flood
Full brown came from the West, and like pale blood   75
Expanded to the upper crimson cloud.

Love, that had robbed us of immortal things,
This little moment mercifully gave,
Where I have seen across the twilight wave
The swan sail with her young beneath her wings.   80

1

Thus piteously Love closed what he begat:
The union of this ever-diverse pair!
These two were rapid falcons in a snare,
Condemned to do the flitting of the bat.
Lovers beneath the singing sky of May,   85
They wandered once; clear as the dew on flowers:
But they fed not on the advancing hours:
Their hearts held cravings for the buried day.
Then each applied to each that fatal knife,
Deep questioning, which probes to endless dole.   90
Ah, what a dusty answer gets the soul
When hot for certainties in this our life!—
In tragic hints here see what evermore
Moves dark as yonder midnight ocean's force,
Thundering like ramping hosts of warrior horse,   95
To throw that faint thin line upon the shore!

GEORGE MEREDITH

377

THE WOODSPURGE

The wind flapped loose, the wind was still,
Shaken out dead from tree and hill:
I had walked on at the wind's will,—
I sat now, for the wind was still.

Between my knees my forehead was,—   5
My lips, drawn in, said not Alas!
My hair was over in the grass,
My naked ears heard the day pass.

My eyes, wide open, had the run
Of some ten weeds to fix upon;   10
Among those few, out of the sun,
The woodspurge flowered, three cups in one.

From perfect grief there need not be
  Wisdom or even memory:
One thing then learnt remains to me,—   15
  The woodspurge has a cup of three.

D. G. ROSSETTI

378

SUDDEN LIGHT

I have been here before,
  But when or how I cannot tell:
I know the grass beyond the door,
  The sweet keen smell,
The sighing sound, the lights around the shore.   5

You have been mine before,—
  How long ago I may not know:
But just when at that swallow's soar
  Your neck turned so,
Some veil did fall,—I knew it all of yore.   10

Then, now,—perchance again! . . .
  O round mine eyes your tresses shake!
Shall we not lie as we have lain
  Thus for Love's sake,
And sleep, and wake, yet never break the chain?   15

D. G. ROSSETTI

379

LOVESIGHT

When do I see thee most, beloved one?
  When in the light the spirits of mine eyes
  Before thy face, their altar, solemnize
The worship of that Love through thee made known?
Or when in the dusk hours, (we two alone,)   5
  Close-kissed and eloquent of still replies
  Thy twilight-hidden glimmering visage lies,
And my soul only sees thy soul its own?

O love, my love! if I no more should see
Thyself, nor on the earth the shadow of thee,   10
  Nor image of thine eyes in any spring,—
How then should sound upon Life's darkening slope
The ground-whirl of the perished leaves of Hope,
  The wind of Death's imperishable wing?

D. G. ROSSETTI

380

SILENT NOON

Your hands lie open in the long fresh grass,—
  The finger-points look through like rosy blooms:
  Your eyes smile peace. The pasture gleams and glooms
'Neath billowing skies that scatter and amass.
All round our nest, far as the eye can pass,   5
  Are golden kingcup-fields with silver edge
  Where the cow-parsley skirts the hawthorn-hedge.
'Tis visible silence, still as the hour-glass.

Deep in the sun-searched growths the dragon-fly
Hangs like a blue-thread loosened from the sky:—   10
  So this wing'd hour is dropt to us from above.
Oh! clasp we to our hearts, for deathless dower,
This close-companioned inarticulate hour
  When two-fold silence was the song of love.

D. G. ROSSETTI

381

My life closed twice before its close;
  It yet remains to see
If Immortality unveil
  A third event to me,

So huge, so hopeless to conceive,   5
  As these that twice befell.
Parting is all we know of heaven,
  And all we need of hell.

EMILY DICKINSON

382

Of all the souls that stand create
I have elected one.
When sense from spirit files away,
And subterfuge is done;

When that which is and that which was   5
Apart, intrinsic, stand,
And this brief tragedy of flesh
Is shifted like a sand;

When figures show their royal front
And mists are carved away,—   10
Behold the atom I preferred
To all the lists of clay!

                                    EMILY DICKINSON

383

A narrow fellow in the grass
Occasionally rides;
You may have met him,—did you not?
His notice sudden is.

The grass divides as with a comb,   5
A spotted shaft is seen;
And then it closes at your feet
And opens further on.

He likes a boggy acre,
A floor too cool for corn.   10
Yet when a child, and barefoot,
I more than once, at morn,

Have passed, I thought, a whip-lash
Unbraiding in the sun,—
When, stooping to secure it,   15
It wrinkled, and was gone.

Several of nature's people
I know, and they know me;
I feel for them a transport
Of cordiality;   20

But never met this fellow,
Attended or alone,
Without a tighter breathing,
And zero at the bone.

EMILY DICKINSON

384

To my quick ear the leaves conferred;
  The bushes they were bells;
I could not find a privacy
  From Nature's sentinels.

In cave if I presumed to hide,   5
  The walls began to tell;
Creation seemed a mighty crack
  To make me visible.

EMILY DICKINSON

385

Hope is the thing with feathers
That perches in the soul,
And sings the tune without the words,
And never stops at all,

And sweetest in the gale is heard;   5
And sore must be the storm
That could abash the little bird
That kept so many warm.

I've heard it in the chillest land,
And on the strangest sea;   10
Yet, never, in extremity,
It asked a crumb of me.

EMILY DICKINSON

386

The last night that she lived,
It was a common night,
Except the dying; this to us
Made nature different.

We noticed smallest things,—   5
Things overlooked before,
By this great light upon our minds
Italicized, as 'twere.

That others could exist
While she must finish quite,   10
A jealousy for her arose
So nearly infinite.

We waited while she passed;
It was a narrow time,
Too jostled were our souls to speak,   15
At length the notice came.

She mentioned, and forgot;
Then lightly as a reed
Bent to the water, shivered scarce,
Consented, and was dead.   20

And we, we placed the hair,
And drew the head erect;
And then an awful leisure was,
Our faith to regulate.

EMILY DICKINSON

387

When I am dead, my dearest,
  Sing no sad songs for me;
Plant thou no roses at my head,
  Nor shady cypress tree:
Be the green grass above me   5
  With showers and dewdrops wet:
And if thou wilt, remember,
  And if thou wilt, forget.

I shall not see the shadows,
  I shall not feel the rain;   10
I shall not hear the nightingale
  Sing on as if in pain:
And dreaming through the twilight
  That doth not rise nor set,
Haply I may remember,   15
  And haply may forget.

CHRISTINA ROSSETTI

388

A PAUSE

They made the chamber sweet with flowers and leaves,
  And the bed sweet with flowers on which I lay;
  While my soul, love-bound, loitered on its way.
I did not hear the birds about the eaves,
Nor hear the reapers talk among the sheaves: 5
  Only my soul kept watch from day to day,
  My thirsty soul kept watch for one away:—
Perhaps he loves, I thought, remembers, grieves.
At length there came the step upon the stair,
  Upon the lock the old familiar hand: 10
Then first my spirit seemed to scent the air
  Of Paradise; then first the tardy sand
Of time ran golden; and I felt my hair
  Put on a glory, and my soul expand.

CHRISTINA ROSSETTI

389

ECHO

Come to me in the silence of the night;
  Come in the speaking silence of a dream;
Come with soft rounded cheeks and eyes as bright
  As sunlight on a stream;
    Come back in tears,   5
O memory, hope, love of finished years.

O dream how sweet, too sweet, too bitter sweet,
  Whose wakening should have been in Paradise,
Where souls brimful of love abide and meet;
    Where thirsting longing eyes   10
    Watch the slow door
That opening, letting in, lets out no more.

Yet come to me in dreams, that I may live
  My very life again though cold in death:
Come back to me in dreams, that I may give   15
  Pulse for pulse, breath for breath:
    Speak low, lean low,
As long ago, my love, how long ago.

CHRISTINA ROSSETTI

390

REMEMBER

Remember me when I am gone away,
  Gone far away into the silent land;
  When you can no more hold me by the hand,
Nor I half turn to go yet turning stay.
Remember me when no more day by day   5
  You tell me of our future that you plann'd:
  Only remember me; you understand
It will be late to counsel then or pray.
Yet if you should forget me for a while
  And afterwards remember, do not grieve: 10
  For if the darkness and corruption leave
A vestige of the thoughts that once I had,
Better by far you should forget and smile
Than that you should remember and be sad.

CHRISTINA ROSSETTI

391

DREAM-LOVE

Young Love lies sleeping
  In May-time of the year,
Among the lilies,
  Lapped in the tender light:
White lambs come grazing,   5
  White doves come building there;
And round about him
  The May-bushes are white.

Soft moss the pillow
  For oh a softer cheek;   10
Broad leaves cast shadow
  Upon the heavy eyes:
There winds and waters
  Grow lulled and scarcely speak;
There twilight lingers   15
  The longest in the skies.

Young Love lies dreaming;
  But who shall tell the dream?

A perfect sunlight
  On rustling forest tips;
Or perfect moonlight   20
  Upon a rippling stream;
Or perfect silence,
  Or song of cherished lips.

Burn odours round him   25
  To fill the drowsy air;
Weave silent dances
  Around him to and fro;
For oh in waking
  The sights are not so fair,   30
And song and silence
  Are not like these below.

Young Love lies dreaming
  Till summer days are gone,—
Dreaming and drowsing   35
  Away to perfect sleep:
He sees the beauty
  Sun hath not looked upon,
And tastes the fountain
  Unutterably deep.   40

Him perfect music
  Doth hush unto his rest,
And through the pauses
  The perfect silence calms:
Oh poor the voices   45
  Of earth from east to west,
And poor earth's stillness
  Between her stately palms!

Young Love lies drowsing
  Away to poppied death;   50
Cool shadows deepen
  Across the sleeping face:
So fails the summer
  With warm delicious breath;
And what hath autumn   55
  To give us in its place?

Draw close the curtains
　　Of branchèd evergreen;
Change cannot touch them
　　With fading fingers sere:　　　　　60
Here the first violets
　　Perhaps will bud unseen,
And a dove, may be,
　　Return to nestle here.

CHRISTINA ROSSETTI

392

SONG

The feathers of the willow
Are half of them grown yellow
　　Above the swelling stream;
And ragged are the bushes,
And rusty now the rushes,　　　　　5
　　And wild the clouded gleam.

The thistle now is older,
His stalk begins to moulder,
　　His head is white as snow;
The branches all are barer,　　　　　10
The linnet's song is rarer,
　　The robin pipeth now.

RICHARD WATSON DIXON

393

WINTER WILL FOLLOW

The heaving roses of the hedge are stirred
By the sweet breath of summer, and the bird
Makes from within his jocund voice be heard.

The winds that kiss the roses sweep the sea
Of uncut grass, whose billows rolling free
Half drown the hedges which part lea from lea.

But soon shall look the wondering roses down
Upon an empty field cut close and brown,
That lifts no more its height against their own.

And in a little while those roses bright,   10
Leaf after leaf, shall flutter from their height,
And on the reaped field lie pink and white.

And yet again the bird that sings so high
Shall ask the snow for alms with piteous cry,
Take fright in his bewildering bower, and die.   15

RICHARD WATSON DIXON

394

THE WIZARD'S FUNERAL

For me, for me, two horses wait,
Two horses stand before my gate!
Their vast black plumes on high are cast,
Their black manes swing in the midnight blast,
Red sparkles from their eyes fly fast.   5
But can they drag the hearse behind,
Whose black plumes mystify the wind?
What a thing for this heap of bones and hair!
Despair, despair!
Yet think of half the world's winged shapes   10
Which have come to thee wondering:
At thee the terrible idiot gapes,
At thee the running devil japes,
And angels stoop to thee and sing
From the soft midnight that enwraps   15
Their limbs, so gently, sadly fair;—
Thou seest the stars shine through their hair.
The blast again, ho, ho, the blast!
I go to a mansion that shall outlast;
And the stoled priest who steps before   20
Shall turn and welcome me at the door.

RICHARD WATSON DIXON

395

SUMMER DAWN

Pray but one prayer for me 'twixt thy closed lips,
  Think but one thought of me up in the stars.
The summer night waneth, the morning light slips,
  Faint and grey 'twixt the leaves of the aspen,
    betwixt the cloud-bars,

That are patiently waiting there for the dawn: 5
   Patient and colourless, though Heaven's gold
Waits to float through them along with the sun.
Far out in the meadows, above the young corn,
   The heavy elms wait, and restless and cold
The uneasy wind rises; the roses are dun;   10
Through the long twilight they pray for the dawn,
Round the lone house in the midst of the corn.
   Speak but one word to me over the corn,
   Over the tender, bow'd locks of the corn.

WILLIAM MORRIS

396

from THE MESSAGE OF THE MARCH WIND

Fair now is the springtide, now earth lies beholding
   With the eyes of a lover the face of the sun;
Long lasteth the daylight, and hope is enfolding
   The green-growing acres with increase begun.

Now sweet, sweet it is through the land to be straying   5
   Mid the birds and the blossoms and the beasts of the field;
Love mingles with love, and no evil is weighing
   On thy heart or mine, where all sorrow is healed.

From township to township, o'er down and by tillage
   Far, far have we wandered and long was the day,   10
But now cometh eve at the end of the village,
   Where over the grey wall the church riseth grey.

There is wind in the twilight; in the white road before us
   The straw from the ox-yard is blowing about;
The moon's rim is rising, a star glitters o'er us,   15
   And the vane on the spire-top is swinging in doubt.

Down there dips the highway, toward the bridge crossing over
   The brook that runs on to the Thames and the sea.
Draw closer, my sweet, we are lover and lover;
   This eve art thou given to gladness and me.   20

WILLIAM MORRIS

397

from THE CHURCHYARD ON THE SANDS

My Love lies in the gates of foam,
  The last dear wreck of shore;
The naked sea-marsh binds her home,
  The sand her chamber door.

The grey gull flaps the written stones,   5
  The ox-birds chase the tide;
And near that narrow field of bones
  Great ships at anchor ride.

Black piers with crust of dripping green,
  One foreland, like a hand,   10
O'er intervals of grass between
  Dim lonely dunes of sand.

A church of silent weathered looks,
  A breezy reddish tower,
A yard whose mounded resting-nooks   15
  Are tinged with sorrel flower. . . .

Strong and alone, my dove, with thee;
  And, tho' mine eyes be wet,
There's nothing in the world to me
  So dear as my regret. . . .   20

Sleep, and forget all things but one,
  Heard in each wave of sea,—
How lonely all the years will run
  Until I rest by thee.

                     WARREN DE TABLEY

398

from A SONG OF THE ROLLING WIND

A song of the fields and a song of the woods,
  And a song of the rolling gale;
A song for my love, and my false, false love,
  To the tune of the crackling hail
    In the teeth of the roaring wind.   5

A song of the clouds and the fallow face,
  Where the wrestling leaves come down,
Of the heart that is changed, and the voice that is gone,
  And the woodland withered brown
    In the drift of the raving wind.   10

A song for me, and a song for thee,
  And never a love between,
And the cold clay-couch of the patient dead
  By the yew tree's inky green,
    In the teeth of the rolling wind. . . .   15

A song, a song, and get thee gone
  For the night runs down with rain,
My throat is dry, and my lute is broke,
  And I never shall love again,
    In the rush of the roaring wind.   20

WARREN DE TABLEY

399

ANTICIPATION

I set my heart to sing of leaves,
  Ere buds had felt the March wind blow:
I laid my head and dreamt of sheaves,
  Ere seedsmen had the heart to sow:
I fancied swallows at the eaves,   5
  And found old nests in pendent snow.

I dreamt a scent of daffodils,
  When frosty shone the village tiles:
Of flowery perfume from the hills,
  When ice had bound the mere for miles: 10
Of kingcups yellowing all the rills,
  When snowdrift silted up the stiles.

I found a barren bush of thorn,
  Where hung last year the sweet field-rose:
I said, no hint of purple morn   15
  The chambers of the east disclose:
Poor heart, poor song, poor pinions torn,
  Flutter and perish in the snows.

I said, a winter, huge and deep,
  Crawls on the bitter, hungry plain: 20
Why should I dream, who cannot sleep,
  Or hope to understand the pain,
Which rolls the doleful tears I weep,
   That Spring is dead, that Love is slain?

WARREN DE TABLEY

400

CHORUS

Before the beginning of years
  There came to the making of man
Time, with a gift of tears;
  Grief, with a glass that ran;
Pleasure, with pain for leaven;   5
  Summer, with flowers that fell;
Remembrance fallen from heaven,
  And madness risen from hell;
Strength without hands to smite;
  Love that endures for a breath;   10
Night, the shadow of light,
  And life, the shadow of death.

And the high gods took in hand
  Fire, and the falling of tears,
And a measure of sliding sand   15
  From under the feet of the years;
And froth and drift of the sea;
  And dust of the labouring earth;
And bodies of things to be
  In the houses of death and of birth;   20
And wrought with weeping and laughter,
  And fashioned with loathing and love
With life before and after
  And death beneath and above,
For a day and a night and a morrow,   25
  That his strength might endure for a span
With travail and heavy sorrow,
  The holy spirit of man.

From the winds of the north and the south
  They gathered as unto strife;   30

They breathed upon his mouth,
  They filled his body with life;
Eyesight and speech they wrought
  For the veils of the soul therein,
A time for labour and thought,   35
  A time to serve and to sin;
They gave him light in his ways,
  And love, and a space for delight,
And beauty and length of days,
  And night, and sleep in the night.   40
His speech is a burning fire;
  With his lips he travaileth;
In his heart is a blind desire,
  In his eyes foreknowledge of death;
He weaves, and is clothed with derision;   45
  Sows, and he shall not reap;
His life is a watch or a vision
  Between a sleep and a sleep.

                              A. C. SWINBURNE

401

A FORSAKEN GARDEN

In a coign of the cliff between lowland and highland,
  At the sea-down's edge between windward and lee,
Walled round with rocks as an inland island,
  The ghost of a garden fronts the sea.
A girdle of brushwood and thorn encloses   5
  The steep square slope of the blossomless bed
Where the weeds that grew green from the graves of its roses
    Now lie dead.

The fields fall southward, abrupt and broken,
  To the low last edge of the long lone land.   10
If a step should sound or a word be spoken,
  Would a ghost not rise at the strange guest's hand?
So long have the grey bare walls lain guestless,
  Through branches and briars if a man make way,
He shall find no life but the sea-wind's, restless 15
    Night and day.

The dense hard passage is blind and stifled
  That crawls by a track none turn to climb

To the strait waste place that the years have rifled
  Of all but the thorns that are touched not of time. 20
The thorns he spares when the rose is taken;
  The rocks are left when he wastes the plain.
The wind that wanders, the weeds wind-shaken,
  These remain.

Not a flower to be pressed of the foot that falls not; 25
  As the heart of a dead man the seed-plots are dry;
From the thicket of thorns whence the nightingale calls not,
  Could she call, there were never a rose to reply.
Over the meadows that blossom and wither
  Rings but the note of a sea-bird's song; 30
Only the sun and the rain come hither
  All year long.

The sun burns sere and the rain dishevels
  One gaunt bleak blossom of scentless breath.
Only the wind here hovers and revels
  In a round where life seems barren as death. 35
Here there was laughing of old, there was weeping,
  Haply, of lovers none ever will know,
Whose eyes went seaward a hundred sleeping
  Years ago. 40

Heart handfast in heart as they stood, 'Look thither,'
  Did he whisper? 'look forth from the flowers to the sea;
For the foam-flowers endure when the rose-blossoms wither,
  And men that love lightly may die—but we?'
And the same wind sang and the same waves whitened, 45
  And or ever the garden's last petals were shed,
In the lips that had whispered, the eyes that had lightened,
  Love was dead.

Or they loved their life through, and then went whither?
  And were one to the end—but what end who knows?
Love deep as the sea as a rose must wither, 50
  As the rose-red seaweed that mocks the rose.
Shall the dead take thought for the dead to love them?
  What love was ever as deep as a grave?
They are loveless now as the grass above them
  Or the wave. 55

All are at one now, roses and lovers,
  Not known of the cliffs and the fields and the sea.
Not a breath of the time that has been hovers
  In the air now soft with a summer to be.   60
Not a breath shall there sweeten the seasons hereafter
  Of the flowers or the lovers that laugh now or weep,
When as they that are free now of weeping and laughter
    We shall sleep.

Here death may deal not again for ever;   65
  Here change may come not till all change end.
From the graves they have made they shall rise up never,
  Who have left nought living to ravage and rend.
Earth, stones, and thorns of the wild ground growing,
  While the sun and the rain live, these shall be;   70
Till a last wind's breath upon all these blowing
    Roll the sea.

Till the slow sea rise and the sheer cliff crumble,
  Till terrace and meadow the deep gulfs drink,
Till the strength of the waves of the high tides humble   75
  The fields that lessen, the rocks that shrink,
Here now in his triumph where all things falter,
  Stretched out on the spoils that his own hand spread,
As a god self-slain on his own strange altar,
    Death lies dead.   80

               A. C. SWINBURNE

402

A MATCH

If love were what the rose is,
  And I were like the leaf,
Our lives would grow together
In sad or singing weather,
Blown fields or flowerful closes,   5
  Green pleasure or grey grief;
If love were what the rose is,
  And I were like the leaf.

If I were what the words are,
  And love were like the tune,   10

With double sound and single
Delight our lips would mingle,
With kisses glad as birds are
   That get sweet rain at noon;
If I were what the words are,   15
   And love were like the tune.

If you were life, my darling,
   And I your love were death,
We'd shine and snow together
Ere March made sweet the weather   20
With daffodil and starling
   And hours of fruitful breath;
If you were life, my darling,
   And I your love were death.

If you were thrall to sorrow,   25
   And I were page to joy,
We'd play for lives and seasons
With loving looks and treasons
And tears of night and morrow
   And laughs of maid and boy;   30
If you were thrall to sorrow,
   And I were page to joy.

If you were April's lady,
   And I were lord in May,
We'd throw with leaves for hours   35
And draw for days with flowers,
Till day like night were shady
   And night were bright like day;
If you were April's lady,
   And I were lord in May.   40

If you were queen of pleasure,
   And I were king of pain,
We'd hunt down love together,
Pluck out his flying-feather,
And teach his feet a measure,   45
   And find his mouth a rein;
If you were queen of pleasure,
   And I were king of pain.

A. C. SWINBURNE

403

THE SELF-UNSEEING

Here is the ancient floor,
Footworn and hollowed and thin,
Here was the former door
Where the dead feet walked in.

She sat here in her chair,   5
Smiling into the fire;
He who played stood there,
Bowing it higher and higher.

Childlike, I danced in a dream;
Blessings emblazoned that day;   10
Everything glowed with a gleam;
Yet we were looking away!

THOMAS HARDY

404

AFTER THE VISIT

Come again to the place
Where your presence was as a leaf that skims
Down a drouthy way whose ascent bedims
   The bloom on the farer's face.

Come again, with the feet   5
That were light on the green as a thistledown ball,
And those mute ministrations to one and to all
   Beyond a man's saying sweet.

Until then the faint scent
Of the bordering flowers swam unheeded away,   10
And I marked not the charm in the changes of day
   As the cloud-colours came and went.

Through the dark corridors
Your walk was so soundless I did not know
Your form from a phantom's of long ago   15
   Said to pass on the ancient floors,

Till you drew from the shade,
And I saw the large luminous living eyes
Regard me in fixed inquiring-wise
    As those of a soul that weighed,   20

    Scarce consciously,
The eternal question of what Life was,
And why we were there, and by whose strange laws
    That which mattered most could not be.

THOMAS HARDY

405

THE HAUNTER

He does not think that I haunt here nightly:
    How shall I let him know
That whither his fancy sets him wandering
    I, too, alertly go?—
Hover and hover a few feet from him   5
    Just as I used to do,
But cannot answer the words he lifts me—
    Only listen thereto!

When I could answer he did not say them:
    When I could let him know   10
How I would like to join in his journeys
    Seldom he wished to go.
Now that he goes and wants me with him
    More than he used to do,
Never he sees my faithful phantom   15
    Though he speaks thereto.

Yes, I companion him to places
    Only dreamers know,
Where the shy hares print long paces,
    Where the night rooks go;   20
Into old aisles where the past is all to him,
    Close as his shade can do,
Always lacking the power to call to him,
    Near as I reach thereto!

What a good haunter I am, O tell him!   25
    Quickly make him know

If he but sigh since my loss befell him
    Straight to his side I go.
Tell him a faithful one is doing
    All that love can do   30
Still that his path may be worth pursuing,
    And to bring peace thereto.

                    THOMAS HARDY

406

AFTER A JOURNEY

Hereto I come to view a voiceless ghost;
    Whither, O whither will its whim now draw me?
Up the cliff, down, till I'm lonely, lost,
    And the unseen waters' ejaculations awe me.
Where you will next be there's no knowing,   5
    Facing round about me everywhere,
        With your nut-coloured hair,
And gray eyes, and rose-flush coming and going.

Yes: I have re-entered your olden haunts at last;
    Through the years, through the dead scenes I have tracked
    you;   10
What have you now found to say of our past—
    Scanned across the dark space wherein I have lacked you?
Summer gave us sweets, but autumn wrought division?
    Things were not lastly as firstly well
        With us twain, you tell?   15
But all's closed now, despite Time's derision.

I see what you are doing: you are leading me on
    To the spots we knew when we haunted here together,
The waterfall, above which the mist-bow shone
    At the then fair hour in the then fair weather,   20
And the cave just under, with a voice still so hollow
    That it seems to call out to me from forty years ago,
        When you were all aglow,
And not the thin ghost that I now fraily follow!

Ignorant of what there is flitting here to see,   25
    The waked birds preen and the seals flop lazily;
Soon you will have, Dear, to vanish from me,
    For the stars close their shutters and the dawn whitens hazily.

Trust me, I mind not, though Life lours,
  The bringing me here; nay, bring me here again!   30
    I am just the same as when
Our days were a joy, and our paths through flowers.

THOMAS HARDY

407

AT CASTLE BOTEREL

As I drive to the junction of lane and highway,
  And the drizzle bedrenches the waggonette,
I look behind at the fading byway,
  And see on its slope, now glistening wet,
    Distinctly yet   5

Myself and a girlish form benighted
  In dry March weather. We climb the road
Beside a chaise. We had just alighted
  To ease the sturdy pony's load
    When he sighed and slowed.   10

What we did as we climbed, and what we talked of
  Matters not much, nor to what it led,—
Something that life will not be balked of
  Without rude reason till hope is dead,
    And feeling fled.   15

It filled but a minute. But was there ever
  A time of such quality, since or before,
In that hill's story? To one mind never,
  Though it has been climbed, foot-swift, foot-sore,
    By thousands more.   20

Primeval rocks form the road's steep border,
  And much have they faced there, first and last,
Of the transitory in Earth's long order;
  But what they record in colour and cast
    Is—that we two passed.   25

And to me, though Time's unflinching rigour,
  In mindless rote, has ruled from sight
The substance now, one phantom figure
  Remains on the slope, as when that night
    Saw us alight.   30

I look and see it there, shrinking, shrinking,
  I look back at it amid the rain
For the very last time; for my sand is sinking,
  And I shall traverse old love's domain
    Never again.   **25**

                THOMAS HARDY

408

    Regret not me;
  Beneath the sunny tree
I lie uncaring, slumbering peacefully.

    Swift as the light
  I flew my faery flight;   **5**
Ecstatically I moved, and feared no night.

    I did not know
  That heydays fade and go,
But deemed that what was would be always so.

    I skipped at morn   **10**
  Between the yellowing corn,
Thinking it good and glorious to be born.

    I ran at eves
  Among the piled-up sheaves,
Dreaming, ' I grieve not, therefore nothing grieves.' **15**

    Now soon will come
  The apple, pear, and plum,
And hinds will sing, and autumn insects hum.

    Again you will fare
  To cider-makings rare,   **20**
And junketings; but I shall not be there.

    Yet gaily sing
  Until the pewter ring
Those songs we sang when we went gipsying.

    And lightly dance   **25**
  Some triple-timed romance
In coupled figures, and forget mischance;

And mourn not me
Beneath the yellowing tree;
For I shall mind not, slumbering peacefully.   30

                              THOMAS HARDY

409

I have loved flowers that fade,
Within whose magic tents
Rich hues have marriage made
With sweet unmemoried scents;
A honeymoon delight,—   5
A joy of love at sight,
That ages in an hour:—
My song be like a flower!

I have loved airs, that die
Before their charm is writ   10
Along a liquid sky
Trembling to welcome it.
Notes, that with pulse of fire
Proclaim the spirit's desire,
Then die, and are nowhere:—   15
My song be like an air!

Die, song, die like a breath,
And wither as a bloom:
Fear not a flowery death,
Dread not an airy tomb!   20
Fly with delight, fly hence!
'Twas thine love's tender sense
To feast; now on thy bier
Beauty shall shed a tear.

                              ROBERT BRIDGES

410

Thou didst delight my eyes:
Yet who am I? nor first
Nor last nor best, that durst
Once dream of thee for prize;
Nor this the only time   5
Thou shalt set love to rhyme.

Thou didst delight my ear:
Ah! little praise; thy voice
Makes other hearts rejoice,
Makes all ears glad that hear;   10
And short my joy: but yet,
O song, do not forget.

For what wert thou to me?
How shall I say? The moon,
That poured her midnight noon   15
Upon his wrecking sea;—
A sail, that for a day
Has cheered the castaway.

ROBERT BRIDGES

411

WINTER NIGHTFALL

The day begins to droop,—
 Its course is done:
But nothing tells the place
 Of the setting sun.

The hazy darkness deepens,   5
 And up the lane
You may hear, but cannot see,
 The homing wain.

An engine pants and hums
 In the farm hard by: 10
Its lowering smoke is lost
 In the lowering sky.

The soaking branches drip,
 And all night through
The dropping will not cease   15
 In the avenue.

A tall man there in the house
 Must keep his chair:
He knows he will never again
 Breathe the spring air: 20

His heart is worn with work;
　　He is giddy and sick
If he rise to go as far
　　As the nearest rick:

He thinks of his morn of life,   25
　　His hale, strong years;
And braves as he may the night
　　Of darkness and tears.

                              ROBERT BRIDGES

412

FELIX RANDAL

Felix Randal the farrier, O he is dead then? my duty all ended,
Who have watched his mould of man, big-boned and hardy-
　　handsome
Pining, pining, till time when reason rambled in it and some
Fatal four disorders, fleshed there, all contended?

Sickness broke him. Impatient he cursed at first, but mended 5
Being anointed and all; though a heavenlier heart began some
Months earlier, since I had our sweet reprieve and ransom
Tendered to him. Ah well, God rest him all road ever he offended!

This seeing the sick endears them to us, us too it endears.
My tongue had taught thee comfort, touch had quenched thy
　　tears,   10
Thy tears that touched my heart, child, Felix, poor Felix Randal;

How far from then forethought of, all thy more boisterous years,
When thou at the random grim forge, powerful amidst peers,
Didst fettle for the great grey drayhorse his bright and battering
　　sandal!

                              GERARD MANLEY HOPKINS

413

PIED BEAUTY

Glory be to God for dappled things—
　　For skies of couple-colour as a brinded cow;
　　　For rose-moles all in stipple upon trout that swim;
Fresh-firecoal chestnut-falls; finches' wings;

Landscape plotted and pieced—fold, fallow, and plough;
　　And áll trádes, their gear and tackle and trim.　　6

All things counter, original, spare, strange;
　　Whatever is fickle, freckled (who knows how?)
　　　With swift, slow; sweet, sour; adazzle, dim;
He fathers-forth whose beauty is past change:　　10
　　　Praise him.

GERARD MANLEY HOPKINS

414

THE LEADEN ECHO AND THE GOLDEN ECHO

THE LEADEN ECHO

How to kéep—is there any any, is there none such, nowhere
　　known some, bow or brooch or braid or brace, láce, latch or
　　catch or key to keep
Back beauty, keep it, beauty, beauty, beauty, . . . from vanishing
　　away?
Ó is there no frowning of these wrinkles, rankéd wrinkles deep,
Dówn? no waving off of these most mournful messengers, still
　　messengers, sad and stealing messengers of grey?
No there's none, there's none, O no there's none,　　5
Nor can you long be, what you now are, called fair,
Do what you may do, what, do what you may,
And wisdom is early to despair:
Be beginning; since, no, nothing can be done
To keep at bay　　10
Age and age's evils, hoar hair,
Ruck and wrinkle, drooping, dying, death's worst, winding sheets,
　　tombs and worms and tumbling to decay;
So be beginning, be beginning to despair.
O there's none; no no no there's none:
Be beginning to despair, to despair,　　15
Despair, despair, despair, despair.

THE GOLDEN ECHO

　　Spare!
There ís one, yes I have one (Hush there!);
Only not within seeing of the sun,
Not within the singeing of the strong sun,　　20
Tall sun's tingeing, or treacherous the tainting of the earth's air.

Somewhere elsewhere there is ah well where! one,
One. Yes I can tell such a key, I do know such a place,
Where whatever's prized and passes of us, everything that's fresh
    and fast flying of us, seems to us sweet of us and swiftly away
    with, done away with, undone,
Undone, done with, soon done with, and yet dearly and danger-
    ously sweet   25
Of us, the wimpled-water-dimpled, not-by-morning-matchèd face,
The flower of beauty, fleece of beauty, too too apt to, ah! to fleet,
Never fleets móre, fastened with the tenderest truth
To its own best being and its loveliness of youth: it is an ever-
    lastingness of, O it is an all youth!
Come then, your ways and airs and looks, locks, maiden gear,
    gallantry and gaiety and grace,   30
Winning ways, airs innocent, maiden manners, sweet looks, loose
    locks, long locks, lovelocks, gaygear, going gallant, girl-
    grace—
Resign them, sign them, seal them, send them, motion them with
    breath,
And with sighs soaring, soaring síghs deliver
Them; beauty-in-the-ghost, deliver it, early now, long before
    death
Give beauty back, beauty, beauty, beauty, back to God, beauty's
    self and beauty's giver.   35
See; not a hair is, not an eyelash, not the least lash lost; every
    hair
Is, hair of the head, numbered.
Nay, what we had lighthanded left in surly the mere mould
Will have waked and have waxed and have walked with the wind
    what while we slept,
This side, that side hurling a heavyheaded hundredfold   40
What while we, while we slumbered.
O then, weary then whý should we tread? O why are we so
    haggard at the heart, so care-coiled, care-killed, so fagged,
    so flashed, so cogged, so cumbered,
When the thing we freely forfeit is kept with fonder a care,
Fonder a care kept than we could have kept it, kept
Far with fonder a care (and we, we should have lost it) finer,
    fonder   45
A care kept.—Where kept? Do but tell us where kept, where.—
Yonder.—What high as that! We follow, now we follow.—
    Yonder, yes yonder, yonder,
Yonder.

GERARD MANLEY HOPKINS

415

GOD'S GRANDEUR

The world is charged with the grandeur of God.
  It will flame out, like shining from shook foil;
  It gathers to a greatness, like the ooze of oil
Crushed. Why do men then now not reck his rod?
Generations have trod, have trod, have trod;   5
  And all is seared with trade; bleared, smeared with toil;
  And wears man's smudge and shares man's smell: the soil
Is bare now, nor can foot feel, being shod.

And for all this, nature is never spent;
  There lives the dearest freshness deep down things;   10
And though the last lights off the black West went
  Oh, morning, at the brown brink eastward, springs—
Because the Holy Ghost over the bent
  World broods with warm breast and with ah! bright wings.

                    GERARD MANLEY HOPKINS

416

PEACE

When will you ever, Peace, wild wooddove, shy wings shut,
Your round me roaming end, and under be my boughs?
When, when, Peace, will you, Peace? I'll not play hypocrite
To own my heart: I yield you do come sometimes; but
That piecemeal peace is poor peace. What pure peace allows   5
Alarms of wars, the daunting wars, the death of it?

O surely, reaving Peace, my Lord should leave in lieu
Some good! And so he does leave Patience exquisite,
That plumes to Peace thereafter. And when Peace here does
    house
He comes with work to do, he does not come to coo,   10
    He comes to brood and sit.

                    GERARD MANLEY HOPKINS

417

THE ODYSSEY

As one that for a weary space has lain
Lull'd by the song of Circe and her wine
 In gardens near the pale of Proserpine,
Where that Æaean isle forgets the main,
And only the low lutes of love complain,   5
 And only shadows of wan lovers pine—
 As such an one were glad to know the brine
Salt on his lips, and the large air again—
So gladly from the songs of modern speech
 Men turn, and see the stars, and feel the free   10
  Shrill wind beyond the close of heavy flowers,
  And through the music of the languid hours
They hear like Ocean on a western beach
 The surge and thunder of the Odyssey.

ANDREW LANG

418

ODE: 'WE ARE THE MUSIC-MAKERS'

We are the music-makers,
 And we are the dreamers of dreams,
Wandering by lone sea-breakers,
 And sitting by desolate streams;
World-losers and world-forsakers,   5
 On whom the pale moon gleams:
Yet we are the movers and shakers
 Of the world for ever, it seems.

With wonderful deathless ditties
We build up the world's great cities,   10
 And out of a fabulous story
 We fashion an empire's glory:
One man with a dream, at pleasure,
 Shall go forth and conquer a crown;
And three with a new song's measure   15
 Can trample an empire down.

We, in the ages lying
  In the buried past of the earth,
Built Nineveh with our sighing,
  And Babel itself with our mirth;   20
And o'erthrew them with prophesying
  To the old of the new world's worth;
For each age is a dream that is dying,
  Or one that is coming to birth.

A. W. E. O'SHAUGHNESSY

419

To S. R. CROCKETT

In reply to a dedication

Blows the wind to-day, and the sun and the rain are flying,
Blows the wind on the moors to-day and now,
Where about the graves of the martyrs the whaups are crying,
My heart remembers how!

Grey recumbent tombs of the dead in desert places,   5
Standing stones on the vacant wine-red moor,
Hills of sheep, and the homes of the silent vanquished races,
And winds, austere and pure:

Be it granted me to behold you again in dying,
Hills of home! and to hear again the call;   10
Hear about the graves of the martyrs the peewees crying,
And hear no more at all.

R. L. STEVENSON

420

IN THE HIGHLANDS

In the highlands, in the country places,
Where the old plain men have rosy faces,
  And the young fair maidens
    Quiet eyes;
Where essential silence cheers and blesses,   5
And for ever in the hill-recesses
  Her more lovely music
    Broods and dies—

O to mount again where erst I haunted;
Where the old red hills are bird-enchanted,   10
  And the low green meadows
    Bright with sward;
And when even dies, the million-tinted,
And the night has come, and planets glinted,
  Lo, the valley hollow   15
    Lamp-bestarr'd!

O to dream, O to awake and wander
There, and with delight to take and render,
  Through the trance of silence,
    Quiet breath!   20
Lo! for there, among the flowers and grasses,
Only the mightier movement sounds and passes;
  Only winds and rivers,
    Life and death.

R. L. STEVENSON

421

IN ROMNEY MARSH

As I went down to Dymchurch Wall,
  I heard the South sing o'er the land;
I saw the yellow sunlight fall
  On knolls where Norman churches stand.

And ringing shrilly, taut and lithe,   5
  Within the wind a core of sound,
The wire from Romney town to Hythe
  Alone its airy journey wound.

A veil of purple vapour flowed
  And trailed its fringe along the Straits;   10
The upper air like sapphire glowed;
  And roses filled Heaven's central gates.

Masts in the offing wagged their tops;
  The swinging waves peal'd on the shore;
The saffron beach, all diamond drops   15
  And beads of surge, prolonged the roar.

As I came up from Dymchurch Wall,
　　I saw above the Downs' low crest
The crimson brands of sunset fall,
　　Flicker and fade from out the west.　　　　20

Night sank: like flakes of silver fire
　　The stars in one great shower came down;
Shrill blew the wind; and shrill the wire
　　Rang out from Hythe to Romney town.

The darkly shining salt sea drops　　　　　25
　　Streamed as the waves clashed on the shore;
The beach, with all its organ stops
　　Pealing again, prolonged the roar.

JOHN DAVIDSON

422

Tell me not here, it needs not saying,
　　What tune the enchantress plays
In aftermaths of soft September
　　Or under blanching mays,
For she and I were long acquainted　　　　5
　　And I knew all her ways.

On russet floors, by waters idle,
　　The pine lets fall its cone;
The cuckoo shouts all day at nothing
　　In leafy dells alone;　　　　　　　　　10
And traveller's joy beguiles in autumn
　　Hearts that have lost their own.

On acres of the seeded grasses
　　The changing burnish heaves;
Or marshalled under moons of harvest　　　15
　　Stand still all night the sheaves;
Or beeches strip in storms for winter
　　And stain the wind with leaves.

Possess, as I possessed a season,
　　The countries I resign,　　　　　　　20
Where over elmy plains the highway
　　Would mount the hills and shine,
And full of shade the pillared forest
　　Would murmur and be mine.

For nature, heartless, witless nature,   25
  Will neither care nor know
What stranger's feet may find the meadow
  And trespass there and go,
Nor ask amid the dews of morning
  If they are mine or no.

A. E. HOUSMAN

423

Far in a western brookland
  That bred me long ago
The poplars stand and tremble
  By pools I used to know.

There, in the windless night-time,   5
  The wanderer, marvelling why,
Halts on the bridge to hearken
  How soft the poplars sigh.

He hears: no more remembered
  In fields where I was known,   10
Here I lie down in London
  And turn to rest alone.

There, by the starlit fences,
  The wanderer halts and hears
My soul that lingers sighing   15
  About the glimmering weirs.

A. E. HOUSMAN

424

The night is freezing fast,
  To-morrow comes December;
    And winterfalls of old
Are with me from the past;
  And chiefly I remember
    How Dick would hate the cold.   5

Fall, winter, fall; for he,
  Prompt hand and headpiece clever,

> Has woven a winter robe,
> And made of earth and sea 10
> His overcoat for ever,
> And wears the turning globe.

A. E. HOUSMAN

425

DAISY

Where the thistle lifts a purple crown
    Six foot out of the turf,
And the harebell shakes on the windy hill—
    O the breath of the distant surf!—

The hills look over on the South, 5
    And southward dreams the sea;
And, with the sea-breeze hand in hand,
    Came innocence and she.

Where 'mid the gorse the raspberry
    Red for the gatherer springs, 10
Two children did we stray and talk
    Wise, idle, childish things.

She listened with big-lipped surprise,
    Breast-deep 'mid flower and spine:
Her skin was like a grape, whose veins 15
    Run snow instead of wine.

She knew not those sweet words she spake,
    Nor knew her own sweet way;
But there's never a bird so sweet a song
    Thronged in whose throat that day! 20

Oh, there were flowers in Storrington
    On the turf and on the spray;
But the sweetest flower on Sussex hills
    Was the Daisy-flower that day!

Her beauty smoothed earth's furrowed face! 25
    She gave me tokens three:—
A look, a word of her winsome mouth,
    And a wild raspberry.

A berry red, a guileless look,
   A still word,—strings of sand!   30
And yet they made my wild, wild heart
   Fly down to her little hand.

For, standing artless as the air,
   And candid as the skies,
She took the berries with her hand,   35
   And the love with her sweet eyes.

The fairest things have fleetest end:
   Their scent survives their close,
But the rose's scent is bitterness
   To him that loved the rose!   40

She looked a little wistfully,
   Then went her sunshine way:—
The sea's eye had a mist on it,
   And the leaves fell from the day.

She went her unremembering way,   45
   She went, and left in me
The pang of all the partings gone,
   And partings yet to be.

She left me marvelling why my soul
   Was sad that she was glad;   50
At all the sadness in the sweet,
   The sweetness in the sad.

Still, still I seemed to see her, still
   Look up with soft replies,
And take the berries with her hand,   55
   And the love with her lovely eyes.

Nothing begins, and nothing ends,
   That is not paid with moan;
For we are born in others' pain,
   And perish in our own.   60

FRANCIS THOMPSON

426

UNWELCOME

We were young, we were merry, we were very very wise,
    And the door stood open at our feast,
When there passed us a woman with the West in her eyes,
    And a man with his back to the East.

O, still grew the hearts that were beating so fast,   5
    The loudest voice was still.
The jest died away on our lips as they passed,
    And the rays of July struck chill.

The cups of red wine turned pale on the board,
    The white bread black as soot.   10
The hound forgot the hand of her lord,
    She fell down at his foot.

Low let me lie, where the dead dog lies,
    Ere I sit me down again at a feast,
When there passes a woman with the West in her eyes,   15
    And a man with his back to the East.

MARY E. COLERIDGE

427

THE WITCH

I have walked a great while over the snow,
And I am not tall nor strong.
My clothes are wet, and my teeth are set,
And the way was hard and long.
I have wandered over the fruitful earth,   5
But I never came here before.
Oh, lift me over the threshold, and let me in at the door!

The cutting wind is a cruel foe.
I dare not stand in the blast.
My hands are stone, and my voice a groan,   10
And the worst of death is past.
I am but a little maiden still,
My little white feet are sore.
Oh, lift me over the threshold, and let me in at the door!

Her voice was the voice that women have,   15
Who plead for their heart's desire.
She came—she came—and the quivering flame
Sank and died in the fire.
It never was lit again on my hearth
Since I hurried across the floor,   20
To lift her over the threshold, and let her in at the door.

MARY E. COLERIDGE

428

ON SUCH A DAY

Some hang above the tombs,
Some weep in empty rooms,
I, when the iris blooms,
    Remember.

I, when the cyclamen   5
Opens her buds again,
Rejoice a moment—then
    Remember.

MARY E. COLERIDGE

429

THE WAY THROUGH THE WOODS

They shut the road through the woods
    Seventy years ago.
Weather and rain have undone it again,
    And now you would never know
There was once a path through the woods   5
    Before they planted the trees,
It is underneath the coppice and heath,
    And the thin anemones.
    Only the keeper sees
That, where the ring-dove broods,   10
    And the badgers roll at ease,
There was once a road through the woods.

Yet, if you enter the woods
    Of a summer evening late,
When the night-air cools on the trout-ring'd pools   15
    Where the otter whistles his mate,

(They fear not men in the woods
  Because they see so few)
You will hear the beat of a horse's feet
  And the swish of a skirt in the dew,   20
  Steadily cantering through
The misty solitudes,
  As though they perfectly knew
The old lost road through the woods . .
But there is no road through the woods.   25

RUDYARD KIPLING

430

CITIES AND THRONES AND POWERS

Cities and Thrones and Powers
  Stand in Time's eye,
Almost as long as flowers,
  Which daily die:
But, as new buds put forth   5
  To glad new men,
Out of the spent and unconsidered Earth
  The Cities rise again.

This season's Daffodil,
  She never hears   10
What change, what chance, what chill,
  Cut down last year's;
But with bold countenance,
  And knowledge small,
Esteems her seven days' continuance   15
  To be perpetual.

So Time that is o'er-kind
  To all that be,
Ordains us e'en as blind,
  As bold as she: 20
That in our very death,
  And burial sure,
Shadow to shadow, well persuaded, saith,
  ' See how our works endure! '

RUDYARD KIPLING

431

DOWN BY THE SALLEY GARDENS

Down by the salley gardens my love and I did meet;
She passed the salley gardens with little snow-white feet.
She bid me take love easy, as the leaves grow on the tree;
But I, being young and foolish, with her would not agree.

In a field by the river my love and I did stand,   5
And on my leaning shoulder she laid her snow-white hand.
She bid me take life easy, as the grass grows on the weirs;
But I was young and foolish, and now am full of tears.

W. B. YEATS

432

THE WILD SWANS AT COOLE

The trees are in their autumn beauty,
The woodland paths are dry,
Under the October twilight the water
Mirrors a still sky;
Upon the brimming water among the stones   5
Are nine and fifty swans.

The nineteenth Autumn has come upon me
Since I first made my count;
I saw, before I had well finished,
All suddenly mount   10
And scatter wheeling in great broken rings
Upon their clamorous wings.

I have looked upon those brilliant creatures,
And now my heart is sore.
All's changed since I, hearing at twilight,   15
The first time on this shore,
The bell-beat of their wings above my head,
Trod with a lighter tread.

Unwearied still, lover by lover,
They paddle in the cold,   20
Companionable streams or climb the air;

Their hearts have not grown old;
Passion or conquest, wander where they will,
Attend upon them still.

But now they drift on the still water,   25
Mysterious, beautiful;
Among what rushes will they build,
By what lake's edge or pool
Delight men's eyes when I awake some day
To find they have flown away?   30

W. B. YEATS

433

SOLOMON TO SHEBA

Sang Solomon to Sheba,
And kissed her dusky face,
' All day long from mid-day
We have talked in the one place,
All day long from shadowless noon   5
We have gone round and round
In the narrow theme of love
Like an old horse in a pound.'

To Solomon sang Sheba,
Planted on his knees,   10
' If you had broached a matter
That might the learned please,
You had before the sun had thrown
Our shadows on the ground
Discovered that my thoughts, not it,   15
Are but a narrow pound.'

Sang Solomon to Sheba,
And kissed her Arab eyes,
' There's not a man or woman
Born under the skies   20
Dare match in learning with us two,
And all day long we have found
There's not a thing but love can make
The world a narrow pound.'

W. B. YEATS

434

THE ROSE TREE

' O words are lightly spoken,'
Said Pearse to Connolly,
' Maybe a breath of politic words
Has withered our Rose Tree;
Or maybe but a wind that blows   5
Across the bitter sea.'

' It needs to be but watered,'
James Connolly replied,
' To make the green come out again
And spread on every side,   10
And shake the blossom from the bud
To be the garden's pride.'

' But where can we draw water,'
Said Pearse to Connolly,
' When all the wells are parched away?   15
O plain as plain can be
There's nothing but our own red blood
Can make a right Rose Tree."

W. B. YEATS

435

DEATH

Nor dread nor hope attend
A dying animal;
A man awaits his end
Dreading and hoping all;
Many times he died,   5
Many times rose again.
A great man in his pride
Confronting murderous men
Casts derision upon
Supersession of breath;   10
He knows death to the bone—
Man has created death.

W. B. YEATS

436

AN ACRE OF GRASS

Picture and book remain,
An acre of green grass
For air and exercise,
Now strength of body goes;
Midnight, an old house   5
Where nothing stirs but a mouse.

My temptation is quiet.
Here at life's end
Neither loose imagination,
Nor the mill of the mind   10
Consuming its rag and bone,
Can make the truth known.

Grant me an old man's frenzy,
Myself must I remake
Till I am Timon and Lear   15
Or that William Blake
Who beat upon the wall
Till Truth obeyed his call;

A mind Michael Angelo knew
That can pierce the clouds,   20
Or inspired by frenzy
Shake the dead in their shrouds;
Forgotten else by mankind,
An old man's eagle mind.

                                    W. B. YEATS

437

NON SUM QUALIS ERAM

Last night, ah, yesternight, betwixt her lips and mine
There fell thy shadow, Cynara! thy breath was shed
Upon my soul between the kisses and the wine;
And I was desolate and sick of an old passion,
    Yea, I was desolate and bow'd my head: 5
I have been faithful to thee, Cynara! in my fashion.

All night upon mine heart I felt her warm heart beat,
Night-long within mine arms in love and sleep she lay;
Surely the kisses of her bought red mouth were sweet;
But I was desolate and sick of an old passion,   10
　　When I awoke and found the dawn was gray:
I have been faithful to thee, Cynara! in my fashion.

I have forgot much, Cynara! gone with the wind,
Flung roses, roses, riotously with the throng,
Dancing, to put thy pale lost lilies out of mind;   15
But I was desolate and sick of an old passion,
　　Yea, all the time, because the dance was long:
I have been faithful to thee, Cynara! in my fashion.

I cried for madder music and for stronger wine,
But when the feast is finish'd and the lamps expire,   20
Then falls thy shadow, Cynara! the night is thine;
And I am desolate and sick of an old passion,
　　Yea, hungry for the lips of my desire:
I have been faithful to thee, Cynara! in my fashion.

                              ERNEST DOWSON

438

DEAD

In Merioneth, over the sad moor
　　Drives the rain, the cold wind blows:
　　Past the ruinous church door,
The poor procession without music goes.

Lonely she wandered out her hour, and died.   5
　　Now the mournful curlew cries
　　Over her, laid down beside
Death's lonely people: lightly down she lies.

In Merioneth, the wind lives and wails,
　　On from hill to lonely hill: 10
　　Down the loud triumphant gales,
A spirit cries *Be strong!* and cries *Be still!*

                              LIONEL JOHNSON

439

from THE BURNING OF THE LEAVES

Now is the time for the burning of the leaves.
They go to the fire; the nostril pricks with smoke
Wandering slowly into a weeping mist.
Brittle and blotched, ragged and rotten sheaves!
A flame seizes the smouldering ruin and bites   5
On stubborn stalks that crackle as they resist.

The last hollyhock's fallen tower is dust;
All the spices of June are a bitter reek,
All the extravagant riches spent and mean.
All burns! The reddest rose is a ghost;   10
Sparks whirl up, to expire in the mist: the wild
Fingers of fire are making corruption clean.

Now is the time for stripping the spirit bare,
Time for the burning of days ended and done,
Idle solace of things that have gone before: 15
Rootless hope and fruitless desire are there;
Let them go to the fire, with never a look behind.
The world that was ours is a world that is ours no more.

They will come again, the leaf and the flower, to arise
From squalor of rottenness into the old splendour,   20
And magical scents to a wondering memory bring;
The same glory, to shine upon different eyes.
Earth cares for her own ruins, naught for ours.
Nothing is certain, only the certain spring.

                                        LAURENCE BINYON

440

FOR A DEAD LADY

No more with overflowing light
Shall fill the eyes that now are faded,
Nor shall another's fringe with night
Their woman-hidden world as they did.

No more shall quiver down the days   5
The flowing wonder of her ways,
Whereof no language may requite
The shifting and the many-shaded.

The grace, divine, definitive,
Clings only as a faint forestalling;   10
The laugh that love could not forgive
Is hushed, and answers to no calling;
The forehead and the little ears
Have gone where Saturn keeps the years;
The breast where roses could not live   15
Has done with rising and with falling.

The beauty, shattered by the laws
That have creation in their keeping,
No longer trembles at applause,
Or over children that are sleeping;   20
And we who delve in beauty's lore
Know all that we have known before
Of what inexorable cause
Makes Time so vicious in his reaping.

                              EDWIN ARLINGTON ROBINSON

441

THE EARLY MORNING

The moon on the one hand, the dawn on the other:
The moon is my sister, the dawn is my brother.
The moon on my left and the dawn on my right.
My brother, good morning: my sister, good night.

                              HILAIRE BELLOC

442

THE DYING SWAN

O silver-throated Swan
Struck, struck! a golden dart
Clean through thy breast has gone
Home to thy heart.
Thrill, thrill, O silver throat!

O silver trumpet, pour
Love for defiance back
On him who smote!
And brim, brim o'er
With love; and ruby-dye thy track   10
Down thy last living reach
Of river, sail the golden light . . .
Enter the sun's heart . . . even teach,
O wondrous-gifted Pain, teach thou
The god to love, let him learn how.   15

                                T. STURGE MOORE

443

THE KINGFISHER

It was the Rainbow gave thee birth,
    And left thee all her lovely hues;
And, as her mother's name was Tears,
    So runs it in thy blood to choose
For haunts the lonely pools, and keep   5
In company with trees that weep.

Go you and, with such glorious hues,
    Live with proud Peacocks in green parks;
On lawns as smooth as shining glass,
    Let every feather show its marks;   10
Get thee on boughs and clap thy wings
Before the windows of proud kings.

Nay, lovely Bird, thou art not vain;
    Thou hast no proud, ambitious mind;
I also love a quiet place   15
    That's green, away from all mankind;
A lonely pool, and let a tree
Sigh with her bosom over me.

                                W. H. DAVIES

444

BORN OF TEARS

A thing that's rich in tears is sweet—
No sounds in all the world are sweeter.
A robin redbreast in the fall,
  The nightingale in June;
The bleating of young lambs in March,   5
  And the violin in tune:
These are the sounds that haunt my ears,
And all of them are born of tears.

A thing that's rich in tears is fair—
No sights in all the world are fairer.   10
How lovely is a summer's eve
  That's full of heavenly light;
When tears of joy, called shooting stars,
  Run down the face of night.
While every rainbow that appears   15
Could say—' My mother's name is Tears.'

W. H. DAVIES

445

EVE

Eve, with her basket, was
Deep in the bells and grass
Wading in bells and grass
Up to her knees,
Picking a dish of sweet   5
Berries and plums to eat,
Down in the bells and grass
Under the trees.

Mute as a mouse in a
Corner the cobra lay,   10
Curled round a bough of the
Cinnamon tall. . . .
Now to get even and
Humble proud heaven and
Now was the moment or   15
Never at all.

'Eva!' Each syllable
Light as a flower fell,
'Eva!' he whispered the
Wondering maid,   20
Soft as a bubble sung
Out of a linnet's lung,
Soft and most silverly
'Eva!' he said.

Picture that orchard sprite,   25
Eve, with her body white,
Supple and smooth to her
Slim finger tips,
Wondering, listening,
Listening, wondering,   30
Eve with a berry
Half-way to her lips.

Oh had our simple Eve
Seen through the make-believe!
Had she but known the   35
Pretender he was!
Out of the boughs he came,
Whispering still her name,
Tumbling in twenty rings
Into the grass.   40

Here was the strangest pair
In the world anywhere,
Eve in the bells and grass
Kneeling, and he
Telling his story low. . . .   45
Singing birds saw them go
Down the dark path to
The Blasphemous Tree.

Oh what a clatter when
Titmouse and Jenny Wren   50
Saw him successful and
Taking his leave!
How the birds rated him,
How they all hated him!
How they all pitied   55
Poor motherless Eve!

Picture her crying
Outside in the lane,
Eve, with no dish of sweet
Berries and plums to eat,   60
Haunting the gate of the
Orchard in vain. . . .
Picture the lewd delight
Under the hill to-night—
' Eva! ' the toast goes round,   65
' Eva! ' again.

RALPH HODGSON

446

THE LISTENERS

' Is there anybody there? ' said the Traveller,
  Knocking on the moonlit door;
And his horse in the silence champed the grasses
  Of the forest's ferny floor:
And a bird flew up out of the turret,   5
  Above the Traveller's head:
And he smote upon the door again a second time;
  ' Is there anybody there? ' he said.
But no one descended to the Traveller;
  No head from the leaf-fringed sill   10
Leaned over and looked into his grey eyes,
  Where he stood perplexed and still.
But only a host of phantom listeners
  That dwelt in the lone house then
Stood listening in the quiet of the moonlight   15
  To that voice from the world of men:
Stood thronging the faint moonbeams on the dark stair,
  That goes down to the empty hall,
Hearkening in an air stirred and shaken
  By the lonely Traveller's call.   20
And he felt in his heart their strangeness,
  Their stillness answering his cry,
While his horse moved, cropping the dark turf,
  'Neath the starred and leafy sky;
For he suddenly smote on the door, even   25
  Louder, and lifted his head:—
' Tell them I came, and no one answered,
  That I kept my word,' he said.

Never the least stir made the listeners,
   Though every word he spake   30
Fell echoing through the shadowiness of the still house
   From the one man left awake:
Ay, they heard his foot upon the stirrup,
   And the sound of iron on stone,
And how the silence surged softly backward,   35
   When the plunging hoofs were gone.

WALTER DE LA MARE

447

AUTUMN

There is a wind where the rose was;
Cold rain where sweet grass was;
   And clouds like sheep
   Stream o'er the steep
Grey skies where the lark was.   5

Nought gold where your hair was;
Nought warm where your hand was;
   But phantom, forlorn,
   Beneath the thorn,
Your ghost where your face was.   10

Sad winds where your voice was;
Tears, tears where my heart was;
   And ever with me,
   Child, ever with me,
Silence where hope was.   15

WALTER DE LA MARE

448

TO A CANDLE

Burn stilly, thou; and come with me.
I'll screen thy rays. Now . . . Look, and see,
Where, like a flower furled,
Sealed from this busy world,
Tranquil brow, and lid, and lip,   5
One I love lies here asleep.

Low upon her pillow is
A head of such strange loveliness—
Gilded-brown, unwoven hair—
That dread springs up to see it there: 10
Lest so profound a trance should be
Death's momentary alchemy.

Venture closer, then. Thy light
Be little day to this small night!
Fretting through her lids it makes   15
The lashes stir on those pure cheeks;
The scarcely-parted lips, it seems,
Pine, but in vain, to tell her dreams.

Every curve and hollow shows
In faintest shadow—mouth and nose;   20
Pulsing beneath the silken skin
The milk-blue blood rills out and in:
A bird's might be that slender bone,
Magic itself to ponder on.

Time hath spread its nets in vain;   25
The child she was is home again;
Veiled with Sleep's seraphic grace.
How innocent yet how wise a face!
Mutely entreating, it seems to sigh,—
' Love made me. It is only I.   30

' Love made this house wherein there dwells
A thing divine, and homeless else.
Not mine the need to ponder why
In this sweet prison I exult and sigh.
Not mine to bid you hence. God knows   35
It was for joy he shaped the rose.'

See, she stirs. A hand at rest
Slips from above that gentle breast,
White as winter-mounded snows,
Summer-sweet as that wild rose . . .   40
Thou lovely thing! Ah, welladay!
Candle, I dream. Come, come away!

WALTER DE LA MARE

449

FARE WELL

When I lie where shades of darkness
Shall no more assail mine eyes,
Nor the rain make lamentation
    When the wind sighs;
How will fare the world whose wonder   5
Was the very proof of me?
Memory fades, must the remembered
    Perishing be?

Oh, when this my dust surrenders
Hand, foot, lip. to dust again,   10
May these loved and loving faces
    Please other men!
May the rusting harvest hedgerow
Still the Traveller's Joy entwine,
And as happy children gather   15
    Posies once mine.

Look thy last on all things lovely,
Every hour. Let no night
Seal thy sense in deathly slumber
    Till to delight   20
Thou have paid thy utmost blessing;
Since that all things thou wouldst praise
Beauty took from those who loved them
    In other days.

                  WALTER DE LA MARE

450

THE DONKEY

When fishes flew and forests walk'd
    And figs grew upon thorn,
Some moment when the moon was blood
    Then surely I was born;

With monstrous head and sickening cry   5
    And ears like errant wings,
The devil's walking parody
    On all four-footed things.

The tatter'd outlaw of the earth,
   Of ancient crooked will;   10
Starve, scourge, deride me: I am dumb,
   I keep my secret still.

Fools! For I also had my hour;
   One far fierce hour and sweet:
There was a shout about my ears,   15
   And palms before my feet.

G. K. CHESTERTON

451

TO EARTHWARD

Love at the lips was touch
As sweet as I could bear;
And once that seemed too much;
I lived on air

That crossed me from sweet things,   5
The flow of—was it musk
From hidden grapevine springs
Down hill at dusk?

I had the swirl and ache
From sprays of honeysuckle   10
That when they're gathered shake
Dew on the knuckle.

I craved strong sweets, but those
Seemed strong when I was young;
The petal of the rose   15
It was that stung.

Now no joy but lacks salt
That is not dashed with pain
And weariness and fault;
I crave the stain   20

Of tears, the aftermark
Of almost too much love,
The sweet of bitter bark
And burning clove.

When stiff and sore and scarred   25
I take away my hand
From leaning on it hard
In grass and sand,

The hurt is not enough:
I long for weight and strength   30
To feel the earth as rough
To all my length.

ROBERT FROST

452

THE ROAD NOT TAKEN

Two roads diverged in a yellow wood,
And sorry I could not travel both
And be one traveller, long I stood
And looked down one as far as I could
To where it bent in the undergrowth;   5

Then took the other, as just as fair,
And having perhaps the better claim,
Because it was grassy and wanted wear;
Though as for that the passing there
Had worn them really about the same,   10

And both that morning equally lay
In leaves no step had trodden black.
Oh, I kept the first for another day!
Yet knowing how way leads on to way,
I doubted if I should ever come back.   15

I shall be telling this with a sigh
Somewhere ages and ages hence!
Two roads diverged in a wood, and I—
I took the one less travelled by,
And that has made all the difference.   20

ROBERT FROST

453

THE RUNAWAY

Once when the snow of the year was beginning to fall,
We stopped by a mountain pasture to say, ' Whose colt? '
A little Morgan had one forefoot on the wall,
The other curled at his breast. He dipped his head
And snorted at us. And then he had to bolt.   5
We heard the miniature thunder where he fled,
And we saw him, or thought we saw him, dim and grey,
Like a shadow against the curtain of falling flakes.
' I think the little fellow's afraid of the snow.
He isn't winter-broken. It isn't play   10
With the little fellow at all. He's running away.
I doubt if even his mother could tell him, " Sakes,
It's only weather." He'd think she didn't know!
Where is his mother? He can't be out alone.'
And now he comes again with clatter of stone,   15
And mounts the wall again with whited eyes
And all his tail that isn't hair up straight.
He shudders his coat as if to throw off flies.
' Whoever it is that leaves him out so late,
When other creatures have gone to stall and bin,   20
Ought to be told to come and take him in.'

ROBERT FROST

454

RELUCTANCE

Out through the fields and the woods
    And over the walls I have wended;
I have climbed the hills of view
    And looked at the world, and descended;
I have come by the highway home,   5
    And lo, it is ended.

The leaves are all dead on the ground,
    Save those that the oak is keeping
To ravel them one by one
    And let them go scraping and creeping   10
Out over the crusted snow,
    When others are sleeping.

And the dead leaves lie huddled and still,
   No longer blown hither and thither;
The last lone aster is gone;   15
   The flowers of the witch-hazel wither;
The heart is still aching to seek,
   But the feet question ' Whither?'

Ah, when to the heart of man
   Was it ever less than a treason   20
To go with the drift of things,
   To yield with a grace to reason,
And bow and accept the end
   Of a love or a season?

                              ROBERT FROST

455

CARGOES

Quinquireme of Nineveh from distant Ophir
Rowing home to haven in sunny Palestine,
With a cargo of ivory,
And apes and peacocks,
Sandalwood, cedarwood, and sweet white wine.   5

Stately Spanish galleon coming from the Isthmus,
Dipping through the Tropics by the palm-green shores,
With a cargo of diamonds,
Emeralds, amethysts,
Topazes, and cinnamon, and gold moidores.   10

Dirty British coaster with a salt-caked smoke stack
Butting through the Channel in the mad March days,
With a cargo of Tyne coal,
Road-rails, pig-lead,
Firewood, iron-ware, and cheap tin trays.   15

                      JOHN MASEFIELD

456

THE GALLOWS

There was a weasel lived in the sun
With all his family,
Till a keeper shot him with his gun
And hung him up on a tree,
Where he swings in the wind and rain,   5
In the sun and in the snow,
Without pleasure, without pain,
On the dead oak tree bough.

There was a crow who was no sleeper,
But a thief and a murderer   10
Till a very late hour; and this keeper
Made him one of the things that were,
To hang and flap in rain and wind
In the sun and in the snow.
There are no more sins to be sinned   15
On the dead oak tree bough.

There was a magpie, too,
Had a long tongue and a long tail;
He could both talk and do—
But what did that avail?   20
He, too, flaps in the wind and rain
Alongside weasel and crow,
Without pleasure, without pain,
On the dead oak tree bough.

And many other beasts   25
And birds, skin, bone, and feather,
Have been taken from their feasts
And hung up there together,
To swing and have endless leisure
In the sun and in the snow,   30
Without pain, without pleasure,
On the dead oak tree bough.

EDWARD THOMAS

457

LIGHTS OUT

I have come to the borders of sleep,
The unfathomable deep
Forest where all must lose
Their way, however straight,
Or winding, soon or late;   5
They cannot choose.

Many a road and track
That, since the dawn's first crack,
Up to the forest brink,
Deceived the travellers,   10
Suddenly now blurs,
And in they sink.

Here love ends—
Despair, ambition ends:
All pleasure and all trouble,   15
Although most sweet or bitter,
Here ends in sleep that is sweeter
Than tasks most noble.

There is not any book   20
Or face of dearest look
That I would not turn from now
To go into the unknown
I must enter, and leave, alone,
I know not how.

The tall forest towers;   25
Its cloudy foliage lowers
Ahead, shelf above shelf;
Its silence I hear and obey
That I may lose my way
And myself.   30

EDWARD THOMAS

458

THISTLEDOWN

This might have been a place for sleep
But, as from that small hollow there
Hosts of bright thistledown begin
Their dazzling journey through the air,
An idle man can only stare.   5

They grip their withered edge of stalk
In brief excitement for the wind;
They hold a breathless final talk,
And when their filmy cables part
One almost hears a little cry.   10

Some cling together while they wait
And droop and gaze and hesitate,
But others leap along the sky,
Or circle round and calmly choose
The gust they know they ought to use.   15

While some in loving pairs will glide,
Or watch the others as they pass,
Or rest on flowers in the grass,
Or circle through the shining day
Like silver butterflies at play.   20

Some catch themselves to every mound,
Then lingeringly and slowly move
As if they knew the precious ground
Were opening for their fertile love:
They almost try to dig, they need   25
So much to plant their thistle-seed.

                                    HAROLD MONRO

459

SHE MOVED THROUGH THE FAIR

My young love said to me, ' My brothers won't mind,
And my parents won't slight you for your lack of kind.'
Then she stepped away from me, and this she did say,
' It will not be long, love, till our wedding day.'

She stepped away from me and she moved through the fair, 5
And fondly I watched her go here and go there,
Then she went her way homeward with one star awake,
As the swan in the evening moves over the lake.

The people were saying no two were e'er wed
But one had a sorrow that never was said, 10
And I smiled as she passed with her goods and her gear,
And that was the last that I saw of my dear.

I dreamt it last night that my young love came in,
So softly she entered, her feet made no din;
She came close beside me, and this she did say, 15
' It will not be long, love, till our wedding day.'

PADRAIC COLUM

460

THE RIVALS

I heard a bird at dawn
Singing sweetly on a tree,
That the dew was on the lawn,
And the wind was on the lea;
But I didn't listen to him, 5
For he didn't sing to me!

I didn't listen to him,
For he didn't sing to me
That the dew was on the lawn,
And the wind was on the lea! 10
I was singing at the time,
Just as prettily as he!

I was singing all the time,
Just as prettily as he,
About the dew upon the lawn, 15
And the wind upon the lea!
So I didn't listen to him,
As he sang upon a tree!

JAMES STEPHENS

461

STILLNESS

When the words rustle no more,
  And the last work's done,
When the bolt lies deep in the door,
  And Fire, our Sun,
Falls on the dark-laned meadows of the floor;   5

When from the clock's last chime to the next chime
  Silence beats his drum,
And Space with gaunt grey eyes and her brother Time
  Wheeling and whispering come,
She with the mould of form and he with the loom of rhyme: 10

Then twittering out in the night my thought-birds flee,
  I am emptied of all my dreams:
I only hear Earth turning, only see
  Ether's long bankless streams,
And only know I should drown if you laid not your hand on me. 15

                                        JAMES ELROY FLECKER

462

THE OLD SHIPS

I have seen old ships sail like swans asleep
Beyond the village which men still call Tyre,
With leaden age o'ercargoed, dipping deep
For Famagusta and the hidden sun
That rings black Cyprus with a lake of fire;   5
And all those ships were certainly so old
Who knows how oft with squat and noisy gun,
Questing brown slaves or Syrian oranges,
The pirate Genoese
Hell-raked them till they rolled   10
Blood, water, fruit and corpses up the hold.
But now through friendly seas they softly run,
Painted the mid-sea blue or shore-sea green,
Still patterned with the vine and grapes in gold.

But I have seen,   15
Pointing her shapely shadows from the dawn
And image tumbled on a rose-swept bay,

A drowsy ship of some yet older day;
And, wonder's breath indrawn,
Thought I—who knows—who knows—but in that same   20
(Fished up beyond Ææa, patched up new
—Stern painted brighter blue—)
That talkative, bald-headed seaman came
(Twelve patient comrades sweating at the oar)
From Troy's doom-crimson shore,   25
And with great lies about his wooden horse
Set the crew laughing, and forgot his course.

It was so old a ship—who knows, who knows?
—And yet so beautiful, I watched in vain
To see the mast burst open with a rose,   30
And the whole deck put on its leaves again.

                                   JAMES ELROY FLECKER

463

HUMMING-BIRD

I can imagine, in some otherworld
Primeval-dumb, far back
In that most awful stillness, that only gasped and hummed,
Humming-birds raced down the avenues.

Before anything had a soul,   5
While life was a heave of Matter, half inanimate,
This little bit chipped off in brilliance
And went whizzing through the slow, vast, succulent stems.

I believe there were no flowers, then   9
In the world where the humming-bird flashed ahead of creation.
I believe he pierced the slow vegetable veins with his long beak.

Probably he was big
As mosses, and little lizards, they say were once big.
Probably he was a jabbing, terrifying monster.

We look at him through the wrong end of the long telescope of
    Time,   15
Luckily for us.

                                   D. H. LAWRENCE

464

What thou lovest well remains,
                        the rest is dross,
What thou lov'st well shall not be reft from thee,
What thou lov'st well is thy true heritage
Whose world, or mine or theirs   5
                        or is it of none?
First came the seen, then thus the palpable
        Elysium, though it were in the halls of hell,
What thou lovest well is thy true heritage.

The ant's a centaur in his dragon world.   10
Pull down thy vanity, it is not man
Made courage, or made order, or made grace,
        Pull down thy vanity, I say pull down.
Learn of the green world what can be thy place
In scaled invention or true artistry,   15
Pull down thy vanity,
                        Paquin pull down!
The green casque has outdone your elegance.

' Master thyself, then others shall thee beare '
        Pull down thy vanity
Thou art a beaten dog beneath the hail,   20
A swollen magpie in a fitful sun,
Half black half white
Nor knowst'ou wing from tail
Pull down thy vanity
                        How mean thy hates   25
Fostered in falsity,
                        Pull down thy vanity,
Rathe to destroy, niggard in charity,
Pull down thy vanity,
                        I say pull down.   30
But to have done instead of not doing
                        this is not vanity
To have, with decency, knocked
That a Blunt should open   35
        To have gathered from the air a live tradition
or from a fine old eye the unconquered flame
This is not vanity.
        Here error is all in the not done,
all in the diffidence that faltered   40

                                EZRA POUND

465

WILTSHIRE DOWNS

The cuckoo's double note
Loosened like bubbles from a drowning throat
Floats through the air
In mockery of pipit, lark and stare.

The stable-boys thud by   5
Their horses slinging divots at the sky
And with bright hooves
Printing the sodden turf with lucky grooves.

As still as a windhover
A shepherd in his flapping coat leans over   10
His tall sheep-crook
And shearlings, tegs and yoes cons like a book.

And one tree-crowned long barrow
Stretched like a sow that has brought forth her farrow
Hides a king's bones   15
Lying like broken sticks among the stones.

ANDREW YOUNG

466

THE FEAR

How often I turn round
To face the beast that bound by bound
Leaps on me from behind,
Only to see a bough that heaves
With sudden gust of wind   5
Or blackbird raking withered leaves.

A dog may find me out
Or badger toss a white-lined snout;
And one day as I softly trod
Looking for nothing stranger than   10
A fox or stoat I met a man
And even that seemed not too odd.

And yet in any place I go
I watch and listen as all creatures do
For what I cannot see or hear,   15
For something warns me everywhere
That even in my land of birth
I trespass on the earth.

ANDREW YOUNG

467

PRELUDE: THE TROOPS

Dim, gradual thinning of the shapeless gloom
Shudders to drizzling daybreak that reveals
Disconsolate men who stamp their sodden boots
And turn dulled, sunken faces to the sky
Haggard and hopeless. They, who have beaten down   5
The stale despair of night, must now renew
Their desolation in the truce of dawn,
Murdering the livid hours that grope for peace.

Yet these, who cling to life with stubborn hands,
Can grin through storms of death and find a gap   10
In the clawed, cruel tangles of his defence.
They march from safety, and the bird-sung joy
Of grass-green thickets, to the land where all
Is ruin, and nothing blossoms but the sky
That hastens over them where they endure   15
Sad, smoking, flat horizons, reeking woods,
And foundered trench-lines volleying doom for doom.

O my brave brown companions, when your souls
Flock silently away, and the eyeless dead
Shame the wild beast of battle on the ridge,   20
Death will stand grieving in that field of war
Since your unvanquished hardihood is spent.
And through some mooned Valhalla there will pass
Battalions and battalions, scarred from hell;
The unreturning army that was youth;   25
The legions who have suffered and are dust.

SIEGFRIED SASSOON

468

HEAVEN

Fish (fly-replete, in depth of June,
Dawdling away their wat'ry noon)
Ponder deep wisdom, dark or clear,
Each secret fishy hope or fear.
Fish say, they have their Stream and Pond;   5
But is there anything Beyond?
This life cannot be All, they swear,
For how unpleasant, if it were!
One may not doubt that, somehow, Good
Shall come of Water and of Mud;   10
And, sure, the reverent eye must see
A Purpose in Liquidity.
We darkly know, by Faith we cry,
The future is not Wholly Dry.
Mud unto mud!—Death eddies near—   15
Not here the appointed End, not here!
But somewhere, beyond Space and Time,
Is wetter water, slimier slime!
And there (they trust) there swimmeth One
Who swam ere rivers were begun,   20
Immense, of fishy form and mind,
Squamous, omnipotent, and kind;
And under that Almighty Fin,
The littlest fish may enter in.
Oh! never fly conceals a hook,   25
Fish say, in the Eternal Brook,
But more than mundane weeds are there,
And mud, celestially fair;
Fat caterpillars drift around,
And Paradisal grubs are found;   30
Unfading moths, immortal flies,
And the worm that never dies.
And in that Heaven of all their wish,
There shall be no more land, say fish.

RUPERT BROOKE

469

THE COMBAT

It was not meant for human eyes,
That combat on the shabby patch
Of clods and trampled turf that lies
Somewhere beneath the sodden skies
For eye of toad or adder to catch.   5

And having seen it I accuse
The crested animal in his pride,
Arrayed in all the royal hues
Which hide the claws he well can use
To tear the heart out of the side.   10

Body of leopard, eagle's head
And whetted beak, and lion's mane,
And frost-grey hedge of feathers spread
Behind—he seemed of all things bred.
I shall not see his like again.   15

As for his enemy, there came in
A soft round beast as brown as clay;
All rent and patched his wretched skin;
A battered bag he might have been,
Some old used thing to throw away.   20

Yet he awaited face to face
The furious beast and the swift attack.
Soon over and done. That was no place
Or time for chivalry or for grace.
The fury had him on his back.   25

And two small paws like hands flew out
To right and left as the trees stood by.
One would have said beyond a doubt
This was the very end of the bout,
But that the creature would not die.   30

For ere the death-stroke he was gone,
Writhed, whirled, huddled into his den,
Safe somehow there. The fight was done,
And he had lost who had all but won.
But oh his deadly fury then.   35

A while the place lay blank, forlorn,
Drowsing as in relief from pain.
The cricket chirped, the grating thorn
Stirred, and a little sound was born.
The champions took their posts again.　　　　40

And all began. The stealthy paw
Slashed out and in. Could nothing save
These rags and tatters from the claw?
Nothing. And yet I never saw
A beast so helpless and so brave.　　　　45

And now, while the trees stand watching, still
The unequal battle rages there.
The killing beast that cannot kill
Swells and swells in his fury till
You'd almost think it was despair.　　　　50

EDWIN MUIR

470

THE CHILD DYING

Unfriendly friendly universe,
I pack your stars into my purse,
And bid you, bid you so farewell.
That I can leave you, quite go out,
Go out, go out beyond all doubt,　　　　5
My father says, is the miracle.

You are so great, and I so small:
I am nothing, you are all:
Being nothing, I can take this way.
Oh I need neither rise nor fall,　　　　10
For when I do not move at all
I shall be out of all your day.

It's said some memory will remain
In the other place, grass in the rain,
Light on the land, sun on the sea,　　　　15
A flitting grace, a phantom face,
But the world is out. There is no place
Where it and its ghost can ever be.

Father, father, I dread this air
Blown from the far side of despair,   20
The cold cold corner. What house, what hold,
What hand is there? I look and see
Nothing-filled eternity,
And the great round world grows weak and old.

Hold my hand, oh hold it fast—   25
I am changing!—until at last
My hand in yours no more will change,
Though yours change on. You here, I there,
So hand in hand, twin-leafed despair—
I did not know death was so strange.   30

EDWIN MUIR

471

SONG

Once my heart was a summer rose
That cares not for right or wrong,
And the sun was another rose, that year,
They shone, the sun and the rose, my dear—
Over the long and the light summer land   5
All the bright summer long.

As I walked in the long and the light summer land
All that I knew of shade
Was the cloud, my ombrelle of rustling grey
Sharp silk, it had spokes of grey steel rain—   10
Hiding my rose away, my dear,
Hiding my rose away.

And my laughter shone like a flight of birds
All in the summer gay,—
Tumbling pigeons and chattering starlings   15
And other pretty darlings, my dear,
And other pretty darlings.

To my heart like a rose, a rain of tears
(All the bright summer long)
Was only the sheen on a wood-dove's breast,   20
And sorrow only her song, my love—
And sorrow only my rest.

I passed a while in Feather Town—
(All the bright summer long)—
The idle wind puffed that town up   25
In air, then blew it down.

I walk alone now in Lead Town
(All in the summer gay . . .)
Where the steady people walk like the Dead—
And will not look my way.   30

For withering my heart, that summer rose,
Came another heart like a sun,—
And it drank all the dew from the rose, my love,
And the birds have forgotten their song
That sounded all summer long, my dear—   35
All the bright summer long.

EDITH SITWELL

472

HEART AND MIND

Said the Lion to the Lioness—' When you are amber dust,—
No more a raging fire like the heat of the Sun
(No liking but all lust)—
Remember still the flowering of the amber blood and bone
The rippling of bright muscles like a sea,   5
Remember the rose-prickles of bright paws
Though we shall mate no more
Till the fire of that sun the heart and the moon-cold bone are one.'

Said the Skeleton lying upon the sands of Time—
' The great gold planet that is the mourning heat of the Sun   10
Is greater than all gold, more powerful
Than the tawny body of a Lion that fire consumes
Like all that grows or leaps . . . so is the heart
More powerful than all dust. Once I was Hercules
Or Samson, strong as the pillars of the seas: 15
But the flames of the heart consumed me, and the mind
Is but a foolish wind.'

Said the Sun to the Moon—' When you are but a lonely white
      crone,
And I, a dead King in my golden armour somewhere in a dark
      wood,

Remember only this of our hopeless love   20
That never till Time is done
Will the fire of the heart and the fire of the mind be one.'

EDITH SITWELL.

473

THE SWANS

In the green light of water, like the day
Under green boughs, the spray
And air-pale petals of the foam seem flowers,—
Dark-leaved arbutus blooms with wax-pale bells
And their faint honey-smells,   5
The velvety syringa with smooth leaves,
Gloxinia with a green shade in the snow,
Jasmine and moon-clear orange-blossoms and green blooms
Of the wild strawberries from the shade of woods.
Their showers   10
Pelt the white women under the green trees,
Venusia, Cosmopolita, Pistillarine—
White solar statues, white rose-trees in snow
Flowering for ever, child-women, half stars
Half flowers, waves of the sea, born of a dream.   15

Their laughter flying through the trees like doves,
These angels come to watch their whiter ghosts
In the air-pale water, archipelagos
Of stars and young thin moons from great wings falling
As ripples widen.   20
These are their ghosts, their own white angels these!
O great wings spreading—
Your bones are made of amber, smooth and thin
Grown from the amber dust that was a rose
Or nymph in swan-smooth waters. But Time's winter falls   25
With snows as soft, as soundless . . . Then, who knows
Rose-footed swan from snow, or girl from rose?

EDITH SITWELL

474

from THE HOLLOW MEN

Eyes I dare not meet in dreams
In death's dream kingdom
These do not appear:
There, the eyes are
Sunlight on a broken column   5
There, is a tree swinging
And voices are
In the wind's singing
More distant and more solemn
Than a fading star.   10

Let me be no nearer
In death's dream kingdom
Let me also wear
Such deliberate disguises
Rat's coat, crowskin, crossed staves   15
In a field
Behaving as the wind behaves
No nearer—

Not that final meeting
In the twilight kingdom.   20

T. S. ELIOT

475

JOURNEY OF THE MAGI

'A cold coming we had of it,
Just the worst time of the year
For a journey, and such a long journey:
The ways deep and the weather sharp,
The very dead of winter.'   5
And the camels galled, sore-footed, refractory,
Lying down in the melting snow.
There were times we regretted
The summer palaces on slopes, the terraces,
And the silken girls bringing sherbet.   10
Then the camel men cursing and grumbling

And running away, and wanting their liquor and women,
And the night-fires going out, and the lack of shelters,
And the cities hostile and the towns unfriendly
And the villages dirty and charging high prices: 15
A hard time we had of it.
At the end we preferred to travel all night,
Sleeping in snatches,
With the voices singing in our ears, saying
That this was all folly.   20

   Then at dawn we came down to a temperate valley,
Wet, below the snow line, smelling of vegetation;
With a running stream and a water-mill beating the darkness,
And three trees on the low sky,
And an old white horse galloped away in the meadow.   25
Then we came to a tavern with vine-leaves over the lintel,
Six hands at an open door dicing for pieces of silver,
And feet kicking the empty wine-skins.
But there was no information, and so we continued
And arrived at evening, not a moment too soon   30
Finding the place; it was (you may say) satisfactory.
   All this was a long time ago, I remember,
And I would do it again, but set down
This set down
This: were we led all that way for   35
Birth or Death? There was a Birth, certainly,
We had evidence and no doubt. I had seen birth and death,
But had thought they were different; this Birth was
Hard and bitter agony for us, like Death, our death.
We returned to our places, these Kingdoms,   40
But no longer at ease here, in the old dispensation,
With an alien people clutching their gods.
I should be glad of another death.

                                                T. S. ELIOT

476

MARINA

What seas what shores what grey rocks and what islands
What water lapping the bow
And scent of pine and the woodthrush singing through the fog
What images return
O my daughter.   5

Those who sharpen the tooth of the dog, meaning
Death
Those who glitter with the glory of the hummingbird, meaning
Death
Those who sit in the stye of contentment, meaning   10
Death
Those who suffer the ecstasy of the animals, meaning
Death

Are become unsubstantial, reduced by a wind,
A breath of pine, and the woodsong fog   15
By this grace dissolved in place

What is this face, less clear and clearer
The pulse in the arm, less strong and stronger—
Given or lent? more distant than stars and nearer than the eye

Whispers and small laughter between leaves and hurrying feet 20
Under sleep, where all the waters meet.
Bowsprit cracked with ice and paint cracked with heat.
I made this, I have forgotten
And remember.
The rigging weak and the canvas rotten   25
Between one June and another September.
Made this unknowing, half conscious, unknown, my own.
The garboard strake leaks, the seams need caulking.
This form, this face, this life
Living to live in a world of time beyond me; let me   30
Resign my life for this life, my speech for that unspoken,
The awakened, lips parted, the hope, the new ships.

What seas what shores what granite islands towards my timbers
And woodthrush calling through the fog
My daughter.   35

T. S. ELIOT

477

BELLS FOR JOHN WHITESIDE'S DAUGHTER

There was such speed in her little body,
And such lightness in her footfall,
It is no wonder her brown study
Astonishes us all.

Her wars were bruited in our high window.   5
We looked among orchard trees and beyond,
Where she took arms against her shadow,
Or harried unto the pond

The lazy geese, like a snow cloud
Dripping their snow on the green grass,   10
Tricking and stopping, sleepy and proud,
Who cried in goose, Alas,

For the tireless heart within the little
Lady with rod that made them rise
From their noon apple-dreams and scuttle   15
Goose-fashion under the skies!

But now go the bells, and we are ready,
In one house we are sternly stopped
To say we are vexed at her brown study,
Lying so primly propped.   20

JOHN CROWE RANSOM

478

DRAGON FLIES

What drinks the dragon fly, that dart of blue light,
The small, the slender one, in June late, or July,
Among the irises, upon the water-lilies, by the bright rock rose
Overhanging the goldfish, dark and yellow in the sunshine?

Drowsy, the tortoise sits by the water edge,   5
On him the air is keener than a razor,
His seat of stone and his shell together getting hotter,
His little webbed feet like darker-dimpled water.

Those blue darts multiply as the day grows warmer,
The leaf-packed lily buds are burst asunder   10
Red-pale and crimson to burn upon the water
Suddenly unfolded. What drinks the dragon fly?

He drinks the limitless, the boundless azure,
Hence is he blue, like the poppy of Himal'ya—
Ten thousand feet high o'er the snow wide-waving   15
Happy like a sea of inland blue water.

Spirits of an alcohol unknown to earth-men,
Delight-drunken fiends half colour, half madness
The Dragon-flies battle, by the fires of their nature
Mid the waves of the wind on the glittering water.   20

W. J. TURNER

479

TALKING WITH SOLDIERS

The mind of the people is like mud,
From which arise strange and beautiful things,
But mud is none the less mud,
Though it bear orchids and prophesying Kings,
Dreams, trees, and water's bright babblings.   5

It has found form and colour and light,
The cold glimmer of the ice-wrapped Poles;
It has called a far-off glow Arcturus,
And some pale weeds, lilies of the valley.

It has imagined Virgil, Helen and Cassandra;   10
The sack of Troy, and the weeping for Hector—
Rearing stark up 'mid all this beauty
In the thick, dull neck of Ajax.

There is a dark Pine in Lapland,
And the great, figured Horn of the Reindeer   15
Moving soundlessly across the snow,
Is its twin brother, double-dreamed,
In the mind of a far-off people.

It is strange that a little mud
Should echo with sounds, syllables, and letters,   20
Should rise up and call a mountain Popocatapetl,
And a green leafed wood Oleander.

These are the ghosts of invisible things;
There is no Lapland, no Helen and no Hector,
And the Reindeer is a darkening of the brain,   25
And Oleander is but Oleander.

Mary Magdalena and the vine Lachrymae Christi,
Were like ghosts up the ghost of Vesuvius,

As I sat and drank wine with the soldiers,
As I sat in the Inn on the mountain,   30
Watching the shadows in my mind.

The mind of the people is like mud:
Where are the imperishable things,
The ghosts that flicker in the brain—
Silent women, orchids, and prophesying Kings,   35
Dreams, trees, and water's bright babblings?

                                        W. J. TURNER

480

THE BURIED CHILD

He is not dead nor liveth
The little child in the grave,
And men have known for ever
That he walketh again;
They hear him November evenings,   5
When acorns fall with the rain.

Deep in the hearts of men
Within his tomb he lieth,
And when the heart is desolate
He desolate sigheth.   10

Teach me then the heart of the dead child,
Who, holding a tulip, goeth
Up the stairs in his little grave-shift,
Sitting down in his little chair
By his biscuit and orange,   15
In the nursery he knoweth.

Teach me all that the child who knew life
And the quiet of death,
To the croon of the cradle-song
By his brother's crib   20
In the deeps of the nursery dusk
To his mother saith.

                            DOROTHY WELLESLEY

481

THE GREATER CATS

The greater cats with golden eyes
Stare out between the bars.
Deserts are there, and different skies,
And night with different stars.
They prowl the aromatic hill,   5
And mate as fiercely as they kill
And hold the freedom of their will
To roam, to live, to drink their fill;
But this beyond their wit know I:
Man loves a little, and for long shall die.   10

Their kind across the desert range
Where tulips spring from stones,
Not knowing they will suffer change
Or vultures pick their bones.
Their strength's eternal in their sight,   15
They rule the terror of the night,
They overtake the deer in flight,
And in their arrogance they smite;
But I am sage, if they are strong:
Man's love is transient as his death is long.   20

Yet oh what powers to deceive!
My wit is turned to faith,
And at this moment I believe
In love, and scout at death.
I came from nowhere, and shall be   25
Strong, steadfast, swift, eternally:
I am a lion, a stone, a tree,
And as the Polar star in me
Is fixed my constant heart on thee.
Ah, may I stay for ever blind   30
With lions, tigers, leopards, and their kind.

V. SACKVILLE-WEST

482

FUTILITY

Move him into the sun—
Gently its touch awoke him once,
At home, whispering of fields unsown.
Always it woke him, even in France,
Until this morning and this snow.   5
If anything might rouse him now
The kind old sun will know.

Think how it wakes the seeds,—
Woke, once, the clays of a cold star.
Are limbs, so dear-achieved, are sides,   10
Full-nerved—still warm—too hard to stir?
Was it for this the clay grew tall?
—O what made fatuous sunbeams toil
To break earth's sleep at all?

WILFRED OWEN

483

ANTHEM FOR DOOMED YOUTH

What passing-bells for these who die as cattle?
   Only the monstrous anger of the guns.
Only the stuttering rifles' rapid rattle
   Can patter out their hasty orisons.
No mockeries for them from prayers or bells,   5
   Nor any voice of mourning save the choirs,—
The shrill, demented choirs of wailing shells;
   And bugles calling for them from sad shires.

What candles may be held to speed them all?
   Not in the hands of boys, but in their eyes   10
Shall shine the holy glimmers of good-byes.
   The pallor of girls' brows shall be their pall;
Their flowers the tenderness of silent minds,
And each slow dusk a drawing-down of blinds.

WILFRED OWEN

484

MINERS

There was a whispering in my hearth,
　　A sigh of the coal,
Grown wistful of a former earth
　　It might recall.

I listened for a tale of leaves　　　　　　　5
　　And smothered ferns;
Frond-forests; and the low, sly lives
　　Before the fawns.

My fire might show steam-phantoms simmer
　　From Time's old cauldron,　　　　　　10
Before the birds made nests in summer,
　　Or men had children.

But the coals were murmuring of their mine,
　　And moans down there
Of boys that slept wry sleep, and men　　15
　　Writhing for air.

And I saw white bones in the cinder-shard.
　　Bones without number;
For many hearts with coal are charred
　　And few remember.　　　　　　　　20

I thought of some who worked dark pits
　　Of war, and died
Digging the rock where Death reputes
　　Peace lies indeed.

Comforted years will sit soft-chaired　　25
　　In rooms of amber;
The years will stretch their hands, well-cheered
　　By our lives' ember.

The centuries will burn rich loads
　　With which we groaned,　　　　　　30
Whose warmth shall lull their dreaming lids
　　While songs are crooned.
But they will not dream of us poor lads
　　Lost in the ground.

WILFRED OWEN

485

A SHEPHERD'S COAT

I woke from death and dreaming.
His absence be the child I carry,
All days, and all years.
Eternally and this night he will deliver me.
Come peace. For he is coming.   5

Time tells a marginal story;
Dilates with midsummer that less than leaf
A mute heart, light heart, blown along the pavement;
Then mortally wintry, sears
The implicit glade—oh universe enough!   10
Orchard in bloom bereaved beyond bereavement.
Yet peace! For now it is gloaming,
Simple and provident, folding the numbered lambs.

No spatial streams no tears
Can melt the insensate piety of grief.   15
Adore instead the untold event still happening;
That miracle be the child I carry,
All days, and all years.
Come other south, come wise and holier thaws,
Enlarge me to inhale so ample a breath;   20
Come peace for he is coming.
Between the lily in bud and the lily opening
Love is, and love redeems.
Come haven, come your hush, horizoning arms.

I shall not want, I wake renewed by death,   25
A shepherd's coat drawn over me.

LILIAN BOWES-LYON

486

THE COOL WEB

Children are dumb to say how hot the day is,
How hot the scent is of the summer rose,
How dreadful the black wastes of evening sky,
How dreadful the tall soldiers drumming by.

But we have speech, that cools the hottest sun, 5
And speech that dulls the hottest rose's scent.
We spell away the overhanging night,
We spell away the soldiers and the fright.

There's a cool web of language winds us in,
Retreat from too much gladness, too much fear: 10
We grow sea-green at last and coldly die
In brininess and volubility.

But if we let our tongues lose self-possession,
Throwing off language and its wateriness
Before our death, instead of when death comes, 15
Facing the brightness of the children's day,
Facing the rose, the dark sky and the drums,
We shall go mad no doubt and die that way.

ROBERT GRAVES

487

IN THE WILDERNESS

Christ of His gentleness
Thirsting and hungering,
Walked in the wilderness;
Soft words of grace He spoke
Unto lost desert-folk 5
That listened wondering.
He heard the bitterns call
From ruined palace-wall,
Answered them brotherly.
He held communion 10
With the she-pelican
Of lonely piety.
Basilisk, cockatrice,
Flocked to his homilies,
With mail of dread device, 15
With monstrous barbèd slings,
With eager dragon-eyes;
Great bats on leathern wings
And poor blind broken things,
Foul in their miseries. 20
And ever with Him went,
Of all His wanderings

Comrade, with ragged coat,
Gaunt ribs—poor innocent—
Bleeding foot, burning throat,   25
The guileless old scapegoat;
For forty nights and days
Followed in Jesus' ways,
Sure guard behind Him kept,
Tears like a lover wept.   30

ROBERT GRAVES

488

THE FOREBODING

Looking by chance in at the open window
    I saw my own self seated in his chair
With gaze abstracted, furrowed forehead,
    Unkempt hair.

I thought that I had suddenly come to die,   5
    That to a cold corpse this was my farewell,
Until the pen moved slowly on the paper
    And tears fell.

He had written a name, yours, in printed letters
    One word on which bemusedly to pore: 10
No protest, no desire, your naked name,
    Nothing more.

Would it be to-morrow, would it be next year?
    But the vision was not false, this much I knew;
And I turned angrily from the open window   15
    Aghast at you.

Why never a warning, either by speech or look,
    That the love you cruelly gave me could not last?
Already it was too late: the bait swallowed,
    The hook fast.   20

ROBERT GRAVES

489

THE MIDNIGHT SKATERS

The hop-poles stand in cones,
  The icy pond lurks under,
The pole-tops steeple to the thrones
  Of stars, sound gulfs of wonder;
But not the tallest there, 'tis said,   5
Could fathom to this pond's black bed.

Then is not death at watch
  Within those secret waters?
What wants he but to catch
  Earth's heedless sons and daughters?   10
With but a crystal parapet
Between, he has his engines set.

Then on, blood shouts, on, on,
  Twirl, wheel and whip above him,
Dance on this ball-floor thin and wan,   15
  Use him as though you love him;
Court him, elude him, reel and pass,
And let him hate you through the glass.

                           EDMUND BLUNDEN

490

WHAT IS WINTER?

The haze upon the meadow
  Denies the dying year,
For the sun's within it, something bridal
  Is more than dreaming here.
There is no end, no severance,   5
No moment of deliverance,
  No quietus made,
Though quiet abounds and deliverance moves
  In that sunny shade.

What is winter? a word,   10
  A figure, a clever guess.
That time-word does not answer to
  This drowsy wakefulness.

The secret stream scorns interval
Though the calendar shouts one from the wall;   15
   The spirit has no last days;
And death is no more dead than this
   Flower-haunted haze.

EDMUND BLUNDEN

491

THE SUNLIT VALE

I saw the sunlit vale, and the pastoral fairy-tale;
The sweet and bitter scent of the may drifted by;
And never have I seen such a bright bewildering green,
   But it looked like a lie,
   Like a kindly meant lie.   5

When gods are in dispute, one a Sidney, one a brute,
It would seem that human sense might not know, might not spy;
But though nature smile and feign where foul play has stabbed
    and slain,
   There's a witness, an eye,
   Nor will charms blind that eye.   10

Nymph of the upland song and the sparkling leafage young,
For your merciful desire with these charms to beguile,
For ever be adored; muses yield you rich reward;
   But you fail, though you smile
   That other does not smile   15

EDMUND BLUNDEN

492

THE OLD JOCKEY

His last days linger in that low attic
That barely lets out the night,
With its gabled window on Knackers' Alley,
Just hoodwinking the light.

He comes and goes by that gabled window   5
And then on the window-pane
He leans, as thin as a bottled shadow—
A look and he's gone again:

Eyeing, maybe, some fine fish-women
In the best shawls of the Coombe 10
Or, maybe, the knife-grinder plying his treadle,
A run of sparks from his thumb!

But, O you should see him gazing, gazing,
When solemnly out on the road
The horse-drays pass overladen with grasses, 15
Each driver lost in his load;

Gazing until they return; and suddenly,
As galloping by they race,
From his pale eyes, like glass breaking,
Light leaps on his face. 20

F. R. HIGGINS

493

THE TRYST

O luely, luely, cam she in
And luely she lay doun:
I kent her be her caller lips
And her breists sae sma' and roun'.

A' thru the nicht we spak nae word 5
Nor sinder'd bane frae bane:
A' thru the nicht I heard her hert
Gang soundin' wi' my ain.

It was about the waukrife hour
Whan cocks begin to craw 10
That she smool'd saftly thru the mirk
Afore the day wud daw.

Sae luely, luely, cam she in,
Sae luely was she gaen;
And wi' her a' my simmer days 15
Like they had never been.

WILLIAM SOUTAR

494

CHOOSING A MAST

This mast, new-shaved, through whom I rive the ropes,
Says she was once an oread of the slopes,
Graceful and tall upon the rocky highlands,
A slender tree, as vertical as noon,
And her low voice was lovely as the silence   5
Through which a fountain whistles to the moon.
Who now of the white spray must take the veil
And, for her songs, the thunder of the sail.

I chose her for her fragrance, when the spring
With sweetest resins swelled her fourteenth ring   10
And with live amber welded her young thews:
I chose her for the glory of the Muse,
Smoother of forms, that her hard-knotted grain,
Grazed by the chisel, shaven by the plane,
Might from the steel as cool a burnish take   15
As from the bladed moon a windless lake.

I chose her for her eagerness of flight
Where she stood tiptoe on the rocky height
Lifted by her own perfume to the sun,
While through her rustling plumes with eager sound   20
Her eagle spirit, with the gale at one,
Spreading wide pinions, would have spurned the ground
And her own sleeping shadow, had they not
With thymy fragrance charmed her to the spot.

Lover of song, I chose this mountain pine   25
Not only for the straightness of her spine
But for her songs: for there she loved to sing
Through a long noon's repose of wave and wing—
The fluvial swirling of her scented hair
Sole rill of song in all that windless air   30
And her slim form the naiad of the stream
Afloat upon the languor of its theme;

And for the soldier's fare on which she fed—
Her wine the azure, and the snow her bread;
And for her stormy watches on the height—   35
For only out of solitude or strife

Are born the sons of valour and delight;
And lastly for her rich exulting life
That with the wind stopped not its singing breath
But carolled on, the louder for its death.   40

Under a pine, when summer days were deep,
We loved the most to lie in love or sleep:
And when in long hexameters the west
Rolled his grey surge, the forest for his lyre,
It was the pines that sang us to our rest   45
Loud in the wind and fragrant in the fire,
With legioned voices swelling all night long,
From Pelion to Provence, their storm of song.

It was the pines that fanned us in the heat,
The pines, that cheered us in the time of sleet,   50
For which sweet gifts I set one dryad free—
No longer to the wind a rooted foe,
This nymph shall wander where she longs to be
And with the blue north wind arise and go,
A silver huntress with the moon to run   55
And fly through rainbows with the rising sun:

And when to pasture in the glittering shoals
The guardian mistral drives his thundering foals,
And when like Tartar horsemen racing free
We ride the snorting fillies of the sea,   60
My pine shall be the archer of the gale
While on the bending willow curves the sail
From whose great bow the long keel shooting home
Shall fly, the feathered arrow of the foam.

                                        ROY CAMPBELL

495

THE ZEBRAS

From the dark woods that breathe of fallen showers,
Harnessed with level rays in golden reins,
The zebras draw the dawn across the plains
Wading knee-deep among the scarlet flowers.
The sunlight, zithering their flanks with fire,   5
Flashes between the shadows as they pass
Barred with electric tremors through the grass
Like wind along the gold strings of a lyre.

Into the flushed air snorting rosy plumes
That smoulder round their feet in drifting fumes,   10
With dove-like voices call the distant fillies,
While round the herds the stallion wheels his flight,
Engine of beauty volted with delight,
To roll his mare among the trampled lilies.

ROY CAMPBELL

496

THE CHRISTMAS TREE

Put out the lights now!
Look at the Tree, the rough tree dazzled
In oriole plumes of flame,
Tinselled with twinkling frost fire, tasselled
With stars and moons—the same   5
That yesterday hid in the spinney and had no fame
Till we put out the lights now.

Hard are the nights now:
The fields at moonrise turn to agate,
Shadows are cold as jet;   10
In dyke and furrow, in copse and faggot
The frost's tooth is set;
And stars are the sparks whirled out by the north wind's fret
On the flinty nights now.

So feast your eyes now   15
On mimic star and moon-cold bauble:
Worlds may wither unseen,
But the Christmas Tree is a tree of fable,
A phoenix in evergreen,
And the world cannot change or chill what its mysteries mean   20
To your hearts and eyes now.

The vision dies now
Candle by candle: the tree that embraced it
Returns to its own kind,
To be earthed again and weather as best it   25
May the frost and the wind.
Children, it too had its hour—you will not mind
If it lives or dies now.

C. DAY LEWIS

497

IS IT FAR TO GO?

Is it far to go?
  A step—no further.
Is it hard to go?
  Ask the melting snow,
  The eddying feather. 5

What can I take there?
  Not a hank, not a hair.
What shall I leave behind?
  Ask the hastening wind,
  The fainting star. 10

Shall I be gone long?
  For ever and a day.
To whom there belong?
  Ask the stone to say,
  Ask my song. 15

Who will say farewell?
  The beating bell.
Will anyone miss me?
  That I dare not tell—
  Quick, Rose, and kiss me. 20

C. DAY LEWIS

498

EAST ANGLIAN BATHE

Oh when the early morning at the seaside
  Took us with hurrying steps from Horsey Mere
To see the whistling bent-grass on the leeside
  And then the tumbled breaker-line appear, 5
On high, the clouds with mighty adumbration
  Sailed over us to seaward fast and clear
And jellyfish in quivering isolation
  Lay silted in the dry sand of the breeze
And we, along the table-land of beach blown
  Went gooseflesh from our shoulders to our knees 10
And ran to catch the football, each to each thrown,
  In the soft and swirling music of the seas.

There splashed about our ankles as we waded
　Those intersecting wavelets morning-cold,
And sudden dark a patch of sea was shaded,   15
　And sudden light, another patch would hold
The warmth of whirling atoms in a sun-shot
　And underwater sandstorm green and gold.
So in we dived and louder than a gunshot
　Sea-water broke in fountains down the ear.   20
How cold the swim, how chattering cold the drying,
　How welcoming the inland reeds appear,
The wood-smoke and the breakfast and the frying,
　And your warm freshwater ripples, Horsey Mere.

JOHN BETJEMAN

499

UPPER LAMBOURNE

Up the ash-tree climbs the ivy,
　Up the ivy climbs the sun,
With a twenty-thousand pattering
　Has a valley breeze begun,
Feathery ash, neglected elder,   5
　Shift the shade and make it run—

Shift the shade toward the nettles,
　And the nettles set it free
To streak the stained Cararra headstone
　Where, in nineteen-twenty-three,   10
He who trained a hundred winners
　Paid the Final Entrance Fee.

Leathery limbs of Upper Lambourne,
　Leathery skin from sun and wind,
Leathery breeches, spreading stables,   15
　Shining saddles left behind—
To the down the string of horses
　Moving out of sight and mind.

Feathery ash in leathery Lambourne
　Waves above the sarsen stone,   20
And Edwardian plantations
　So coniferously moan
As to make the swelling downland,
　Far-surrounding, seem their own.

JOHN BETJEMAN

500

SONG

Warm are the still and lucky miles,
White shores of longing stretch away,
The light of recognition fills
    'The whole great day, and bright
The tiny world of lovers' arms.   5

Silence invades the breathing wood
Where the drowsy limbs a treasure keep,
Now greenly falls the learned shade
    Across the sleeping brows
And stirs their secret to a smile.   10

Restored! Returned! The lost are born
On seas of shipwreck home at last:
See! In the fire of praising burns
    The dry dumb past, and we
The life-day long shall part no more.   15
                W. H. AUDEN

501

Lay your sleeping head, my love,
Human on my faithless arm;
Time and fevers burn away
Individual beauty from
Thoughtful children, and the grave   5
Proves the child ephemeral:
But in my arms till break of day
Let the living creature lie,
Mortal, guilty, but to me
The entirely beautiful.   10

Soul and body have no bounds:
To lovers as they lie upon
Her tolerant enchanted slope
In their ordinary swoon,
Grave the vision Venus sends   15
Of supernatural sympathy,

Universal love and hope;
While an abstract insight wakes
Among the glaciers and the rocks
The hermit's sensual ecstasy.   20

Certainty, fidelity
On the stroke of midnight pass
Like vibrations of a bell,
And fashionable madmen raise
Their pedantic boring cry: 25
Every farthing of the cost,
All the dreaded cards foretell,
Shall be paid, but from this night
Not a whisper, not a thought,
Not a kiss nor look be lost.   30

Beauty, midnight, vision dies:
Let the winds of dawn that blow
Softly round your dreaming head
Such a day of sweetness show
Eye and knocking heart may bless,   35
Find the mortal world enough;
Noons of dryness see you fed
By the involuntary powers,
Nights of insult let you pass
Watched by every human love.   40

W. H. AUDEN

502

Fish in the unruffled lakes
The swarming colours wear,
Swans in the winter air
A white perfection have,
And the great lion walks   5
Through his innocent grove;
Lion, fish, and swan
Act, and are gone
Upon Time's toppling wave.

We till shadowed days are done,   10
We must weep and sing
Duty's conscious wrong,
The Devil in the clock,
The Goodness carefully worn

For atonement or for luck;   15
We must lose our loves,
On each beast and bird that moves
Turn an envious look.

Sighs for folly said and done
Twist our narrow days;   20
But I must bless, I must praise
That you, my swan, who have
All gifts that to the swan
Impulsive Nature gave,
The majesty and pride,   25
Last night should add
Your voluntary love.

                                   W. H. AUDEN

503

A TOAST

The slurred and drawled and crooning sounds,
The blurred and suave and sidling smells,
The webs of dew, the bells of buds,
The sun going down in crimson suds—
    This is on me and these are yours.   5

The bland and sculped and urgent beasts,
The here and there and nowhere birds,
The tongues of fire, the words of foam,
The curdling stars in the night's dome—
    This is on me and these are yours.   10

The face and grace and muscle of man
The balance of his body and mind,
Who keeps a trump behind his brain
Till instinct flicks it out again—
    This is on me and these are yours.   15

The courage of eyes, the craft of hands,
The gay feet, the pulse of hope,
The will that flings a rope—though hard—
To catch the future off its guard—
    This is on me and these are yours.   20

The luck and pluck and plunge of blood,
The wealth and spilth and sport of breath,
And sleep come down like death above
The fever and the peace of love—
    This is on me and these are yours.   25

               LOUIS MACNEICE

504

NOSTALGIA

In cock-wattle sunset or grey
Dawn when the dagger
Points again of longing
For what was never home
We needs must turn away   5
From the voices that cry ' Come '—
That under-sea ding-donging.

Dingle-dongle, bells and bluebells,
Snapdragon solstice, lunar lull,
The wasp circling the honey   10
Or the lamp soft on the snow—
These are the times at which
The will is vulnerable,
The trigger-finger slow,
The spirit lonely.   15

These are the times at which
Aloneness is too ripe
When homesick for the hollow
Heart of the Milky Way
The soundless clapper calls   20
And we would follow
But earth and will are stronger
And nearer—and we stay.

               LOUIS MACNEICE

505

JUNE THUNDER

The Junes were free and full, driving through tiny
Roads, the mudguards brushing the cowparsley,
Through fields of mustard and under boldly embattled
    Mays and chestnuts

Or between beeches verdurous and voluptuous   5
Or where broom and gorse beflagged the chalkland—
All the flare and gusto of the unenduring
    Joys of a season

Now returned but I note as more appropriate
To the maturer mood impending thunder   10
With an indigo sky and the garden hushed except for
    The treetops moving.

Then the curtains in my room blow suddenly inward,
The shrubbery rustles, birds fly heavily homeward,
The white flowers fade to nothing on the trees and rain comes 15
    Down like a dropscene.

Now there comes the catharsis, the cleansing downpour
Breaking the blossoms of our overdated fancies
Our old sentimentality and whimsicality
    Loves of the morning.   20

Blackness at half-past eight, the night's precursor,
Clouds like falling masonry and lightning's lavish
Annunciation, the sword of the mad archangel
    Flashed from the scabbard.

If only you would come and dare the crystal   25
Rampart of rain and the bottomless moat of thunder,
If only now you would come I should be happy
    Now if now only.

                                        LOUIS MACNEICE

506

THE PRISONERS

Far far the least of all, in want,
Are these,
The prisoners
Turned massive with their vaults and dark with dark.

They raise no hands, which rest upon their knees,   5
But lean their solid eyes against the night,
Dimly they feel
Only the furniture they use in cells.

Their Time is almost Death. The silted flow
Of years on years   10
Is marked by dawns
As faint as cracks on mud-flats of despair.

My pity moves amongst them like a breeze
On walls of stone
Fretting for summer leaves, or like a tune   15
On ears of stone.

Then, when I raise my hands to strike,
It is too late,
There are no chains that fall
Nor visionary liquid door   20
Melted with anger.

When have their lives been free from walls and dark
And airs that choke?
And where less prisoner to let my anger
Like a sun strike?   25

If I could follow them from room to womb
To plant some hope
Through the black silk of the big-bellied gown
There would I win.

No, no, no,   30
It is too late for anger,
Nothing prevails
But pity for the grief they cannot feel.

STEPHEN SPENDER

507

Poor girl, inhabitant of a strange land
Where death stares through your gaze,
As though a distant moon
Shone through midsummer days
With the skull-like glitter of night: 5

Poor child, you wear your summer dress
And your shoes striped with gold
As the earth wears a variegated cover
Of grass and flowers
Covering caverns of destruction over   10
Where hollow deaths are told.

I look into your sunk eyes,
Shafts of wells to both our hearts,
Which cannot take part in the lies
Of acting these gay parts.   15
Under our lips, our minds
Become one with the weeping
Of the mortality
Which through sleep is unsleeping.

Of what use is my weeping?   20
It does not carry a surgeon's knife
To cut the wrongly multiplying cells
At the root of your life.
It can only prove
That extremes of love   25
Stretch beyond the flesh to hideous bone
Howling in hyena dark alone.

Oh, but my grief is thought, a dream,
To-morrow's gale will sweep away.
It does not wake every day   30
To the facts which are and do not only seem:
The granite facts around your bed,
Poverty-stricken hopeless ugliness
Of the fact that you will soon be dead.

STEPHEN SPENDER

508

SEASCAPE

There are some days the happy ocean lies
Like an unfingered harp, below the land.
Afternoon gilds all the silent wires
Into a burning music of the eyes.
On mirroring paths between those fine-strung fires   5
The shore, laden with roses, horses, spires,
Wanders in water, imaged above ribbed sand.

The azure vibrancy of the air tires
And a sigh, like a woman's, from inland
Brushes the golden wires with shadowing hand   10
Drawing across their chords some gull's sharp cries
Or bell, or gasp from distant hedged-in shires:
These, deep as anchors, the silent wave buries.

Then, from the shore, two zig-zag butterflies,
Like errant dog-roses cross the hot strand   15
And on the ocean face in spiralling gyres
Search for foam-honey in reflected skies.
They drown. Witnesses understand
Such wings torn in such ritual sacrifice,

Remembering ships, treasures and cities.   20
Legendary heroes, plumed with flame like pyres
On flesh-winged ships fluttered from their island
And them the sea engulfed. Their coins and eyes
Twisted by the timeless waves' desires,
Are, through the muscular water, scarcely scanned   25
While, above them, the harp assumes their sighs.

STEPHEN SPENDER

509

TO MY MOTHER

Most near, most dear, most loved and most far,
Under the window where I often found her
Sitting as huge as Asia, seismic with laughter,
Gin and chicken helpless in her Irish hand,

Irresistible as Rabelais, but most tender for   5
The lame dogs and hurt birds that surround her,—
She is a procession no one can follow after
But be like a little dog following a brass band.

She will not glance up at the bomber, or condescend
To drop her gin and scuttle to a cellar,   10
But lean on the mahogany table like a mountain
Whom only faith can move, and so I send
O all my faith and all my love to tell her
That she will move from mourning into morning.

                                        GEORGE BARKER

510

SUMMER SONG

I looked into my heart to write
    And found a desert there.
But when I looked again I heard
Howling and proud in every word
    The hyena despair.   5

Great summer sun, great summer sun,
    All loss burns in trophies;
And in the cold sheet of the sky
Lifelong the fishlipped lovers lie
    Kissing catastrophes.   10

O loving garden where I lay
    When under the breasted tree
My son stood up behind my eyes
And groaned: Remember that the price
    Is vinegar for me.   15

Great summer sun, great summer sun,
    Turn back to the designer:
I would not be the one to start
The breaking day and the breaking heart
    For all the grief in China.   20

My one, my one, my only love,
    Hide, hide your face in a leaf,
And let the hot tear falling burn
The stupid heart that will not learn
    The everywhere of grief.   25

Great summer sun, great summer sun,
   Turn back to the never-never
Cloud-cuckoo, happy, far-off land
Where all the love is true love, and
   True love goes on for ever.   30

GEORGE BARKER

511

THE WILD TREES

O the wild trees of my home,
forests of blue dividing the pink moon,
the iron blue of those ancient branches
with their berries of vermilion stars.

In that place of steep meadows   5
the stacked sheaves are roasting,
and the sun-torn tulips
are tinders of scented ashes.

But here I have lost
the dialect of your hills,   10
my tongue has gone blind
far from their limestone roots.

Through trunks of black elder
runs a fox like a lantern,
and the hot grasses sing   15
with the slumber of larks.

But here there are thickets
of many different gestures,
torn branches of brick and steel
frozen against the sky.   20

O the wild trees of home
with their sounding dresses,
locks powdered with butterflies
and cheeks of blue moss.

I want to see you rise   25
from my brain's dry river,
I want your lips of wet roses
laid over my eyes.

O fountains of earth and rock,
gardens perfumed with cucumber,   30
home of secret valleys
where the wild trees grow.

Let me return at last
to your fertile wilderness,
to sleep with the coiled fernleaves   35
in your heart's live stone.

                              LAURIE LEE

512

APRIL RISE

If ever I saw blessing in the air
    I see it now in this still early day
Where lemon-green the vaporous morning drips
    Wet sunlight on the powder of my eye.

Blown bubble-film of blue, the sky wraps round   5
    Weeds of warm light whose every root and rod
Splutters with soapy green, and all the world
    Sweats with the bead of summer in its bud.

If ever I heard blessing it is there
    Where birds in trees that shoals and shadows are   10
Splash with their hidden wings and drops of sound
    Break on my ears their crests of throbbing air.

Pure in the haze the emerald sun dilates,
    The lips of sparrows milk the mossy stones,
While white as water by the lake a girl   15
    Swims her green hand among the gathered swans.

Now, as the almond burns its smoking wick,
    Dropping small flames to light the candled grass;
Now, as my low blood scales its second chance,
    If ever world were blessed, now it is.   20

                              LAURIE LEE

513

from THE PLACE AND THE PERSON

From the far horizon, and breaking in triumph towards him,
A ship comes forth, with supernatural haste
Parting the waters; and with grace the waves
Draw from her painted sides. Seductively
She flourishes her dazzling burden of sails
Which without wind or tide approach the harbour.
He sees her, and rises and cries, ' Again, again!
This ship will go to-morrow, and I shall go with it! '
And to the empty hovels he turns, but the dancers
Do not emerge, and their movements cannot be heard.   10
He calls to them: ' This ship will go to-morrow.
And if I am in your debt, to whatever degree,
Tell me at once, for I depart to-morrow.
I shall not wait for the unreturning vessels
Of you who dance your dances on this shore.   15
This is my ship; its name I do not know.
And since, if you ask the first dog in the street,
It will know enough to tell you I am helpless,
An impotent and wretched, and can do little or nothing,
And least of all for myself, do me this final act,   20
Who have never done me anything so gentle:
Find me the time of this golden ship's departure,
For, paralysed, I wish most earnestly to get
Early on board. Find me and tell me when.'

The ship draws closer, triumphant and unconcerned,   25
Unpiloted, and with the deliverer's smile,
And confidently cargoed with a love
That has broken through virgin seas to seek and find him,
Wherefore it gleams more brightly, wherefore it glitters.
The ropes are quickly thrown to where the harbour   30
Gladly receives them; the gang-planks quickly descend
And women in green and purple come from the deck
Descend to the jetty, bearing a burden of oil,
And some with flowers, and all of these they dispose
Close to his feet, and withdraw. The ship fills the harbour, 35
And to the ship they return. It gleams more brightly,
And its gleam is the gleam of yet another deception.
For look, the sails, their powerful and striding canvas,
And the riding fortress of timber which is the hull,

Are changing there in the sunlight, undone and mastered   **40**
As all is undone and mastered that comes this way;
Dislimning, falling, dissolving, canvas to satin,
Satin to sunlight turning, wood to paper,
The masts to cobwebs, women to wraith and phantom,
Failing mirage of the noontime, sunlight to sea,   **45**
Cobweb and satin to sunlight, sunlight to sun,
The empty harbour an unattended altar
For the barren, unblest marriage of sun and sea. . . .

                                        HENRY REED

514

FERN HILL

Now as I was young and easy under the apple boughs
About the lilting house and happy as the grass was green,
  The night above the dingle starry,
   Time let me hail and climb
   Golden in the heydays of his eyes,   **5**
And honoured among wagons I was prince of the apple towns
And once below a time I lordly had the trees and leaves
  Trail with daisies and barley
   Down the rivers of the windfall light.

And as I was green and carefree, famous among the barns   **10**
About the happy yard and singing as the farm was home,
  In the sun that is young once only,
   Time let me play and be
   Golden in the mercy of his means,
And green and golden I was huntsman and herdsman, the calves   **15**
Sang to my horn, the foxes on the hills barked clear and cold,
  And the sabbath rang slowly
   In the pebbles of the holy streams.

All the sun long it was running, it was lovely, the hay-
Fields high as the house, the tunes from the chimneys, it was air   **20**
  And playing, lovely and watery
   And fire green as grass.
   And nightly under the simple stars
As I rode to sleep the owls were bearing the farm away,
All the moon long I heard, blessed among stables, the nightjars   **25**
  Flying with the ricks, and the horses
   Flashing into the dark.

And then to awake, and the farm, like a wanderer white
With the dew, come back, the cock on his shoulder; it was all
   Shining, it was Adam and maiden,   30
      The sky gathered again
   And the sun grew round that very day.
So it must have been after the birth of the simple light
In the first, spinning place, the spellbound horses walking warm
   Out of the whinnying green stable   35
      On to the fields of praise.

And honoured among foxes and pheasants by the gay house
Under the new made clouds and happy as the heart was long,
   In the sun born over and over,
      I ran my heedless ways,   40
   My wishes raced through the house-high hay
And nothing I cared, at my sky blue trades, that time allows
In all his tuneful turning so few and such morning songs
   Before the children green and golden
      Follow him out of grace,   45

Nothing I cared, in the lamb white days, that time would take me
Up to the swallow thronged loft by the shadow of my hand,
   In the moon that is always rising,
      Nor that riding to sleep
   I should hear him fly with the high fields   50
And wake to the farm forever fled from the childless land.
Oh as I was young and easy in the mercy of his means,
      Time held me green and dying
   Though I sang in my chains like the sea.

DYLAN THOMAS

515

WATER MUSIC

   Deep in the heart of the lake
   Where the last light is clinging
   A strange foreboding voice
   Is patiently singing.

   Do not fear to venture   5
   Where the last light trembles
   Because you were in love.
   Love never dissembles.

Fear no more the boast, the bully,
The lies, the vain labour.   10
Make no show for death
As for a rich neighbour.

What stays of the great religions?
An old priest, an old birth.
What stays of the great battles?   15
Dust on the earth.

Cold is the lake water
And dark as history.
Hurry not and fear not
This oldest mystery.   20

This strange voice singing,
This slow deep drag of the lake,
This yearning, yearning, this ending
Of the heart and its ache.

ALUN LEWIS

516

WINTER GARDEN

The season's anguish, crashing whirlwind, ice,
Have passed, and cleansed the trodden paths
That silent gardeners have strewn with ash.

The iron circles of the sky
Are worn away by tempest;   5
Yet in this garden there is no more strife:
The Winter's knife is buried in the earth.
Pure music is the cry that tears
The birdless branches in the wind.
No blossom is reborn. The blue   10
Stare of the pond is blind.

And no-one sees
A restless stranger through the morning stray
Across the sodden lawn, whose eyes
Are tired of weeping, in whose breast   15
A savage sun consumes its hidden day.

DAVID GASCOYNE

517

WILLIAM WORDSWORTH

No room for mourning: he's gone out
Into the noisy glen, or stands between the stones
Of the gaunt ridge, or you'll hear his shout
Rolling among the screes, he being a boy again.
He'll never fail nor die   5
And if they laid his bones
In the wet vaults or iron sarcophagi
Of fame, he'd rise at the first summer rain
And stride across the hills to seek
His rest among the broken lands and clouds.   10
He was a stormy day, a granite peak
Spearing the sky; and look, about its base
Words flower like crocuses in the hanging woods,
Blank though the dalehead and the bony face.

SIDNEY KEYES

NOTES TO
THE GOLDEN TREASURY

BY FRANCIS TURNER PALGRAVE

SUMMARY OF BOOK FIRST

THE Elizabethan Poetry, as it is rather vaguely termed, forms the substance of this Book, which contains pieces from Wyatt under Henry VIII to Shakespeare midway through the reign of James I, and Drummond who carried on the early manner to a still later period. There is here a wide range of style;—from simplicity expressed in a language hardly yet broken in to verse,—through the pastoral fancies and Italian conceits of the strictly Elizabethan time,—to the passionate reality of Shakespeare: yet a general uniformity of tone prevails. Few readers can fail to observe the natural sweetness of the verse, the single-hearted straightforwardness of the thoughts:—nor less, the limitation of subject to the many phases of one passion which then characterized our lyrical poetry,—unless when, as with Drummond and Shakespeare, the ' purple light of Love ' is tempered by a spirit of sterner reflection.

It should be observed that this and the following Summaries apply in the main to the Collection here presented, in which (besides its restriction to Lyrical Poetry) a strictly representative or historical Anthology has not been aimed at. Great excellence, in human art as in human character, has from the beginning of things been even more uniform than Mediocrity, by virtue of the closeness of its approach to Nature:—and so far as the standard of Excellence kept in view has been attained in this volume, a comparative absence of extreme or temporary phases in style, a similarity of tone and manner, will be found throughout:—something neither modern nor ancient, but true in all ages, and, like the works of Creation, perfect as on the first day.

PAGE NO.

    l. 4. *Rouse Memnon's mother:* Awaken the Dawn from the dark Earth and the clouds where she is resting. Aurora in the old mythology is mother of Memnon (the East), and wife of Tithonus (the appearances of Earth and Sky during the last hours of Night). She leaves him every morning in renewed youth, to prepare the way for Phoebus (the Sun), whilst Tithonus remains in perpetual old age and greyness.

28 — l. 27. *by Peneüs' streams:* Phoebus loved the Nymph Daphne whom he met by the river Peneüs in the vale of Tempe. This legend expressed the attachment of the Laurel (Daphne) to the Sun, under whose heat the tree both fades and flourishes.

    It has been thought worth while to explain these allusions, because they illustrate the character of the Grecian Mythology which arose in the Personification of natural phenomena, and was totally free from those debasing and ludicrous

PAGE	NO.	
28	—	ideas with which, through Roman and later misunderstanding or perversion, it has been associated.
—	—	l. 31. *Amphion's lyre*: He was said to have built the walls of Thebes to the sound of his music.
—	—	l. 39. *Night like a drunkard reels*: Compare *Romeo and Juliet*, Act II, Scene 3: ' The grey-eyed morn smiles,' etc.
29	4	l. 10. *Time's chest*: in which he is figuratively supposed to lay up past treasures. So in *Troilus*, Act III, Scene 3, ' Time hath a wallet at his back,' etc.
30	5	A fine example of the highwrought and conventional Elizabethan Pastoralism, which it would be ludicrous to criticize on the ground of the unshepherdlike or unreal character of some images suggested. Stanza 6 was probably inserted by Izaak Walton.
32	9	This Poem, with 25 and 94, is taken from Davidson's *Rhapsody*, first published in 1602. One stanza has been here omitted, in accordance with the principle noticed in the Preface. Similar omissions occur in 45, 87, 100, 128, 160, 165, 227, 235. The more serious abbreviation by which it has been attempted to bring Crashaw's ' Wishes ' and Shelley's ' Euganean Hills ' within the limits of lyrical unity is commended with much diffidence to the judgement of readers acquainted with the original pieces.
36	15	This charming little poem, truly ' old and plain, and dallying with the innocence of love ' like that spoken of in *Twelfth Night*, is taken with 5, 17, 20, 34, and 40, from the most characteristic collection of Elizabeth's reign, *England's Helicon*, first published in 1600.
36	16	Readers who have visited Italy will be reminded of more than one picture by this gorgeous Vision of Beauty, equally sublime and pure in its Paradisaical naturalness. Lodge wrote it on a voyage to ' the Islands of Terceras and the Canaries '; and he seems to have caught, in those southern seas, no small portion of the qualities which marked the almost contemporary Art of Venice,—the glory and the glow of Veronese, or Titian, or Tintoret when he most resembles Titian, and all but surpasses him.
—	—	l. 1. *The clear* is the crystalline or outermost heaven of the old cosmography. For *resembling* (l. 7) other copies give *refining*: the correct reading is perhaps *revealing*.
37	—	l. 43. *for a fair there's fairer none*: If you desire a Beauty, there is none more beautiful than Rosalynde.
38	18	l. 10. *that fair thou owest*: that beauty thou ownest.
41	22	l. 9. *my . . . thy* is here conjecturally printed for ' thy . . . my.' A very few similar corrections of (it is presumed) misprints have been made: as *men* for *me*, 41. l. 3; *dome* for *doom*, 275. l. 25; with two or three more less important.
41	23	ll. 7, 8. *the star . . . Whose worth's unknown, although his height be taken*: apparently, Whose stellar influence is uncalculated although his angular altitude from the plane of the astrolabe or artificial horizon used by astrologers has been determined.
43	27	l. 9. *keel*: skim.
44	29	l. 8. *expense*: waste.

PAGE   NO.

45   30   **l. 5.** *Nativity, once in the main of light*: when a star has risen and entered on the full stream of light;—another of the astrological phrases no longer familiar.

—   —   **l. 7.** *Crooked* eclipses: as coming athwart the Sun's apparent course.

Wordsworth, thinking probably of the *Venus* and the *Lucrece*, said finely of Shakespeare: ' Shakespeare *could* not have written an Epic; he would have died of plethora of thought.' This prodigality of nature is exemplified equally in his Sonnets. The copious selection here given (which, from the wealth of the material, required greater consideration than any other portion of the Editor's task) contains many that will not be fully felt and understood without some earnestness of thought on the reader's part. But he is not likely to regret the labour.

45   31   **l. 11.** *upon misprision growing*: either, granted in error, or, on the growth of contempt.

46   32   With the tone of this Sonnet compare Hamlet's ' Give me that man That is not passion's slave,' etc. Shakespeare's writings show the deepest sensitiveness to passion:—hence the attraction he felt in the contrasting effects of apathy.

46   33   **l. 4.** *grame*: sorrow. It was long before English Poetry returned to the charming simplicity of this and a few other poems by Wyatt.

47   34   **l. 23.** Pandion in the ancient fable was father to Philomela.

49   38   **l. 4.** *ramage*: confused noise.

50   39   **l. 4.** *censures*: judges.

50   40   By its style this beautiful example of old simplicity and feeling may be referred to the early years of Elizabeth.

—   —   **l. 3.** *late*: lately.

52   41   **l. 9.** *haggards*: the least tameable hawks.

53   44   **l. 2.** *cypres* or cyprus,—used by the old writers for *crape*; whether from the French *crespe* or from the Island whence it was imported. Its accidental similarity in spelling to *cypress* has, here and in Milton's *Penseroso*, probably confused readers.

54-55   46-47   ' I never saw anything like this funeral dirge,' says Charles Lamb, ' except the ditty which reminds Ferdinand of his drowned father in *The Tempest*. As that is of the water, watery; so this is of the earth, earthy. Both have that intenseness of feeling, which seems to resolve itself into the element which it contemplates.'

57   51   **l. 8.** *crystal*: fairness.

58   53   This ' Spousal Verse ' was written in honour of the Ladies Elizabeth and Katherine Somerset. Although beautiful, it is inferior to the *Epithalamion* on Spenser's own marriage,— omitted with great reluctance as not in harmony with modern manners.

—   —   **l. 27.** *feateously*: elegantly.

60   —   **l. 121.** *shend*: put out.

61   —   **l. 145.** *a noble peer*: Robert Devereux, second Lord Essex, then at the height of his brief triumph after taking Cadiz:

PAGE	NO.	
61	—	hence the allusion following to the Pillars of Hercules, placed near Gades by ancient legend.
61	53	l. 157. *Eliza*: Elizabeth.
62	—	l. 173. *twins of Jove*: the stars Castor and Pollux.
—	—	l. 174. *baldric*, belt; the zodiac.
64	57	A fine example of a peculiar class of Poetry;—that written by thoughtful men who practised this Art but little. Wotton's 72, is another. Jeremy Taylor, Bishop Berkeley, Dr. Johnson, Lord Macaulay, have left similar specimens.

SUMMARY OF BOOK SECOND

THIS division, embracing the latter eighty years of the seventeenth century, contains the close of our Early poetical style and the commencement of the Modern. In Dryden we see the first master of the new: in Milton, whose genius dominates here as Shakespeare's in the former book,—the crown and consummation of the early period. Their splendid Odes are far in advance of any prior attempts, Spenser's excepted: they exhibit the wider and grander range which years and experience and the struggles of the time conferred on Poetry. Our Muses now give expression to political feeling, to religious thought, to a high philosophic statesmanship in writers such as Marvell, Herbert, and Wotton; whilst in Marvell and Milton, again, we find the first noble attempts at pure description of nature, destined in our own ages to be continued and equalled. Meanwhile the poetry of simple passion, although before 1660 often deformed by verbal fancies and conceits of thought, and afterward by levity and an artificial tone, produced in Herrick and Waller some charming pieces of more finished art than the Elizabethan: until in the courtly compliments of Sedley it seems to exhaust itself, and lie almost dormant for the hundred years between the days of Wither and Suckling and the days of Burns and Cowper.— That the change from our early style to the modern brought with it at first a loss of nature and simplicity is undeniable: yet the far bolder and wider scope which Poetry took between 1620 and 1700, and the successful efforts then made to gain greater clearness in expression, in their results have been no slight compensation.

PAGE	NO.	
70	62	l. 64. *whist*: hushed.
71	—	l. 89. *Pan*: used here for the Lord of all.
74	—	l. 191. *Lars and Lemures*: household gods and spirits of relations dead.
—	—	l. 194. *Flamens*: Roman priests.
—	—	l. 199. *that twice-batter'd god*: Dagon.
—	—	l. 213. *Osiris*, the Egyptian god of Agriculture (here, perhaps by confusion with Apis, figured as a Bull), was torn to pieces by Typho and embalmed after death in a sacred chest. This myth, reproduced in Syria and Greece in the legends of Thammuz, Adonis, and perhaps Absyrtus, represents the annual death of the Sun or the Year under the influences of the winter darkness. Horus, the son of Osiris, as the New Year, in his turn overcomes Typho.—It suited the genius of Milton's time to regard this primeval poetry

PAGE NO.

74 — and philosophy of the seasons, which has a further reference to the contest of Good and Evil in Creation, as a malignant idolatry. Shelley's Chorus in *Hellas*, ' Worlds on worlds,' treats the subject in a larger and sweeter spirit.

— — l. 215. *unshower'd*: as watered by the Nile only.

77 64 *The Late Massacre*: the Vaudois persecution, carried en in 1655 by the Duke of Savoy. This ' collect in verse,' as it has been justly named, is the most mighty Sonnet in any language known to the Editor. Readers should observe that, unlike our sonnets of the sixteenth century, it is constructed on the original Italian or Provençal model,—unquestionably far superior to the imperfect form employed by Shakespeare and Drummond.

77 65 Cromwell returned from Ireland in 1650. Hence the prophecies, not strictly fulfilled, of his deference to the Parliament, in ll. 81-96.

This Ode, beyond doubt one of the finest in our language, and more in Milton's style than has been reached by any other poet, is occasionally obscure from imitation of the condensed Latin syntax. The meaning of st. 5 is ' rivalry or hostility are the same to a lofty spirit, and limitation more hateful than opposition.' The allusion in st. 11 is to the old physical doctrines of the nonexistence of a vacuum and the impenetrability of matter:—in st. 18 to the omen traditional connected with the foundation of the Capitol at Rome. The ancient belief that certain years in life complete natural periods and are hence peculiarly exposed to death, is introduced in st. 26 by the word *climacteric*.

81 66 *Lycidas*. The person lamented is Milton's college friend Edward King, drowned in 1637 whilst crossing from Chester to Ireland.

Strict Pastoral Poetry was first written or perfected by the Dorian Greeks settled in Sicily; but the conventional use of it, exhibited more magnificently in *Lycidas* than in any other pastoral, is apparently of Roman origin. Milton, employing the noble freedom of a great artist, has here united ancient mythology with what may be called the modern mythology of Camus and Saint Peter,—to direct Christian images.—The metrical structure of this glorious poem is partly derived from Italian models.

— — l. 15. *Sisters of the sacred well*: the Muses, said to frequent the fountain Helicon on Mount Parnassus.

82 — l. 54. *Mona*: Anglesea, called by the Welsh Inis Dow¹¹ or the Dark Island, from its dense forests.

— — l. 55. *Deva*: the Dee, a river which probably derived its magical character from Celtic traditions: it was long the boundary of Briton and Saxon.—These places are introduced, as being near the scene of the shipwreck.

82 66 l. 58. *Orpheus* was torn to pieces by Thracian women.

83 — ll. 68. 69. *Amaryllis* and *Neaera*: names used here for the love-idols of poets: as *Damoetas* previously for a shepherd.

— — l. 75. *the blind Fury*: Atropos, fabled to cut the thread of life.

PAGE	NO.	
83	—	ll. 85, 86. *Arethuse* and *Mincius*: Sicilian and Italian waters here alluded to as synonymous with the pastoral poetry of Theocritus and Virgil.
—	—	l. 88. *oat*: pipe, used here like Collins's *oaten stop*, No. 146, l. 1, for *Song*.
—	—	l. 96. *Hippotades*: Aeolus, god of the Winds.
—	—	l. 99. *Panope*: a Nereid. The names of local deities in the Hellenic mythology express generally some feature in the natural landscape, which the Greeks studied and analysed with their usual unequalled insight and feeling. *Panope* represents the boundlessness of the ocean-horizon when seen from a height, as compared with the limited horizon of the land in hilly countries such as Greece or Asia Minor.
—	—	l. 103. *Camus*: the Cam; put for King's University.
—	—	l. 106. *that sanguine flower*: the Hyacinth of the ancients; probably our Iris.
—	—	l. 109. *The pilot*: Saint Peter, figuratively introduced as the head of the Church on earth, to foretell ' the ruin of our corrupted clergy, then in their heighth ' under Laud's primacy.
84	—	l. 128. *the wolf*: Popery.
—	—	l. 132. *Alpheus*: a stream in Southern Greece, supposed to flow underseas to join the Arethuse.
84	66	l. 138. *swart star*: the Dogstar, called swarthy because its heliacal rising in ancient times occurred soon after mid-summer.
85	—	l. 159. *moist vows*: either tearful prayers, or prayers for one at sea.
—	—	l. 160. *Bellerus*: a giant, apparently created here by Milton to personify Bellerium, the ancient title of the Land's End.
—	—	l. 161. *the great Vision*: the story was that the Archangel Michael had appeared on the rock by Marazion in Mount's Bay which bears his name. Milton calls on him to turn his eyes from the south homeward, and to pity Lycidas, if his body has drifted into the troubled waters off the Land's End. Finisterre being the land due south of Marazion, two places in that district (then by our trade with Corunna probably less unfamiliar to English ears) are named,—*Namancos* now Mujio in Galicia, *Bayona* north of the Minho, or perhaps a fortified rock (one of the *Cies* Islands) not unlike Saint Michael's Mount, at the entrance of Vigo Bay.
—	—	l. 170. *ore*: rays of golden light.
—	—	l. 189. *Doric*: Sicilian, pastoral.
88	70	*The assault* was an attack on London expected in 1642, when the troops of Charles I reached Brentford. ' Written on his door ' was in the original title of this sonnet. Milton was then living in Aldersgate Street.
—	—	l. 10. *The Emathian conqueror*: When Thebes was destroyed (335 B.C.) and the citizens massacred by thousands, Alexander ordered the house of Pindar to be spared. He was as incapable of appreciating the Poet as Lewis XIV of appreciating Racine: but even the narrow and barbarian mind

PAGE	NO.	
88	—	of Alexander could understand the advantage of a showy act of homage to Poetry.
89	—	ll. 12, 13. *the repeated air Of sad Electra's poet*: Amongst Plutarch's vague stories, he says that when the Spartan confederacy in 404 B.C. took Athens, a proposal to demolish it was rejected through the effect produced on the commanders by hearing part of a chorus from the Electra of Euripides sung at a feast. There is, however, no apparent congruity between the lines quoted (167-8, ed. Dindorf) and the result ascribed to them.
90	73	This high-toned and lovely Madrigal is quite in the style, and worthy of, the ' pure Simonides.'
91	75	Vaughan's beautiful though quaint verses should be compared with Wordsworth's great Ode, No. 287.
92	76	l. 6. *Favonius*: the spring wind.
92	77	l. 2. *Themis*: the goddess of justice. Skinner was grandson by his mother to Sir E. Coke:—hence, as pointed out by Mr. Keightley, Milton's allusion to the *bench*.
—	—	l. 8. Sweden was then at war with Poland, and France with the Spanish Netherlands.
94	79	l. 28. *Sidneian showers*: either in allusion to the conversations in the *Arcadia*, or to Sidney himself as a model of ' gentleness ' in spirit and demeanour.
98	84	*Elizabeth of Bohemia*: daughter to James I, and ancestor to Sophia of Hanover. These lines are a fine specimen of gallant and courtly compliment.
99	85	Lady M. Ley was daughter to Sir J. Ley, afterwards Earl of Marlborough, who died March, 1628-9, coincidently with the dissolution of the third Parliament of Charles's reign. Hence Milton poetically compares his death to that of the Orator Isocrates of Athens, after Philip's victory in 328 B.C.
103-104	92-93	These are quite a Painter's poems.
107	99	*From Prison*: to which his active support of Charles I twice brought the high-spirited writer.
111	105	Inserted in Book II as written in the character of a Soldier of Fortune in the seventeenth century.
112	106	*waly waly*: an exclamation of sorrow, the root and the pronunciation of which are preserved in the word *caterwaul*. *Brae*, hillside: *burn*, brook: *busk*, adorn. *Saint Anton's Well*: at the foot of Arthur's Seat by Edinburgh. *Cramasie*, crimson.
113	107	l. 7. *burd*, maiden.
115	108	*corbies*, crows: *fail*, turf: *hause*, neck: *theek*, thatch.—If not in their origin, in their present form this and the two preceding poems appear due to the seventeenth century, and have therefore been placed in Book II.
117	111	The remark quoted in the note to No. 47 applies equally to these truly wonderful verses, which, like *Lycidas*, may be regarded as a test of any reader's insight into the most poetical aspects of Poetry. The general differences between them are vast: but in imaginative intensity Marvell and Shelley are closely related.—This poem is printed as a translation in Marvell's works: but the original Latin is obviously

117   —   his own. The most striking verses in it, here quoted as the
book is rare, answer more or less to stanzas 2 and 6:—

> Alma Quies, teneo te! et te, Germana Quietis
> Simplicitas! vos ergo diu per Templa, per urbes,
> Quaesivi, Regum perque alta Palatia frustra.
> Sed vos Hortorum per opaca silentia longe
> Celarant Plantae virides, et concolor Umbra.

119, 122 112   *L'Allegro* and *Il Penseroso*. It is a striking proof of Milton's
113   astonishing power that these, the earliest pure Descriptive
Lyrics in our language, should still remain the best in a style
which so many great poets have since attempted. The
Bright and the Thoughtful aspects of Nature are their
subjects: but each is preceded by a mythological introduction in a mixed Classical and Italian manner. The meaning of the first is that Gaiety is the child of Nature; of the
second, that Pensiveness is the daughter o. Sorrow and
Genius.

119   112   l. 2. Perverse ingenuity has conjectured that for *Cerberus*
we should read *Erebus*, who in the Mythology is brother at
once and husband of Night. But the issue of that union is
not Sadness, but Day and Aether:—completing the circle
of primary Creation, as the parents are both children of
Chaos, the first-begotten of all things. (Hesiod.)

—   —   l. 36. *the mountain nymph*; compare Wordsworth's Sonnet,
No. 210.

120   —   l. 62. is in *apposition* to the preceding, by a grammatical
license not uncommon with Milton.

—   —   l. 67. *tells his tale*: counts his flock.

—   —   l. 80. *Cynosure*: the Pole Star.

—   —   ll. 83 *sqq. Corydon, Thyrsis*, etc.; shepherd names from the
old Idylls.

122   —   l. 132. *Jonson's learned sock*: the gaiety of our age would
find little pleasure in his elaborate comedies.

—   —   l. 136. *Lydian airs*: a light and festive style of ancient
music.

122   113   l. 3. *bestead*: avail.

123   —   l. 19. *starr'd Ethiop queen*: Cassiopeia, the legendary Queen
of Ethiopia, and thence translated amongst the constellations.

124   —   l. 59. *Cynthia*: the Moon: her chariot is drawn by dragons
in ancient representations.

—   —   l. 88. *Hermes*, called Trismegistus, a mystical writer of the
Neo-Platonist school.

—   —   l. 99. *Thebes*, etc.: subjects of Athenian Tragedy.

—   —   l. 102. *buskin'd*: tragic.

125   —   l. 104. *Musaeus*: a poet in Mythology.

—   —   l. 109. *him that left half-told*: Chaucer, in his incomplete
' Squire's Tale.'

—   113   l. 116. *great bards*: Ariosto, Tasso, and Spenser are here
intended.

—   —   l. 123. *frounced*: curled.

—   —   l. 124. *the Attic Boy*: Cephalus.

PAGE NO.

127 114 Emigrants supposed to be driven towards America by the Government of Charles I.

128 — ll. 23–4. *But apples*, etc. A fine example of Marvell's imaginative hyperbole.

128 115 l. 6. *concent*: harmony.

SUMMARY OF BOOK THIRD

It is more difficult to characterize the English Poetry of the eighteenth century than that of any other. For it was an age not only of spontaneous transition, but of bold experiment: it includes not only such divergencies of thought as distinguish the *Rape of the Lock* from the *Parish Register*, but such vast contemporaneous differences as lie between Pope and Collins, Burns and Cowper. Yet we may clearly trace three leading moods or tendencies:—the aspects of courtly or educated life represented by Pope and carried to exhaustion by his followers; the poetry of Nature and of Man, viewed through a cultivated, and at the same time an impassioned frame of mind by Collins and Gray:—lastly, the study of vivid and simple narrative, including natural description, begun by Gay and Thomson, pursued by Burns and others in the north, and established in England by Goldsmith, Percy, Crabbe, and Cowper. Great varieties in style accompanied these diversities in aim: poets could not always distinguish the manner suitable for subjects so far apart: and the union of the language of courtly and of common life, exhibited most conspicuously by Burns, has given a tone to the poetry of that century which is better explained by reference to its historical origin than by naming it, in the common criticism of our day, artificial. There is, again, a nobleness of thought, a courageous aim at high and, in a strict sense, manly excellence in many of the writers:—nor can that period be justly termed tame and wanting in originality, which produced poems such as Pope's *Satires*, Gray's *Odes* and *Elegy*, the ballads of Gay and Carey, the songs of Burns and Cowper. In truth Poetry at this as at all times was a more or less unconscious mirror of the genius of the age: and the brave and admirable spirit of inquiry which made the eighteenth century the turning-time in European civilization is reflected faithfully in its verse. An intelligent reader will find the influence of Newton as markedly in the poems of Pope, as of Elizabeth in the plays of Shakespeare. On this great subject, however, these indications must here be sufficient.

PAGE NO.

141 123 *The Bard*. This Ode is founded on a fable that Edward I, after conquering Wales, put the native Poets to death.—After lamenting his comrades (st. 2, 3) the Bard prophesies the fate of Edward II and the conquests of Edward III (4): his death and that of the Black Prince (5): of Richard II, with the wars of York and Lancaster, the murder of Henry VI (the *meek usurper*), and of Edward V and his brother (6). He turns to the glory and prosperity following the accession of the Tudors (7), through Elizabeth's reign (8): and concludes with a vision of the poetry of Shakespeare and Milton.

— — l. 13. *Glo'ster*: Gilbert de Clare, son-in-law to Edward. *Mortimer*, one of the Lords Marchers of Wales.

PAGE	NO.	
141	123	l. 35. *Arvon*: the shores of Carnarvonshire opposite Anglesey.
142	—	l. 57. *She-wolf*: Isabel of France, adulterous Queen of Edward II.
143	—	l. 87. *towers of Julius*: the Tower of Londoi, built in part, according to tradition, by Julius Caesar.
—	—	l. 93. *bristled boar*: the badge of Richard III.
—	—	l. 99. *Half of thy heart*: Queen Eleanor died soon after the conquest of Wales.
—	—	l. 109. *Arthur*: Henry VII named his eldest son thus, in deference to British feeling and legend.
145	125	l. 5. The Highlanders called the battle of Culloden, Drumossie.
145	126	*lilting*, singing blithely: *loaning*, broad lane: *bughts*, pens: *scorning*, rallying: *dowie*, dreary: *daffing* and *gabbing*, joking and chatting: *leglin*, milk-pail: *shearing*, reaping: *bandsters*, sheaf-binders: *runkled*, wrinkled: *lyart*, grizzled: *fleeching*, coaxing: *gloaming*, twilight: *bogle*, ghost: *dool*, sorrow.
147	128	The Editor has found no authoritative text of this poem, in his judgement superior to any other of its class in melody and pathos. Part is probably not later than the seventeenth century: in other stanzas a more modern hand, much resembling Scott's, is traceable. Logan's poem (127) exhibits a knowledge rather of the old legend than of the old verses. —*Hecht*, promised—the obsolete *hight*: *mavis*, thrush: *ilka*, every: *lav'rock*, lark: *haughs*, valley-meadows: *twined*, parted from: *marrow*, mate: *syne*, then.
149	129	The Royal George, of 108 guns, whilst undergoing a partial careening in Portsmouth Harbour, was overset about 10 a.m. Aug. 29, 1782. The total loss was believed to be near 1000 souls.
151	131	A little masterpiece in a very difficult style: Catullus himself could hardly have bettered it. In grace, tenderness, simplicity, and humour it is worthy of the Ancients; and even more so, from the completeness and unity of the picture presented.
155	136	Perhaps no writer who has given such strong proofs of the poetic nature has left less satisfactory poetry than Thomson. Yet he touched little which he did not beautify: and this song, with 'Rule, Britannia' and a few others, must make us regret that he did not more seriously apply himself to lyrical writing.
157	140	l. 1. *Aeolian lyre*: the Greeks ascribed the origin of their Lyrical Poetry to the colonies of Aeolis in Asia Minor.
158	—	l. 17. *Thracia's hills*: supposed a favourite resort of Mars.
—	—	l. 21. *feather'd king*: the Eagle of Jupiter, admirably described by Pindar in a passage here imitated by Gray.
—	—	l. 27. *Idalia* in Cyprus, where *Cytherea* (Venus) was especially worshipped.
—	—	l. 53. *Hyperion*: the Sun. St. 6–8 allude to the Poets of the islands and mainland of Greece, to those of Rome and of England.
160	—	l. 115. *Theban Eagle*: Pindar.

PAGE	NO.	
162	141	l. 75. *chaste-eyed Queen*: Diana.
163	142	l. 5. *Attic warbler*: the nightingale.
165	144	*sleekit*, sleek: *bickering brattle*, flittering flight: *laith*, loath: *pattle*, ploughstaff: *whiles*, at times: *a daimen-icker*, a corn-ear now and then: *thrave*, shock: *lave*, rest: *foggage*, aftergrass: *snell*, biting: *but hald*, without dwelling-place: *thole*, bear: *cranreuch*, hoarfrost: *thy lane*, alone: *a-gley*, off the right line, awry.
169	147	Perhaps the noblest stanzas in our language.
173	148	*stoure*, dust-storm: *braw*, smart.
174	149	*scaith*, hurt: *ent*, guard: *steer*, molest.
175	151	*drumlie*, muddy: *birk*, birch.
176	152	*greet*, cry: *daurna*, dare not.—There can hardly exist a poem more truly tragic in the highest sense than this: nor, except Sappho, has any Poetess known to the Editor equalled it in excellence.
177	153	*fou*, merry with drink: *coost*, carried: *unco skeigh*, very proud: *gart*, forced: *abeigh*, aside: *Ailsa Craig*, a rock in the Firth of Clyde: *grat his een bleert*, cried till his eyes were bleared: *lowpin*, leaping: *linn*, waterfall: *sair*, sore: *smoor'd*, smothered: *crouse* and *canty*, blithe and gay.
178	154	Burns justly named this ' one of the most beautiful songs in the Scots or any other language.' One verse, interpolated by Beattie, is here omitted:—it contains two good lines, but is quite out of harmony with the original poem. *Bigonet*, little cap—probably altered from *beguinette*: *thraw*, twist: *caller*, fresh.
179	155	*airts*, quarters: *row*, roll: *shaw*, small wood in a hollow, spinney: *knowes*, knolls.
180	156	*jo*, sweetheart: *brent*, smooth: *pow*, head.
181	157	*leal*, faithful: *fain*, happy.
182	158	Henry VI founded Eton.
187	161	The Editor knows no Sonnet more remarkable than this, which, with 162, records Cowper's gratitude to the lady whose affectionate care for many years gave what sweetness he could enjoy to a life radically wretched. Petrarch's sonnets have a more ethereal grace and a more perfect finish; Shakespeare's more passion; Milton's stand supreme in stateliness, Wordsworth's in depth and delicacy. But Cowper's unites with an exquisiteness in the turn of thought which the Ancients would have called Irony, an intensity of pathetic tenderness peculiar to his loving and ingenuous nature.—There is much mannerism, much that is unimportant or of now exhausted interest in his poems: but where he is great, it is with that elementary greatness which rests on the most universal human feelings. Cowper is our highest master in simple pathos.
189	163	l. 19. *fancied green*: cherished garden.
190	164	Little more than his name appears recoverable with regard to the author of this truly noble poem. It should be noted as exhibiting a rare excellence—the climax of simple sublimity.

PAGE   NO.

190   —   It is a lesson of high instructiveness to examine the
essential qualities which give first-rate poetical rank to lyrics
such as ' To-morrow ' or ' Sally in our Alley,' when compared with poems written (if the phrase may be allowed) in
keys so different as the subtle sweetness of Shelley, the
grandeur of Gray and Milton, or the delightful Pastoralism
of the Elizabethan verse. Intelligent readers will gain hence
a clear understanding of the vast imaginative range of
Poetry;—through what wide oscillations the mind and the
taste of a nation may pass;—how many are the roads which
Truth and Nature open to Excellence.

Summary of Book Fourth

It proves sufficiently the lavish wealth of our own age in Poetry, that
the pieces which, without conscious departure from the standard of
Excellence, render this Book by far the longest, were with very few
exceptions composed during the first thirty years of the nineteenth
century. Exhaustive reasons can hardly be given for the strangely sudden
appearance of individual genius: but none, in the Editor's judgement,
can be less adequate than that which assigns the splendid national
achievements of our recent poetry to an impulse from the follies and
wars that at the time disgraced our foreign neighbours. The first French
Revolution was rather, in his opinion, one result, and in itself by no
means the most important, of that far wider and greater spirit which
through inquiry and doubt, through pain and triumph, sweeps mankind
round the circles of its gradual development: and it is to this that we
must trace the literature of modern Europe. But, without more detailed
discussion on the motive causes of Scott, Wordsworth, Campbell, Keats,
and Shelley, we may observe that these Poets, with others, carried to
further perfection the later tendencies of the century preceding, in
simplicity of narrative, reverence for human Passion and Character in
every sphere, and impassioned love of Nature:—that, whilst maintaining
on the whole the advances in art made since the Restoration, they renewed the half-forgotten melody and depth of tone which marked the
best Elizabethan writers:—that, lastly, to what was thus inherited they
added a richness in language and a variety in metre, a force and fire
in narrative, a tenderness and bloom in feeling, an insight into the finer
passages of the Soul and the inner meanings of the landscape, a larger
and wiser Humanity,—hitherto hardly attained, and perhaps unattain-
able even by predecessors of not inferior individual genius. In a word,
the nation which, after the Greeks in their glory, has been the most
gifted of all nations for Poetry, expressed in these men the highest
strength and prodigality of its nature. They interpreted the age to itself
—hence the many phases of thought and style they present:—to
sympathize with each, fervently and impartially, without fear and without fancifulness, is no doubtful step in the higher education of the Soul.
For, as with the Affections and the Conscience, Purity in Taste is
absolutely proportionate to Strength:—and when once the mind has
raised itself to grasp and to delight in Excellence, those who love most
will be found to love most wisely.

PAGE	NO.	
195	166	l. 11. *stout Cortez*: History requires here *Balboa*: (A. T.) It may be noticed that to find in Chapman's Homer the ' pure serene ' of the original, the reader must bring with him the imagination of the youthful poet;—he must be ' a Greek himself,' as Shelley finely said of Keats.
199	169	The most tender and true of Byron's smaller poems.
200	170	This Poem, with 236, exemplifies the peculiar skill with which Scott employs proper names:—nor is there a surer sign of high poetical genius.
216	191	The Editor in this and in other instances has risked the addition (or the change) of a Title, that the aim of the voices following may be grasped more clearly and immediately.
222	198	l. 4. *nature's Eremite*: like a solitary thing in Nature.— This beautiful Sonnet was the last word of a poet deserving the title ' marvellous boy ' in a much higher sense than Chatterton. If the fulfilment may ever safely be prophesied from the promise, England appears to have lost in Keats one whose gifts in Poetry have rarely been surpassed. Shakespeare, Milton, and Wordsworth, had their lives been closed at twenty-five, would (so far as we know) have left poems of less excellence and hope than the youth who, from the petty school and the London surgery, passed at once to a place with them of ' high collateral glory.'
224	201	It is impossible not to regret that Moore has written so little in this sweet and genuinely national style.
224	202	A masterly example of Byron's command of strong thought and close reasoning in verse:—as the next is equally characteristic of Shelley's wayward intensity, and 204 of the dramatic power, the vital identification of the poet with other times and characters, in which Scott is second only to Shakespeare.
233	209	Bonnivard, a Genevese, was imprisoned by the Duke of Savoy in Chillon on the lake of Geneva for his courageous defence of his country against the tyranny with which Piedmont threatened it during the first half of the seventeenth century.—This noble Sonnet is worthy to stand near Milton's on the Vaudois massacre.
234	210	Switzerland was usurped by the French under Napoleon in 1800: Venice in 1797 (211).
236	215	This battle was fought Dec. 2, 1800, between the Austrians under Archduke John and the French under Moreau, in a forest near Munich. *Hohen Linden* means *High Limetrees*.
240	218	After the capture of Madrid by Napoleon, Sir J. Moore retreated before Soult and Ney to Corunna, and was killed whilst covering the embarkation of his troops. His tomb, built by Ney, bears this inscription—' John Moore, leader of the English armies, slain in battle, 1809.'
251	229	The Mermaid was the club-house of Shakespeare, Ben Jonson, and other choice spirits of that age.
252	230	*Maisie*: Mary. Scott has given us nothing more complete and lovely than this little Song, which unites simplicity and dramatic power to a wildwood music of the rarest quality.

PAGE	NO.	
252	—	No moral is drawn, far less any conscious analysis of feeling attempted:—the pathetic meaning is left to be suggested by the mere presentment of the situation. Inexperienced critics have often named this, which may be called the Homeric manner, superficial, from its apparent simple facility: but first-rate excellence in it (as shown here, in 196, 156, and 129) is in truth one of the least common triumphs of Poetry. —This style should be compared with what is not less perfect in its way, the searching out of inner feeling, the expression of hidden meanings, the revelation of the heart of Nature and of the Soul within the Soul,—the Analytical method, in short,—most completely represented by Wordsworth and by Shelley.
257	234	*correi*: covert on a hillside; *cumber*: trouble.
258	235	Two intermediate stanzas have been here omitted. They are very ingenious, but, of all poetical qualities, ingenuity is least in accordance with pathos.
269	243	This Poem has an exaltation and a glory, joined with an exquisiteness of expression, which place it in the highest rank amongst the many masterpieces of its illustrious Author.
278	252	l. 24. *interlunar swoon*: interval of the Moon's invisibility.
283	256	l. 11. *Calpe*: Gibraltar.
—	—	l. 21. *Lofoden*: the Maelstrom whirlpool off the N.W. coast of Norway.
285	257	This lovely Poem refers here and there to a ballad by Hamilton on the subject better treated in 127 and 128.
297	268	l. 10. *Arcturi*: seemingly used for *northern stars*.
—	—	l. 21. *And wild roses*, etc. Our language has no line modulated with more subtle sweetness. A good poet *might* have written *And roses wild*,—yet this slight change would disenchant the verse of its peculiar beauty.
299	270	l. 81. *Ceres' daughter*: Proserpine.
—	—	l. 82. *God of Torment*: Pluto.
301	271	This impassioned Address expresses Shelley's most rapt imaginations, and is the direct modern representative of the feeling which led the Greeks to the worship of Nature.
310	274	The leading idea of this beautiful description of a day's landscape in Italy is expressed with an obscurity not infrequent with its author. It appears to be,—On the voyage of life are many moments of pleasure, given by the sight of Nature, who has power to heal even the worldliness and the uncharity of man.
311	—	l. 58. Amphitrite was daughter to Ocean.
—	—	l. 76 *Sun-girt* City: It is difficult not to believe that the correct reading is *Seagirt*. Many of Shelley's poems appear to have been printed in England during his residence abroad: others were printed from his manuscripts after his death. Hence probably the text of an English Poet after 1600 contains so many errors. See the Note on No. 9.
315	275	l. 21. *Maenad*: a frenzied Nymph, attendant on Dionysus in the Greek mythology.
—	—	l. 39. Plants under water sympathize with the seasons of the land, and hence with the winds which affect them.

PAGE	NO.	
317	276	Written soon after the death, by shipwreck, of Wordsworth's brother John. This Poem should be compared with Shelley's following it. Each is the most complete expression of the innermost spirit of his art given by these great Poets: —of that Idea which, as in the case of the true Painter (to quote the words of Reynolds), ' subsists only in the mind: The sight never beheld it, nor has the hand expressed it; it is an idea residing in the breast of the artist, which he is always labouring to impart, and which he dies at last without imparting.'
318	—	l. 50. *the Kind*: the human race.
319	278	l. 13. Proteus represented the everlasting changes, united with ever-recurrent sameness, of the Sea.
320	279	l. 1. *the royal Saint*: Henry VI.

NOTES TO ADDITIONAL POEMS

BY C. DAY LEWIS

PAGE	NO.	
343	298	l. 1. *Stygian set*: the dead. l. 3. *Charon*: the ferryman who conveyed the souls of the dead across the river Styx.
349	310	l. 7. *Phoenix*: a mythical, unique bird, living for five or six hundred years in the Arabian desert, then burning itself to ashes on a funeral pyre, from which it emerged with its youth renewed to live through the next cycle of years.
351	312-5	William Barnes wrote many of his poems in the Dorset dialect.
351	312	l. 5. *drong*, a narrow way: l. 9. *jay*, joy: l. 17. *shill*, shrill: l. 17. *whiver*, hover.
352	313	l. 17. *rig*, climb: l. 19. *parrock*, a small field: l. 22. *yoller*, yellow: l. 25. *gil'cups*, buttercups: l. 36. *vlees*, flies: l. 49. *alassen*, lest.
353	314	l. 1. *clote*, yellow water-lily: l. 5. *allers*, alders: l. 19. *vo'k*, folk: l. 25. *mores*, stalk.
354	315	l. 10. *het*, heat: l. 25. *vaice*, voice.
357	320	*Brahma*: the supreme God of Hindu mythology; the Divine reality, of which all else is only a manifestation.
358	321	l. 18. *Parian*: the marble of Paros was famed among the ancients for its whiteness.
—	—	l. 21. *maugre*: in spite of.
359	323	l. 1. *Theocritus*: Greek pastoral poet of the 3rd century B.C.
366	329	*Kraken*: a mythical, gigantic sea-monster.
367	331	l. 7. *Danae*: legendary princess, to whom Zeus came down in a shower of gold.
368	333	Tithonus was a mortal, married to Eos, goddess of the morning, who obtained immortality for him but forgot to ask that he should also be granted immortal youth.
384 386 387	345 348 349	These poems were part of the Gondal saga—the chronicle of an imaginary country written by Emily and her sister Anne. Though they refer to imaginary characters, they convey the essence of Emily Brontë's personality and experience. We give them in the original text: Charlotte Brontë, when revising her sister's poems for publication, made a number of alterations, changing, for example, ' all-wearing ' to ' all-severing ' and ' Angora's shore ' to ' that northern shore ' (345, 11, 4 and 6).
387	349	It has been noted how closely this passage follows the stages of the mystics' experience.
389	354	*Amours de Voyage*, Clough's masterpiece, is in the form of letters, written chiefly by a young man travelling in Italy to a friend in England. It offers the most successful use of the hexameter in English poetry.

PAGE NO.

392 358   The full title of this poem is *A Requiem for Soldiers Lost in Ocean Transports*. The Requiem, as also 357, 359 and 361, was inspired by the American Civil War.

393 360   The subject of this poem is Abraham Lincoln.

395 363   l. 28. *melick*, a kind of grass: l. 51. *mote*, might: l. 73. *scorpe*, hill or cliff-face: l. 101. *eygre*, a tidal wave.

404 366   Philomela, ravished by Tereus, king of Thrace, took a terrible revenge upon him; then, fleeing his rage, was turned into a nightingale.

— —   l. 21. Tereus had cut out Philomela's tongue and secretly imprisoned her: but she wove her story on a web and had it conveyed to her sister, Procne, Tereus's wife, who rescued her and participated in her revenge. In this line, Arnold seems to have confused the two sisters.

416 376   *Modern Love* explores the relationship of a young husband and wife whose love has died but who are still bound together by memories of it and by their efforts to behave towards each other in a responsible, civilised way. The poem is a masterpiece of psychological penetration.

420 381-6   Emily Dickinson, the New England recluse, was an exact contemporary of Christina Rossetti. She wrote once, ' If I read a book and it makes my whole body so cold no fire can ever warm me, I know it is poetry. If I feel physically as if the top of my head were taken off, I know this is poetry. These are the only ways I know it.' Her own best work, so curt, packed, hard-hitting, passes this test triumphantly.

427 393   The wonderfully effective last line of this poem may remind some readers of Meredith's ' The small bird stiffens in the low starlight.' ' Low ' and ' bewildering ' are instances of the epithet used at full imaginative stretch.

437 403   Hardy looks back to his childhood home at Lower Bockhampton.

438 405-7   Three of the 1912-1913 poems, written after the death of his first wife, when Hardy was over 70. These exquisite love-poems fully bear out his own lines

> But Time, to make me grieve,
> Part steals, lets part abide,
> And shakes this fragile frame at eve
> With throbbings of noontide.

444 412   Hopkins, whose poetic language and rhythms have profoundly influenced English verse from the time when his poems were first published, posthumously, in 1918, was a Jesuit priest.

444 413   l. 2. *brinded*: brindled.

447 416   l. 4. *to own my heart* = to my own heart.

— —   l. 7. *reaving Peace* = when he takes Peace away.

449 419   l. 3. *whaups*: curlews.

460 434   l. 2. Pearse and Connolly were leaders of the Easter Rebellion in Dublin, 1916. Both were executed.

PAGE   NO.

463   440   Charming verse breaks through, in lines 13-14, to a deeper level and becomes memorable poetry.

464   442   Yeats tells us that in Part 3 of his poem, *The Tower*, he ' unconsciously echoed one of the loveliest lyrics of our time —Mr. Sturge Moore's " Dying Swan." '

468   446   Familiar as it is, *The Listeners* remains an object lesson in variety, subtlety and rightness of rhythm.

473   452   Robert Frost's supreme gift is for arguing with himself musically, for blending the colloquial with the lyrical.

476   456-7 Edward Thomas, too often dismissed as another Georgian ' nature-poet,' was, with the exception of Wilfrid Owen, the most individual and naturally gifted of the poets killed in the first World War.

480   462   l. 23: Ulysses.

482   464   From the Pisan Cantos (No. 81): the subject of this Canto is, Mr. H. W. Kenner tells us, ' Artist-explorers.' The Pisan Cantos are partly drawn from Ezra Pound's experiences in an internment camp.

—   —   l. 29: *rathe*: quick.

483   465   l. 9. *windhover*: kestrel.

486   469   One of the most remarkable allegorical poems of modern times.

490   473   ll. 12-16, Dr. Sitwell tells us, are ' a rough adaptation into English of a prose passage by Paul Eluard.'

491   474   " *The Hollow Men* is the ghost of a play. It might be called also the ghost of a poem, since all the poetic elements are reduced to their barest essentials. . . . The image which dominates the centre of the poem is the image of eyes. The central sections are about being looked at and not being looked at; about eyes that look upon us with reproach or judge us, eyes that seem to smile upon us or look on us with serenity; and about gazing at a stony eyeless face, or groping in a darkness where we neither see nor are seen."
                                        Helen Gardner: *The Art of T. S. Eliot.*

492   476   " . . . the whole poem is penetrated with the Christian hope, the fulfilment of the promise ' Behold I make all things new ' . . . The voyage in *Marina* discovers in the ocean an island, and sees again a beloved face. Its theme is not the immortality of the soul, but resurrection."
                                        Helen Gardner: *The Art of T. S. Eliot.*

505   493   l. 2. *luely*, quietly: l. 3. *caller*, cold: l. 9. *waukrife*, alert: l. 11. *smool'd*, stole away: l. 12. *daw*, dawn.

517   507   The subject is a woman stricken with mortal disease.

522   513   This wonderfully sustained, long-breathed passage has, for its central image, the ship of illusion. One way to interpret this image (no doubt there are others) is to see it as the illusion that a man, by changing his country, his environment, can change his nature.

INDEX OF WRITERS

Including dates of birth and death and titles of poems. Where a poem is untitled, the first line is given in italics.

545

INDEX OF TITLES AND FIRST LINES

GLOSSARY OF POETIC TERMS

(Compiled by the General Editor)

ACATALECTIC Name given to a metre having the full number of syllables. The following is an example of an *iambic tetrameter acatalectic, i.e.,* a metre which consists of four complete iambuses.

It was | a lov | er and | his lass | (*See* Poem No. 8)

ACCENT In prosody, rhythmical stress on single syllables.

ACCIDENCE That part of grammar which treats of inflections, or the different forms words can take.

ALEXANDRINE Verse with twelve syllables and six feet or stresses, *e.g.,*

They love to steal a march, nor lightly risk the lure.

The name is probably derived from French poems on Alexander the Great written in this metre.

ALLITERATION The repetition of a stressed consonantal sound in closely successive words to give poetical effect to a line or passage, *e.g.,*

The moan of doves in immemorial elms,
And murmuring of innumerable bees.

from *The Princess* by Tennyson.

AMPHIBRACH A metrical foot of three syllables, a long between two short ones, or stressed between two unstressed, *e.g.,*

The sunset | at last and | the twilight | are dead;

and | the darkness | is breathless.

ANACRUSIS Unaccented syllables usually at the beginning of a line introductory to the normal rhythm, *e.g.,*

The wind | is pip | ing loud | my boys |,

The light | ning flash | es free— |

While the holl | ow oak | our pal | ace is |,

Our her | itage | the sea |.   (*See* Poem No. 205)

ANAPAEST A metrical foot which consists of two unstressed syllables followed by a stressed syllable, *e.g.,*

At the corn | er of Wood | Street when

day | light ap-pears.   (*See* Poem No. 251)

571

ANASTROPHE A changing of the normal order of words for rhetorical effect, *e.g., Came the snow.*

APHONIC Not sounded.

APOSTROPHE A digression in speech or writing for the purpose of addressing a person or thing, absent or present, *e.g.,*

> *Long Scrolls of Paper solemnly he waves,*
> *With Characters, and Figures dire inscrib'd,*
> *Grievous to Mortal Eyes;* (ye Gods avert
> Such Plagues from Righteous Men!) *Behind him stalks*
> *Another Monster, not unlike himself.*

ARCHAISM An out-of-date word, *e.g., yclept* for *called.*

ARSIS (opposite of *thesis*) In verse, the stressed part of a foot. Stressed syllables are said to be *in arsis*, the unstressed *in thesis.*

ASSONANCE The rhyming of the vowel sound alone, irrespective of the consonant (or sound) which follows it: *e.g., base* and *face*—true rhyme: *base* and *fade*—assonance.

BALLAD A simple narrative poem in short stanzas, or a simple, sentimental song each verse of which is sung to the same tune. Originally a song sung to accompany a dance.

BALLAD METRE Ancient and elaborate French verse-form, which was revived in France and Britain during the 19th century. It consists of three stanzas of eight (or ten) lines and an envoy of four (or five) lines. Only three (or four) rhymes are used and they are in the same order in each stanza. Each stanza and the envoy ends with the same line.

BATHOS A passage which is intended to impress, but which defeats its purpose because of an incongruous association of ideas, *e.g.,*

> *The piteous news, so much it shocked her*
> *She quite forgot to send the doctor.*　　　Wordsworth.

BLANK VERSE Any unrhymed verse, but especially unrhymed verse of ten syllables, or five iambic feet.

CAESURA A rhythmic break, usually about the middle of the metrical line, *e.g.,*

> *. . . Two vast and trunkless legs of stone*
> *Stand in the desert.* | *Near them on the sand*
> *Half sunk, a shatter'd visage lies . . .* (See Poem No. 246)

CINQUAIN A *pentastich*, *i.e.,* Five consecutive lines of verse.

COUPLET A *distich*. Two successive lines of rhyming verse, usually with the same metrical form, used especially for sharp or epigrammatic effect.

DACTYL A foot of three syllables, the first stressed, the others unstressed. The following is an example of *dactylic verse*:

> *Make no deep | scrutiny | into her | mutiny.*

DIALECT A local form of speech distinguished from standard speech by peculiarities of accent, idiom or vocabulary. (*See* Poems Nos. 139, 150, 152, 154, etc.)

DIMETER A metrical line consisting of two feet.

DIPODY A double foot.

DISTICH *See* COUPLET.

ELEGIACS Couplets in Greek and Latin verse, each consisting of alternate hexameter and pentameter lines.

ELEGY A song of mourning in elegiac verse; in general any poem expressing grief or melancholy reflection.

ELISION The omission of a vowel or syllable in pronunciation, *e.g.*,

> *Th' applause of listening senates to command.*

ENJAMBMENT The continuation of a sentence beyond the end of a couplet into the first line of the next.

ENVOY A postscript to a poem, most frequently in fewer lines than the preceding stanzas.

EPIGRAM A short, witty, or satirical poem.

EPODE *See* PINDARIC ODE.

EPOPEE An epic poem or poetry.

EUPHONY A combination of sounds which produces a pleasing effect.

FEMININE ENDING Name given to an unstressed syllable at the end of an iambic or anapaestic line, *e.g.*,

> iambic: *The fount | ains ming | le with | the riv | er*

> anapaestic: *So the flowers | come to bloom | in the warmth | of the sun | mer*

FOOT The unit of metre; a division of a metrical line consisting of two or three stressed and unstressed syllables.

HEMISTICH Half a line of poetry.

HENDECASYLLABLE A metre having lines of eleven syllables, *e.g.*, Dante's *terza rima*.

HEPTASTICH Seven consecutive lines of verse.

HEROIC The verse form in which the accepted heroic poetry of any particular language is written, *e.g.*, in English the line of ten syllables and five stresses, whether in rhymed couplets (Pope and Dryden) or blank verse (Milton).

HEXAMETER The Greek and Latin heroic metre, consisting of six feet, four dactyls or spondees, a dactyl and a spondee.

HOMOPHONE A *paranym*; a word which sounds like another but is spelt differently and has a different meaning, *e.g.*, *thyme* and *time*.

IAMBUS A metrical foot composed of a stressed syllable preceded by an unstressed syllable. The following is an example of iambic verse:

> *When I | have fears | that I | may cease | to be |*   (*See* Poem No. 199)

IAMBIC PENTAMETER The most common form of English verse (five iambic feet) used by Chaucer, Shakespeare, Milton, etc.

ICTUS Rhythmical or metrical stress.

LAMPOON Formerly a drinking song, now a satire, in verse or prose, usually upon an individual.

LIQUIDS Name given to the sounds *l*, *r*, and sometimes *m* and *n*.

LYRIC Any short poem, divided into stanzas, in which the writer gives expression to his own thoughts and emotions.

MEASURE A metrical unit (*e.g.*, a foot or double foot) used to determine the length of a line of verse. Thus a *monometer, dimeter, trimeter, tetrameter, pentameter, hexameter*, etc., consist respectively of one, two, three, four, five, six, etc., measures.

METRE Any form of rhyme in verse, measured by the character and number of its feet.

MONOMETER A line or verse consisting of one metrical unit.

MONOSTICH One line of poetry.

OCTASTICH *See* OCTAVE.

OCTAVE Eight consecutive lines of verse; also called *octastich, huitain* or *octet*.

OCTET *See* OCTAVE.

OCTOSYLLABICS Eight-syllable rhyming metre, *e.g.*,

> ′   ′   ′   ′
> *I gazed—and gazed—but little thought*
> ′   ′   ′   ′
> *What wealth the show to me had brought.*   (*See* Poem No. 253)

ODE In Greek drama, a song sung by the chorus, often accompanied by music and dancing. Now usually a rhymed poem of irregular form, written to celebrate a special occasion, in honour of a particular person, or on a special theme, *e.g.*, Poems Nos. 255, 256, 275, 287.

OTTAVA RIMA An eight-lined stanza, with eleven syllables to the line in Italian (ten in English), invented by Boccaccio and now the accepted Italian heroic metre. The rhyme-sequence is *abababcc*.

OXYMORON A rhetorical figure in which two terms, ordinarily contradictory, are combined in one phrase or sentence, *e.g.*, in Tennyson's *Lancelot and Elaine*,

> *His honour rooted in dishonour stood*
> *And faith unfaithful kept him falsely true.*

PARODY A facetious imitation of an author's style.

PENTAMETER A line of five feet of which the first half may be dactylic or spondaic and the second must consist of two dactyls. It is used alternatively with the hexameter in elegiac verse. In English prosody, any line consisting of five feet.

PENTASTICH *See* CINQUAIN.

PERSONIFICATION A figure of speech in which personal qualities are attributed to an abstraction, *e.g.*,

> *Can Honour's voice provoke the silent dust,*
> *Or Flattery soothe the dull cold ear of Death?*   (*See* Poem No. 147)

PINDARIC ODE The triumphal choric ode as written by the Greek poet Pindar. This is best represented in English poetry by Gray's poems *The Progress of Poesy* and *The Bard*. (Poems Nos. 140 and 123.) The ode consists of nine stanzas divided into three groups of three.

POETIC LICENCE The latitude allowed to poets in regard to grammatical construction, and occasionally to the use of facts, but denied to the writers of prose, *e.g.*, Byron's: *There let him lay* (instead of *lie*).

PROSODY That branch of grammar which treats of the laws of versification, *i.e.*, rhyme, metre, accent, etc.

PROSOPOPEIA   A rhetorical device by which inanimate or non-human things are addressed as persons, *e.g.*,

> *Yet once more, O ye laurels, and once more*
> *Ye myrtles brown, with ivy never sere,*   (*See* Poem No. 66)

PYRRHIC   In Classical verse, a metrical foot of two short syllables.

QUATORZAIN   Fourteen consecutive lines of verse.

QUATRAIN   Four consecutive lines of verse; also called a *tetrastich* or *quartet.*

QUINZAIN   Fifteen consecutive lines of verse.

RHYME   Identity of sound in the end-words or syllables of two or more lines of verse.

RHYTHM   The measured recurrence of accented and unaccented syllables.

RONDEAU   A metrical form of thirteen lines (Villon, ten), with only two rhymes, variously placed. The opening words (usually half the line) recur at the end of the eighth line (the sixth in Villon) and at the end, but do not enter the rhyme-scheme. The metre is usually eight-syllabled, with four stresses, although Swinburne devised a form of his own.

RONDEL   A variant of the *rondeau* with a refrain consisting of the whole of the first line, or of the first two lines. The first two recur after the sixth line and either one or both at the end. Accordingly the length may be thirteen or fourteen lines.

ROUNDEL   The English form of *rondeau* and *rondel*. Swinburne's version has nine lines and a refrain after the third and last.

RUNE   Strictly, a Finnish poem, or part of one, especially of the *Kalevala*.

SAPPHICS   Sapphic verse; a Greek metre used by Sappho and imitated (in Latin) by Horace. The English sapphic stanza consists of three lines of five beats followed by a short line.

SATIRE   The use of sarcasm or ridicule as a weapon against political institutions, etc.

SCAN   To analyse metrically the feet in a line. The number of feet is reckoned from the number of stresses and not from the number of syllables.

SEPTENARIUS   A line of verse consisting of seven feet.

SESTET   Six consecutive lines of verse; also called *hexastich, sixain, sextain,* or *sextet.*

SEXTET   *See* SESTET.

SIBILANT   Name given to any of the sounds *s*, *z*, *sh*, and *zh* (as in *pleasure*).

SIMILE   A figure of speech in which one thing is directly compared with another. It is usually introduced by *as* or *like*, *e.g.*,

> *I wandered lonely as a cloud*
> *That floats on high o'er vales and hills*   (*See* Poem No. 253)

SIXAIN   *See* SESTET.

SONNET   A poem of fourteen iambic lines which may be arranged in one of several ways: (1) the *Petrarchan* (*see* Poems Nos. 161, 166, 245, 266, 278), consists of an octave (eight lines rhyming) *abbaabba* and a sestet (six lines) with two or three rhymes variously arranged. There is a break in continuity between octave and sestet, and in this respect the *Petrarchan* sonnet differs from (2) the *Miltonic*, in which the break is not always observed. (*See* Poems Nos. 64, 71.) (3) *Shakespearian*. This consists of three quatrains each with two independent rhymes followed by a rhyming couplet. (*See* Poems Nos, 3, 4, 10, 11, 12, 13 ,14, etc.)

SPENSERIAN STANZA   *See* STANZA.

SPONDEE   In Classical verse, a metrical foot consisting of two long syllables, *e.g.*, *dmén*. In English a foot of two stressed syllables employed only in direct imitations of Classical measures.

SPRUNG RHYTHM   A phrase invented by the poet, Gerard Manley Hopkins, to describe " the rhythm of common speech and of written prose, when rhythm is perceived in them."

STANZA   A group of four or more rhymed verse-lines serving as a pattern for a longer poem. The *Spenserian Stanza* (*e.g.*, in the *Faerie Queene*) consists of nine lines, the first eight of ten syllables and the last of twelve, rhyming *ababbcbcc*.

TERZA RIMA   In English verse, lines of five iambic feet with an extra syllable; *e.g.*, Shelley's *Ode to the West Wind* (Poem No. 275).

TETRAMETER   A line of verse consisting of four feet.

TETRASTICH   *See* QUATRAIN.

TRIBRACH   A foot of three short syllables.

TRIMETER   A line of verse consisting of three feet.

TRIPLET   Three consecutive lines of verse; also called a *tristich* or *tercet*.

TRIOLET   An eight line poem rhyming *abaaabab*, in which the first line is repeated in lines four and seven and the second line is repeated at the end.

TRISTICH   *See* TRIPLET.

TROCHAIC   A verse consisting of trochees, *e.g.*,

$$\acute{D}\textit{ew-drops} \mid \textit{are the} \mid \textit{gems of} \mid \textit{morning}.$$

TROCHEE   A metrical foot consisting of a stressed syllable followed by an unstressed, *e.g.*, *daughter, body*.

VERSE   In prosody this means *one line* of poetry as well as a number of such lines.

VERS LIBRE   Verse (often unrhymed) in which the ordinary rules of prosody are disregarded.

VILLANELLE   Poem of five (or more) tercets and a quatrain. There are only two rhymes, one in the middle lines of the tercets and the second line of the quatrain, and the other everywhere else. The first line recurs at the end of the second and fourth tercets, the third line at the end of the third and fifth tercets, and the quatrain ends with the first and third lines. Examples are to be found in the work of Austin Dobson.